Living in History

EDINBURGH CRITICAL STUDIES IN AVANT-GARDE WRITING
SERIES LIST
Series Editors: Georgina Colby and Eric B. White

Published

Literary History and Avant-Garde Poetics in the Antipodes: Languages of Invention
A. J. Carruthers

Living in History: Poetry in Britain, 1945–1979
Luke Roberts

www.edinburghuniversitypress.com/series-edinburgh-critical-studies-in-avant-garde-writing

Living in History
Poetry in Britain, 1945–1979

Luke Roberts

EDINBURGH
University Press

Edinburgh University Press is one of the leading university presses in the UK. We publish academic books and journals in our selected subject areas across the humanities and social sciences, combining cutting-edge scholarship with high editorial and production values to produce academic works of lasting importance. For more information visit our website: edinburghuniversitypress.com

© Luke Roberts 2024

Edinburgh University Press Ltd
13 Infirmary Street
Edinburgh EH1 1LT

Typeset in 11/13pt Adobe Sabon by
Cheshire Typesetting Ltd, Cuddington, Cheshire, and
printed and bound in Great Britain

A CIP record for this book is available from the British Library

ISBN 978 1 3995 1985 4 (hardback)
ISBN 978 1 3995 1987 8 (webready PDF)
ISBN 978 1 3995 1988 5 (epub)

The right of Luke Roberts to be identified as the author of this work has been asserted in accordance with the Copyright, Designs and Patents Act 1988, and the Copyright and Related Rights Regulations 2003 (SI No. 2498).

Contents

Acknowledgements vi

Introduction: Living in History 1

PART I

1. Possessing the Landscape: Kamau Brathwaite in England, 1950–1955 15

2. Lovely, Flaring Destruction: J. H. Prynne, Charles Olson, Edward Dorn 43

3. The Avant-Garde of Their Own People: Poetry and Exile, 1959–1975 75

PART II

4. Driven Out of the Town: Homosexuality and the British Poetry Revival 105

5. Living in Feminism: Denise Riley and Wendy Mulford 135

6. Yout Rebels: Refusal and Self-Defence 1970–1979 164

7. Grave Police Music: Anti-Carceral Poetics 192

8. Fear of Retribution: Anna Mendelssohn 217

Coda: The Kind of Poetry I Want 239

Select Bibliography 248
Index 263

Acknowledgements

I wrote most of this book in the same room as Amy Tobin, sometimes at the same table. Her company improved it all beyond words, the whole way through.

I discussed the argument of each chapter with David Grundy, and this dialogue gave shape to my thinking, especially during the phases of lockdown where we would take long walks across London. Tom Crompton and Dom Hale both read and commented on drafts, and I'm grateful for their friendship and example.

I'm appreciative to so many friends for conversation and sustenance that I can't list them all here. But for particularly relevant inspiration at crucial junctures, I'm indebted to Sara Crangle, Jackqueline Frost, Peter Gizzi, Danny Hayward, Owen Holland, Sam Ladkin, Felicity Roberts, and Azad Sharma.

My work on this book has been supported in numerous ways by the camaraderie of the English Department at King's College London. Again, happily, there are too many people to mention. But I'm especially appreciative of Sita Balani, Amy De'Ath, Seb Franklin, Carl Kears, Catherine Kelly, Christine Okoth, and the UCU picket line faithful.

The students who took my classes over the years I was doing this research are owed the biggest thanks of all. The shared insights, collective guesswork, gentle disbelief and sudden enthusiasm of the classroom has contributed immeasurably to my understanding of what's at stake in poetry.

Thanks to Georgina Colby, Eric White, and the team at Edinburgh University Press for shepherding this book to completion. Dan Jones and Polly Jones generously gave me their permission for the cover.

My parents, Daphne and Mark, took me on many minor pilgrimages to Sparty Lea, to Briggflatts, to the Hugh MacDiarmid monument in Langholm. Mark Roberts died in June 2023, just as I was making my final edits. His quiet enthusiasm is irreplaceable.

Archivists and librarians at the following institutions helped with my research: the Bishopsgate Institute; the British Library; Brunel University Special Collections; Cambridge University Library; King's College London Special Collections; and May Day Rooms. I am especially grateful to the latter for their online resources.

Chapter 4 started out as a conference paper at 'Queer Publishing / Publishing Queer', Senate House Library, 11 October 2018. My thanks to Leila Kassir. It was published as 'Driven Out of the Town: Homosexuality and the British Poetry Revival' in *ELH*, and comments from the anonymous reviewers were vital, as were comments from Connie Scozzaro.

An earlier draft of Chapter 7 appeared as 'Grave Police Music' in *The Journal of British and Irish Innovative Poetry*. It originated as a paper at the 'Secret Poetry' symposium, Northumbria University, 29–30 April 2016. Thanks to Jo Walton for editorial suggestions. The present chapter incorporates some material from my 'Strategies of Survival: Experimental Poetry in Britain, 1980–2000', in *British Literature in Transition: Accelerated Times*, ed. Eileen Pollard and Berthold Schoene (Cambridge: Cambridge UP, 2018).

Chapter 6 was presented at the Marxism in Culture seminar, Institute of Historical Research, London, in December 2022. Thanks to Larne Abse Gogarty for the invitation, and to the audience for the stimulating discussion and feedback.

Chapter 8 was published, in slightly different form, as 'Fear of Retribution' in *The Journal of British and Irish Innovative Poetry*. I am grateful to the anonymous peer reviewer and to Eleanor Careless and especially Vicky Sparrow for patient edits and careful reading. An earlier version was given as a conference paper at the Anna Mendelssohn Symposium, University of Sussex, February 2017. Thanks again to Eleanor and Vicky. I presented it, also, at the Centre for Modern Poetry, University of Kent, 2017: thanks to Juha Virtanen and Nell Perry, excellent hosts.

Aspects of the Introduction and Coda were given as a paper at the Marxism in Culture Seminar, Institute of Historical Research, London, 23 November 2018. Thanks to Marina Vishmidt, and to the fellow panellists Amy De'Ath, Sean O'Brien and Samuel Solomon. It was pivotal for this book.

In memory of Mark Roberts
(1950–2023)

Introduction: Living in History

'The avant-garde worships history,' writes Fanny Howe towards the end of her early-1990s sequence *O'Clock*, sounding a mixture of scornful and wry. Announcing her disaffection, she aligns herself with 'the others' who 'choose mystery', before declaring: 'So far, God, this may be my last / book of unreconstructed poetry.'[1] Well acquainted with the literary avant-gardes of her native North America, Howe wrote most of *O'Clock* while staying in Newbliss, County Monaghan, a few miles from the military checkpoints of the Northern Irish border.[2] Her lines navigate the arbitrary and the precise, crackling with restless intensity. Almost all of the poems in the sequence carry timestamps ('5:58', '3:08', '23:19'), either signalling the commencement of writing or its completion. Through these liturgical hours we're presented with the slow ecstatic coming of spring, the unfurling and recoil of memory, sleepless grappling with injustice. The work is acutely aware, painfully so, that while we might choose the terms of our consolation, our options are violently enforced and restricted. 'Massacres continue in Greysteel and Palestine', she notes, with history bitterly present.[3]

For Howe – agnostic Catholic and small 'c' communist – poetry dwells in contradiction. It's at once solitary and social, sacred and material, riven with doubt and belief. One poem in *O'Clock*

---

[1] Fanny Howe, *O'Clock* (London: Reality Street, 1995), 101.
[2] A recently published prose text from this period details Howe's travels through Britain and Europe for work. Fanny Howe, *London-Rose / Beauty Will Save the World* (Brussels: Divided, 2022). For Howe's reception in Britain, see the special issue of *Spectacular Diseases* 11 (1999).
[3] Howe, *O'Clock*, 92.

('Tuesday the Second') records a visit to Highgate Cemetery, and begins:

> The stains of blackberries near Marx's grave
> do to color what eyes do to everything.
> Help me survive my own presence, open to the elements.[4]

These lines *are* mysterious. The sensuous trace of the blackberries seems almost too much to bear, as they spill beyond the outline of their form. The language rustles and murmurs, held together by the weight of Marx's funerary gaze. In spite of herself, the poet turns to think of her own survival, her vulnerability and exposure. When Howe writes 'Help me', is she addressing poetry, Marx or God? Does it matter? Is this what she means by 'unreconstructed' poetry – spare, beautiful, desperate?

As this quite literal return to Marx would suggest, the sequence as a whole works through the post-Soviet tectonic shifts of the end of the last century. Most of all, Howe is preoccupied by the disasters of colonialism still unfolding in her ancestral homeland. The second half of 'Tuesday the Second' turns to the late stages of the Troubles, giving a highly compressed analysis of the Provisional Irish Republican Army (IRA): 'Guerrilla war, terror: / the tactics of landless neo-realists'. These juxtapositions of the aesthetic and the political don't seem to have designs as such on the reader, but the tone is hard to gauge. Though Howe tends against despair, gloom is always at the edges, ready to sweep in. Caught between the avant-garde and the neo-realists, where does that leave the poet, 'a lonely communist', hands stained with blackberries?[5] Poems can be a means of evading a predicament; sometimes they're a way of sinking deeper in.

This book won't have much to say about the worship of history. In fact, many of the poets in the following chapters were *students* of history, producing work about social struggles and writing materialist analyses of society alongside their poetic productions.[6] But I'm interested in Howe's separation of the avant-garde and the

---

[4] Ibid., 66.
[5] Ibid., 74.
[6] For example: Edward Kamau Brathwaite, *The Development of Creole Society in Jamaica, 1770–1820* (London: Clarendon, 1971); Tom Pickard, *Jarrow March* (London: Allison & Busby, 1982); Denise Riley, *War in the Nursery: Theories of the Child and Mother* (London: Virago, 1983); Bill Griffiths, *Pitmatic: The Talk of the Northeast Coalfield* (Newcastle: Northumbria UP, 2007). See also J. H. Prynne's speculative investigation of Bronze Age value, 'A Note On Metal' (1968), collected in his *Poems* (Hexham: Bloodaxe, 2015), 127–32.

others, her divided loyalties, her specifically leftist critique. Until very recently, critical accounts of British poetry in the later twentieth century have been organised around a putative opposition between the avant-garde and mainstream, originating in the fabled 'poetry wars' of the 1970s.[7] In brief: between 1971 and 1977, a large group of poets – headed by Eric Mottram, Professor in American Literature at King's College London – took over the Poetry Society and its journal *Poetry Review*. The work Mottram published in *Poetry Review* stood for the inheritance of modernist aesthetic experiment; the rediscovery of radical currents of English romanticism; and the incorporation of new forms and ideas from the United States. This period – and latterly this period *style* – came to be known as the 'British Poetry Revival'.[8]

The taxonomy of the avant-garde is notoriously messy, and there are many other terms vying for competition: 'late modernist', 'the underground', 'neo-modernist', 'post-avant' and 'linguistically innovative' have all been used with varying degrees of traction.[9] These terms often work to differentiate writers *within* the avant-garde, sometimes pedantically, but historically their use in Britain has been to signal a deviation from the bland conservatism of The Movement poets and the apprentice laureates of Faber & Faber.[10] I do not intend to retread this ground, which tends to emphasise a primary contradiction based on aesthetic technique. Rather than a purportedly radical avant-garde and conservative mainstream, I am interested in the question of political commitment. In the following chapters we will meet writers involved in anarchist groups, the Communist Party, anti-colonial movements, Women's Liberation and the British Black Panther Movement. This brings into focus a range of neglected concerns – other contradictions – around race, class and gender.

---

[7] For the definitive account see Peter Barry, *Poetry Wars: British Poetry of the 1970s and the Battle for Earls Court* (Cambridge: Salt, 2006).

[8] See Eric Mottram, 'The British Poetry Revival', in *New British Poetries: The Scope of the Possible*, ed. Robert Hampson and Peter Barry (Manchester: Manchester UP, 1993); Barry MacSweeney, 'The British Poetry Revival, 1965–1979', *South East Arts Review* (1979): 33–46.

[9] My preference is probably closest to the mocking term coined by Stephen Rodefer in a freewheeling and satirical lecture from the early 2000s: 'Contemporary, Avant-Garde, & Experimental', or CAGE. Stephen Rodefer, 'The AGE in its CAGE', *Chicago Review* 51/52: 4/1 (2006): 108–22.

[10] For some of the influential work on this question, see Andrew Crozier, 'Resting on Laurels', in *British Culture of the Postwar: An Introduction to Literature and Society, 1945–1999*, ed. Alistair Davies and Alan Sinfield (London: Routledge, 2000), 192–204; Andrew Duncan, *The Failure of Conservatism in Modern British Poetry* (Cambridge: Salt, 2006).

In the ugly light of Brexit, what's most striking about the British Poetry Revival is that it implies a national project of cultural renewal, a problem I'll return to in this Introduction and across the book as a whole. Thanks to the concerted work of a new generation of scholars and activists, revisionist histories of British poetry are beginning to gather pace. In a series of crucial interventions following the founding of the Race & Poetry & Poetics in the UK (RAPAPUK) research group, Sandeep Parmar analysed the 'pervasive whiteness' of the avant-garde in Britain.[11] This whiteness has been reproduced at all levels: from practitioners to critics, from literary histories to theory and poetics. Important parts of Parmar's argument are structured around a discussion of lyric subjectivity and authenticity, and demonstrate how this area of formal contest between the avant-garde and mainstream has worked to exclude discussions of race. Yet she also writes in an aside: 'But perhaps the problem is not formal or generic, but more broadly rooted in how individual voices are read within national idealisations of the state and its singular or pluralistic cultures.'[12]

My argument in the following chapters is an attempt to address this problem. I focus on poets who were born between the 1930s and the early 1950s, and trace the ambivalent identifications and compromised horizons that were provoked by the new formations of the welfare state. From nationalisation of heavy industry to educational reforms, the extension of social provision to the reconstitution of empire, these changes created specific and novel conditions for the production and reception of poetry. Rather than an idealised vision of post-war social democracy, I emphasise the ideological and repressive apparatuses of the capitalist state, the dynamics of colonialism and imperialism, and the logics of race, gender and sexuality. While I don't ignore questions of form, and work via the close reading of individual poems, the history I present here is one of social antagonism.

The book progresses in broadly chronological order, bracketed by the election of Clement Attlee's Labour Government in 1945 and the advent of Thatcherism in 1979. I transgress these dates when necessary, particularly as I try to think about the history of the recent

---

[11] Sandeep Parmar, 'Still Not a British Subject: Race and UK Poetry', *Journal of British and Irish Innovative Poetry* 12(1), no. 33 (2020): 1–44 (4). See also Parmar, 'Not a British Subject: Race and Poetry in the UK', *LA Review of Books* (6 December 2015), online: https://lareviewofbooks.org/article/not-a-british-subject-race-and-poetry-in-the-uk/ [Accessed 25 October 2023].

[12] Parmar, 'Still Not a British Subject', 13.

present. Faced with unremitting attacks on public institutions since the financial crisis of 2008 and the imposition of fiscal austerity, the left in Britain has often relied on sentimental and nostalgic accounts of the origins of the welfare state. The Corbyn movement – the closest socialists have come to power in generations – had to continually struggle to free itself from the idiom typified by the Ken Loach documentary *The Spirit of '45* (2013).[13] While Loach's film presents many moving accounts of pre-war poverty and highlights the limits of nationalisation as opposed to workers' control, it wholly sidesteps the process of underdevelopment and wealth extraction that underpinned the British state's capabilities. It presents a history of the working class in Britain that is entirely white. Among dozens of contributors, none are from the African, Caribbean or South Asian diaspora. No people of colour are presented on screen. As Kojo Koram has argued, this 'romantic mythology' of post-war social democracy has been 'a key tool in the erasure of Empire'.[14]

In Part I of *Living in History*, I focus on the persistence of empire in post-war Britain. Chapter 1, 'Possessing the Landscape', examines poems written by Kamau Brathwaite while he was a student in England in the early 1950s. While his later activism with the Caribbean Artists Movement (CAM) is becoming well known, I position his work in a political trajectory that starts with Frantz Fanon and culminates in 1968, when the Guyanese revolutionary Walter Rodney was banned from entering Jamaica. Chapter 2, 'Lovely, Flaring Destruction' triangulates work by J. H. Prynne, Charles Olson and Edward Dorn, and reads Prynne's tentative mid-1960s Marxism in conjunction with British and US relations. I pay particular attention to the way the university facilitated student exchange through Fulbright Fellowships and other examples of soft power. Chapter 3, 'The Avant-Garde of Their Own People', draws together exiled writers of the early 1960s and 1970s. These include the Trinidadian Communist Claudia Jones, the African National Congress activist Mazisi Kunene and the Chilean poet and artist Cecilia Vicuña.

As these chapter summaries suggest, and as the subtitle of this book implies, this is an account of poetry *in* Britain, rather than an attempt to expand or redefine 'British poetry' as such. I have followed

---

[13] The former Labour shadow chancellor John McDonnell cites the film in his discussion of the problems of nationalisation and bureaucracy in John McDonnell, ed., *Economics for the Many* (London: Verso, 2020), xv.

[14] Kojo Koram, *Uncommon Wealth: Britain and the Aftermath of Empire* (London: John Murray, 2022), 89.

Keith Tuma's description of the latter as a 'field of contradictory practices', always contested and subject to revision, and I have consciously attempted to weaken the boundaries of citizenship and nationality as principles for study.[15] But equally, I resist the false conciliations or self-congratulation of a merely liberal gesture towards inclusivity. At least one poet in this study – the South African Arthur Nortje, who died in 1970 awaiting leave to remain in the UK – was hastened to their death by the border regime of the British state. It's not the aim of this book to revivify or expand 'the experimental' by simply incorporating non-white authors into the field: my objective is to problematise that field and instigate new associations and more complex lineages.[16] At the most simple level of historical comprehension, our understanding of the poetry of the post-war period will continue to be distorted and incomplete if it ignores the work of migrants, exiles, students on scholarships and Commonwealth subjects whose citizenship was regulated by the racist immigration policies of subsequent governments, whether Labour or Conservative.[17]

To reiterate: the formation of the welfare state in 1945 was not only, as Ralph Miliband had it, 'the "ransom" the working classes had been able to extract from their rulers'.[18] The Second World War had taken an extremely heavy toll on the British economy. In the memorable words of C. L. R. James, referring to the Marshall Plan loans of 1948, 'Britain lives by blood-plasma from the United States'.[19] When the terms of the agreement provoked a sterling crisis in 1947, Labour introduced a set of austerity measures, including wage freezes, ration reductions and strike-breaking. In addition to Marshall Plan aid – itself a broad strategy of anti-communism, enthusiastically adopted by the Labour Foreign Office under Ernest Bevin – the Attlee Government relied on its own colonial economics.[20] The austerity budget, delivered by Stafford Cripps, involved 'a seven-fold increase in net invisible earnings between 1948/9 and 1952/3'

---

[15] Keith Tuma, *Fishing by Obstinate Isles: Modern and Postmodern British Poetry and American Readers* (Evanston: Northwestern UP, 1998), 23.

[16] For a brilliant critique of the racial politics of 'the experimental' in a US context, see Natalia Cecire, *Experimental: American Literature and the Aesthetics of Knowledge* (Baltimore: Johns Hopkins UP, 2019).

[17] See Nadine El-Enany, *(B)ordering Britain: Law, Race, and Empire* (Manchester: Manchester UP, 2020).

[18] Ralph Miliband, *The State and Capitalist Society* (London: Weidenfeld & Nicholson, 1969), 109–10.

[19] C. L. R. James, *Notes on Dialectics: Hegel, Marx, Lenin* (Westport, CT: Lawrence Hill, 1981), 226.

[20] For an analysis of Bevin, see John Saville, *The Politics of Continuity: British Foreign Policy and the Labour Government, 1945–46* (London: Verso, 1993).

in order to maintain the expenditures of the British state.[21] These 'invisible earnings' were extracted from the colonies.

My readings in the following chapters are centred on Britain, but gesture towards a global narrative of rupture and discontinuity. In the 1965 poem by J. H. Prynne which gives this book its title, he appears to meditate on the transformation of shore into coast: that is, the process of accumulated settlement and boundary-marking that produces the imagined outline of a nation.[22] It ends with an enigmatic surge of feeling:

> Walk on it, being a line, of rest
> and distinction, a hope now lived up
> to, a coast in awkward
> singular desires
> thigh-bone of the
> world[23]

The poem stringently avoids specifying a geographic location, but implicitly stages a revision of Matthew Arnold's 'Dover Beach'. In a radio talk from 1963, Prynne had criticised the 'elegiac cocoon' of Arnold and his Victorian contemporaries such as Tennyson, analysing the way their verse-technique performed a sustained melancholic withdrawal from the world into 'a self-generating ambience of regret'.[24] The very awkwardness of the line breaks in 'Living in History' seem designed to avoid this trap: we're taken by surprise, perhaps like the lapping wave that suddenly rushes further than we thought to expect.

But Prynne shares more with Arnold at this point than he might wish. Paul Gilroy has described Arnold's 'geo-piety', and how 'Dover Beach' posits 'a geological tempo to which he gives the reader access'.[25] This is achieved and regulated via 'the right dosage of Hellenism'.[26] In Prynne's poem, I take the final lines to be an allusion

---

[21] Ron Ramdin, *The Making of the Black Working Class in Britain* (London: Verso, 2017), 69.

[22] A few days before enclosing a copy of 'Living in History' to the American poet Charles Olson, Prynne wrote him a letter unfavourably discussing a book by C. A. M. King, *Beaches and Coasts* (London: Edward Arnold, 1959). Prynne, Letter to Charles Olson, 23 November 1965, in *The Collected Letters of Charles Olson and J.H. Prynne*, ed. Ryan Dobran (Albuquerque: U of New Mexico P, 2017), 138–9.

[23] J. H. Prynne, *Poems*, 41.

[24] J. H. Prynne, 'The Elegiac World in Victorian Poetry', *The Listener* (14 February 1963), 290–1 (291). This is a transcript of a broadcast for the BBC Radio *Third Programme*.

[25] Paul Gilroy, *Postcolonial Melancholia* (New York: Columbia, 2004), 91.

[26] Ibid.

to the Hellenic designation of the *omphalos* stone at Delphi as 'navel of the world'.[27] This manoeuvre is bathetic: Britain is imagined as a femur, and the reader starts to imagine the corresponding shin bone of the world, the kneecap of the world, the knuckle, faintly ridiculous. But this image-complex makes an uneasy association between land and body, the white cliffs of Dover now subsumed into the blanched skeletal evidence of belonging.

It's as if in this poem Prynne is poised, waiting for history to register. If Arnold and Tennyson were the poets of an empire in ascendancy, whose atrocities registered only unconsciously in their work, Prynne writes through the long interregnum of imperial decline. His work has slowly and painfully come to reckon with this, treating language itself as a historical register of corruption, exploitation and violence, from the Vietnam War to the invasion of Iraq. Since 2016, Prynne has returned to something like the site of 'Living in History' again and again, reckoning with the coast as the site of murderous 'distinction' by the Home Office and the European Union (EU). In his late sequences, the 'shore' is always accompanied by the *offshore* manoeuvres of capital and the desperate flight of refugees across the Mediterranean Sea and the English Channel.[28]

How did we get here? Writing during the protracted social crisis of Thatcherism – a crisis we still live with – Stuart Hall soberly remarked that 'the very expansion of the state, for which many on the left worked so hard, turned out to be a very contradictory experience'.[29] In Part II of *Living in History*, I trace these experiences through the emergence of liberation struggles around gender, sexuality and race, and the direct engagement by poets with the carceral apparatus of the state. My interpretation of this work has been informed by my own experiences. I began writing this book in 2016. I remember the morning after the Brexit referendum I was supposed to visit the Bill Griffiths material in Eric Mottram's archives. Instead,

---

[27] See, for instance, Pindar in his Pythian Ode 6: 'as we proceed to the enshrined / navel of the loudly rumbling earth'. *Pindar: Olympian Odes / Pythian Odes*, ed. and trans. William H. Race (Cambridge, MA: Harvard Loeb, 1997), 315.

[28] For example *Of the Abyss* (Cambridge: Materials, 2017), and *Sea Shells Told* (Cambridge: Face Press, 2022). For an analysis of the former, see John Kerrigan, 'Lampedusa: Migrant Tragedy', *Cambridge Journal of Postcolonial Literary Inquiry* 8, no. 2 (2021), 138–57.

[29] Stuart Hall, 'The State – Socialism's Old Caretaker', in *The Hard Road To Renewal: Thatcherism and Crisis of the Left* (London: Verso, 1988), 222.

that evening I attended a solidarity march which started at the Altab Ali memorial park in Whitechapel, named after a Bangladeshi textile worker murdered in 1978, and which headed over London Bridge to the headquarters of News UK (formerly News International), whose media titles had been instrumental in whipping up racist and xenophobic sentiment. Late in the summer, like Fanny Howe, I visited Marx's grave, though I don't recall any blackberries.

In the period 2015–2019 there was a huge upsurge in socialist electoralism around Jeremy Corbyn's Labour Party, which often swept away distinctions between different leftist blocs and currents. At the same time, the movement for police and prison abolition surged through the Black Lives Matter uprisings, climaxing in 2020. This sometimes led to compromised positions of the kind that Hall identifies. The Labour Party manifesto of 2017 involved investment in the NHS and education, and commitments to more progressive immigration policies, but also involved funding for 10,000 extra police officers. The state is not simply an instrument to be won, but an internally divided ensemble of competing fractions and powers. When the left has to *defend* the progressive vestiges of the welfare state, try and save it from further hollowing out, it can become hard to imagine wholly *transforming* the state, never mind seeking its revolutionary abolition.[30] And the 'progressive' aspects of the welfare state – the NHS, for instance – are by no means immune to being mobilised for nativist ends.[31] During the first Covid-19 pandemic lockdown in 2020, as the Tories instigated ritual applause for NHS workers – a kind of pageantry usually reserved for either royalty or the military – it seemed clear that we had entered a new phase of melancholic nationalist attachment.[32]

But these various developments – marked by real radical openings and new fronts and struggles – have been immensely clarifying, making it possible to think things about poetry that weren't possible to think before, and to see historical shifts and patterns emerge and concretise. To return once more to Howe, this is one way in which poems are 'open to the elements', weathered by the

---

[30] For a recent analysis, see Sita Balani, Gargi Bhattacharyya, Nadine El-Enany, Adam Elliott-Cooper, Dalia Gebrial, Kojo Koram, Kerem Nisancioglu and Luke de Neronha, *Empire's Endgame: Racism and the British State* (London: Pluto, 2021).
[31] See Des Fitzgerald, Amy Hinterberge, John Narayan and Ros Williams, 'Brexit as Heredity Redux: Imperialism, Biomedicine and the NHS in Britain', *The Sociological Review* 68, no. 6 (2020): 1161–78.
[32] This apparent enthusiasm has since been tempered by widespread industrial action in the NHS, featuring strikes across the entire workforce.

times in which they're written and the time in which they're read. I don't pretend to have written a balanced or comprehensive survey of poetry across Britain. There are many more poets I would have liked to have written about, and who might have carried parts of the story that follows. It's also true that I focus to a large extent on London, with Cambridge as its satellite. This is in part because my previous book, *Barry MacSweeney and the Politics of Post-War British Poetry: Seditious Things*, addressed the post-industrial situation of the North of England and regionally felt commitments to trades union politics.[33] But it's also because the dynamics of this book are keenly registered in the metropolitan centres of the imperial core.[34] As my opening evocation of Howe in the partitioned island of Ireland should suggest, I am conscious throughout this book of the British state as a colonial entity, a fact that repeatedly impinges on the political imaginary of the poets.

In Chapter 4, 'Driven Out of the Town', I bring together the neglected work of Harry Fainlight with the love poems Lee Harwood wrote for John Ashbery during their brief relationship in 1965–1966. Situating these authorships in relation to the Sexual Offences Act 1967, which partially decriminalised sexual contact between men, I consider the apparent absence of a tradition of queer experimental poetry in Britain comparative to the United States. Tracing the homophobic reception of Fainlight and Harwood, I come to analyse the emergence in the latter's work of a kind of empire nostalgia running in parallel to his disavowal of homosexuality. In Chapter 5, 'Living in Feminism', I work through the literary historiography of the feminist movement in Britain, focusing on the socialist work of Denise Riley and Wendy Mulford. I give an extended reading of one of Riley's most famous poems, 'A note on sex and the reclaiming of language', addressing her allegorical deployment of racial figures, and I read Mulford's coalitional politics through her practice of citation.

Chapter 6, 'Yout Rebels', concentrates on two examples of politically engaged publishing in 1970s London. The first is the work of the Hackney-based social centre and publisher Centerprise, read through the work of the twelve-year-old poet Vivian Usherwood. The second is Linton Kwesi Johnson's involvement in the collective

---

[33] Luke Roberts, *Barry MacSweeney and the Politics of British Poetry: Seditious Things* (London: Palgrave, 2017).

[34] For some recent work on the dispersed networks of the avant-garde, see Ross Hair, *Avant-Folk: Small Press Poetry Networks From 1950 to the Present* (Liverpool: Liverpool UP, 2016), and Greg Thomas, *Border Blurs: Concrete Poetry in England and Scotland* (Liverpool: Liverpool UP, 2019).

around the journal *Race Today*. I analyse specific theorising about the position of young Black people in Britain in the 1970s as they faced violence from the police and street fascist organisations. The final two chapters continue to address the carceral state. In Chapter 7, 'Grave Police Music', I examine the anti-prison writings and activism of Bill Griffiths, and place him in dialogue with Tom Pickard's writing about his time in Brixton Prison and John James's address to Irish political prisoners at Long Kesh. In Chapter 8, 'Fear of Retribution', I focus on the work of Anna Mendelssohn, who was imprisoned in the 1970s due to her association with the militant leftist group the Angry Brigade, who carried out a series of bombings in the wake of the anti-trades union Industrial Relations Act 1971 and the escalation of the British military presence in Northern Ireland. The difficulty of her work, overdetermined by biography and damaged by political persecution, prompts me to reflect on my own methodology, and to return to the question of the contemporary context from which I write.

In the Coda I return to some of the issues I've outlined here, via readings of poems by Jackie Kay and Hugh MacDiarmid. But as Carolyn Steedman reminds us, 'The poetics of history teaches us that there may be endings, but there is no end'.[35] What's at stake is the future; there is always further history to be made.

---

[35] Carolyn Steedman, *Poetry for Historians* (Liverpool: Liverpool UP, 2018), 236.

Part I

Chapter 1

Possessing the Landscape: Kamau Brathwaite in England, 1950–1955

At the beginning of my research, and as it goes on, I accumulate materials. A copy of Anne Walmsley's classic *The Caribbean Artists Movement, 1966–1972*, withdrawn from the University of North London. A copy of the Bogle L'Ouverture edition of *Journey to an Illusion: The West Indian in Britain* by Donald Hinds, withdrawn from the Wandsworth Library Services. A copy of Paul Gilroy's *Small Acts*, withdrawn from the University of Northumbria. A copy of Edward Kamau Brathwaite's *Third World Poems*, stamped 'Multicultural Resource Centre'. These objects are bittersweet. Their existence is evidence of activist achievements in publishing, in education, and in literature and art. Here is the transformative Caribbean presence in Britain, here are complex solidarities and identities, flourishing and irrefutable. But after ten years and counting of austerity, it's hard not to read these traces of deaccession as evidence of the calculated and ongoing erosion of institutional and collective memory. Since 2010 over 800 libraries have closed in Britain.[1] More than 700 youth centres have been shut down.[2] The marketisation of the universities has left post-1992 institutions under-resourced, and subject to course cuts and department closures. The social catastrophe of Covid-19 is likely to reverberate for a generation, and will do further damage to the fragile ecology of small press publishers, bookshops and community organisations that rely on government

---

[1] Adele Walton, 'The Quiet Disappearance of Britain's Public Libraries', *Tribune* (17 January 2021), online: https://tribunemag.co.uk/2021/01/the-quiet-disappearance-of-britains-public-libraries [Accessed 10 April 2023].
[2] Sally Weale, 'Youth services suffer 70% funding cut in less than a decade', *The Guardian* (20 January 2020), online: theguardian.com/society/2020/jan/20/youth-services-suffer-70-funding-cut-in-less-than-a-decade [Accessed 18 September 2021].

funding for support. Though in recent years prestigious British literary prizes have been awarded to Anthony (Vahni) Capildeo, Kei Miller, Roger Robinson and Anthony Joseph, this recognition has taken place in a bleak landscape of setbacks.

But perhaps struggle is always like this, unfolding, as Gordon Rohlehr put it, somewhere between 'trophy and catastrophe'.[3] Kamau Brathwaite understood this more than most. His influence is vast: his organisational work with the Caribbean Artists Movement (CAM) and his editorial roles with *Savacou* and *Bim*; his historical research and scholarship, including *The Folk Culture of the Slaves in Jamaica*; his oversight of the educational textbooks, *The People Who Came*; his legendary talks and lectures, most famously *The History of the Voice*; and above all and in everything the poetry, more than twenty volumes of righteous invention and visionary experiment. Yet from the late 1970s onwards, Brathwaite was increasingly beset by tragedy: the assassination of friends and comrades such as Walter Rodney and Michael Smith; the sudden death of Doris Brathwaite, his first wife and collaborator; extensive damage to his archives and his home during Hurricane Gilbert in 1988; his own violent assault at the hands of gunmen in Kingston. This was 'the time of salt', or as he called it in *Trench Town Rock* (1994), 'the Age of Dis. Distress Despair & Disrespect. Distrust Disrupt Distruction'.[4] After Jamaica he left for the United States, where he taught for more than a decade, becoming Professor of Comparative Literature at NYU. Though his work found supportive audiences and sympathetic publishers, including New Directions and Wesleyan, his suffering continued through 'the second time of salt' or what he called his 'cultural lynching'.[5] Objects went missing from his apartment in New York, including his Musgrave Medal, awarded by the Jamaican Government in 2006. These were traumatic events, culminating in his hospitalisation in 2008, and his permanent return to Barbados.

But if his suffering was Job-like, Brathwaite also became something close to the ambivalent figure of a Black Noah he had evoked at the conclusion of *Rights of Passage* (1967).[6] His hope throughout the 1990s and 2000s was to establish a cultural centre in Barbados at his home, Cow Pastor, and to salvage from his precarious archives

---

[3] Gordon Rohlehr, 'Trophy and Catastrophe', *The Shape of That Hurt* (Port of Spain: Longman Trinidad, 1992).
[4] Kamau Brathwaite, *Trench Town Rock* (Providence: Lost Road, 1994), 73.
[5] See Brathwaite, 'The Second Time of Salt', *Scritture Migranti* 5 (2011).
[6] See Gordon Rohlehr, *Pathfinder: Black Awakening in the Arrivants of Edward Kamau Brathwaite* (Tunapuna: Gordon Rohlehr, 1981), 54–7.

a Caribbean library of Alexandria.[7] In Britain, his later work was supported and published by Bloodaxe, Salt and Peepal Tree Press, and he was one of few poets to find readers across the rarely overlapping poetry scenes of the UK. Yet even so, and despite his inclusion on the GCSE curriculum since 1998, Brathwaite remains under-read, and there are questions about how his work is framed. In the original NEAB/AQA exams anthology, his poems appeared in the 'Other Cultures and Traditions' section, set apart from 'English Literary Heritage', and this othering has yet to be undone.[8] Oxford University Press has allowed his first trilogy, collected as *The Arrivants* (1973), to slip out of print. In 2001, the OUP *Anthology of Twentieth-Century British and Irish Poetry* was greeted by a hostile mention in *Poetry Review*, calling him 'E.K. Resentment'.[9] While *The Guardian* at least gave him an obituary, the paper neglected to review any of his books in the twenty-first century. As late as 2008, *The Times* treated his inclusion on the syllabus as an excuse to raise a patronising eyebrow at education reform.[10]

None of this is surprising. As Bill Schwarz has recently argued, we are surrounded by 'faux histories', the stories Britain likes to tell about itself, always structured by the 'discontinuous presence' of a white ethnic populism.[11] In its diffuse form, this takes shape as *'not caring to remember'*.[12] The last few years have seen successful attempts to challenge this pervasive imperial amnesia, from the Rhodes Must Fall campaign in 2015 to the toppling of Bristol's Colston statue by Black Lives Matter protestors in 2020. But these protests, which are in themselves arguments about history, have been met with extensive government opposition. The Department for Digital, Culture, Media and Sport has rebuked such staid institutions

---

[7] For a reading of the long aftermath of Hurricane Gilbert and the status of Brathwaite's archives, see Sonya Posmentier, *Cultivation and Catastrophe: The Lyric Ecology of Modern Black Literature* (Baltimore: Johns Hopkins UP, 2017), 181–212.

[8] For Brathwaite's inclusion in the National Curriculum, see Asha Rogers, *State Sponsored Literature: Britain and Cultural Diversity After 1945* (Oxford: Oxford UP, 2020), 174–8.

[9] Sean O' Brien, 'Bizzaro's Bounty', *Poetry Review* 91, no. 2 (2001): 110.

[10] 'What's on the Syllabus?', Phil Beadle interviewed by Francesca Steele, *The Times*, supplement (2 January 2008). Brathwaite's name appears in a quiz, pairing poets (for example, Brathwaite and Blake) and asking the reader to guess which is on the AQA syllabus. The big reveal that this is a trick question and that the syllabus is 'perfectly balanced' simply reinforces the position of Brathwaite, Moniza Alvi, John Agard, Sujata Bhatt and Tatamkhulu Afrika as a kind of punchline.

[11] Bill Schwarz, 'Forgetfulness: England's Discontinuous Histories', in *Embers of Empire in Brexit Britain*, ed. Stuart Ward and Astrid Rasch (London: Bloomsbury, 2019), 55.

[12] Ibid., 50. Emphasis in the original.

as the National Trust and Heritage England for merely issuing reports on the ties between country houses and historic buildings and the slave trade. To turn Rohlehr's phrase another way, the British establishment is desperate to obfuscate the material links between the trophies of empire and the catastrophes of the Middle Passage. For a younger generation in Britain, these links are no longer deniable, their glorification is intolerable; a new stance towards history is beginning to take shape.

This chapter reads Brathwaite's early work as a part of this history, focusing on one of the first poems he wrote in England: 'The Day the First Snow Fell'. Brathwaite referred to this poem in talks throughout his life, and he revised and reversioned it over a period of more than fifty years. I use this poem to illuminate Brathwaite's first residence in England in the early 1950s and his time as a student. This formative experience has been overshadowed, understandably, by Brathwaite's later involvement with CAM, and the publication of *Rights of Passage* (1967) and *Masks* (1968) while Brathwaite was living in London and pursuing doctoral research. This crucial period of Brathwaite's life and writing has benefited from Walmsley's invaluable study of CAM, Rohlehr's *Pathfinder: Black Awakening in The Arrivants of Edward Kamau Brathwaite*, and the many essays on Brathwaite's early books. But all of Brathwaite's scattered fragments are important, even his seemingly 'aberrant' juvenilia.[13] Speaking in 1994, Brathwaite recalled his first embodied encounter with snow as an 'environmental shock [...] leading to new metaphorical riddim'.[14] In the following I consider Brathwaite's complex acclimatisation to England, and his rhythms, metaphorical and otherwise.

Lawson Edward Brathwaite, one of only four Barbados Scholars that year, travelled to England on the SS Willemstad, docking at Plymouth on 2 October 1950. In her description of his departure, Brathwaite's sister Mary recalls that prior to the construction of the deep-water port at Bridgetown in 1956, travellers from Barbados had to go out in a launch boat to board big passenger ships. It was dramatic: 'when our mother discovered that his passport and other important papers

---

[13] See Lee M. Jenkin's excellent discussion, '*X/Self*: Kamau Brathwaite at the Crossroads', in *Aberration in Modern Poetry*, ed. Lucy Collins and Steven Matterson (Jefferson: McFarland, 2012), 144–60.

[14] Kamau Brathwaite, 'Newstead to Neustadt', *World Literature Today* 68, no. 4 (1994): 656.

had been left behind, I had to run back down the gangway [...] to retrieve the folder with the paper, and get back to the ship'.[15] In the autobiographical *Sun Poem* (1982/2001), Brathwaite describes setting sail 'w/ his back to the land & the house / where he live' thinking 'what his mother wd say / if he didnt come back'.[16] He would be away from the Caribbean for ten years, completing an undergraduate degree in history at Pembroke College, Cambridge, followed by a graduate diploma in education. He sailed from Liverpool to Akorati in February 1955, working as an education officer during the prelude to and early years of Ghana's independence in 1957. After a teaching stint at the University of West Indies (UWI), he returned to Britain in 1965 to research for his PhD at the University of Sussex.

In 1950 there were around 7,500 overseas students in Britain, with more than 4,000 coming from the British Commonwealth.[17] Some 1,000 of these students were from the West Indies, up from 166 in 1939.[18] At the close of the Second World War, the Colonial Office had made access to tertiary education a priority. The findings of the Asquith Committee, *Report of the Commission on Higher Education in the Colonies*, had argued for the immediate establishment of a university in the West Indies, and made broad recommendations for the maintenance and expansion of scholarship systems in the interim.[19] The Committee's reasoning was explicit:

> The immediate objective is to produce men and women who have the standards of public service and capacity for leadership which the progress of self-government demands, and to assist in satisfying the need for persons with the professional qualifications required for the economic and social development of the Colonies.[20]

Uprisings across the West Indies in the 1930s had set the gears of decolonisation into motion, but this process was going to be long and

---

[15] Mary E. Morgan, 'Highway to Vision: This Sea Our Nexus', *World Literature Today* 68, no. 4 (1994): 668.
[16] Brathwaite, *Ancestors* (New York: New Directions, 2001), 195.
[17] Hilary Perraton, *A History of Foreign Students in Britain* (London: Palgrave, 2014), 84.
[18] A. J. Stockwell, 'Leaders, Dissidents and the Disappointed: Colonial Students in Britain as Empire Ended', *The Journal of Imperial and Commonwealth History* 36, no. 3 (2008): 491.
[19] The Barbados Scholarship, which Brathwaite received, was established a result of educational reforms in 1875. See Shirley Gordon, 'Documents Which Have Guided Educational Policy In The West Indies: The Mitchinson Report, Barbados, 1875', *Caribbean Quarterly* 9, no. 3 (September 1963): 33–43.
[20] *Report of the Commission on Higher Education in the Colonies* (London: HM Stationery Office, 1945), 104.

drawn out, countered and defused by British bureaucracy. As Sylvia Wynter noted many years later, 'the university has no self which is not imposed on it by circumstances', and those circumstances were determined in a large part by the administrators of empire.[21]

Brathwaite's experience in England was not typical of West Indian migrants in the 1950s. His scholarship stipend gave him economic security for at least three years, and the Cambridge system of porters, cleaners and dining halls was a far cry from the conditions described by contemporaries such as Sam Selvon and George Lamming. Even within the broader student population, the residential system of Cambridge colleges meant that his position differed in crucial ways from West Indians studying at the University of London. Facing discrimination and exploitation from private landlords, accommodation in the capital had long been a site of antagonism for students of colour, providing an opportunity for political organisation and solidarity. Shyamji Krishnavarma's India House in Highgate, 'a political nerve centre for Indian revolutionary nationalists', became a template for groups in the 1930s.[22] The West African Student Union (WASU) established its own Africa House hostel in Camden, and vigorously opposed the opening of the 'official' Colonial Office accommodation Aggrey House in 1934.[23] The West Indian Students Union (WISU) formed in 1945, and members were involved in disputes at residences including Nutford House in Marble Arch and the Collingham Gardens building at Earl's Court. In July 1951 WISU members were involved in a major example of eviction resistance at the Hans Crescent Hostel, which only ended after the intervention of the Secretary of State for the Colonies, Labour MP Jim Griffiths.[24]

The mood at Oxbridge was rather different. There were far fewer Black students, and social life was further stratified by college affiliations and the rituals of class privilege. In Michael Banton's account, the student societies were markedly less politically active than those in London such as WASU and WISU. Where the London students had been 'leaders of colonial protest', at Oxbridge they mainly 'presided over social gatherings'.[25] But making use of the doctoral work

[21] Sylvia Wynter, 'We Must Learn to Sit Down Together and Talk About a Little Culture', *Jamaica Journal* 2, no. 4 (December 1968): 26.
[22] Priyamvada Gopal, *Insurgent Empire: Anticolonial Resistance and British Dissent* (London: Verso, 2019), 210.
[23] Christian Høgsberg, *C.L.R. James in Imperial Britain* (Durham, NC: Duke UP, 2014), 88.
[24] Stockwell, 'Leaders, Dissidents and the Disappointed', 498–9.
[25] Michael Banton, *White and Coloured: The Behaviour of British People Towards Coloured Immigrants* (New Brunswick: Rutgers, 1959), 146.

of Sheila Webster, Banton catalogues the racist attitudes of both students and staff in the Oxbridge system.[26] In Brathwaite's telling, he was unprepared for this: he understood himself as a 'Citizen of the World', versed in Shakespeare, T. S. Eliot, the *Hebrides* overture of Felix Mendelssohn and Gustav Holst's *Planets*, only to be met with rejection.[27] This included the social world of the poetry scenes and drama clubs, and extended to his syllabus and studies:

> My history at Cambridge spent its time talking about the open field system and Medieval coins: that was the basic thrust of the lectures. I once brought up the subject of Eric Williams and the tutor got very upset and said he was a communist and I should not bring up that subject again. So Eric Williams was lost too.[28]

Faced with a conservative and alienating institution, an unwelcoming student body and hostile tutors, Brathwaite would 'Prepare to fight ... / with pen & ink & pencil-point / The whole mad University'.[29]

Before it was gathered in *Other Exiles* (1975), 'The Day the First Snow Fell' was published in at least four places: *Delta*, a student magazine from Cambridge, in 1953; *Bim*, the legendary Barbadian journal edited by Brathwaite's mentor Frank Collymore, in June 1953; in a special commemorative issue of *Caribbean Quarterly* marking the formation of the West Indies Federation in 1958; and in a poetry supplement in *The London Magazine*, edited by Derek Walcott in 1965. Brathwaite refers to it obliquely in his famous lecture *The History of the Voice* and discusses it at some length in *Barabajan Poems* (1994). He revised and republished it for the last time in *Golokwati 2000*, a kind of self-curated selected poems and

---

[26] Sheila Webster, *Negroes at Bluebrick: An Analysis of the Problems of Assimilation of African and West Indian Students in the Universities of Oxford and Cambridge*, unpublished B.Litt, Oxford University; Bodleian Library Thesis 20155.

[27] Brathwaite, *Barabajan Poems* (Kingston and New York: Savacou North, 1994), 56. Hereafter *Barabajan*, with citations in text.

[28] Victor L. Chang, ed., *Three Caribbean Poets on Their Work* (Kingston: UWIP, 1993), 11. Williams's *Capitalism and Slavery*, first published by the University of North Carolina in 1944, would not find a British publisher until the Andre Deutsch edition in 1964. Elsewhere, Brathwaite describes trying to get hold of C. L. R. James's *Black Jacobins*, only to be told that it was a work of fiction. Brathwaite, *Golokwati 2000* (Kingston and New York: Savacou North, 2002), unpaginated.

[29] 'The Exile', unpublished poem quoted by Brathwaite in *Barabajan* 299. Brathwaite dates it 1953, the year of his graduation.

autobiographical commentary issued to celebrate the poet's seventieth birthday. There, the poem is subtitled 'continuous tense revision', and moves the action into an ongoing present: the poem is still with him, and still resonates as unfinished business. Readers of Brathwaite will be familiar with his biting puns and wordplay, and perhaps we can detect in this '*continuous tense* revision' an echo of Fanon's famous assertion that 'confronted with the colonial order the colonized subject is in a permanent state of tension'.[30] I want to examine this poem at some length, drawing out Brathwaite's account of the composition and context, before going on to consider the development of Brathwaite's political positions in the 1970s.

Here is how the poem appeared in *Delta*:

THE DAY THE FIRST SNOW FELL

I

The day the first snow fell I floated to my birth
Of feathers falling by my window; touched earth
And melted touched again and left a little touch of light
And everywhile we touched till earth was white.

II

Wood was now black or white
White world was bright at night
And water was black wood
Carved into two white swans.

III

Birth was black water
Where the white swans bend
Death was black winter
Where the white wood ends.

IV

The day the first snow fell I floated to my death
Of feathers fallen by my window; left
Love unmelted loved again to touch the little left of light
And everywhere we left while love was white.[31]

---

[30] Frantz Fanon, *The Wretched of the Earth*, trans. Constance Farrington (New York: Grove Press, 2004), 16. Brathwaite has alluded to this: 'it was Fanon, I think, echoed by Tsitsi Dangarembga (1988) [...] who speaks of colonialism as a "nervous condition" / this **Conversations** is really my first (& unexpected, unintentioned) effort to deal w/ my personal relationship to this.' *ConVERSations* (Minneapolis: XCP (Cross Cultural Poetics), 1999), 49.

[31] The first issue of *Delta* carries no date, but the second issue appears in Spring 1954. In several places, Brathwaite dates the poem's publication as 1951, but I think this is unlikely.

As the title suggests, the poem was prompted by Brathwaite's first experience of snowfall in December 1950.[32] This was a relatively common subject for poets from the Caribbean making trips to colder climates. Claude McKay's 'The Snow Fairy', published in *Harlem Shadows* (1922), is a beautiful double-sonnet moving from the 'revolt and riot' of falling snowflakes to the warm memory of a lover with 'passion all aflame'.[33] St-John Perse's war-time *Neiges*, a long meditative prose poem, takes snow as the starting point for the renewal of the world.[34] Shake Keane, from St Vincent – who played in Joe Harriot's group in London in the late 1950s and early 1960s – uses snow as a source of inter-island banter, making fun of the Bermudan who 'when he first see snow in New York / how he run outside and bring back a handful / put it in the frying pan and fry it / just so'.[35] But Brathwaite here works by intense condensation and seriousness. We are in a world of boundaries, definitions and thresholds, a strange landscape rich with allegorical implication.

Brathwaite appeared in the first two issues of *Delta*, both towards the end of his time in England. It was a prestigious undergraduate magazine, proximate to the literary establishment. In the later 1950s, *Delta* became a venue for Philip Hobsbaum's influential 'Group' poets, and published early work by, among others, Ted Hughes and Sylvia Plath. In 1951, Brathwaite himself had appeared in an anthology of Cambridge writers from the Fortune Press, the legendary and slightly louche publishers of Dylan Thomas and soon-to-be dominant Movement writers Philip Larkin and Kingsley Amis.[36] But while Brathwaite was friends with Peter Redgrove, founding editor of *Delta*, and friendly with Hughes, he was very much adjacent to any kind of 'scene'.[37] In *Barabajan Poems*, Brathwaite describes 'the two

---

[32] It was a particularly cold month, with the *Times* reporting that 'the snowfalls this month have been more severe than in any December since 1937'. 'Heavy December Snowfall', *The Times* (16 December 1950).

[33] Claude McKay, *Harlem Shadows* (New York: Harcourt, 1922), 76–7.

[34] St-John Perse, 'Snows (Neiges)', trans. Denis Devlin, *The Sewanee Review* 53, no. 2 (1945): 186–97.

[35] Shake Keane, 'Roundtrip', *The Angel Horn* (Philipsburg: House of Nehesi, 2005), 10. This important long poem, written 1975–1977, is a sustained reflection on migrant communities in Notting Hill in the 1950s and Keane's return to St Vincent in the early 1970s.

[36] *Poetry from Cambridge, 1947–1950*, ed. Peter Morris Green (London: The Fortune Press, 1951). Brathwaite contributes 'A Caribbean Theme', parts of which would be reworked into 'Calypso' and 'The Emigrants' in *Rights of Passage* (1967). He also contributes an uncollected poem, 'River Bay Revisited'.

[37] For Redgrove's involvement in *Delta* and his friendship with Brathwaite, see Neil Roberts, *A Lucid Dreamer: The Life of Peter Redgrove* (London: Jonathan Cape, 2012), 70–2.

white swans of a literary Cambridge of among others, Thom Gunn, Peter Redgrove' and another half a dozen names (59). It's possible, then, to read the middle stanzas of 'The Day the First Snow Fell' as an anxious self-reference to Brathwaite's position and literary prospects. He is the 'black wood' being 'carved into two white swans'. In an important later poem, 'Ogun', Brathwaite portrays his uncle, a carpenter, who on Sundays works on a figural carving, transforming 'knotted hurts' into the 'emerging woodwork image of his anger'.[38] In that poem, wood is presented as an elemental resource which can disclose ancestral memories. But here the swans are inert: they merely 'bend'. I want to read this as an image of deference and genuflection, and suggest that the swans are the undergraduate poets playing the game of patronage and self-promotion, ruffling what Brathwaite calls 'clever conceit within "formal" forms [...] not my thang' (*Barabajan*, 303–4). In all the other magazine versions, this line reads 'where the white *wood* bends' (emphasis added), suggesting that this was a barb Brathwaite initially reserved for his fellow undergraduate readers, and later came to settle on in *Other Exiles*.

Yet this bending and revision works another way, raising the question of mutability. In this poem, everything is moving and everything is still; everything seems to change and stay the same. The poem is full of action: falling, floating, melting, touching, carving, loving. These verbs swirl around the repeated nouns – snow, feathers, wood, water, swans – with the last three of these placed, in the middle two stanzas, in a series of copula equations. These equations – x was y – quicken the pace, and we're unsure if water *became* black wood, or simply *looked like* black wood. The images flicker, and we recall Aimé Césaire: 'In the image A is no longer A [...] In the image A can be not-A.'[39] But the freedom to metamorphose is consistently undermined, or at least bracketed by the deployment of seeming oppositions: black/white, birth/death, night/day. Though we know that each of these terms can move into the other, the poem seems to hold them apart. The effect is woozy, a reverie of equivalence and displacement, underpinned by a brooding sense that black reverts to black and white reverts to white. The poem works like a snowglobe: however much we shake it, once the motion settles we're met with the same structure, the same scene fixed in place. And yet the desire

---

[38] Brathwaite, *The Arrivants: A New World Trilogy* (Oxford: Oxford UP, 1973), 243.
[39] Aimé Césaire, 'Poetry and Knowledge' (1945), in *Refusal of the Shadow: Surrealism and the Caribbean*, ed. Michael Richardson, trans. Krysztof Fijałowski and Michael Richardson (London: Verso, 1996), 142.

to touch and love and melt protests against this, searching for reciprocity and a less fleeting and provisional form of relation.

These struggles and contradictions are enacted at the formal level of rhyme and metre. Even in this very early poem, we can see Brathwaite's extraordinary prosodic dexterity.[40] He seems to float the stresses of the opening line, an Alexandrine, through a cluster of rhymes and half-rhymes: I/my, snow/floated, first/birth. The next line continues this sound-patterning, and adds two very strong caesuras after 'feather' and 'window'. These pauses let the sounds linger and mingle in the ear. The third line stretches to seven stresses, a whole breath out, like condensation in the cold air. The stanza rounds off with a line of unmistakeable iambic pentameter. We'll return to this in a moment, but it's worth noting that this line delivers an image of rhymed whiteness on a very large scale: 'the earth was white'. The middle stanzas seem formed almost in reaction against this: 'the earth was white' is the 'environmental shock' which sets off the series of equations outlined above ('Birth was black water', 'Death was black winter'), all in three-beat lines, heavy with emphasis. The closing stanza returns us to the opening metrical set, and again ends with a line of iambic pentameter, resolving in another strong image of whiteness: 'love was white'.[41] There is no ambiguity about where the stress or rhyme falls. 'White' hangs in the air, pronounced like a rictus grin.[42]

I dwell on these prosodic aspects because I want to suggest that Brathwaite is already trying to escape the 'tyranny of the pentametre' he would later analyse in *The History of the Voice* (30). In this lecture – first given in 1976, and printed in two slightly different forms in the 1980s – he demonstrates how poets in the Caribbean have worked to throw off imposed European models of literary expression. Presenting a range of examples, including legendary calypsonian The Mighty Sparrow, the popular poet Louise Bennett and younger Rastafari poets such as Bongo Jerry, Brathwaite celebrates the realisation of what he calls 'nation language', a vernacular poetry adequate at last to the social reality of the Caribbean. The pentameter – which Brathwaite at one point calls 'the socio-colonial

---

[40] For an overview of Brathwaite's prosody and an original theory of 'cellular' scansion, see Ben Etherington, 'Cellular Scansion: Creolization as Poetic Practice in Brathwaite's *Rights of Passage*', *Thinking Verse* 3 (2013): 188.
[41] Later revisions alter this line to 'but all the world was dark while earth was white'.
[42] Compare Brathwaite's description of 'teeth and lips tight and closed around the mailed fist of a smile' of middle-class speech in *The History of the Voice* (London: New Beacon, 1984), 27. Hereafter '*HV*'.

pentameter' (*HV* 41) – represents the whole edifice of naturalised colonial domination. To use the language of the essay, it had to be broken down, fragmented and attacked. In the most persistent term, Brathwaite analyses how various poets *eroded* the pentameter, as if the pentameter were the white cliffs of Dover or a monument to be worn away. The tactics Brathwaite analyses are diverse, and range from the cricket commentator John Arlott to Marianne Moore's syllabics to the language of the Kumina priestess Miss Queenie. The scale of the task requires the use of every available resource.

In one of the most famous passages, Brathwaite analyses how the colonial education system shaped and restricted the available 'perceptual models'. He writes:

> in terms of what we write, our perceptual models, we are more conscious (in terms of sensibility) of the falling of the snow, for instance – the models are all there for the falling of the snow – than of the force of the hurricanes which take place every year. In other words, we haven't got the syllables, the syllabic intelligence, to describe the hurricane, which is our own experience, whereas we can describe the imported alien experience of the snowfall. It is that kind of situation we are in. (*HV* 9)

In the version published in England – by John La Rose and Sarah White's New Beacon Press, Brathwaite's comrades from CAM – he at this point inserts the first stanza of 'The Day the First Snow Fell'.[43] On the one hand, this implicates Brathwaite's early work in the perpetuation of forms of consciousness that have been superseded by nation language. But perhaps, on the other, it also suggests that in this early poem Brathwaite is already coming to terms with and struggling against what he calls 'the terrible terms meted out for universality' (*HV* 20). He describes elsewhere, in a stark description of the racism of the university literary scene, that because he was Black, his fellow poets and editors:

> could not see how this person could have written it. For them, therefore, it was a mock man poem, it was not real. And their problem was they were insisting that I should write 'real' poems about my own

[43] There are two extant versions of the essay: the version in *Roots* (Ann Arbor: U of Michigan P, 1993) – first published in Cuba in 1986 – and the expanded New Beacon pamphlet *The History of the Voice*, reprinted in 1995. My sense is that the New Beacon version is the later and 'definitive' instance, because it includes a long bibliography and a memorial dedication to Michael Smith, and it extends several footnotes. Brathwaite's work challenges any easy notion of closure, but the textual history of the essay demands further scholarly attention.

ghetto, and I, coming from Little England, felt that my poetry should be universal, the poetry of the world, not realizing that the true universal poetry for a Caribbean person is the Caribbean poem.[44]

The pentameter lines which declare 'earth was white' and 'love was white' *already know this*, with a sharp and wounding irony, and the poem as a whole is a painful working through and working out of the dimensions of his alienation.

Before returning to this argument, we should note a further and related reference to snow in *The History of the Voice*: the schoolchild who writes 'the snow was falling on the canefields' (9). Like several of Brathwaite's other phrases ('the hurricane does not roar in pentameters', 'the unity is submarine', 'the tyranny of the pentameter'), this has become something of an aphorism. There are at least two books which use it as a title.[45] In the version of *The History of the Voice* published in *Roots*, the child's attempt to have 'both cultures at once' is understood as an example of creolisation.[46] The child – faced with the imposition of a colonial education – has made an adaptation. In the past, West Indian schoolchildren wrote, following the textbook, 'the snow was falling on the playing fields of Shropshire'. Now they write 'the snow was falling on the canefields'. This is, of course, absurd, and stands as evidence of the suppression of adequate 'perceptual models' for writing the Caribbean environment. Yet it's also an example of creative resistance – or better, perhaps, as Brathwaite calls it elsewhere, 'creative ambivalence' – in a compromised position.[47]

Brathwaite developed his concept of creolisation in his doctoral work, *The Development of Creole Society in Jamaica, 1770–1820* (1971), and in lectures and essays including *Contradictory Omens: Cultural Diversity and Integration in the Caribbean* (1974). It is a widely debated and contested term, an overview of which lies beyond the scope of this chapter.[48] But it's important to note

---

[44] *Three Caribbean Poets on their Work*, 8.
[45] Judith Raiskin, *Snow on the Cane Fields: Women's Writing and Creole Subjectivity* (Minneapolis: U of Minnesota P, 1995); Ian Dieffenthaller, *Snow on the Sugar Cane: The Evolution of West Indian Poetry in Britain* (Newcastle: Cambridge Scholars, 2009).
[46] *Roots*, 263–4. In *Roots* the child is gendered: '*She* was trying to have both cultures at the same time.'
[47] Brathwaite, *Contradictory Omens: Cultural Diversity and Integration in the Caribbean* (Mona: Savacou, 1974), 16.
[48] For an excellent recent discussion, see Aaron Kamugisha, *Beyond Coloniality: Citizenship and Freedom in the Caribbean Intellectual Tradition* (Bloomington: Indiana UP, 2019), 76–113.

Brathwaite's emphasis on creolisation as an ongoing process: a shifting set of cultural dynamics set in motion by the colonisation of the Caribbean and by the Middle Passage. The child's experience in the classroom raises the question of imitation and authenticity. It is an uneasy and ambiguous example, sitting on the boundary between acculturation ('the process of absorption of one culture by another') and interculturation ('a process of intermixture and enrichment, each to each').[49] Though Brathwaite doesn't argue it this way, it's possible to see a poetic logic at work: at the end of the production process, which would typically take place overseas, granulated sugar looks like snow.[50] And beyond that still – holding at arm's length the portent of climate breakdown – the very unreality of the image can itself be understood as a powerful form of protest: as René Ménil wrote, 'the land of the marvellous is the most stunning revenge we have'.[51]

But it would be a mistake to downplay Brathwaite's indignation at how educational institutions shape, distort and deny forms of self-consciousness and knowledge. In his discussion of Sparrow's calypso 'Dan is the Man in the Van', Brathwaite talks about *Nelson's West Indian Reader*, the school textbooks he read as a child in 1930s Barbados. These were compiled by J. O. 'Captain' Cutteridge, who rose to become Director of Education in Trinidad and Tobago before retiring to the Isle of Man.[52] Sparrow refers to him directly in 'Dan is the Man', declaring 'Cutteridge wanted to keep us in ignorance!' and the *Readers* appear in novels by V. S. Naipaul and Merle Hodge.[53] In the volumes of *Nelson's Reader* I have seen – dating from 1928 but still in use in the 1960s – there is a persistent belittling of the West Indies, often brazenly so. In one written task, students are asked:

---

[49] *Contradictory Omens*, 11.
[50] In 'Didn't He Ramble', Brathwaite, describing crop burning, writes 'black snow falls from my heaven'; *The Arrivants*, 24.
[51] René Ménil, 'Introduction to the Marvellous' (1941), in *Refusal of the Shadow*, 91.
[52] Robert Fraser, *Literature, Music and Cosmopolitanism: Culture as Migration* (London: Palgrave, 2018), 170. For the definitive background see Carl C. Campbell, *The Young Colonials: A Social History of Education in Trinidad & Tobago, 1834–1939* (Kingston: UWIP, 1996).
[53] According to Gordon Rohlehr, Cutteridge also sat on the Trinidad Board of Censors, and had been satirised in a calypso by Atilla in the 1930s. See Rohlehr, *Calypso & Society in Pre-Independence Trinidad* (Port of Spain: Rohlehr, 1990), 285. Cutteridge's successor as Director of Education, Captain E. W. Daniel, was also lampooned by Growling Tiger in 'Daniel must go!' (1950).

> What common customs in the West Indies are very foolish?
> Explain why they are foolish and why they may do harm rather than good.⁵⁴

The repudiation of this question can be heard later both in Sparrow's ridicule ('they teach me like a fool / the things they teach me / a shoulda been a block-headed mule' (*HV* 24)) and in Brathwaite's determination to take common customs seriously in his historical and social criticism.

In another quiz we see the terms of opposition and equivalence I've argued 'The Day the First Snow Fell' grapples with and protests against, here operating in full effect:

> GOOD is to BAD as WHITE is to
> CLEAN, <u>BLACK</u>, WICKED, RED.⁵⁵

This is the model answer for a list of 25 logic-exercises, so that the student working alone will follow the heading: good equated with white, bad equated with black. And though the expression might be more subtle and refined, these are the terms for the racism of the literati at the university; the tutor who dismisses Eric Williams; the critic who calls you, offhandedly, E. K. Resentment. We can hear it echoing there, behind 'Birth was black water / Where the white swans bend / Death was black winter / Where the white wood ends.'

The 'environmental shock' Brathwaite examines in 'The Day the First Snow Fell' is registered through a particular sensation: floating. I've already described how the pattern of stress seems to hover, but really *everything* in this poem floats, from snow to feathers, wood to swans. Though the opening stanza touches the earth for balance, we sense that the poet has simply drifted out of his study window, reaching through the glass and dissolving into snow. The repeated emphasis on 'light' is optical, but also takes part, surreptitiously, in creating a mood of suspension. It is vertiginous. The poet and theorist D. S. Marriott has, in another context, described the 'uncanny, weightless state of non-being' that we find in the work

---

⁵⁴ *Nelson's West Indian Readers: Book Four* (London: Thomas Nelson, 1966), 72.
⁵⁵ Ibid., 242.

of Frantz Fanon.[56] Though it's unlikely Brathwaite had read it as he was writing the poem – it was first published in 1952 – we find within the phenomenological argument of *Black Skin, White Masks* numerous aerial motifs. These include trampolines, high jumps and springboards, even (at least in the Markmann translation) the introduction of a helicopter to the analytic session.[57] On his return to the Caribbean, the Martinican who has travelled to France practically levitates, with his 'almost aerial way of walking'.[58] More than once the ground gives way: 'in all truth, I tell you, my shoulders slipped out of the framework of the world, my feet could no longer touch the ground'.[59] The alienation produced by colonialism is gravitational: it holds the subject down until it doesn't; the colonised person is thrown, continually, into and out of another's orbit, a body in space, attracted and repelled.

These motifs climax in the profound statement of resolve in the concluding chapter:

> I should remind myself that the real *leap* consists in introducing invention into existence.
> In the world through which I travel, I am endlessly creating myself.
> I am a part of Being to the extent that I go beyond it.[60]

To leap into invention, to go beyond being, to construct a new selfhood: this is the revolutionary propulsion that Fanon commits to and would explore until his death in 1961. We can understand the dominant motion in 'The Day the First Snow Fell' – falling and floating – in Fanon's terms. It is the condition of being acted upon, a reaction-formation which melts on contact, not yet seized or understood. In a review of *Other Exiles*, Kenneth Ramchand identifies 'a figurative complex' in Brathwaite's earliest poems and argues that 'the key idea of this complex is that of a fall'.[61] Brathwaite stumbles, rather than leaps. But 'The Day the First Snow Fell' – which

---

[56] David Marriott, *Haunted Life: Visual Culture and Black Modernity* (New Brunswick: Rutgers, 2007), 33. See also Marriott, 'No Lords A-Leaping: Fanon, C.L.R. James, and the Politics of Invention', *Humanities* 3, no. 4 (2014): 517–45.

[57] 'If a Negro comes up in the first session, he must be removed at once; to that end, suggest a stairway or a rope to the patient, or propose that he let himself be carried off in a helicopter'. Fanon, *Black Skin, White Masks*, trans. Charles Lamm Markmann (London: Pluto, 2008), 147.

[58] *Black Skin, White Masks*, trans. Richard Philcox (New York: Grove Press, 2008), 4.

[59] *Black Skin, White Masks*, trans. Markmann, 106.

[60] Ibid., 179.

[61] Kenneth Ramchand, 'The Pounding in His Dark: Edward Brathwaite's Other Poetry', *Tapia* (2 January 1977): 7.

Ramchand doesn't address – half-rhymes with Fanon, in a kind of desperate pact. Recall that in *Black Skin, White Masks* the famous encounter with the child on the train who cries 'Regarde, le nègre!' takes place on a winter's day; the shivering body is misrecognised as trembling with rage. In a different part of the same world, Kamau Brathwaite floats to his death, loving still to touch the light.[62]

In a poem composed around the same time as 'The Day the First Snow fell', then known as 'Caribbean Theme', Brathwaite finds his feet. These are the famous lines he would later rework into 'Calypso' in *Rights of Passage*:

> The stone had skidded, arched and bloomed into islands
> Cuba and San Domingo
> Jamaica and St. Christopher[63]

The stresses here don't float; they skip in what Brathwaite calls 'a skimming motion' (*HV* 18). In later revisions, the stone's flight is 'arc'd', but here it's *arched*, like the foot and the spine of the poet who throws the stone out onto the water. The stance is strong; there's no collapsing back into the imperial marching of the pentameter, but instead the blooming of the *kaiso* rhythm, 'the actual rhythm and the syllables, the very body work, in a way, of the language'.[64] That this poem, long acknowledged as central to Brathwaite's writing, coexists with 'The Day the First Snow Fell' is important. It's tempting to think of the summer here as the negation of the winter, the stone as negation of the snow. But Brathwaite's work doesn't quite operate or develop like this. As the 'continuous tense revision' suggests, Brathwaite keeps the work in process, holding all the terms open for later recovery or renewal.[65]

Brathwaite's time in England in the 1950s has remained underresearched. The most extensive treatment has been by Peter J. Kalliney

---

[62] Brathwaite called the poem 'a suicide note' in his Judith E. Wilson lecture at Cambridge in 2005. See Jenkins, 'X/Self: Kamau Brathwaite at the Crossroads', 148.
[63] Brathwaite, 'A Caribbean Theme', *Poetry from Cambridge, 1947–1950*, 9–13 (9). Reprinted (with significant differences) in *Golokwati 2000* in what Brathwaite calls the '1950 Zurich Version'.
[64] 'The History of the Voice', *Roots*, 265. The New Beacon edition, perhaps anticipating Brathwaite's increasing interest in the possibility of computer technology in composition, replaces the body with 'the very software of the language' (*HV* 9).
[65] See the discussion of 'equilibrium' and 'disequilibrium' in Brathwaite, 'Metaphors of Underdevelopment: A Proem for Hernan Cortez', in *The Art of Kamau Brathwaite*, ed. Stewart Brown (Bridgend: Seren, 1995), 231–53.

in his *Commonwealth of Letters: British Literary Culture and the Emergence of Postcolonial Aesthetics*. This is an impressive and sometimes disarming book, which focuses on the interstitial phase between high modernism (1920s–1930s) and the emergence of postcolonial literature as such in the 1970s. Alongside this argument about periodisation, Kalliney examines collaborations and competition within and between metropolitan and colonial intellectuals, mostly taking place in London. He portrays his subjects as 'literary professionals', working across state institutions such as the BBC and commercial publishing firms including Faber & Faber.[66]

One of the persistent claims of the book is that these aren't straightforward instruments of capitalist domination: rather, following Pierre Bourdieu, they can be understood as complex sites of cultural production, which were often used tactically or strategically by colonial writers. Kalliney suggests, in an elaboration on C. L. R. James's autobiographical reflections in *Beyond a Boundary*: 'The field of literature, as on the field of cricket, was one of the few places in which black and white competitors could meet on terms of relative, if not absolute, equality.'[67] Although our first reaction might be to say that another term for 'relative equality' is simply 'inequality', Kalliney asks his reader to defer these sharper judgements. Literature is to be understood as a site of healthy competition rather than sharp antagonism; a friendly game, rather than a system.

The centrepiece of Kalliney's argument – the preface by the series editors calls it 'entirely persuasive' – is a reading of the affinities between Brathwaite's work as a poet and critic and the literary and cultural criticism of F. R. Leavis.[68] The pairing makes sense. For a student at Cambridge between 1950 and 1955, Leavis was an imposing presence. In fact, it's hard to overestimate the extent to which Leavis set the terms of the debate in post-war Britain. For figures such as Raymond Williams (ten years older than Brathwaite) and Stuart Hall (two years younger), Leavis was the main figure to contend with. His commitment to the 'great tradition' – Hall called Leavis 'its gatekeeper, its refiner, its gardener'[69] – was one of the primary objects that cultural studies had to work to clear away. His anti-Marxism, too, remained hegemonic: as late as 1983, Terry Eagleton

---

[66] Peter J. Kalliney, *Commonwealth of Letters* (Oxford: Oxford UP, 2013), 67.
[67] Ibid., 25. For a critical reading of James's analysis of sport, see Cedric J. Robinson, *Black Marxism* (Chapel Hill: U of North Carolina P, 2000), 266–9.
[68] Kalliney, *Commonwealth of Letters*, ix.
[69] Stuart Hall, *Cultural Studies 1983: A Theoretical History* (Durham, NC: Duke UP, 2016), 15.

would suggest, ruefully, that 'English students in England today are "Leavisites" whether they know it or not'.[70]

Brathwaite was not a Marxist. In a letter to BBC producer Henry Swanzy in 1953, Brathwaite positioned himself as an avowed Leavisite: 'I am Dr Leavis' man,' writes the young poet and aspiring critic, 'Because in him I found a road to run my attitude to literature on.'[71] For Kalliney, this stands as evidence that all roads – for at least the next two decades of Brathwaite's writing life – must lead back to Leavis. He draws parallels between their respective rhetorical styles; he notes their shared ambivalence towards educational institutions; he stages equivalences and continuity between key terms in Leavis' and Brathwaite's work. In this reading, Leavis' emphasis on 'the living language' becomes a precursor to Brathwaite's ideas about nation language and vernacular literature in the Caribbean. Brathwaite's assertion of a 'little tradition' in the West Indies is no longer a retort or repudiation to the 'great tradition', but rather evidence of affiliation.

Most notably, Kalliney argues that where Leavis looks back to the lost rural ideal of an 'organic community' (subject to extensive critique by Raymond Williams in *Culture and Society*), Brathwaite – along with Ngũgĩ wa Thiong'o – cultivates an 'authentic, oppositional folk culture' which 'could still be constructed in Barbados or Kenya'.[72] We can see here how the spatial relationship between an industrialised imperial core and an underdeveloped periphery carries with it a temporal logic. Forms of culture apparently belonging to an earlier stage of capitalist development persist in Barbados and Kenya. In Kalliney's argument, Brathwaite recognises Leavis' portrayal of the lost 'organic community' of pre-industrial Britain as the present situation of the Caribbean. It is another instance of his 'entanglement with Leavisite thought' (93). This downplays, I think, the extent to which Brathwaite subverted, repurposed and transformed the cultural apparatus as he *dis*-entangled himself from inherited critical models. As a historian, poet and cultural activist, Brathwaite would repeatedly address the temporal distortions brought about by the process of capitalist modernity. The Warwick Research Collective has argued in recent work on combined and uneven development: 'To grasp the nettle here means recognising

---

[70] Terry Eagleton, *Literary Theory: An Introduction* (Oxford: Blackwell, 1983), 31.
[71] Quoted in Kalliney, *Commonwealth of Letters*, 77. For another reading of this letter, see Glyne A. Griffith, *The BBC and the Development of Anglophone Caribbean Literature, 1943–1958* (London: Palgrave, 2016), 134.
[72] Kalliney, *Commonwealth of Letters*, 80.

that capitalist development does not smooth away but rather produces unevenness, systematically and as a matter of course.'[73] There simply are no level playing fields, anywhere, in the capitalist world system.

But it's possible, and even rewarding, as Kalliney's study implies, to read Brathwaite with Leavis in mind. Certainly, Brathwaite read Leavis' criticism, especially that on T. S. Eliot, a pervasive influence on Brathwaite's poetry until at least the 1970s. The image of snowfall and feathers in 'The Day the First Snow Fell' owes something to the 'white feathers in the snow' of Eliot's *Gerontion*, which Leavis had glossed: 'A bunch of feathers blown in the gale, it brings home poignantly the puny helplessness of the individual life.'[74] For Brathwaite, 4,000 miles from home, we can imagine that this sense of desolation would be redoubled. In his essay 'Timehri' (1970), Brathwaite again refers to the snow, writing: 'When I saw my first snowfall I felt that I had come into my own; I had arrived; I was possessing the landscape.'[75] But again, this moment of possession collapses in the face of disinterest from his peers, a loneliness both emotional and aesthetic. In an interview with Nathaniel Mackey, Brathwaite explains how *late* he discovered the work of figures such as Césaire – whose *Cahier* 'had been written when I was nine years old and living in the same backyard of his sea' – how long it took to get to Langston Hughes, Nicolás Guillén, Léon Damas.[76] Though he disavowed and overcame the English canon, his early reading – guided by Leavis and Eliot – deserves further attention.[77]

Curiously, Kalliney makes no mention of Brathwaite's story 'The Professor', drafted in 1954 and published in 2007 in the customary Sycorax Video Style of his later work: the text is set in two columns and several different fonts, moving between narrative, self-commentary and asides to the reader.[78] The title refers to Leavis, and the story – which shuttles backwards and forwards between two

---

[73] Warwick Research Collective, *Combined and Uneven Development: Towards a New Theory of World-Literature* (Liverpool: Liverpool UP, 2015), 12.
[74] F. R. Leavis, *New Bearings in English Poetry* (London: Chatto, 1950), 86–7.
[75] Brathwaite, 'Timehri', *Savacou* 2 (1970): 37.
[76] Nathaniel Mackey, 'An Interview with Kamau Brathwaite', *The Art of Kamau Brathwaite*, 13–32.
[77] For example, the unusual archaism 'everywhile' in 'The Day the First Snow Fell' – which becomes 'everywhere' by the time of *Other Exiles* – is probably an allusion to the metaphysical poet Richard Crashaw. Crashaw, Brathwaite's Pembroke College predecessor, writes 'But everywhere, and everywhile / Is one consistent solid smile' in his 'Hymn for the Epiphany'.
[78] See Brathwaite, *DS(2): Dreamstories* (New York: New Directions, 2007), 3–13. Hereafter *DS2*.

different meetings – is worth outlining in detail. Brathwaite admires Leavis and attends his lectures and seminars. He arranges to meet Leavis for a one-on-one talk, and presents him with an essay he's been working on, 'The Nature of West Indian Sensibility', in the hope that Leavis will take an interest in the poetry of Brathwaite's contemporaries, including George Lamming, Wilson Harris, Eric Roach, Shake Keane and Derek Walcott.[79] Although Brathwaite is self-deprecating about the essay (he describes it as 'shamelessly Leavisittian' (*DS2* 9)), he is wounded by the fact that Leavis finds the whole prospect of West Indian poetry beneath 'serious consideration. Since for him there was no **new bearings** there – no **rootedness**' (*DS2* 9).

A year passes, and Brathwaite is out walking on an autumn day. He bumps into F. R. and Q. D. Leavis, 'wearing thick brown << Marks & Spencer coats', with Brathwaite dressed in 'eternal Cambridge corduroy' (*DS2*). The Leavises beckon him over, and they spend time at the foot of a tree, at ease with each other, talking seriously and then chatting until it's time to go their separate ways. F. R. and Q. D. leave first. Brathwaite sets off, in the drizzle, through some woods, and then the denouement takes place. He hears F. R. Leavis in respiratory distress, 'a terrible wretching noise of something tearing body & soul' (*DS* 11), and Brathwaite freezes, separated from him by a screen of trees. On the other side, he hears Q. D.'s footsteps rushing for help. Brathwaite is faced with a painful dilemma, because he knows that 'she wd despise & hate me if i came. it wd be > stripping him of all his skin & dignity association' (12). Brathwaite sinks further into his hiding place, where the story leaves him, listening to the silence of the dark wood and the raindrops dripping on the leaves.

The story is told perfectly, an anecdote revised over fifty years into something mythic. The young West Indian intellectual, wounded and betrayed, leaves the old order to die out, half tragedy, half excruciating English comedy of manners. It is in no way a simple repudiation of Leavis and the Leavisite methodology and tradition. Brathwaite doesn't 'reject' Leavis, even if – as the story implies – he left him choking for breath on the Cambridge backs, the two separated at the point of 'skin & dignity'. Brathwaite pays excessive attention to Leavis' body, which moves with 'quick syntax steps', hazel eyes, thin

---

[79] This is the list of names Brathwaite gives in *Golokwati 2000*. Brathwaite implies that the essay was written as a paper to be read for the West Indian Society in Cambridge, was never published and was likely lost in the damage caused by Hurricane Gilbert.

dry lips, hands, high forehead: but they never touch. The structuring force of whiteness, its dominance, holds them apart. But Leavis *does* reject Brathwaite, and the story is in part about this drama of recognition and mis-recognition, and the kind of knowledge it produces. We end with Brathwaite literally invisible to the Leavises, but in a position which allows him to hear them and see them.

This returns us again to the question of combined and uneven development. Brathwaite and Leavis are brought together in what Brathwaite calls the 'still imperial / feudal' structure of the university (*DS2* 10). Between them lies Leavis' fantasies of an organic community in Britain's pre-industrial past and Brathwaite's cognisance of the history of slavery and dispossession in the West Indies. When the story is set – between 1953 and 1954 – sugar rationing had just ended; the Commonwealth Sugar Agreement of 1951 gave Britain preferential access to West Indian sugar exports, with prices set below the market value and opportunities for the extension of privatisation under the auspices of Tate & Lyle and the United Fruit Company.[80] What lies ahead of them? The West Indies Federation, the Independence of Barbados; the moribund and melancholy decline of empire. How can these histories be made commensurate? Fredric Jameson evokes Ernst Bloch's phrase, 'nonsynchronous synchronicity' or the 'simultaneity of the non-simultaneous'.[81] Perhaps we can recall again Brathwaite's 'continuous tense revision', a temporal disruption to match the discrepancies produced by late capitalism.

These political questions became increasingly important to Brathwaite. Though neocolonialism stifled the newly independent nations of the Caribbean, socialism in West Africa – particularly Nyerere's Tanzania and Nkrumah's Ghana – brought with it new hopes for social transformation and intense debate about what form the new states and societies should take. In his review of Walter Rodney's classic *How Europe Underdeveloped Africa* (1973), Brathwaite challenges Rodney's methodology, arguing:

> It would be a mistake therefore, to take it that European superstructures are an end of the matter, bringing man to his highest level of civilization and consciousness. And certain it is that *How Europe Underdeveloped Africa* was not set out to make this point. Very much the contrary. And yet (tyranny of the model) this is just what

---

[80] See Belinda Coote, *The Hunger Crop: Poverty and the Sugar Industry* (Oxford: Oxfam, 1987), 39.
[81] Fredric Jameson, 'Third World Literature in the Era of Multi-National Capitalism' (1986), in *Allegory and Ideology* (London: Verso, 2019), 190.

happens in/to the book. Over and over we find our brother, trapped with his modernist/progressive dialectic, talking about the escalation of African societies from their primal/primitive structures into something newer, more complex, more 'efficient' (i.e. exploitative of resources, less subsistent, less like their original model.)[82]

The tyranny of the model; the tyranny of the pentameter. For Brathwaite, Rodney's Marxist teleology – despite intentions to the contrary – still retains Europe as its centre of gravity, and he bristles in comradely frustration. Brathwaite's seven-year stay in Ghana had transformed his understanding of the relationship between Africa and the Caribbean, which he would go on to outline in the central section of *The Arrivants* trilogy, *Masks* (1968), in his PhD work and in the 1970s talk 'The African Presence in Caribbean Literature'.

The published version of the talk recalls the 'obscure miracle of connection' Brathwaite felt when, on his return from Ghana and living in St Lucia, he recognised in a seasonal drought the dust of the Saharan harmattan winds.[83] Brathwaite's climatic revelation gave him an understanding of Black diasporic history which would require the invention and rediscovery of a different conceptual apparatus, a counter to Hegel's notorious declaration that in Africa 'history is in fact out of the question'.[84] The harmattan is felt as a direct riposte to Hegel's claim that 'the true theatre of history is [...] the temperate zone' and specifically 'its northern half'.[85] Brathwaite's revelation points, too, to a formal difference between his approach and Rodney's: it is a poetics of history contending with a science of history, each a part of the whole.[86] The terms that Brathwaite goes on to develop in the 1970s, including creolisation, tidalectics and nation language, are part of his contribution to this argument and debate.

[82] Brathwaite, 'Dialect and Dialectic', *African Studies Association of the West Indies Bulletin* 6 (1973): 92.
[83] Brathwaite, 'The African Presence in Caribbean Literature', *Daedalus* 103, no. 2 (1974): 73–109. This is in itself a citation of the liner notes to Brathwaite's LP recording, *Rights of Passage* (Argo, 1968).
[84] G. W. F. Hegel, *Lectures on the Philosophy of World History: Introduction*, trans. H. B. Nisbet (Cambridge: Cambridge UP, 1982), 176.
[85] G. W. F. Hegel, *The Philosophy of History*, trans. J. Sibree (Mineola: Dover, 1956), 80.
[86] As David Scott says: 'Rodney and Brathwaite here map rival positions within a black radical *tradition* [...] they are engaged in contending interpretations of what is equally perceived to be a common possession, namely, the present of an African past.' 'On the Very Idea of a Black Radical Tradition', *Small Axe* 17, no. 1 (2013), 1–6, 5. See also the excellent reading by Andrew J. Douglas, '"The Brutal Dialectics of Underdevelopment": Thinking Politically with Walter Rodney', *The CLR James Journal* 23, nos. 1–2 (2017): 245–66.

Brathwaite's second residence in England, accompanied by his wife Doris (Zea Mexican) lasted from 1965 to 1968, and involved him in an extraordinary ongoing dialogue with his close comrades John La Rose and Andrew Salkey, historian and novelist Orlando Patterson, visual artists such as Aubrey Williams and Ronald Moody, and many, many others. One of the persistent features of Anne Walmsley's account of CAM is the emphasis on debate and productive argument, carried out both in public settings and informal gatherings, the sheer amount of talk and writing going on. Brathwaite's poetry was central to the momentum of the group. One of the inaugural events for CAM was Brathwaite's public reading of *Rights of Passage* on 3 March 1967, presented by New Beacon Books. A few months later, in July, Kwame Ture (Stokely Carmichael) spoke at the Dialectics of Liberation Conference at the Roundhouse, and for Brathwaite 'magnetised a whole set of splintered feelings that had long been seeking a node'.[87] At the same time, he was researching and compiling his doctoral work, situating his work in relation to Elsa Goveia at UWI, M. G. Smith in California and Patterson, who'd recently completed his PhD at the London School of Economics (LSE). In March of 1968, the Labour Government – who had banned Ture after his speech in 1967 – further restricted Commonwealth immigration, which had been curtailed by the Commonwealth Immigration Act 1962. That spring Enoch Powell gave his 'Rivers of Blood' speech to the Conservative Association in Birmingham, flaunting the central place of racism in British political discourse. The last CAM conference in England before Brathwaite's departure to take up a teaching post at UWI-Mona was dominated by arguments about political commitment and Black power.

One of the final resolutions at the CAM conference was to send a cable to the Jamaican Government in protest at the banning of literature by Carmichael, Malcolm X and Elijah Muhammad.[88] Following Hailie Selassie's visit to Jamaica in 1966 and an emboldened and strengthened Rastafarian movement, the Jamaican Government began a process of slum clearances.[89] In an atmosphere of increasing trades union activity, the Government declared

---

[87] Quoted in Ashley Dawson, *Mongrel Nation: Diasporic Culture and the Making of Postcolonial Britain* (Ann Arbor: U of Michigan P, 2007), 50.

[88] Anne Walmsley, *The Caribbean Artists Movement, 1966–1972* (London: New Beacon, 1992), 187–9.

[89] See Rupert Lewis, 'Walter Rodney: 1968 Revisited', *New Currents in Caribbean Thought* (September 1994): 7–56.

a State of Emergency. Running parallel to CAM's organising in London among the intelligentsia, Walter Rodney – a lecturer at UWI – was going out and talking to the people, 'grounding' with young Rastafarians.[90] This sense of *grounding* instead of *floating* is crucial: there could be no return to the specific form of alienation that Brathwaite had experienced as a young man. The grounding was a kind of leap. Brathwaite arrived back in early October, and Jamaica was almost immediately thrown into the 'Rodney Affair': the Government refused the Guyanese-born Rodney entry to the country, as he returned from a Congress of Black Writers in Canada. The country erupted into mass protest, giving specific political form to the decade's consciousness-raising and empowerment.

It's vital to situate Brathwaite's work within this political trajectory. Kalliney's study consistently downplays the political commitment of Brathwaite's work, emphasising often his doubt and hesitancy. I don't want to dismiss this: but I would suggest that it's often a working-through of doubt.[91] In his reading of the poem 'Anvil' for instance, one of the concluding poems in *Islands*, Kalliney concentrates on the 'fateful attitude' of old Tom, who couldn't bring himself to 'strike / the white // slave master down' (*Arrivants* 250). But in the final section of the poem – which Kalliney ignores – we find 'His terror, caged', pacing and turning and pacing. And then Brathwaite presents a direct challenge to his readers:

Which one

of you,
with doubt-

ing, peer-
ing faces,

will return
to where this

future paces
and dare

to let it out?
(253)

---

[90] Walter Rodney, *The Groundings with My Brothers* (London: Bogle L'Ouverture, 1969).
[91] And as Fanon reminds us, 'the body is surrounded by an atmosphere of certain uncertainty'. *Black Skin, White Masks*, trans. Markmann, 83.

Brathwaite's 'doubt' here is a component of social movements, rather than a quality of private failure or creative dilemma. 'Which one / of you' both situates the reader in a multitude and raises the question of self-transformation: which *part* of you will return to redeem the failures or fulfil the promises of an earlier generation? The poem ends with a rhetorical question because Brathwaite knows that the answer lies in the streets: as he writes in *The History of the Voice*, 'It is not language, but people, who make revolutions' (*HV* 13).

Yet Kalliney makes the argument – in reference to the Association for Commonwealth Literature and Language Studies Conference (ACLALS) in January 1971 – that 'Brathwaite's opening address at the ACLALS shows in condensed form the extent of his entanglement with Leavisite thought'.[92] At the risk of sounding like one of the Marxist dolts who Leavis chides for wanting things to be simple, this reading makes too much of the wrong details.[93] The conference, at UWI-Mona, came after major student unrest on campus the previous year, with a student occupation of the Creative Arts Centre lasting from February to April 1970. Concomitant was the Black Power Revolution in Trinidad, emerging from the St Augustine Campus of UWI and presenting a major challenge to the authority of Eric Williams. The debates at ACLALS, and the meaning of Leavis within them, can't be understood without reference to the context of a revolutionary situation and ensuing political repression. Kenneth Ramchand's article 'Concern for Criticism' (June 1970) devotes almost half its pages to an encomium on the Leavisite method, and uses Leavis to chastise Sylvia Wynter for subjecting literature to 'socio-political commentary'.[94] Wynter's coruscating reply, 'Creole Criticism – A Critique', says that Ramchand is using Leavis 'as a stalking-horse against Gordon Rohlehr's critical essay on Naipaul'.[95] Where Kalliney assumes that the 'presumed antagonist' of the committed writer at the ACLALS conference was 'the white scholar', in fact much of the ambivalence is between Indo-Caribbean writers

---

[92] Kalliney, *Commonwealth of Letters*, 93.
[93] For instance: 'for most Marxists, the attraction of Marxism is simplicity: it absolves from the duty of wrestling with complexities: above all, the complexities introduced if one agrees that cultural values – human ends – need more attention than they get in the doctrine, strategy and tactics of the Class War.' Leavis, *For Continuity* (Cambridge: The Minority Press, 1933), 5.
[94] Kenneth Ramchand, 'Concern for Criticism', *Caribbean Quarterly* 16, no. 2 (June 1970): 59.
[95] Sylvia Wynter, 'Creole Criticism: A Critique', *New World Quarterly* 4, no. 4 (1970): 12–36.

(Ramchand and Naipaul) and the advocates of Black power, including Wynter, Rohlehr and Brathwaite.[96] Rohlehr, for his part, wrote in the radical newspaper *Tapia*, 'Our context is simply not Leavis's'.[97]

The context is Rodney. Brathwaite's controversial anthology of new poets in *Savacou*, Nos. 3/4, showcasing nation language *avant la lettre*, includes a number of young Rastafarians who had been present at Rodney's groundings. These include Bongo Jerry (Robin Small), Audvil King and Ras Dizzy. As Brathwaite described it later, this was 'post-Independence consciousness (sufferer, Rasta, black, Marxist, guerrilla)'.[98] Far from snow, far from the blooming summer, Jerry writes:

> BLACK ELECTRIC STORM
>   IS HERE
> How long you feel "fair to fine
> (WHITE)" would last?[99]

Grounding, in Jerry's poem, sets the speaker in circuit with atmospheric Blackness. Brathwaite was inspired by these young writers and these moments of possibility, soon to be crushed under the weight of heavy manners and emergencies across the 1970s. In his elegy for Rodney, assassinated in Guyana in 1980, Brathwaite talks about 'how bonny baby bellies grow doom laden dungeon / grounded down to groaning in their hunger'.[100] From floating to leaping; from grounding to grounded down and groaning. This is a pattern we recognise, and one that recurs in the discovery of political commitment, the movement to political action and the experiences of defeat.

But Stuart Hall, speaking in 1996, described the transformation of Jamaica in the 1970s:

> When I'd come back in the '70s, people were speaking patois everywhere, you'd turn on the radio and people were speaking patois. I'd been prevented from speaking patois my entire life. This is a black

---

[96] Kalliney, *Commonwealth of Letters*, 94.
[97] Gordon Rohlehr, 'Afterthoughts', *Tapia* 23 (26 December 1971). Reprinted in *My Strangled City and Other Essays* (San Juan, Trinidad: Longman, 1992), 141.
[98] Brathwaite 'The Love Axe/L: Developing a Caribbean Aesthetic, Part Two', *Bim* 16, no. 2 (1977): 104.
[99] Bongo Jerry, 'Mabrak', *Savacou* 3/4 (1971): 14. See Jerry's reflections on Rodney in 'The Conscious Youth', in *The Groundings with My Brothers* (London: Verso, 2019).
[100] Brathwaite, *Third World Poems* (Harlow: Longman, 1983), 63.

Jamaica for the first time. Jamaica was not black before that. It became possible to be black in Jamaica at the end of the '60s.[101]

Hall, unlike Brathwaite, settled permanently in Britain, where over the course of his lifetime it also became possible, in this sense, to be Black and British. Brathwaite was a vital part of this, laying the groundwork for the cultures of rebellion and resistance I'll return to in Chapter 6. More than simply providing an example, or giving inspiration, his work is like an element, an atmosphere: the snow still falling, the stone still skidding, present, continuous, tense.

---

[101] Stuart Hall, 'Politics, Contingency, Strategy: An Interview with David Scott', in *Essential Essays: vol. 2*, ed. David Morley (Durham, NC: Duke UP, 2019), 242–3.

Chapter 2

Lovely, Flaring Destruction: J. H. Prynne, Charles Olson, Edward Dorn

> There is a great deal of whirlyblade about feeling, about increasing it.
> CHARLES OLSON[1]

For more than fifty years now, the political significance of J. H. Prynne's poetry has been hesitantly contested by Marxist literary critics in Britain. His work, for the most part composed and published as pamphlet-length sequences, has progressed dialectically: each discrete unit a fresh negation, with new limits discovered and transgressed. For his longstanding readers, these are *events*: little seismic tremors which sometimes result in flurries of discussion and debate. Gathered together in the ever-expanding editions of his collected *Poems*, the reader is presented with accumulated strata of radical thought.[2] But ever since Terry Eagleton's assessment of *Kitchen Poems* (1968) – recognising that this was 'a new political poetry', which seemed to 'critique the spiritual structure of neo-capitalism' but failed to 'communicate' – it seems that Prynne has never quite become the Marxist poet his critics might want him to be.[3] He is too romantic for the modernists; too Maoist for the Adornoites; too difficult for the populists; too aloof for the insurrectionists.

---

[1] Charles Olson, 'Quantity in Verse, and Shakespeare's Late Plays' (1956/1965), in *Collected Prose*, ed. Donald Allen and Benjamin Friedlander (Berkeley: U of California P, 1997), 281.
[2] J. H. Prynne, *Poems* (Edinburgh and London: Agneau 2, 1982); *Poems* (South Fremantle: Fremantle Arts Centre Press; Newcastle Upon Tyne: Bloodaxe Books, 1999); 2nd enlarged edition, 2005; 3rd enlarged edition, 2015. Page references in text refer to the 3rd edition.
[3] Terry Eagleton, 'Recent Poetry', *Stand* 10, no. 1 (1968): 73.

Yet from the vantage point of the twenty-first century, Prynne's politics seem relatively clear. His anti-capitalism has long been recognised. For poets and critics influenced by Gillian Rose in the 1990s, his work became emblematic of a late modernist rebuke to the supposed end of history.[4] For others, Prynne was engaged in strategies of subversion and resistance in a lineage traced back to Guy Debord and the Situationist International.[5] His anti-imperialism, evident in Vietnam War-era texts such as *Wound Response* (1974) has been consistent: his opposition to the invasion and occupation of Afghanistan in 2001 and of Iraq in 2003 was scathing and enraged, and took place in exchange with younger poets and activists in Cambridge and London.[6] His idiosyncratic anti-humanism, an admixture of an early engagement with Heidegger, a long commitment to the dialectics of nature in Mao and Engels, and more recently the work of psychoanalyst Wilfred Bion, has been increasingly evident.[7] He has shown little interest in feminism or in liberation struggles around sexuality, and the degree to which his work articulates a meaningful anti-racist position remains to be seen.

But Prynne is that rare thing: a poet who has grown more radical with age, more explicit, more demonstrative in his political solidarity. In the summer of 2010, he published a brief text called 'No Universal Plan for a Good Life', outlining in measured declarative sentences his striving towards 'truthful living' and 'directed political consciousness and commitment', suggesting that these were necessary facets if one was 'to be in and across all things a poet'.[8] The text was published by writers associated with the Maoist insurgency in Nepal, evidence of his serious engagement with non-Western literary cultures and with the political struggles of the Global South. In autumn 2011, Prynne marked the publication of his dizzying long poem *Kazoo*

---

[4] This tendency is most evident in *Parataxis* magazine, edited by Drew Milne between 1991 and 2001, shadowed and contested by *fragmente*, edited by Anthony Mellors and Andrew Lawson.

[5] See for instance Ben Watson, *Art, Class and Cleavage* (London: Quartet, 1998), and Iain Sinclair's framing of Prynne and others in *Conductors of Chaos* (London: Picador, 1996).

[6] See Joshua Stanley, 'J.H. Prynne's Romanticism: Wordsworth and the Dawn of Neoliberalism', *Textual Practice* 35, no. 7 (2020): 1087–1108, DOI: 10.1080/0950236X.2020.1731586. For the anti-war context post-2001, see *Quid* magazine, edited by Keston Sutherland.

[7] See 'On Peter Larkin', *No Prizes* 2 (2013); 'The Poet's Imaginary', *Chicago Review* 58 no. 1 (2013); 'A Note to Josh Kotin and Jeff Dolven', *No Prizes* 4 (2015).

[8] 'No Universal Plan for a Good Life', in *Sahitya Ra Jeevan Darshan* [*A Collection of the Expressions*], ed. Rajan Prasad Pokharel (Kathmandu: Madan and Geeta, July 2010).

Dreamboats, Or, On What There Is, closer to home. He gave a rare public reading to a student occupation at the University of Cambridge, where he has taught since 1961, sharing a bill with the legendary Marxist feminist Selma James. I was there that night, and for a time it all made sense: something like what Prynne's contemporary Tom Raworth described as 'the true centre, where art is pure politics'.[9] But this raises the question of wish-fulfilment, of over-identification and perhaps equally strong dis-identification, which is latent in much of the reception of Prynne's work and too often goes unacknowledged. Because of his long teaching career at Cambridge, many of Prynne's critics are his ex-students, many of whom have also had careers inside the university apparatus. Inevitably, they bring with them credulities and rivalries, taking up their parts in a sprawling family romance.

This chapter tries to get back to somewhere near the beginning, and to follow the first years of Prynne's writing life as a serious poet. I examine how his political formation emerges and unfolds through his correspondence and friendships with the American poets Charles Olson and Edward Dorn, and across the poems published in the worksheet *The English Intelligencer* and its associated milieu. This ground has been covered before. Neil Pattison, in his introduction to *Certain Prose of the English Intelligencer* (2012), and Alex Latter, in *Late Modernism and the English Intelligencer: On the Poetics of Community* (2015), have mapped how transatlantic exchanges at the start of the 1960s helped to produce a vital culture of politically engaged poetry in Britain. Keston Sutherland, Richard Owens and David Herd have all also written incisively on the inheritances and divergences specific to the relationship between Prynne and Olson.[10] In what follows I focus on how these exchanges were mediated and structured by histories of empire, race and nation, and I identify moments of ambivalence, disavowal and friction.

I am interested specifically in a phrase Prynne uses in a letter to Olson in 1964, written amid the passing of the US Civil Rights Act. He asks:

---

[9] Tom Raworth, 'Letters from Yaddo' (1971), in *Earn Your Milk: Collected Prose* (Cambridge: Salt, 2009), 115.

[10] Keston Sutherland, 'XL Prynne', in *Complicities: British Poetry, 1945–2007*, ed. Sam Ladkin and Robin Purves (Prague: Litteraria Pragensia, 2007), 43–74; Richard Owens, 'The Practical Limits of Daylight', in *Sauvage: Essays on Anglophone Poetry* (Kenmore: BlazeVox, 2020), 115–32; David Herd, '"To take the whole condition of something': On Prynne Reading Olson', in *For the Future: Poems and Essays in Honour of J.H. Prynne*, ed. Ian Brinton (Bristol: Shearsman, 2016), 196–215.

Emotionally how can anyone help being a near-Marxist (what with [Barry] Goldwater and that [William] Scranton man around); I thought that piece in Mainstream by Leroi J. was as good a punch as we're likely to see, a quick, knowing, passionate jab.[11]

Leroi J. is LeRoi Jones, soon to change his name to Amiri Baraka. The piece in 'Mainstream' is a piece in *Midstream*, 'What Does Non-Violence Mean?', an urgent call to arms following the church bombing in Birmingham, Alabama, and the assassination of activist Medgar Evers. In his gloss of this passage, Keston Sutherland writes: 'Whatever Prynne at this point thought anyone ought to be, he clearly did not think he ought to be it "emotionally".'[12] I want to allow for the possibility that Prynne's poetry escaped his better judgement. Across the poems collected as *The White Stones* (1969), which he began writing the year after he sent this letter to Olson, Prynne often writes about feelings, and does so usually in close proximity to a line break:

>   back to the place
> where I feel it[13]
>
>   or feel it
> as you walk[14]
>
>   what we
> do feel[15]
>
>   She feels
> the glimpse[16]
>
>   How
> I feel[17]
>
>   I
>
> can feel[18]

---

[11] J. H. Prynne, Letter to Charles Olson, 25 June 1964, in *The Collected Letters of Charles Olson and J.H. Prynne*, ed. Ryan Dobran (Albuquerque: U of New Mexico P, 2017), 100. Hereafter cited as *Letters*.
[12] Sutherland, 'XL Prynne', 57.
[13] 'The Stranger, Instantly', *Poems*, 40.
[14] 'The Holy City', *Poems*, 43.
[15] 'The Western Gate', *Poems*, 48.
[16] 'Love in the Air', *Poems*, 56.
[17] 'From End to End', *Poems*, 62.
[18] 'Señor Vázquez Speaking and Further Soft Music to Eat By', *Poems*, 97.

>   I feel the
> blood[19]
>   this
> is not our feeling[20]

Line breaks are decisive; they are also moments of doubt, ambiguity, deferral. A feeling is not the same as an emotion, and it may be the case that to remain in undifferentiated feeling is a way of avoiding becoming 'emotional' in the negative sense diagnosed by Sutherland. Sutherland's interest is in the development of radical *thought* in Prynne's work; but perhaps an attention to feeling will open out in unexpected ways.

To borrow a term from Raymond Williams, Prynne's teacher at Cambridge, whom he seems to have disliked, we might identify 'emotional near-Marxism' as the *structure of feeling* that Prynne's early writing moves within and sometimes against.[21] To use the language of Prynne's early poetry, perhaps this is the *quality* or *condition* of his thought. To return to the phrasing in the letter: Prynne's feelings are provoked by racism in the United States; he makes sense of his feelings by turning to a critique of non-violence, admiring Baraka's 'passionate jab' as he might have admired recent World Heavyweight Muhammad Ali.[22] Prynne's feelings are *reactive*: he can't help them; they are or ought to be collective feelings ('how can anyone'); he names this feeling 'near-Marxist', as if Marxism was incompatible with certain emotions or threw those emotions into doubt. Can we trace an aetiology of this feeling, the fleeting possibility of the 'emotional near-Marxist'? What was its origin? Where did it go?

∽

---

[19] 'Acquisition of Love', *Poems*, 111.

[20] 'As it Were an Attendant', *Poems*, 124.

[21] Prynne remarks in a rare interview: 'I don't think I would ever have thought of myself as inclined towards Marxist opinions when I was a student. I certainly objected to Raymond Williams's ideologies when he was my teacher.' Jeff Dolven and Joshua Kotin, interview with J. H. Prynne, 'The Art of Poetry No. 101', *The Paris Review* 218 (Fall 2016): 186. Hereafter *Paris Review*. Much of the incidental biographical information in this chapter, not always cited, is corroborated in this interview.

[22] In correspondence with Edward Dorn in May 1962, Baraka describes receiving a supportive letter from Prynne during an obscenity case involving the magazine he edited with Diane di Prima, *The Floating Bear*: 'He helped with the F.B. obscenity case, too, with a really positive letter, unsolicited, which I read for the grand jury.' Claudia Moreno Pisano, *Amiri Baraka and Edward Dorn: The Collected Letters* (Albuquerque: U of New Mexico P, 2013), 87.

Prynne wrote to Olson for the first time in November 1961. He was twenty-five years old and had recently returned to Cambridge after spending a year at Harvard on a Frank Knox Memorial Fellowship. Knox, a newspaper man and Secretary of the Navy during the Second World War, died in 1944. His widow established the fellowship in order to promote 'a devotion to the democratic ideal' through scholarly exchange between the United States and the British Commonwealth.[23] Though Prynne appears to have shown little interest in Harvard itself, preferring to split his time between Boston's Grolier Bookshop and automat diners, his experiences in America were crucial. It was during this stay that he had firsthand exposure to the new poetry, making contact with figures such as Cid Corman, editor of *Origin*, and accessing the magazines of the burgeoning mimeograph revolution. He travelled to America again in 1965 to teach a summer school, and in a letter to Olson in 1967 – which I will discuss in detail below – Prynne describes feeling, to his surprise, 'homesick for America'.[24] This is a concise description of what the Knox Fellowship, along with initiatives like the Fulbright Program (which facilitated visits by Prynne's students Andrew Crozier and John Temple to SUNY Buffalo in 1964, and Dorn's Lectureship at Essex in 1965) was designed to do. University exchanges were strategic aspects of the post-war expansion of American soft power, in which 'a putatively universalistic idealism was wed to a nationalist cultural program'.[25] Prynne's enthusiasm and ambivalence about American poetry and America itself must be understood within a specific interstices: the waxing US Empire and its waning British counterpart.

Prior to his undergraduate study, Prynne had been called up for National Service, a form of conscription enacted by the post-war Labour Government in 1948. National Servicemen were almost immediately deployed to suppress the national liberation struggles in the newly formed Federation of Malaya, and were used against the Mau Mau in Kenya and in the Cypriot War of Independence. Prynne was conscripted in 1956, and narrowly avoided being sent to Suez, spending the majority of his tour in West Germany. The Suez Crisis – which signalled both the weakness of British imperial power on the

---

[23] For further information on the Frank Knox Memorial Fellowship, see: www.frank knoxfellowships.org.uk/ [Accessed 18 September 2021].

[24] Prynne to Olson, 15 October 1967, *Letters*, 222. Original emphasis.

[25] Sam Lebovic, 'From War Junk to Educational Exchange: The World War II Origins of the Fulbright Program and the Foundations of American Cultural Globalism, 1945–1950', *Diplomatic History* 37, no. 2 (April 2013): 311.

world stage and the willingness of British governments to attempt large imperial wars – was decisive for Prynne's generation. After the nationalisation of the Suez Canal in July 1956, Britain colluded with France and Israel to invade Egypt in November. They failed to win American backing, leading to what Harold Macmillan – then Chancellor of the Exchequer and soon to be Conservative Prime Minister – called 'the Anglo-American schism'.[26] In actuality this was no schism at all, merely a realignment: from this moment onwards, British foreign policy would be subordinate to American interests. For Stuart Hall, four years older than Prynne, the Suez debacle was the 'moment of truth'. It laid bare the urgency of the task facing socialists: to try and think beyond the confines of a complacent '"welfare" philosophy', all too content to leave the structures of the imperial state intact.[27]

From 1957, National Service would be phased out, meaning that Prynne was among the last of his poetic contemporaries to have served in the army. In some respects, this makes his formative experience closer to figures such as Donald Davie, or even F. R. Leavis, than to the younger poets around him from the mid-1960s onwards.[28] The American poet Tom Clark (recipient of a Fulbright in 1965), in letters home from Cambridge in 1963, tells his parents about 'Mr. Prynne', who is 'smart & interesting' and 'very English'. Clark appears to have been convinced by his fellow students that Prynne has 'served as an officer in British army elite detachment, "Polish cavalry" (?)'.[29] We can see that to students within the university, Prynne was a representative of recent history, even as that history was overlaid with gossip, rumour and fantasy.

Olson, meanwhile, more than twice Prynne's age, had been involved in the Roosevelt election campaign of 1944, but had turned down a post in the administration. As Ben Hickman has recently argued, though this is often conceptualised as Olson's 'break' with

---

[26] See John Newsinger, *The Blood Never Dried: A People's History of the British Empire* (London: BookMarks, 2013), 189.

[27] Stuart Hall, 'The New Conservatism and the Old' (1957), in *Selected Political Writings*, ed. Sally Davidson, David Featherstone, Michael Rustin and Bill Schwarz (Durham, NC: Duke UP, 2017), 26.

[28] For Prynne's relationship to Davie, Leavis and the intellectual tradition of the University of Cambridge, see Louis Goddard, 'J.H. Prynne in Context: 1955–1975' (unpublished PhD thesis, University of Sussex, 2016).

[29] Tom Clark, 'Letters Home From Cambridge, 1963–65', Jacket Magazine (December 2002), online: http://jacketmagazine.com/20/clark-letters.html [Accessed 18 September 2021]. Prynne's close friend John James appears to joke about this in his poem 'Talking in Bed', where he refers to 'our / national service in the Polish cavalry'. James, *Striking the Pavilion of Zero* (London: Ian McKelvie, 1975), 13.

politics and his turn to poetry, this wasn't a clean break but a tumultuous and complex transition.[30] Olson's pedagogy and aesthetics are often a politics by other means, riven with contradictions. After quitting his post in the Office for War Information, and while still based in Washington, DC, Olson was one of the first poets to visit Ezra Pound, then incarcerated at St Elizabeth's on treason charges after his wartime broadcasts of fascist propaganda. His study of Herman Melville, *Call Me Ishmael*, published in 1947, carries a dedication to Pound, but the following year he would break off contact, ultimately refusing to play along with Pound's racism. His final letter offers Pound a rebuke, challenging his theories of racial 'degeneration' (or 'decomposition'), and invoking the history of European immigration to North America and the legacies of settler colonialism:

> But brother: we get decomposed here. We are not decomposition via the Atlantic.
> [...]
> Yr gd damn Europeans (I speak of my ancestors) (and yrs) acted from the start like a fucking bunch of G.I.s on leave in invaded country. Holiday.[31]

Olson's telegraphic style, learned from Pound, means that there is almost always something to unpick, something left unresolved. When he writes 'We are not decomposition via the Atlantic', he is, within the context of the letter, not referring to the transatlantic slave trade but to European migration. Pound's extreme anti-Black racism, including his collaboration with white supremacist terrorists such as John Kasper, would emerge later; in 1947 he was primarily known as an antisemite. Olson tries to counter Pound's biological and cultural racism with an appeal to morality, and his argument fails to land. He claims kinship with Pound ('brother') and iterates a common European ancestry underpinned by a shared complicity in the genocide of Native peoples. But this is something Pound would simply repudiate: 'Wot Olson don't know IZ, I hate Swedes as much as I do Jewz.'[32]

But the occluded comparison between European migration and the forced transportation of Africans in the slave trade is something

---

[30] Ben Hickman, *Crisis and the U.S. Avant-Garde: Poetry and Real Politics* (Edinburgh: Edinburgh UP, 2015), 66–90.
[31] Olson, Letter to Pound, 8 February 1948, in *Selected Letters of Charles Olson*, ed. Ralph Maud (Berkeley: U of California P, 2001), 75.
[32] Quoted in George Butterick, ed., *The Complete Correspondence of Charles Olson and Robert Creeley* (Santa Rosa: Black Sparrow, 1980), vol. 1, 147.

that structures much of Olson's thinking. In *Call Me Ishmael* he outlines an essentially mythic understanding of the United States, in which 'We are the last "first" people', imbued with a tragic destiny to expand and fulfil the meaning of the West.[33] A *Maximus* poem from 1966 is typical of how this logic works during his writing in the Civil Rights era:

> my father a Swedish
> wave of
> migration after
> Irish? like Negroes
> now like Leroy and Malcolm
> X the final wave
> of wash upon this
> desperate
> ugly
> cruel
> Land this Nation
> which never
> lets anyone
> come to
> shore:[34]

This is a passionate indictment of the nation, which strives towards the possibilities of multiracial solidarity. Olson recognises what David R. Roediger and James R. Barrett have analysed as the 'racial inbetween-ness' of working-class European migrants to the United States in the late nineteenth century through to the 1920s.[35] Lines earlier, he draws on the living memory of the persecution his father faced as a union organiser, and the poem gathers together anger and love into a great passage of indignation. But as Kirsty Singer observes, Olson attempts to 'render the American shore as common ground' by 'imagining the radically divergent historical experiences they inhabit as analogous'.[36] This is enacted prosodically in the passage quoted above: the 'sh' sounds in 'Swedish', 'migration',

---

[33] Olson, *Collected Prose*, 19.
[34] Charles Olson, *The Maximus Poems*, ed. George F. Butterick (Berkeley: U of California P, 1985), 497.
[35] James R. Barrett and David R. Roediger, 'Inbetween Peoples: Race, Nationality, and the "New Immigrant" Working Class', in Barrett, *History from the Bottom Up* (Durham, NC: Duke UP, 2017), 145–74.
[36] Kirsty Singer, '"what insides are": history – gravitational and unrelieved', in *Staying Open: Charles Olson's Sources and Influences*, ed. Joshua Hoeynck (Wilmington: Vernon Art and Science, 2019), 137.

'Irish' and 'nation', and the vowels of 'Negro' and 'Leroy' all resolve in the climactic word 'shore'. Underpinning this are the cluster of trochees, 'Swedish', 'Irish', 'Negroes' and 'Malcolm', that climax in 'Nation'. Though Olson was no 'naïve democrat', any more than Melville was, the counterpart of his mythic view of America is an idealism which emerges even in the most moving moments of anger and critique.[37] After all, Olson *does* write from the shore, and it *does* matter whether your arrival on shore is traced to the hold or the deck, and who that shore belonged to in the first place. Olson redeems the nation even as he damns it.

The reason I linger on this moment is because Olson's influence on poetry in Britain was immense. After he joined the faculty at Black Mountain College, becoming its rector from 1951 to 1957, his ideas were disseminated among many of the poets with whom he came into contact: Robert Creeley, Edward Dorn, Jonathan Williams and John Wieners, to name only the more prominent. In 1960, as Prynne was arriving in the United States on the Knox Fellowship, Olson and the Black Mountain Poets would take pole position in Donald Allen's *New American Poetry* anthology. Prynne would later recall that his copy 'fell to pieces out of intensive use'.[38] Prynne and his contemporaries, perhaps especially those who contributed to *The English Intelligencer*, came to understand their own work via a shared reading of Olson and the idea of America and American poetry that he represented. I suggest that this mediation creates a kind of double-occlusion, where Olson's anxieties and blockages about race in America filter back in peculiar ways to the poets in England, where the social category of whiteness operated differently and was undergoing its own changes in the 1960s.

To give an example of what I mean, this is a poem by John Temple (who was born in Stockton-on-Tees in 1942), which was published in Britain in 1968:

POEM
Jubilee is the word that pro
nounces, my life &
unites the people of the earth—the only
word that helps
me, as a living
person see where Malcolm X

---

[37] Olson, *Collected Prose*, 60.
[38] *Paris Review*, 180.

>   was going when they killed him, namely
>   that the plight of a lost
>   people in a north american
>   wilderness & the
>   reunification w. the homeland is a lost
>   cause (or a bypassed
>   one
>   because the world has
>   moved, as the poet sd. in another
>   context, on.[39]

Rather than a developed political position, this poem seems to register a partial moment of identification, at once both grandiose and self-effacing. The young poet John Temple is trying to understand 'where Malcolm X / was going when they killed him'. The word 'jubilee' – with its Biblical origins, its etymology rooted in the Hebrew word for trumpet and its strong association with African American song and emancipation – 'unites the people of the earth', rather than dividing them on racial, religious or cultural grounds. This is the movement away from separatism and towards unity that Malcolm X was beginning to pursue following his completion of the Hajj in 1964, before his assassination in February 1965. The following lines appear to hand over to Olson, 'the poet', with whom Temple studied at Buffalo in 1965.[40] Temple's readers would have immediately recognised these final lines and the irony they suggest, because they refer to the theory of continental drift, central to Olson's poetics, on which I'll elaborate later in this chapter. The idea of returning to the homeland is undercut by the movement of the earth itself: the world has moved on.

So we have a young English poet looking across the Atlantic to the Civil Rights struggle, balancing the figure of Malcolm X against the sayings of Charles Olson. This, I contend, is a *typical* experience for the poets associated with *The English Intelligencer*. Andrew Crozier, also a visitor to Buffalo, writes in the first poem in *Loved Litter of Time Spent*, composed during his American stay:

>   The Americans go by in their cars
>   I am standing at the bus stop

---

[39] John Temple, *Rothschild's Lapwing* (London: Ferry, 1968), unpaginated.
[40] Temple had visited Olson at Gloucester in January 1966, and is mentioned in *The Maximus Poems* by name in the poem immediately adjacent to Olson's lines on Malcolm X, quoted above. Temple has suggested to me in an email that this is in fact an allusion to Edward Dorn. Email to the author, 10 August 2022.

> I go by in Fred's van
> Three Negroes are standing at the bus stop[41]

Race in America is visible, remarkable in a literal sense. The poem triangulates a series of ambivalent relationships: Crozier and 'Three Negroes' occupy the same space but at different times. They are not 'The Americans'. Yet 'Fred's van' allows Crozier to assimilate, to join one of the 'insulating cars' and leave the multiracial bus stop behind. Nothing comparable seems to register in Britain. The period in which Prynne corresponded with Olson (1961–1970) and *The English Intelligencer* was operative (1966–1968) saw the independence of Jamaica, Trinidad, Barbados and other Caribbean nations; the Unilateral Declaration of Independence and white-minority rule in Rhodesia in 1965; the beginning of Civil Rights campaigns in the North of Ireland; mass protests against the Vietnam War in 1968. These events have hardly grazed the critical reception of the work.

Prynne's letters to Olson, which I'll return to throughout this chapter, are audacious, passionate and loving, ending, as both Keston Sutherland and Alex Latter have argued, in disenchantment. Though some of this feeling was reciprocated, as Prynne's influence is felt across the 'gloomy Republic' Olson constructs in *Maximus IV, V, VI* (1968) and the poems posthumously collected as *The Maximus Poems: Volume Three* (1975), the relationship was never on an equal footing. Prynne's ostensible reason for making contact was to solicit work for *Prospect* magazine, which he had taken over from Elaine Feinstein, an early correspondent of Olson's in England. Feinstein, whose family were Russian Jews, remained in the orbit of the young men of *The English Intelligencer*, warning them in the very first issue against any notions of 'fictional "Englishness"', asking, 'What could be nastier?'.[42] But what Prynne finds in Olson's poetry goes far beyond the parameters of simple literary interest. He writes:

> It will surely sound foolishly ecstatic, but you cannot imagine the sense of fabled release, the expansiveness, the new air. Most of it was new; but reading your various things was like reading for the first time the back of my hand. IN COLD HELL, IN THICKET speaks

---

[41] Andrew Crozier, *All Where Each Is* (Edinburgh and London: Agneau 2, 1985), 19.
[42] Elaine Feinstein, 'Correspondence' [1966], in *Certain Prose of the English Intelligencer*, ed. Neil Pattison, Reitha Pattison and Luke Roberts (Cambridge: Mountain, 2014), 3.

for me out of the fast centre, I know why the traceries and knots
and topology of the imagination, the arching spaces, the instant that
flows, the law of outward and object, the care and use of one's eyes,
I know why they turn as they must, fill out the necessary & musical
spaces; you cannot imagine with what intense excitements I have
been drawn to – RECOGNITION.[43]

The same letter will find him reaching for *Anna Karenina* to describe
the scale and particularity of his response and feeling. This shock
of recognition was not reserved for Olson alone. Prynne also found
something like it in Dorn, his other sustained and crucial American
correspondent and friend, who would prove in many ways a much
more important presence in Prynne's writing life. More than forty
years after the letter to Olson, speaking at Dorn's memorial service in
2000, Prynne described his first encounter with the work as follows:

But when I read those early books of Ed's, I recognised at once
exactly every word and every line break, what they were about, and
it was a great eye opener and ear opener to me, and we were fast
friends from that moment onwards.[44]

Though no longer 'foolishly ecstatic', the language Prynne uses
remains constant: it is the language of fate and destiny, the bodily
shock of finding what you needed to find. Here at last are 'some men
that focus / on the true intentness' and they will each change the
other's life.[45]

As Ryan Dobran notes in the introduction to the Olson-Prynne
letters, the 'asymmetrical interaction' that develops across the corre-
spondence is most evident in Prynne's research into the Weymouth
and London Port Books. Olson was interested in these shipping
records for what they could tell him about the early-seventeenth-
century settlement of the Massachusetts Bay Colony, the fulcrum
from which the whole *Maximus* project billows and unfolds.
He was specifically interested in two English merchants of the
Atlantic, Maurice Thomson and Matthew Craddock. They were
members of what Robert Brenner has called the 'colonial entre-
preneurial leadership', crucial to the history of dispossession and
capital accumulation across the East Coast of North America, the

---

[43] Prynne, Letter to Charles Olson, 4 November 1961, *Letters*, 11.
[44] J. H. Prynne, 'Afterword', in Edward Dorn, *Collected Poems*, ed. Jennifer Dunbar
Dorn with Justin Katko, Reitha Pattison and Kyle Waugh (Manchester: Carcanet,
2012), 938.
[45] Prynne, 'For a Quiet Day', *Poems*, 58.

West Coast of Africa and the West Indies.[46] About a year into the correspondence, Olson mentions his dormant hopes to travel to Weymouth to examine the maritime records for himself. This kind of work – what Olson calls *istorin*, finding out for oneself – was fundamental to the composition of the *Maximus* poems, its vast scale and sometimes inscrutable leaps. As Prynne reflected in 1969, the whole project worked through a 'panic-stricken encyclopaedic impulse' via the medium of 'primary writing'.[47] Because of Olson's freewheeling and often inebriated talks – the Reading at Berkeley in 1965, or his *Paris Review* interview – it's easy to forget that he was a skilled and brilliant researcher. He was, after all, the person responsible for tracking down Melville's library. The reader of the letters is left with the impression that Prynne is both trying to keep Olson on course, sending him reading lists, books, hard-to-find articles and recent research, and at the same time presenting Olson with a kind of test. According to Ralph Maud's research, Prynne sent Olson at least thirty fascicles of offprints and other assemblages, additions to the heaving tables and bookshelves of Olson's apartment on Fort Square. In Maud's typically astute phrasing, 'it meant something to Olson to have this kind of abundance in the house; he was bargaining for poems from a position of strength'.[48] Like a fisherman, he widens his net; he uses research as bait; he catches his poems.

The asymmetry works in both directions. Prynne, even at the outset of his career, is capable of complex and multifaceted research. He jumps at the chance to assist Olson with the Port Books; not only does he have geographical proximity on his side, he also has some status as a member of the university, a 'Cambridgeite' as Olson calls him (*Letters* 68), or a 'Caius man', as Prynne puts it in reference to a colleague (150). In his first letter to Olson, quoted above, Prynne's refrain was 'I know ...', and from the start, without perhaps even meaning to, Prynne demonstrates that he *knows better*, both literally and figuratively, than his counterpart. He is, or will soon be, better than Olson is at knowing, at finding out, at the systematic comprehension of a field or area of study. Take 1963: in January, Prynne writes to Olson from the Public Record Office (PRO) in London, where he is examining the Port Books, many of which are in bad

---

[46] Robert Brenner, *Merchants and Revolution: Commercial Change, Political Conflict, and London's Overseas Traders, 1550–1653* (London: Verso, 2003), 114.

[47] Prynne, 'Review of Charles Olson, *Maximus IV, V, VI*', *The Park* 4/5 (1969): 66.

[48] Ralph Maud, *Charles Olson's Reading* (Carbondale: Southern Illinois UP, 1996), 153.

repair, damaged by 'dirt & dust, and what looks like rats' (51). In April, he is chasing the PRO for the production of microfilms of the relevant volumes to Olson's interests. He sends these to Olson in May, with a note reading 'I hope these contain at least part of what you want' (63). In November 1963 he reports that he spent part of the summer in the British Museum, reading about Maurice Thomson, and forwards his correspondence with the Guildhall Library in the City of London, where records of customs and excise are kept. In between, he found the time to compile an outline bibliography of the archaeologist of Mesoamerica John Lloyd Stephens, prompted by a reading of Olson's *Mayan Letters*. These are differences in temperament: Prynne is orderly, methodical, precise; Olson is wild, charismatic, improvisatory. What Olson wants is material for poems; what Prynne wants is for Olson to come to England to look at the Port Books himself, a suggestion that Olson spends five years studiously evading.

While the letters give some insight into the dynamics of the relationship, the Port Books research is important for another reason. As Aldon Nielsen has argued:

> Olson's major contribution to the racial discourse in poetry, however, is in his use of historical materials regarding the slave trade, an aspect of history which the student of Gloucester could not very well ignore. It is common practice in *The Maximus Poems* for Olson to make his attack upon racism through the deployment of historical records demonstrating the monstrosity of the slave trade and praising those who opposed it, and *Maximus* is free of the complicating notes of prejudice which counteract the effect of similar strategies in Pound.[49]

If we follow this interpretation we reach a tantalising conclusion: that what J. H. Prynne is helping Olson to do is to 'make his attack upon racism' by extending Olson's understanding of Craddock and Thomson. Ten years prior to his application to establish a fishing colony at Cape Ann, Thomson was shipping enslaved persons from West Africa to St Kitts; a few years later he was financing the sugar plantations of Barbados.[50] Soon after, his faction of commercial interests would support the English Revolution and the overthrowing of the monarchy, becoming one of the most ferocious driving forces in the transition out of feudalism and into empire-building.

---

[49] Aldon Lynn Nielsen, *Reading Race: White American Poets and the Racial Discourse in the Twentieth Century* (Athens, GA: U of Georgia P, 1990), 146.
[50] See David McNally, *Blood and Money: War, Slavery, and Empire* (Haymarket Books, 2020).

Prynne's relationship to Olson, again, takes place in the nexus of inter-imperial relations, all the way down to the rat-eaten ledgers of three centuries prior.

But nothing in Prynne's published writing on the *Maximus Poems*, or indeed in his correspondence with Olson, suggests that he read the poems in this way. Notwithstanding the work of Frances Rose-Troup, it was only with Robert Brenner's research, beginning in the 1970s and published in full in 1993, that the networks of Thomson and Craddock were first systematically plotted and understood.[51] Likewise, the work of Peter Linebaugh and Marcus Rediker, and most importantly that of Paul Gilroy, would transform the understanding of the history of the Atlantic and its study in the late 1980s.[52] Olson's Atlantic, like Ahab's whale, is white; there is no many-headed hydra, only Maximus. In Keston Sutherland's influential interpretation, Prynne's long renegotiation of his debt to Olson will, by the 1990s, come to view the figure of Maximus as coeval with American imperialism.[53] This conclusion was far from inevitable. Though Prynne makes explicit references in the letters to empire – the 'U.S. Air Force brooding over the land' in 1964 (*Letters* 110), the British exit from Aden in 1966 (168) or indeed the question of civil rights – there's a romantic intensity which tends to outshine the details. As Sutherland says, we need to 'understand how impressive and beautiful Olson's ideas were' to Prynne; and these ideas, at this time, don't include using the historical materials of the slave trade and its groundwork in order to critique contemporary racial capitalism.

But returning to the question of feeling, I want to suggest that we can identify a perverse anti-imperialist challenge latent in Prynne's research into the Port Books. In an interview the day after the Berkeley Poetry Conference, quoted in Dobran's introduction, Olson describes receiving a 'catalog' from Prynne, with 'all the goddamn records of all the boats that crossed the Atlantic Ocean after Columbus that might have a bearing on entering Gloucester Harbor' (9). Olson's talk is good-humoured, comical and wily: he explains how he solved the problem of this mass of data in a single elegant passage:

---

[51] See Robert Brenner, 'The Civil War Politics of London's Merchant Community', *Past & Present* 58 (February 1973), 53–107.

[52] Peter Linebaugh and Marcus Rediker, 'The Many-Headed Hydra: Sailors, Slaves, and the Atlantic Working Class in the Eighteenth Century', *Journal of Sociology* 3, no. 3 (1990): 225–52; Paul Gilroy, *The Black Atlantic* (London: Verso, 1993).

[53] Sutherland, 'XL Prynne', 71.

Lovely, Flaring Destruction: J. H. Prynne, Charles Olson, Edward Dorn   59

> And now let all the ships come in
> pity and love the Return the Flower
> the Gift and the Alligator catches
> – and the mind go forth to the end of the world[54]

So much for Prynne's research. But in a passage that Dobran avoids, Olson relays the following anecdote about himself and his first wife Elizabeth Kaiser:

> In fact, he shipped me a catalog in Wyoming last year with the razor, airmail, and the razor – Bet and I were in bed when I was reading the goddamn thing, and I almost did what I did today with his razor that he cuts catalogs with so that he reads in all – he knows the books and everything.[55]

He had relayed the same story earlier, in a letter to Prynne in June 1964, three months after Betty was killed in a car crash:

> Please keep me informed on anything + all things—including such crazy matters [and I believe it was the last night or Two of Bet's life] that a razor blade fell out of one those two catalogues you sent me (a significance meant of all but it was a complete evidence of your own rate of speed—which I showed her—that you paid for the transport air mail to here of that Single Edge! (*Letters* 99)

Prynne has absent-mindedly left the blade he has used to trim and assemble the fascicle in the airmail parcel. Wrapped up in the gift is something sharp; the research culminates in an act of aggression. And Olson, who had made great use of Freud in *Call Me Ishmael*, surely understands this aggression, situating the story in the marital bed. In this telling, the conflict is animated by an Oedipal threat and the fear of castration; the slip of the razor and other 'crazy matters' are associated by Olson with the loss of Betty. The whole thing is so obvious it hardly needs to be spelled out.

But perhaps it's possible to read this scenario in another way, and to suggest that Prynne's unconscious aggression is directed at the Maximus who idealises America and promulgates a mythic understanding of the United States. Prynne's slip of the blade targets the shoreline, cutting both ways. The Port Books, which are the raw data of colonisation and imperialism, *should* wound the poem, derail it. Olson assimilates this material all too easily, and the triumphal

---

[54] Olson, *The Maximus Poems*, 120.
[55] Olson, 'Reading at Berkeley – the Day After', in *Muthologos*, ed. Ralph Maud (Vancouver: Talonbooks, 2010), 194.

announcement that *all the ships come in* doesn't ring out with anything like, say, Édouard Glissant's beautiful vision – 'our boats are open and we sail them for everyone' – but instead celebrates, unwittingly, the consolidation of American Empire.[56] It is, after all, in his reply to Olson's letter about the razor and the catalogue that Prynne describes the feeling of being 'emotionally [...] near-Marxist', a feeling which he must intuit that Olson doesn't share. If Prynne is tempted by Marxism in the mid-1960s – as he says in an early poem, 'the Marxist comet burns with / such lovely, flaring destruction' (*Poems* 17) – Olson has long since decisively rejected 'goddamned boring Marxian "commie" crap' (*Letters* 146). What I suggest here is that inside Prynne's feelings of 'homesickness' for America, his loyalty and love of Olson, there is a great deal of antagonism. This may be Oedipal, but it's also ideological: it is the dawning of a political commitment.

Though my reading here is evidently speculative, the tendency I'm describing is generally accepted by Prynne's critics. As Sutherland has so convincingly argued, Prynne quotes from Olson's poetry throughout the 1970s, subjecting it to critique, deflation, satire and detournement. My modification is twofold: firstly, that this antagonism is detectable from the start; and secondly, as I'll go on to show, that the presence of Edward Dorn in England from 1965 onwards transforms Prynne's understand of both poetry and politics. Critics – perhaps especially those who studied with Prynne – tend to find in his work an unshakeable consistency, finding meaning ingeniously secreted in even the most intransigent material. What I want to stress is that for Prynne, the 1960s were a period of disavowal followed by intense and sometimes fraught activity.[57] This is not a smooth process, and is marked by often contradictory and competing allegiances, deep anxieties and insecurities. He loves the new American poetry, but he is not an American poet. He is a young university lecturer, but he is unsure of his career prospects.[58] He understands his facilities in the language, but he doesn't know where it might lead him. Nowhere are these dilemmas more evident than in the question of continental drift.

[56] Édouard Glissant, *Poetics of Relation*, trans. Betsy Wing (Ann Arbor: U of Michigan P, 1997), 9.
[57] Prynne had published and almost immediately disowned his first book, *Force of Circumstance* (London: Routledge, 1962).
[58] 'You can have no idea how hostile the parochial mediocrity of an English university can be,' he writes in his second letter to Olson (*Letters* 16).

Lovely, Flaring Destruction: J. H. Prynne, Charles Olson, Edward Dorn

To try out our excavation from another angle, we might say that the problem with Charles Olson, and his greatest gift also, is that he makes everything seem like it ought to connect. As he writes in the *Maximus Poems*, dreaming of the priestly castes of Ancient Greece:

> All night long
> I was a Eumolpidae
> as I slept
> putting things together
> which had not previously
> fit[59]

Or a few pages later:

> I looked up and saw
> its form
> through everything
> – it is sewn
> in all parts, under
> and over[60]

These dreams and visions of unification, of putting things together and sewing things up, can be intoxicating. We can identify an ecstatic crescendo for this process in the mid-1960s, as Olson, Prynne and Dorn reacted to the discovery that the theory of continental drift, proposed by the geologist Alfred Wegener in the 1920s, had been confirmed by advances in geophysics. According to George Butterick, Wegener's vision of a united landmass, referred to as Pangaea or Gondwanaland, had been known to Olson in some shape or form since 1939.[61] In England, these ideas surfaced in popular nature writing, referenced for example by Jacquetta Hawkes in her post-war mythopoetic vision *A Land*.[62] In the 1960s, papers by J. Tuzo Wilson brought new developments to the attention of Olson and Prynne, and then in late 1965, Prynne read *A Symposium on Continental Drift*, the proceedings of a conference at the Royal Society. These papers have detailed accounts of new methods of ocean mapping, studies of the Earth's magnetic field and an analysis of the distribution of fauna and minerals on either side of the

---

[59] Olson, *The Maximus Poems*, 327.
[60] Ibid., 343.
[61] Butterick traces this back to a note Olson made while reading Thomas Mann's *Joseph and His Brothers*. See Butterick, *A Guide to the Maximus Poems of Charles Olson* (Berkeley: U of California P, 1980), 239.
[62] Jacquetta Hawkes, *A Land* (Harmondsworth: Pelican, 1959).

Atlantic. All pointed to the same conclusion: Wegener was right. The Atlantic had once been closed.

As Alex Latter has demonstrated, Prynne and Dorn arranged to have a copy of the proceedings sent to Olson, and a shared preoccupation with the study of continental drift can be traced in the cartographic imagery on the covers of Prynne's *Kitchen Poems* (1968), Dorn's *North Atlantic Turbine* (1967) and Olson's *Maximus, IV, V, VI* (1968), which uses a Wegener map sourced by Prynne. In a note to his English contemporaries referring to the *Symposium*, Prynne stated that 'the political and personal relevance of this volume has to be surveyed to be believed'.[63] In his accompanying poem, 'The Wound, Day and Night' – which he inscribed inside the gift copy for Olson – Prynne writes:

> Age by default: in some ways this must
> be solved. The covenants that bind
> into the rock, each to the other
> are for this, for the argon dating
>   by song as echo of the world.
>   O it runs sweetly by, and prints over
>   the heart; I am supremely happy,
> the whole order set in this, the
> proper guise, of a song.

'I am supremely happy'. There is no line break here to interrupt the feeling, as elsewhere in *The White Stones*, no hesitancy. In fact, this moment stands out in *The White Stones* as a rare moment of achieved and named emotion: elsewhere there is a great deal of hope and hoping, there are glimpses of joy, but this is the only moment Prynne calls happiness. Prynne is happy, and it is continental drift that makes him so. Why is this the case? In Guy Davenport's eloquent summary of Olson's career, continental drift is 'a comprehensive symbol of disintegration, of man's migratory fate, of the tragic restlessness of history'.[64] But for Prynne something has been solved, and the poets with this knowledge could 'suppress the / breaks', could 'dissolve the bars to it and let run / the hopes' and be reborn in the 'image   of love' (*Poems* 64).

What about the 'personal and political relevance' of the volume? Where Prynne's research into the Port Books has an indirect and

---

[63] J. H. Prynne, 'A Communication' (1966), in *Certain Prose of the English Intelligencer*, 5.
[64] Guy Davenport, *The Geography of the Imagination* (New York: North Point, 1981), 86.

latent political valence, the cosmic scale of continental drift surely overwhelms most political epistemologies. I suggest there are at least five reasons for the appeal: (1) It provides a means of reimagining the relationship between North America and Britain which antedates and dwarfs the temporary arrangements of NATO, Vietnam, military bases and the bomb; (2) The vision of a primary continental unity is, in itself, prelapsarian and Edenic. As Prynne signs off a letter to Olson, in awed tones: 'What Wegener could have done with the original unison of language' (*Letters* 177). Pangaea is earth before the fall, like language before Babel; (3) The scientific evidence for continental drift *confirms a poetic intuition*, and thus emboldens poetry: if this is true, then 'the whole order' could be set in song, and Prynne, Olson and Dorn could be the ones to do it; (4) It forms a kind of post-empire consolation, in which the dominion of Britain, greatly reduced, is found to connect and extend across the Atlantic after all; (5) It performs a specific affective function: paradoxically, given that it involves the closing of the Atlantic in the imagination, the image of primary continental unity is an example of what Wegener's contemporary Sigmund Freud would call 'oceanic feeling'.

It's the last of these that I want to emphasise, bearing in mind that Prynne's geological imaginary was shaped in part by a reading of the psychoanalytic criticism of Adrian Stokes.[65] The theory of continental drift acknowledges a breach – the continents have separated, the landmass is no longer whole – but it invites us to imagine repair and completion. We put things together; everything fits, everything adds up. The primary unity without 'breaks' in which we might dissolve and become flushed with hope is called 'happiness' in J. H. Prynne's poem. But we might also see it as a type of oceanic feeling. In *Civilization and Its Discontents*, Freud begins with a quizzical analysis of his friend Romain Rolland's account of a feeling which Rolland – himself an atheist – believes is the source of religious sentiment. In Freud's summary: 'It is a feeling which he would like to call a sensation of "eternity", a feeling as of something limitless, unbounded – as it were, "oceanic".'[66] This is certainly how it can sometimes feel reading *The White Stones*, even if only momentarily,

---

[65] Stokes talks about oceanic feeling in 'Form in Art: A Psychoanalytic Interpretation', *The Journal of Aesthetics and Art Criticism* 18, no. 2 (1959):193–203. For a compelling contemporary perspective, see Jackie Wang's lecture, 'Oceanic Feeling and Communist Affect', Riga Bicentennial of Contemporary Art 2020, online: https://youtu.be/ma6y2IFDfUY [Accessed 24 October 2023].

[66] Sigmund Freud, *Civilization and Its Discontents* (1930), trans. Joan Riviere, rev. ed. (London: Hogarth, 1963), 1.

grasped for a moment and then undone. It is the feeling of 'an indissoluble bond, of being one with the external world as a whole'.[67] In a letter to Dorn, Prynne calls Olson's Berkeley reading 'beautiful as scripture', and in some way *Maximus*, with its visions of creation and paradise, falling always between history and myth, makes most sense if understood as a religious poem.[68]

With continental drift, with oceanic feeling, the ambivalence towards Olson disappears, the demarcations of inside and outside, East and West, America and England: all are suspended. But this could only ever be temporary. In one of the wildest passages of the letters, written after Olson had finally visited England in 1967, and after which Prynne could never quite recover these limitless, unbounded bonds, Prynne writes:

> We do of course both realise that we were held off, here, and you most poignantly from as you say even the normal purchase of gravity, from what should have been the closing or reach over of a fantastic accident: the mid-atlantic cordilleras could have been ours, we could have stood there without drowning or defeat (or any of that female Hapsburg nonsense) and even Europa herself could have settled into something called <u>the re-emergence of land</u>.
> Instead there's a slice of meat, severed and bleeding at both shores, and we talk of home. A week ago it was clear and frosty for the first time, the earth beginning solid and giving that free movement through the air, not invited with old summer persistence: chaste weather, indeed. I mean, I thought about children of certain particular ages & tempers, and I was also <u>homesick</u> for the United States of America.[69]

Here a whole transformation has taken place. Prynne and Olson's meeting should have been as cataclysmic as the unification of the continents, or the sublime vision of the mid-Atlantic as a mountain range, the poets triumphant on ridge and peak. The passage is almost, but not quite, a parody of lines in Blake's great revolutionary vision *America*, 'those vast shady hills between America & Albion's shore / now barred out by the Atlantic sea'.[70] But instead a sourness is given free rein, from the inscrutable misogyny about 'female Hapsburg nonsense' to the contemptible domestic sphere in which someone

---

[67] Ibid., 2.
[68] Quoted in Alex Latter, *Late Modernism and the English Intelligencer: On the Poetics of Community* (London: Bloomsbury, 2015), 98.
[69] Prynne, Letter to Charles Olson, 15 October 1967, *Letters*, 222. Original emphasis.
[70] See Peter Linebaugh, 'All the Atlantic Mountains Shook', *Labour / Le Travail* 10 (Autumn, 1982): 87–121.

serves you roast beef. No more feeling oceanic, with 'the earth beginning solid': Prynne and Olson themselves are the wounded ones, the bleeding meat on either shore. At this point Olson becomes switched out for the United States of America, in the uncanny confession of homesickness. How did we get here from supreme happiness? 'We cannot fall out of this world,' writes Freud.[71] 'Love the world – and stay inside it,' commands Charles Olson.[72] To which Edward Dorn, who we'll now turn, offers a reply: 'the earth as primary object / must be destroyed'.[73]

Dorn arrived in England in September 1965 after a turbulent, pivotal summer. With the photographer Leroy McLucas, he had travelled on assignment among the Shoshone people of the Great Basin, across the states of Nevada and Wyoming. He completed *The Shoshoneans*, the resulting book, during his transatlantic crossing. Accompanying him on the boat along with his family was J. H. Prynne, travelling back from teaching the Buffalo summer school. Prynne and Olson's Atlantic crossing was always fantasy; here was the real thing. Dorn had in mid-July attended the Berkeley Poetry Conference, speaking in place of his friend Baraka, who, following the assassination of Malcolm X earlier in the year, had disaffected from the white poetry world. These were complicated and humbling experiences for Dorn, woven through with shame and a redrawing of his commitments. Between the book and his talk, titled 'The Poet, the People, the Spirit', Dorn outlines his ethical coordinates. Against race or nation or community, he will attend to the position of the outsider and the stranger. 'The man who doesn't belong in a community,' he told the crowd at Berkeley, 'is probably the man to pay attention to.' His loyalty to the disenfranchised would later have its limits: his homophobia during the AIDS crisis was unforgivable, and his contrarianism during the Balkans wars led him to pledge his support of Serbian ethnic cleansing. The arc of his work follows the traditional slide of the satirist into bitter reaction. But in 1965, the summer of the Watts uprising and the first search and destroy missions in Vietnam, Dorn

---

[71] Freud quotes Christian Dietrich Grabbe's 1835 play *Hannibal*: 'Ja, aus der Welt warden wir nicht fallen. Wir sind einmal darin' ('Indeed, we shall not fall out of this world. We are in it once and for all'). Prynne quotes the first part of these lines, in German, in his early 1970s poem 'The King of Spain', *Poems*, 188.
[72] Olson, *The Maximus Poems*, 582.
[73] Dorn, *Collected Poems*, 247. Hereafter *Collected*, with citations in the text.

strains against his own whiteness, his position as a poet and as an American. He is searching, self-conscious, vigilant. 'Most of us are not American,' he says; 'I want to ask myself if a poet exists.'[74]

Dorn had many enthusiastic readers in England, including Donald Davie – who, at Prynne's instigation, had secured Dorn's teaching post at the new University of Essex – and Tom Raworth, with whom he had been corresponding for half a decade. He would publish three books in England in as many years (*Geography* (1965), *From Idaho Out* (1965) and *The North Atlantic Turbine* (1967)), and he remains a lasting influence on British poetry. Though Olson has long been acknowledged as a primary referent, it's Dorn's cadences that the reader will catch in the work of figures such as Lee Harwood, Barry MacSweeney and John Hall.[75] But despite friends and a ready audience, in England Dorn continued to meditate on what it meant to be an outsider, to be dislocated and estranged. Though he had disavowed America at Berkeley, in England his position as an American was unavoidable, registering in language, habit and sensibility. The poems he wrote between 1965 and 1967, collected in *The North Atlantic Turbine*, work these disturbances up into a frequently acerbic commentary on Anglo-American commerce, the complacency of the old empire and the vulgarity of the new.

It's worth describing, briefly, the movement of the book. Dorn begins in an elegiac mode, with the poem 'Thesis' forming a plaintive address to the Northern Canadian territories of Aklavik. With its refrain 'Only the illegitimate are beautiful', it seems to revive the possibilities of the great romantic ode (*Collected* 233). It was the only poem by an American to be published in *The English Intelligencer*, and was well known enough to be grist for in-jokes in the 'spoof issue' prepared by Raworth and Anselm Hollo.[76] After two poems ranging from Croydon, South London to Hadrian's Wall in the North (where Dorn hung out with Tom Pickard and Basil Bunting), we come to 'A Theory of Truth: The North Atlantic Turbine', written, a note tells us, between summer and December 1966, with the help of Dorn's wife Helene. I will discuss this poem at greater

---

[74] Edward Dorn, 'The Poet, The People, The Spirit', in *The Shoshoneans*, expanded edition, ed. Matthew Hofer (Albuquerque: U of New Mexico P, 2018), 157.
[75] For background see Keith Tuma, 'Ed Dorn and England', *The Gig* 6 (2000): 41–54.
[76] Referring to a gathering of poets organised by Barry MacSweeney and J. H. Prynne in Sparty Lea, the spoof issue carries the notice: 'On June 1st a dozen or so poets are going to walk from the village of Sparty Lea in Northumberland to Aklavik in memory of their old comrades.' *Certain Prose of the English Intelligencer*, 114.

length in a moment. The longest poem in the book, the twenty-page and six-part 'Oxford', follows Dorn on a visit to the university town. Among the English ruling class in their natural habitat, his persistent reaction is disgust. The poet travels by train and remarks:

> The woman opposite me
> by no other act than Murder
> is permitted existence.
> (*Collected* 250)

Perhaps he was thinking of Baraka's play *The Dutchman*, in which a white woman on a subway kills a Black man. Here the murder is at one remove, outsourced. But it's telling that Dorn manages to treat the male undergraduates of the university with less scorn: he admits, shamefacedly, to being 'dazzled by learning'. It's not clear if Dorn was being deliberately, calculatedly misogynistic in the opening ploys of 'Oxford'. He and his contemporaries frequently mobilise a critique of capitalism and consumerism around the figure of women, the moral accusation often expressed via metaphors of sex work. These were homosocial groupings, and the politics they articulated were circumscribed by their homogeneity.

The second half of the book commences with a short poem about the assassination of Hendrik Verwoerd, Prime Minister of apartheid South Africa, which Dorn calls 'a message' (*Collected* 269). The Keatsian 'Wait by the door awhile Death there are others' moves through dream to waking and back again, and ends with the fabular account of 'Pedro', a Brazilian stowaway who has become stateless and who will 'ply the seas, a captive there / until he dies' (275). Dorn identifies with this figure, claiming: 'He is the man we all are and yet he doesn't exist' (276). But Pedro did exist; Dorn read about him in the newspaper, and would have learned that he was probably called Mantoani Alcide, and could have guessed he was likely seeking refuge after the Brazilian military coup of 1964.[77] Throughout *The North Atlantic Turbine* Dorn makes poems out of the news, as Prynne was doing at the same time in his *Kitchen Poems* (1968), several of which were composed at the Dorn kitchen table in Essex. As the book draws to a close, the unsettled and transitional quality of the volume is apparent: 'An idle visitation' is a vignette that becomes

---

[77] See 'Modern Flying Dutchman in London', *The Times* (6 October 1965); 'News in Brief', *The Times* (7 October 1965); 'News in Brief', *The Times* (27 September 1966); 'From Day to Day', *The Times* (18 October 1966). In the last two of these articles, Alcide is referred to only as 'Pedro'.

Gunslinger, the mock epic that would occupy Dorn for much of the next ten years; and the book ends with the masterful 'The Sundering U.P. Tracks', which returns to Leroy McLucas and the Shoshonean project. It is a painful reckoning of how race intercedes in their relationship, comes between them, governs their respective navigations of the town of Pocatello. It ends with a rhetorical question, and an equally rhetorical reply:

> You talk of color?
> O cosmological america, how well
> and with what geometry
> you teach your citizens
>
> (284)

Dorn's work is as beautiful as it is ugly. Like Olson, he is no Marxist, whether emotionally or otherwise, and his writing refuses the strictures of political commitment, instead expressing a volatile critique. He is interested in going too far, pushing limits, wrapping the offensive in seemingly effortless cool, while also *taking* offence at the seemingly innocuous. It is a great achievement, and difficult to accept.

I want to suggest that the 'Turbine' of the title, as it appears in 'A Theory of Truth', is quite precisely a satirical reimagining of the theory of continental drift and the kind of historical research Prynne had undertaken on Olson's behalf. For Dorn, the ecstatic revelation of continental drift – what I have called a species of oceanic feeling – is mystification. The geophysicists and poets can debate to their hearts' content what mechanism it is that drives the movements of the earth, from convection currents to rotational pull, or the eventual consensus on tectonic plates. Dorn knows that what makes the world go round is money:

> "We need *all* the money. The money
> has to be total and it has to be totally deflated
> It must be worth everything. One man
> must have *all* of it. *All* men
> must have *all* of it. Every man
> must, and will, or he will kill,
> have *all* the money.
>
> (243)

In one short, beautiful poem, Olson had written of migratory patterns of animals, plants and men ('constant in history') evoking both Gertrude Stein and the conclusion of Dante's *Paradiso*: 'This / is the rose is the rose is the rose of the world'.[78] Dorn replies: 'This is no rose / this is the turbine' (240). The turbine is a force of negation.

Olson was led to the Port Books because he was preoccupied with origins; but as Dorn says, 'There is no beginning / unless the end / has been reached' (240). Olson could have listened to John Temple's parroted advice: the earth has moved on, pulped and broken by the turbine. From England, Dorn can see further than Olson. He writes in the opening lines:

> not *includes* west Africa
> *goes to* west Africa
> rum slaves and crude molasses
> Wilberforce a standard trick
> of conscience, what i.e.,
> can be *thought* of man
> as he ventures
> part of Bristol is still rich.
> (240)

Chewed up and spat out, Dorn tries to account for the three sides of the triangular trade as the turbine sweeps up everything in its path. No fantasies of unity or repair, but instead a burlesque vision of destruction, starting with blowing up zoo animals with dynamite and climaxing with the statement, 'The earth has been destroyed'(247). The poem ends, as it has to, with Vietnam, but it does so with an awful pun: 'End-O-China' (248). There is no consolation here, except, perhaps, the consolation that comes from giving up on consolation.

Prynne's *Kitchen Poems* (1968) were written in close proximity to the poems Dorn published in *The North Atlantic Turbine*. He composed the five of them in relatively quick succession, publishing them in *The English Intelligencer* magazine between March 1966 and March 1967. They are discursive and argumentative poems, which mount a less satirically gleeful but no less scathing critique of the state of affairs. They grow directly from Dorn's company, and the mutual exchange of ideas and argument between the two men. In June 1966 – the same month Dorn begins writing 'A Theory of

---

[78] Olson, *The Maximus Poems*, 565. A broadside of Olson's handwritten manuscript of this passage was published in the UK by Andrew Crozier's Ferry Press in 1971.

Truth' – Prynne sends Olson a new poem, 'Die A Millionaire', which he says he wrote in Dorn's kitchen after an evening with Dorn and Robert Creeley (*Letters* 189). While the other poets slept, Prynne constructed a winding and knotty argument about want and need as social categories. This is the territory of Marx in the *Economic and Philosophic Manuscripts* of 1844: 'The need for money is therefore the true need produced by the modern economic system, and it is the only need which the latter produces.'[79] As Marx explains, the capitalist mode of production ever decreases the minimal needs of the worker, who is thought to be able to do without light, fresh air or cleanness. But as Agnes Heller reminds us, in a dialectical fashion, 'production creates new needs'.[80]

Towards the beginning of 'Die a Millionaire' Prynne writes:

> Imperialism was just
> an old, very old name for that
> idea, that what you want, you by
> historic process or just readiness
> to travel, also "need"—and
> need is of course the sacred daughter
> through which you improve, by
> becoming more extensive.
>
> (*Poems* 13)

As Alan Marshall has suggested, Prynne's high ironic style in *Kitchen Poems* – and in this passage in particular – diagnoses a 'metaphysics of imperialism'.[81] This is a complementary strand to Eagleton's 'critique of the spiritual structure of neo-capitalism' I quoted in the Introduction. We might argue against Prynne here, and say that in 1966, imperialism was undergoing a transformation. The previous year, Kwame Nkrumah had diagnosed *neocolonialism* as the latest and last stage of imperialism, just as Lenin fifty years earlier had seen imperialism as the highest stage of capitalism. Raymond Williams, Stuart Hall and E. P. Thompson would argue in the *May Day Manifesto*, prepared in 1967 and expanded in 1968, that the way Britain was establishing relations with its ex-colonies was, quite precisely, 'a new imperialism'.[82] Prynne's weary finitude here

---

[79] Karl Marx, *Economic and Philosophic Manuscripts of 1844* (Moscow: Progress, 1959), 116.
[80] Agnes Heller, *The Theory of Need in Marx* (London: Verso, 2018), 40.
[81] Alan Marshall, 'Drift, Loss, and Return in the Poetry of J.H. Prynne', *Études Britanniques Contemporaines* 27 (2005): 142.
[82] Raymond Williams, ed., *May Day Manifesto* (London: Verso, 2018), 68–72.

is compounded by the weak puns at the line-ending: 'Imperialism was just,' he momentarily announces; 'what you want, you *buy*' he says, and the poem rattles with the echoes of voices of shopkeepers or Tory MPs, too clever for its own good.[83]

But for all the definitive posture here, this is really the *beginning* of Prynne's serious thought about the mechanisms of contemporary capitalism. He will, in *The White Stones*, quote from Rudolf Hilferding's *Finance Capital* (1910), in order to critique the New York art market while he heats up a can of Campbell's Tomato Soup.[84] Via Dorn's collaborations with Gordon Brotherston and the Latin American Department at Essex, he will be kept abreast of the revolutionary struggles there – for example, the role of Fabio Vasquez Castario and the National Liberation Army (ELN) in uprisings in Colombia, which Prynne refers to in 'Señor Vazquez Speaking and Further Soft Music to Eat By'.[85] What begins as citation and reference becomes subject and theme, and by the mid-1970s Prynne is writing works such as *Wound Response* (1974), which harshly confront the war in Vietnam. This is a path of education and transcultural exchange, which will steadily and slowly accumulate. It was not inevitable that J. H. Prynne should commence the 2010s by publishing in Maoist journals in Nepal or reading in occupied buildings with Selma James. This is evidence of a long, slow and often inconsistent political education, which has for the most part taken place at a remove from practical political organising, instead growing from the reading and writing of poetry.

I want to bring this chapter to a close by looking at *The English Intelligencer*, which played a decisive role in the trajectory of Prynne's political positions. I have already alluded to Elaine Feinstein's early rebuke to the nationalist overtones of the title of the worksheet. Despite her warning, a kind of 'fictional Englishness' does abound in the worksheet, including visions of Stonehenge and Morris dancers, real ale and the rest of it. But there is also an erratic internationalism and at least some contending with the legacies of the British Empire. In the same letter she argues:

---

[83] I owe this insight to Alan Marshall.
[84] The passage from Hilferding reads: 'the transfer of capitalistic production / to the foreign market frees the latter completely from / the limitations imposed by its own consumer capacity'. Prynne, 'Foot and Mouth', *Poems*, 107. As far as I'm aware, this is Prynne's own translation.
[85] Tom Raworth would translate a 1967 interview with Castario in John Gerassi, ed., *Towards Revolution*, 2 vols. (London: Weidenfeld & Nicholson, 1971), vol. 2. Brotherston and Dorn compiled and translated *Our Word: Guerrilla Poems from Latin America* (London: Cape Goliard, 1968).

You letting in a presumably (?) visiting African, and excluding some obvious visiting Americans seems a deliberate piece of illogic which answers your need to assert some independence of the prevailing American culture.[86]

This is an intriguing letter, because it raises the possibility of a counterfactual version of *The English Intelligencer* which *was* orientated towards African writers, or had, say, made contact with the Caribbean Artists Movement rather than being dominated by the influence of American poetry, fraught with self-scrutiny about the place of Britain in the world. After all, poets including Henry Owuor-Anyumba, later a collaborator with Ngũgĩ wa Thiong'o, had also been students of J. H. Prynne.[87] But the *Intelligencer* mailing list of contributors was exclusively white, like almost every poetry magazine of the British Poetry Revival. The African Feinstein is referring to is most likely John Hall, who was born in what was then Northern Rhodesia, where his father was Secretary of State for Native Affairs.[88] Hall writes to the *Intelligencer* in September 1966, with the opening salvo: 'Poetry is like nation – I distrust it – that is, for us there should be no such thing as the state of poetry, & least of all of the nation's poetry, British poetry.'[89] He goes on to quote from 'Diamonds in the Air', placing it in dialogue with 'At Betancourt' by Amiri Baraka. There is here, I think, a missed moment, when the poets could have wrestled with the British Empire specifically rather than imperialism *per se*, which became America's responsibility as the Vietnam War continued. But they were writing in a broader culture that was doing everything it could to forget and to continue to forget British responsibility for colonial crimes. They would, each in their own way, come to reckon with these legacies in the decades that followed, through the Troubles in Northern Ireland, the jingoism, racism and nationalism of Thatcherism, and the renewal of the 'special relationship' of Anglo-American imperialism in the New Labour era.

These poets remained ambivalent, sceptical and, at least in some senses, opposed to a national identity. In 1987, in the preface to

---

[86] *Certain Prose of the English Intelligencer*, 3.
[87] Neil Kirkham, 'Keeping a Culture Alive: Henry Owuor Anyumba', *Once a Caian* 13 (2013): 24–5. Prynne is quoted in this article, describing Anyumba as a 'serious and highly motivated student'.
[88] Stuart Montgomery, editor of Fulcrum Press, was also born in Northern Rhodesia.
[89] John Hall, 'Some Notes for the Biographies of Poems Written and Unwritten', *The English Intelligencer*, Series 1, no. 8 (1966). Reprinted in *Certain Prose of the English Intelligencer*, 16. See also Hall's Letter, 1 April 1967, to Peter Riley, which discusses migration in Southern Africa, *Certain Prose of the English Intelligencer*, 100–3.

A Various Art, the first anthology to make the work of *The English Intelligencer* contributors available to a wider public, Andrew Crozier wrote: 'it is not an anthology of English, let alone British poetry'.[90] Of the seventeen contributors, one is Scottish (Veronica Forrest-Thomson, who was born in Malaya, and is the only woman in the anthology) and one is Anglo Welsh-Irish (John James). What, then, does he mean? Partly he implies that this poetry has been *suppressed*, and denied its rightful inheritance of the national tradition, displaced by Larkin and Hughes. We might say, more or less accurately, that 'it is an anthology of men's poetry', 'it is an anthology of poetry by white people' or 'it is an anthology of poetry by the university-educated'. But it's also as if the 'English' in *The English Intelligencer* was simply a stage to be passed through, a temporary entrenchment after the encounter with Americans and America, to be followed by disaffection. The final issue of *The English Intelligencer* follows something like this trajectory, as it announces that the poets are going to attend the Grosvenor Square demonstration of March 1968. It is the supersession of the worksheet, the turn to politics that never quite arrived. Perhaps Crozier simply remembered John Hall's words from twenty years earlier: poetry is like nation, nation is like poetry. Distrust it.

Although Prynne often fulminated against the *Intelligencer*, it was indispensable to the development of his work. All but thirteen of the fifty-eight poems in *The White Stones* saw print in its pages, along with the entirety of *Kitchen Poems* and various letters, comments and assemblages. Any serious study of post-war British poetry must attend to the network of the *Intelligencer*, and the fraught community it instantiated. But as Gillian Rose warned, it is easy to fall in love with the idea of community and give up on communism.[91] Yet at least some of the people that Prynne met through the *Intelligencer* were, or became, communists. As I have described elsewhere at length, the poets of post-war generation had strong intellectual

---

[90] Andrew Crozier, 'Introduction', *A Various Art*, ed. Crozier and Tim Longville (Manchester: Carcanet, 1987), 11. In a letter to Douglas Oliver dated 30 November 1987, Prynne takes extreme umbrage against this claim, calling it 'The silliest talk I have heard for a long time'. Prynne suggests that Crozier's meekness is a sop to the publishing industry and is politically defeatist. Prynne proposes the alternative title: *English Poetry and the Poetry of England, 1960–1985*. See Joe Luna, ed., *The Correspondence of Douglas Oliver and J.H. Prynne* (Amsterdam: The Last Books, 2022), 111–13.

[91] 'We have given up on communism – only to fall more deeply in love with the idea of "the community"'. Gillian Rose, *Mourning Becomes the Law* (Cambridge: Cambridge UP, 1996), 15.

affiliations with both the Communist Party historians such as E. P. Thompson, Christopher Hill and Eric Hobsbawm, and the wider New Left.[92] John James and Wendy Mulford joined the Party. Who was more 'emotionally Marxist' than Barry MacSweeney? Almost all were on or of the left. In the collective project of communist and socialist poetry in Britain, we find the painful working out, again and again, where it is we might start from, and where we might go. As Prynne writes in one of the many moments in *The White Stones* where the feeling is so intense it could only be called revolutionary, even as it disavows revolution: it is 'learning / to wish always for more' (*Poems* 53).

---

[92] See Roberts, *Barry MacSweeney and the Politics of Post-War British Poetry: Seditious Things* (London: Palgrave, 2017).

Chapter 3

The Avant-Garde of Their Own People: Poetry and Exile, 1959–1975

Before introducing the main subjects of this chapter, it's worth restating the trajectories and crossings we've encountered so far. Kamau Brathwaite sailing from Barbados to England to Ghana; J. H. Prynne travelling from Cambridge to Harvard and back; Edward Dorn making the trip to Essex from the American Midwest. In each case, these journeys were facilitated by university scholarships and undertaken in relative prosperity and security. But they were also symbolically resonant, their meanings overdetermined. Brathwaite was a representative of the Black diaspora, tracing an arc of trial and spiritual renewal. Prynne was at the ambivalent crux of inter-empire contest, trying to negotiate literary inheritance and political commitment. Dorn was seeking to disaffiliate from any schema of national belonging. In the previous chapter, I made glancing reference to Mantoani Alcide, a stowaway on the Oakwood cargo ship in 1965. Aside from Dorn's poem, 'Wait by the door awhile death there are others', Alcide's story appears in a handful of 'News in Brief' items in *The Times*, each of which reports on his lack of identity papers and resulting inability to make landfall at port. Over the course of these stories he loses his name, becoming known only as 'Pedro', and his nationality – initially reported as Brazilian, subsequently Argentinian – becomes increasingly uncertain. His final appearance in the newspaper, to the best of my knowledge, comes in a Reuters news report from September 1966. Three small paragraphs detail his transfer to a quarantine centre in Perth, Australia, ending with what would be, for anyone following the story, something of a refrain: 'because he has no identity documents he is classed as an illegal immigrant in every port'.[1]

---

[1] 'From Day to Day', *The Times* (18 October 1966).

Would it be possible to tell the story of post-war British poetry – or, rather, *poetry in post-war Britain* – from a position closer to the stowaway than the Fulbright? The major structuring division in our literary criticism remains the split between the mainstream and the avant-garde, with its various shibboleths: closed vs open form; a transparent or a troubled lyric subjectivity; rhymed vs free verse; referential vs non-referential language, and various other ways of sorting the sheep from the goats and the wheat from the chaff. The urgency of these arguments has faded over time, and the incorporation of 'experimental' technique into creative writing degrees means that, in the present moment, much of the formal distinction no longer applies. But what this division represents is an insistence on the political significance of aesthetic practice. The governing fiction of the avant-garde is that political conservatism goes hand in hand with aesthetic conservatism. This is obviously wishful thinking: open any left-wing anthology of the past century and you're sure to find contributors who believe form stops at 'The Masque of Anarchy'; and of course, the avenues of modernist poetry are littered with fascists, eugenicists and bigots. But the history of this argument should be understood as a *demand*: the poets must turn the reactionary politics of Pound and Eliot on their heads, seize the new possibilities – poems containing history, fragments shored against ruins – and advance a different programme. Part of the story of post-war British poetry is, precisely, the emergence of a socialist modernism and the contradictions this entails. But do these inheritors of modernism inherit modernism's condition of exile? On the contrary, with their British Poetry Revival and their *English Intelligencer*, they seem all too at home.[2] They might *talk* about exile, a little transcendental homelessness or perhaps nomadic lines of flight, but they simply protest too much. Where *are* the exiles? Where *are* the stateless, the émigrés?

Writing in 1941, Hannah Arendt argued that 'refugees from every nation, driven as they are from country to country, have become

---

[2] We can understand both *The English Intelligencer* and the British Poetry Revival as emblematic of the dilemmas of English modernism proposed by Jed Etsy: 'if English culture was too national for a thriving intercultural modernism, it was *also not national enough*. This buried element of the problem becomes visible when we reread English modernism in terms of the imperial hollowing-out of national culture'. *A Sinking Island: Modernism and National Culture in England* (Princeton: Princeton UP, 2004), 35. That is, the emergence of post-war socialist modernism takes place from *within* the hollowed-out national culture, asserting and reformulating 'Englishness' and 'Britishness' in relation to European and North American avant-gardes.

the avant-garde of their own people'.³ The context, of course, was not speculation about literary modernism, but mass displacement in Nazi-occupied Europe and the Zionist project in British Mandate Palestine. But the idea, an avant-garde of refugees, of the stateless, in post-war Britain – is it possible? Think of Kurt Schwitters in a detention centre on the Isle of Man, then dying the day after he received British citizenship in 1948. Or Amelia Rosselli, orphaned by the Mussolini regime and educated in London, writing her first poems in English – her mother tongue – desperate with warnings from 'my revolutionary heart'.⁴ Or Dambudzo Marechera, the Zimbabwean novelist and poet, thrown out of Oxford University after an arson attempt in 1977, whose experience of exile led him to declare: 'If you write for a specific nation or a specific race, then fuck you.'⁵ A study of these writers and others like them would surely offer up new forms of linguistic innovation and experiment, different chronologies and cartographies.

This chapter makes a start on such a project. I begin by focusing on Claudia Jones, and make links between her work and that of the South African poet Mazisi Kunene, and his role within the 'external mission' of the African National Congress (ANC) in exile.⁶ I then introduce the work of Arthur Nortje, another South African, who was not directly involved in political activism but consistently portrays the painful experience of being displaced. He writes in a brief poem, shortly after his arrival in Britain in 1966, 'I am saying I am sorry / I spilled across your borders'.⁷ Finally I look at the work undertaken by the poet and artist Cecilia Vicuña following the military coup in her native Chile in 1973. Her book *Saborami*, produced

---

³ Hannah Arendt, 'Active Patience' (1941), in *The Jewish Writings*, ed. Jerome Kohn and Ron H. Feldman (New York: Shockhen, 2007), 141. The same phrasing, with 'vanguard' for 'avant-garde' and the qualifier '– if they keep their identity' appears in the celebrated 'We Refugees' (1943). I am indebted to Lyndsey Stonebridge's discussion in *Placeless People: Writing, Rights, and Refugees* (Oxford: Oxford UP, 2018), 1–45.

⁴ Amelia Rosselli, *Sleep: Poesie in Inglese*, ed. Emmanuela Tandello (Milan: Garzanti, 2020), 124. Rosselli's work in English – around a hundred poems – deserves more attention from anglophone scholars. For the life of her mother, Marion Cave Rosselli, see Isabelle Richet, *Women, Antifascism and Mussolini's Italy* (London: Bloomsbury, 2018).

⁵ Flora Veit-Wild, *Dambudzo Marechera: A Source-Book on His Life and Work* (Harare: U of Zimbabwe P, 1992), 221.

⁶ Stephen Ellis, *External Mission: The ANC in Exile, 1960–1990* (Oxford: Oxford UP, 2013).

⁷ Arthur Nortje, 'Spring Feeling', *Dead Roots* (London: Heinemann, 1973), 37. Hereafter *Dead Roots*, with citation in text.

by the collaborative Beau Geste Press in the month of the coup, is an unapologetic spilling across borders, vividly experimental and politically militant. Though none of these writers were stowaways – Kunene, Nortje and Vicuña at least all also came on university scholarships – each became exiled in Britain and none could return home.

The Trinidadian communist activist Claudia Jones died in London on Christmas Day, 1964. She had arrived in Britain in 1955 after being deported from the United States due to her political activism, and was in continuous ill health as a result of her repeated periods of incarceration. Her numerous achievements in Britain included establishing the *West Indian Gazette*, and organising the community response to racist violence in Notting Hill, the foundation of the modern-day Notting Hill Carnival. A member of the Communist Party of Great Britain (CPGB) and the Caribbean Labour Congress, she was a pivotal and influential figure. She also wrote poetry, and as the scholarship of Carol Boyce Davies has made clear, poetry was a central resource in Jones's intellectual and emotional life.

It's no surprise, then, to see the prominence of poetry in her memorialisation. On 27 February 1965, following the internment of her ashes at Highgate Cemetery (famously, 'to the left of Karl Marx'), a public meeting was held at St Pancras Town Hall.[8] It was chaired by Mazisi Kunene, then known as Raymond Kunene, one of the chief representatives of the ANC in Europe and later poet laureate of South Africa. The event included recitations, by the actors Bari Jonson and Earl Cameron, of poems by Langston Hughes ('Let America Be America Again') and the Guyanese revolutionary Martin Carter ('Death of a Comrade'). Peter Blackman, veteran member of the CPGB and author of the extraordinary long poem *My Song is For All Men*, read his 'To Claudia' and also gave a speech.[9] There were further performances by the singer, actor and songwriter Nadia Cattouse, along with Peggy and Pete Seeger.[10]

---

[8] See Carole Boyce Davies, *Left of Karl Marx: The Political Life of Black Communist Claudia Jones* (Durham, NC: Duke UP, 2007).

[9] Peter Blackman, *My Song is For All Men* (London: Lawrence & Wishart, 1952). Collected in Blackman, *Footprints*, ed. Chris Searle (Ripon: Smokestack, 2013). Blackman's wife, Winifred, was one of the first Black nurses in England and later became involved in lesbian activism. See her contribution to Selma James, ed., *Strangers and Sisters: Women, Race, & Immigration* (Bristol: Falling Wall, 1985), 141–6.

[10] See Marika Sherwood, *Claudia Jones: A Life in Exile* (London: Lawrence & Wishart, 1999), 164–72.

In his statement on behalf of the ANC – printed in Jones's *Gazette* – Kunene writes:

> The death of Claudia Jones has deprived the liberation movements all over the world of one of the most dynamic and most militant fighters. [...] Claudia as we knew her belonged to the forefront of the struggle against imperialism, colonialism, and fascism. She at no time stood aside when the fight was on, be it the struggle of the Afro-Americans in the USA, the Africans in Angola, South Africa, Algeria or Asians in South Africa [...] She attacked uncompromisingly the lies that beset the British society, and personally organised demonstrations and campaigned against the Immigration Act.[11]

That Kunene's description of Jones's multiple solidarities ends with her resistance to the 1962 Commonwealth Immigration Act is important. This legislation removed the right of Commonwealth citizens to settle in Britain, and introduced a vouchers system based on a distinction between 'skilled' and 'unskilled' labour. It was not only intended to limit non-white immigration, but as an act of legislation it *produced* the 'immigrant' from the remains of the British Commonwealth subject.[12] In the analysis of A. Sivanandan, these measures 'took discrimination out of the market-place and gave it the sanction of the state', and 'made racism respectable and clinical by institutionalising it'.[13] As I've said, Jones herself had been through the traumatic experience of deportation and understood both the border and the question of citizenship as a site of antagonism. Kunene, who had grown up with the pass laws of apartheid South Africa, and as a member of the ANC (proscribed in South Africa since 1960), also understood the discriminatory practices of the state, and how racism becomes enshrined in laws, statutes and acts.

Joseph Keith, writing about Jones, has theorised what he calls the condition of *alienage*. This is the exclusion from 'legal, social, and cultural forms of national membership', and 'marks

---

[11] Raymond Kunene, 'World Liberation Movement Loss', in Buzz Johnson, *'I Think of My Mother': Notes on the Life and Times of Claudia Jones* (London: Karia, 1985), 165.

[12] See Nadine El-Enany, *(B)ordering Britain: Law, Race, and Empire* (Manchester: Manchester UP, 2020).

[13] A. Sivanandan, 'Race, Class, and the State: The Political Economy of the Immigration' (1976), in *Catching History on the Wing: Race, Culture and Globalisation* (London: Pluto, 2008), 73. For Jones's analysis, see 'The Caribbean Community in Britain' (1964), in *Claudia Jones: Beyond Containment*, ed. Carole Boyce Davies (Banbury: Ayebia, 2011), 171–4.

the boundaries against which the conceptual and political terms of national belonging are in part defined and secured'.[14] The term is helpful for two reasons. First, exile, which can in some cases be elective, carries with it the idea of return and reincorporation into national belonging. Even if this is impossible, we tend to understand exile in relation to an ideal form, a narrative shape. Alienage, however, reminds us of the state's role in the production of the stateless, and with its echo of *marronage* implies a particular form of racialisation. Second, the impersonal logic of alienage – legalistic, bureaucratic, biopolitical – resists recuperation. It is a process that carries on behind our backs and over our heads and in plain view. And this process, in all its subtlety and crudeness, continues even after death. Following the Black Lives Matter uprisings in 2020, it was announced that Cecil Rhodes House, an estate in Camden a short walk from St Pancras Town Hall, was finally to be renamed. Jones's name, along with the great Pan-Africanist leader George Padmore, was among the suggestions for a replacement. But the residents, perhaps weary of controversy, opted for the blandest possible 'Park View House'.[15]

I was reminded of a poem Jones wrote in 1958, which begins:

> There are some things one always remembers...
> The hurts – especially the little ones
> The cruelty of cruelness, the harshness
> of reality.

The appropriate monument to Claudia Jones would not be the renaming of an already existing structure, but the dismantling of, for example, the Napier Barracks immigration detention centre or the Yarl's Wood Immigration Removal Centre. This is part of the 'harshness / of reality': the everyday and ongoing production of alienage by the border regimes of Europe and inside the national territory. The poem ends with what I take to be an allusion to Wordsworth's 'Lines Written in Early Spring':

> But one remembers till
> It hurts remembering too...

---

[14] Joseph Keith, *Unbecoming Americans: Writing Race and Nation from the Shadows of Citizenship, 1945–60* (New Brunswick: Rutgers, 2013), 4–5.
[15] Matthew Weaver, 'Goodbye Cecil Rhodes: House renamed to lose link to British empire builder in Africa', *The Guardian* (18 March 2021), online: www.theguardian.com/uk-news/2021/mar/18/goodbye-cecil-rhodes-house-renamed-to-lose-link-to-british-empire-builder-in-africa [Accessed 18 September 2021].

> The plans, the buds of forgotten dreams...
> The fleetness of Summer and
> The suddenness of Autumn...

For 'that sweet mood when pleasant thoughts / Bring sad ones to the mind' we have the act of remembering until it hurts, and the wistfulness is undercut – or is it confirmed? – by autumn's sudden onset. But as Jay Bernard and Walt Hunter note in their discussion of this poem, the syntax of 'It hurts remembering too...' is richly suggestive.[16] It hurts *to* remember, but the person who remembers also seems to *cause hurt* to 'remembering' as such. The pun between 'one remembers' and 'remembering too' (remembering 'two') sets up fraught questions: does remembering lead us towards or away from the collective? Can you negate hurt by hurting? When I hurt do you hurt too? Hurt sits ambiguous, disturbing our attachments, and these questions don't resolve. It's not simply that recall is imperfect, and that to remember does damage to the content of the memory; it's about form.

Writing almost twenty-five years later, Fredric Jameson would announce in a famous crescendo that 'History is what hurts, it is what refuses desire and sets inexorable limits to individual as well as collective praxis'.[17] We see that for Jones, *memory* is what hurts, prior to or adjacent to history. Memory is also *where* it hurts, and this is tied to the standpoint of alienage, which must – acknowledging the constitutive formations of race, gender and sexuality with class – complicate almost every term of Jameson's claim. Whose desire does history refuse? Whose praxis? I take Jones's poem as an electrifying comradely rejoinder, a reminder of human agency and the revolutionary potency of memory, something like Enzo Traverso's description of 'a Marxist *countermemory*' which 'should focus on the engulfed happiness of humankind, joining utopia as a promise of freedom'.[18] This is a poetics. Boyce Davies, glossing a letter from Elizabeth Gurley Flynn, explains that Jones's extended period of poetic composition was during her imprisonment at Alderson in West Virginia in 1954–1955. On release, she doubted that the authorities would allow her to take her papers with her, so she

---

[16] Jay Bernard and Walt Hunter, 'Roses Full of Flame: The Poems of Claudia Jones', Young Poets Network, online: https://ypn.poetrysociety.org.uk/features/roses-full-of-flame-the-poems-of-claudia-jones/ [Accessed 18 September 2021].
[17] Fredric Jameson, *The Political Unconscious* (Abingdon: Routledge, 2002), 88.
[18] Enzo Traverso, *Left-Wing Melancholia: Marxism, History, and Memory* (New York: Columbia, 2016), 70.

committed her poems to memory. On the train to New York, with her deportation certain, she wrote them down again.[19] Nearly sixty years after her death, living memory of Claudia Jones is drawing to a close; and so her poetry now comes to us as memory's gift to history, each line hurting back.

In a memoir of his time as editor of Heinemann's African Writers Series, James Currey introduces Mazisi Kunene with the following vignette:

> Ros de Lanerolle told me how, during endless ANC meetings in London at the beginning of the 1960s, she would become aware out of the corner of her eye that Mazisi Kunene was writing, writing, writing poetry in Zulu. Under the name Raymond Kunene he was supposed, as official ANC representative in Europe, to be doing something about the freedom struggle. Instead he was slipping away from his life of exile into drawing on what he had heard from his grandmother.[20]

This is a familiar scenario: the poet who turns away from the demands of political struggle and towards the consolation of poetry. But it underestimates both Kunene's practical political activism in London in the 1960s and the place of poetry within the cultural wing of the freedom struggle. Kunene describes his *great*-grandmother, Maqendayana Nthuli, as 'one of the greatest oral historians and narrators of legends I have ever met', and her memories and stories contributed to his two great epic poems: *Shaka the Great* and *Anthem of the Decades*.[21] For Kunene, adhering to a Zulu cosmology which places high importance on communion with ancestors, the stakes of memory and forgetting are different: 'Then the memory persists and punishes / Those who dare forget the moment of their awakening', he writes in a poem titled 'Breaking off from tradition'.[22] For Tim Woods – who observes the centrality of memorialisation and memory in the work of exiled South African poets – Kunene's work

---

[19] Boyce Davies, *Left of Karl Marx*, 109–10.
[20] James Currey, *Africa Writes Back: The African Writers Series & The Launch of African Literature* (Oxford: James Currey, 2008), 237.
[21] Mazisi Kunene, *Anthem of the Decades* (London: Heinemann, 1981), ix.
[22] Mazisi Kunene, 'Breaking off From Tradition', *The Ancestors of the Sacred Mountain* (London: Heinemann, 1982), 55. For his discussion of African cosmologies see 'Problems in African Literature', *Research in African Literatures* 23, no. 1 (Spring 1992): 27–44.

insists on tradition as 'a source of political strength, rather than force for conservative inaction'.[23] He wrote in isiZulu, and insisted on the importance of African languages, but he translated his work into English for publication. This process became increasingly important after he was added, in 1966, to the list of writers banned by the apartheid regime.[24] While he is now recognised in South Africa as a major poet, his work is no longer in print in Britain and is not widely known. This is symptomatic of a broad forgetfulness about the presence of African poets in Britain in the 1950s and 1960s.[25] As such, in what follows I try to illuminate both Kunene's role in the ANC and his literary activism.

Kunene came to England on a Christian Action scholarship organised by Canon John Collins in 1959.[26] He had completed an MA at the University of the Natal on Zulu poetry and was teaching in Lesotho. In a 1988 interview, Kunene reported some ambivalence about accepting the scholarship – which would involve pursuing doctoral work at the School of Oriental and African Studies (SOAS) – but says that 'the ANC told me I must go there and start the boycott movement'.[27] He was duly elected as an officer of the South Africa Boycott Committee in September 1959.[28] This movement, a loose network of churches, student groups, trade unionists, peace campaigners and Communist, Labour and Liberal Party activists, had in fact been in existence since the early 1950s. But it would become formalised as the Anti-Apartheid Movement (AAM) in the wake of the Sharpeville massacre in March 1960, when sixty-nine protestors were killed by the South African police. Soon after Sharpeville, Kunene published two poems in *Writers Against Apartheid*, a broadsheet including work by Scottish communists Hamish Henderson and Hugh MacDiarmid, the Irish poet

---

[23] Tim Woods, *African Pasts: Memory and History in African Literatures* (Manchester: Manchester UP, 2007), 191.
[24] Peter D. MacDonald, *The Literature Police: Apartheid Censorship and Its Cultural Consequences* (Oxford: Oxford UP, 2009), 48.
[25] For instance, in the Penguin *Modern Poetry From Africa* anthology, popular enough to be reprinted half a dozen times in the 1960s, a full quarter of the contributors had spent significant time in Britain, usually as students. Gerald Moore and Ulli Beier, eds., *Modern Poetry From Africa*, rev. ed. (Harmondsworth: Penguin, 1973).
[26] Some correspondence about Kunene's scholarship is available in the digital archive at Wits. See 'South African Institute of Race Relations (SAIRR), 1892–1974', Collection AD1715, Item 12.11.2, online: www.historicalpapers.wits.ac.za//inventories/inv_pdfo/AD1715/AD1715-1 2-1 1-2 -002-jpeg.pdf [Accessed 18 September 2021].
[27] 'An Interview With Mazisi Kunene', *Commonwealth (Dijon)* 14, no. 2 (1992): 37.
[28] Elizabeth M. Williams, *The Politics of Race in Britain and South Africa* (London: I.B. Tauris, 2015), 30.

Louis MacNeice, the Caribbean writer and activist Andrew Salkey and many others. Kunene's poem 'This Day', signed 'In Exile, London 1960', appears on the front page next to the Magnum Agency photographer Ian Berry's famous reportage photographs of the dead. The poem is written from the perspective of the 'Children of Sharpeville' and begins by alluding to the Bantu Education act ('lips cracking [...] / with the mouthings of a slave's education') and the Coalbrook mining disaster of January 1960, which left more than 400 workers dead. The poem moves from 'songs sung underneath the collapsing mines' to the closing invocation of 'our hymn, the song of Liberty'. Foreshadowing the central importance of music to the cultural resistance to apartheid, Kunene's poem makes song the continuum between the living and dead, poised between the requirements of mourning and the necessity of action.

Four years later, Hamish Henderson – the first translator of Antonio Gramsci's prison letters into English – would write his folksong 'Rivonia', named after the treason trial of Nelson Mandela, Walter Sisulu, Govan Mbeki and other members of the ANC. Kunene, by then the ANC representative in London, was responsible for forwarding the song to the main office of the ANC in Dar es Salaam, where it became well known, and wrote to Henderson that 'song has, after all, been from time immemorial the most potent form of expressing protest'.[29] MacDiarmid, who famously engaged in a lengthy feud with Henderson over the status of folk music, also contributed two poems to *Writers Against Apartheid*, both of which rework lines from his Spanish Civil War-era *The Battle Continues*.[30] This book-length poem, finally published in 1957, attacks the South African poet Roy Campbell, a supporter of the Franco regime. The poem is by turns hilarious and tedious, brilliantly scatological and foolishly self-contradicting. The fifty or so lines excerpted and modified as 'Let Africa Flourish' begin with some jokes about the sphincters of ruling National Party politicians François Erasmus, Eric Louw and Hendrik Verwoerd, and then asks:

> Why do I support the African National Congress
> And want complete independence

---

[29] Timothy Neat, *Hamish Henderson: Poetry Becomes People* (Edinburgh: Birlinn, 2012).

[30] For the Henderson–MacDiarmid disputes, see Corey Gibson, *The Voice of the People: Hamish Henderson and Scottish Cultural Politics* (Edinburgh: Edinburgh UP, 2015), 9–44.

And want universal adult suffrage
In all the African countries?

He goes on to explain his commitment to active democracy, which must 'always be on the attack', and reminds his reader of 'the great historical task of the working class' to undo the 'monstrous distortion of the faculties of man'.[31] MacDiarmid would continue to support the ANC into the 1970s, providing a foreword to the important anthology *Poets to the People: South African Freedom Poems*, edited by Barry Feinberg.[32]

Kunene's second poem in *Writers Against Apartheid* appears on the back page, and reiterates the struggle:

> The rains will be levelling the mounds we have dedicated to liberty
> The torrential mixture will raise the chest with the waves,
> There will be thick summers smelling decay,
> We shall be like mushrooms after thunderbolt postmortems.
> Our day is longer than this swelling smoke
> We shall endure, regrow from the uncultivated fields
> Because we are the weeds on the oppressors nights.[33]

In a note to a later poem commemorating Canon Collins, Kunene explains that mushrooms symbolise 'the idea of growth and cleansing'.[34] It's as if the poem begins where 'This Day' left off: after the singing 'dedicated to liberty', time will pass and the seasons will change. From the graves of martyrs (the 'mounds'), the resistance will grow, whether like mushrooms or weeds. In his introduction to the John Berger and Anna Bostock translation of Aimé Césaire's *Return to My Native Land*, Kunene identifies a recurrent image for the Martinican poet: 'the breaking of earth by the peasant represents

---

[31] Hugh MacDiarmid, 'Let Africa Flourish', *Writers Against Apartheid* (1960), unpaginated. For the corresponding passage see MacDiarmid, *The Battle Continues* (Edinburgh: Castle Wynd, 1957), 86–7.

[32] Hugh MacDiarmid, 'Foreword', *Poets to the People: South African Freedom Poems*, ed. Barry Feinberg (London: Allen & Unwin, 1974). One of the most interesting poets included in the anthology is 'A.N.C. Kumalo', the pseudonym of Ronnie Kasrils, founding member of the armed wing of the anti-apartheid movement, Umkhonto We Sizwe (MK). His poems were published in the ANC magazine *Sechaba* as well as *African Communist*, the organ of the South African Communist Party (SACP). For his crucial role in London, see Ken Keable, ed., *The London Recruits: The Secret War Against Apartheid* (London: Merlin, 2012).

[33] Mazisi Kunene, 'Aftermath', *Writers Against Apartheid*, ed. Iain White (1960), unpaginated.

[34] Ian Henderson, ed., *Canon Collins: Man of Christian Action* (Cambridge: Lutterworth, 1976), 130.

the whole process whereby new forms of life emerge'.[35] Kunene's 'thunderbolt postmortem' is indicative of the symbolic register in which his shorter poems work: cataclysmic and compressed, with moments of sudden illumination piercing the obscurity. From a Marxist perspective, Kunene could be accused of effacing labour, and writing from the perspective of gods and emperors rather than the peasantry and the proletariat.[36] In truth, these two poems – neither of which are included in his *Zulu Poems* of 1970 – are unusually direct, clearly commenting on an immediate political event. Ntongela Masilela recalls Kunene suggesting, in the mid-1970s, that 'he would never write any poetry against apartheid because it was beneath his dignity'.[37] His work, then, is rarely 'reactive' protest poetry, but instead mounts a vastly elevated mythic register, given fullest expression in his epic works. For Kunene, apartheid is only the latest episode in the history of the colonisation of the African continent, and the task of the writer involves total refusal and total transformation.

Within the offices of the London ANC, Kunene was closely allied to Oliver Tambo, who would become President of the ANC after the death of Chief Luthuli in 1967. Kunene was active on many fronts, for instance speaking with Claudia Jones at Conway Hall in June 1963 at a solidarity meeting for the March on Washington for Jobs and Freedom, and protesting with Jones, Jan Carew and others at the US Embassy after the murder of Medgar Evers.[38] He travelled all over Europe, making particularly important links with the left in Sweden.[39] According to Sfiso Mxolisi Ndlovu, Kunene was in part responsible for finding a publisher for the transcript of Mandela's Rivonia trial speech.[40] Although he was surely already on their radar, these activities brought him to the attention of the British

---

[35] Mazisi Kunene, 'Introduction' in Aimé Césaire, *Return to My Native Land*, trans. John Berger and Anna Bostock (Harmondsworth: Penguin, 1969), 15.
[36] John Haynes presents a critique of this kind in 'Kunene's Shaka and The Idea of the Poet as Teacher', *Ariel: A Review of International English Literature* 18, no. 1 (1987): 39–50.
[37] See the book-length interview with Ntongela Masilela in Dike Okoro, *New Perspectives on Mazisi Kunene* (Milwaukee: Cirrus, 2015). This book is indispensable for anglophone readers of Kunene, and I am indebted to it for my understanding of Kunene's work.
[38] Sherwood, *Claudia Jones: A Life in Exile*, 100, 121 n65.
[39] Tor Sellström, *Sweden and National Liberation in South Africa* (Uppsala: Nordiska Afrikainstitutet, 2003), 111.
[40] Sifiso Mxolisi Ndlovu, 'The ANC and the World, 1960–1970', in *The Road to Democracy in South Africa, vol. 1, 1960–1970*, ed. SADET (Cape Town: Zebra Press, 2004), 551.

state, with the Foreign Office labelling him a communist in late 1964.[41] There's some irony to this designation, because Kunene was decidedly on the African Nationalist rather than Marxist wing of the ANC. As his work with Claudia Jones and members of the CPGB indicate, he was non-sectarian, but these orientations and alliances would become increasingly complex – and increasingly fraught – as the decade wore on.

Ndlovu notes, importantly, that Kunene was committed to raising money for the Umkhonto We Sizwe (MK) troops stationed in Tanzania in the later 1960s, apparently setting himself the 'ridiculous target' of raising £1 million.[42] He published theoretical interventions on the armed struggle, including in March 1965 'The End of Non-Violence: A Tactic Not a Doctrine'. Though MK had formed in 1961, and represented the armed wing of both the ANC and the South African Communist Party, between the catastrophe of the Rivonia arrests and the difficulty in establishing the external mission, the opportunity for armed uprising within South Africa had been minimal. Kunene's argument makes clear the mounting sense of urgency, as he ends by discussing the inevitability of civil war, gravely writing that 'There comes a point when life itself is not worth living'.[43]

In June 1967, as the MK troops were working with the Zimbabwean African People's Union (ZAPU) to make incursions in Southern Rhodesia, Kunene published a call to arms in the ANC journal *Sechaba*:

> Was I wrong when I thought
> All shall be avenged?
> Was I wrong when I thought
> The rope of iron holding the neck of young bulls
> Shall be avenged?

The anaphora continues, as Kune dispenses with 'love', 'forgiveness', 'progress' and 'goodness', and ends with a vision of global anti-imperial struggle:

> Was I wrong to ignite the earth
> And dance above the stars

---

[41] Arianna Lissoni, 'The African Liberation Movements in Exile, c.1945–1970' (unpublished PhD thesis, SOAS, 2008), 8.

[42] Ndlovu, 'The ANC and the World', 556.

[43] Mazisi Kunene, 'Non-Violence: A Tactic Not a Doctrine', *The New African* 4, no. 1 (March 1965): 4–7. The typesetting of this article can lead to some confusion: it's printed in parallel with an article by Matthew Nkoana of the Pan Africanist Congress (PAC).

Watching Europe burn with its civilization of fire,
Watching America disintegrate with its gods of steel,
Watching the persecutors of mankind turn into dust
Was I wrong? Was I wrong?[44]

Written in the context of the Tet Offensive in Vietnam and the conclusion of the guerrilla war in Yemen, Kunene's work of this period presents an internationalist outlook, informed by his work as an ANC emissary. The same issue of *Sechaba* prints part one of Kunene's presentation to the Afro-Asian Writers' Conference held in Beirut in March 1967. He describes the development of the 'socially based lyric' as one of the most 'potent forms for conveying revolutionary thought'.[45] In part two he goes on to provide a brief materialist history of uneven access to printing presses and the emergence of censorship in South Africa, ending with a call to revolutionary action.[46]

As these examples make clear, Kunene wrote outwards from his London base, addressing both ANC cadres and other groups involved in liberation struggles. But he also acted as a node within Britain, making it possible to draw connecting lines, as I've been doing here, between major figures like MacDiarmid, Césaire and Jones. But the experience of exile took its toll. He wrote to Tambo in 1968:

> I could not agree with you more, London politics are the politics of the scavengers. They eat up and devour the bones with an almost impersonal relish. One cannot help feeling that the exile mentality operates more in London than any other part of the world, so that people go round in huge ... motions of action and then settle down in a blanket of desert dust.[47]

The aftermath of the MK-ZAPU military campaigns of 1967–1968 was bitter. Many freedom fighters were captured and killed, and there were serious questions about the lack of resources and the

---

[44] Mazisi Kunene, 'Thought on June 26', *Sechaba* 1, no. 6 (June 1967): 16. The poem was also published in *Lotus: Afro-Asian Writers*. I have quoted from the revised version published in *Zulu Poems* (New York: Africana, 1970), 41. There are minor differences in line arrangement and diction. The ANC's traditional day for inaugurating campaigns and protests was 26 June.

[45] Kunene [unsigned], 'Literature and Resistance in South Africa', *Sechaba* 1, no. 6 (June 1967): 17–18.

[46] Kunene [unsigned], 'Literature and Resistance in South Africa, Part Two', *Sechaba* 1, no. 7 (July 1967): 12, 16–18.

[47] Kunene to Oliver Tambo, incorrectly dated 12 January 1958. Quoted in Ndlovu, 'The ANC and the World', 567.

overall strategy of the ANC. These came to a head at the Morogoro Conference in Tanzania in late April 1969, and a series of suspensions and expulsions in the years following. Though this didn't fall along neat factional lines, there was a realignment of the ANC-SACP alliance, particularly around the question of opening up the ANC to a multiracial membership. In the ensuing recriminations, Kunene was replaced in the London office by Reg September, and members he was close to – known as 'the Gang of Eight' – were expelled in 1975.[48]

Kunene left London in the early 1970s, moving to the United States with his wife Mathabo Kunene, where they started a family and he began a long teaching career at UCLA.[49] He remained a member of the ANC, working as a Director of Finance. But he also went on to make a number of provocative public statements in support of the Zulu Inkatha Party, which have perhaps contributed to his relative marginal status in histories of the ANC in London. As Edward Said reminds us, the 'achievements of exile are permanently undermined by the loss of something left behind forever'.[50] Kunene's shorter, more occasional poems, have been eclipsed by the epic work he published after his move to the United States. Perhaps this is because Kunene's trajectory follows the form of an epic: exiled in England, exiled in the United States, he eventually returned home to a liberated South Africa in 1993, laid to rest in 2006 in his ancestral homelands.

Arthur Nortje, born on the Western Cape in 1942, presents a very different story. Where Kunene embodied the cultural and political struggle of the anti-apartheid movement, Nortje was unable to commit. Where Kunene celebrated his Blackness and his ancestral inheritance, Nortje wrestled with uncertainty over the identity of his father, and ambivalence over his status as a Coloured (biracial) South African. Kunene wrote in isiZulu; Nortje in an Afrikaans-inflected English. Kunene aspired to the epic; Nortje was drawn to the confessional lyric. Kunene became poet laureate and died in a

[48] See Luli Callinicos, *Oliver Tambo: Beyond the Engeli Mountains* (Claremont, South Africa: David Phillip, 2004), 339–41.
[49] Mathabo Kunene contributes, along with their daughter Lamakhosi Kunene, to Hilda Bernstein's collection of oral histories, *The Drift: The Exile Experience of South Africans* (London: Jonathan Cape, 1994), 458–65.
[50] Edward Said, *Reflections on Exile and Other Essays* (London: Granta, 2001), 175.

free South Africa; Nortje died in Oxford in 1970, the whereabouts of his grave unknown until 2017.[51]

In part, this is about timing. As Mark Israel has argued, London in the 1960s 'became a building site for the construction of exile', and suggests that in 1960 'most political activists who had left South Africa did not call themselves exiles [...] In 1965 most did'.[52] Nortje arrived in autumn 1965 with a scholarship to study English at Jesus College, Oxford. He had already completed a degree at the University of the Western Cape, and had been awarded an Mbari Prize for his poetry by the club associated with the Nigerian-based *Black Orpheus* magazine. In the estimation of Dennis Brutus – his former schoolteacher, speaking in 1968 – Nortje was 'far and away the best poet to come out of South Africa'. He goes on to suggest that the condition of exile has provided Nortje with a particular aesthetic latitude:

> It seems that ever since he came to Britain roughly a year and a half ago, he wrote keeping himself well in check because he was afraid that if we spoke out and then had to return to South Africa, he would go to prison – as I am sure he would have to. Now he has resigned himself to not going home. Since he made this acceptance his poetry has acquired a tremendous freedom.[53]

This sense of resignation is important. Brutus was a militant. During his arrest in 1963 he'd been shot in the stomach, and he spent eighteen months imprisoned on Robben Island. Nortje would report in a later poem that 'what isn't told / is how a warder kicked the stitches open'. In the same poem, Nortje calls himself 'too nominal an exile / to mount such intensities of song'.[54] Somewhere between the writing of this poem for Brutus and Brutus's speech, Nortje seems to have become resigned enough to stop being a 'nominal' exile, and to have joined the ranks for real.

The fear of repercussions within South Africa were, of course, well founded. James Currey recalls the launch event for Nortje's posthumous *Dead Roots* in 1973, published alongside Brutus's

---

[51] See Selwyn Milborrow, 'Repatriating Arthur Nortje', online:https://arthurnortje.wordpress.com/2019/03/11/a-call-for-the-repatriation-of-arthur-nortje-selwyn-milborrow/ [Accessed 25 October 2023].

[52] Mark Israel, *South African Political Exile in the United Kingdom* (London: Palgrave, 1999), 140, 142.

[53] Dennis Brutus, 'Protest Against Apartheid', in *Protest and Conflict in African Literature*, ed. Cosmo Pieterse and Donald Munro (London: Heinemann, 1969), 99.

[54] Nortje, 'Autopsy', *Dead Roots*, 53.

A Simple Lust, novels by D. M. Zwelonke and Modikwe Dikobe, an academic study by Albie Sachs and a new edition of Mandela's *No Easy Walk to Freedom* with a foreword by Ruth First. First was assassinated by South African security services in Mozambique in 1982; Sachs was injured by a car bomb in 1988; all the other writers except Nortje had been in prison.[55] Nortje was never involved in anti-apartheid activism in any practical sense.[56] His autobiographical 'Oxford Journal', an extraordinary document of his arrival in England and subsequent travels to Toronto, memorably records his difficulties with Oxford student organisations such as the Joint Action Committee Against Racial Intolerance (JACARI):

> Like – I've got this batch of Jacari membership-for-the-term cards lying on the table. 2/- each. In the end I'll simply throw them out the window & pay the £2 or so out of pocket.[57]

For comparison, he wryly describes elsewhere stealing money from the coffee funds in the common room in order to buy a ticket for Michelangelo Antonioni's *Red Desert*.[58] Nortje's work is saturated with this kind of minor scandal and discrepancy, moments of embarrassment and awkwardness which brush up against the desperate seriousness of his situation. The delicacy of his phrasing can be achingly beautiful, and the clarity of his self-address falls somewhere between accusation and entreaty.

In 'London Impressions', written in 1966, Nortje begins with quatrains:

> Out of the Whitehall shadows I pass
> into a blaze of sun as sudden as fountains.
> Between the bronze paws of a lion
> a beatnik stretches his slack indifferent muscles.
>
> (*Dead Roots* 56)

---

[55] James Currey, *Africa Writes Back*, 188–9.

[56] David Bunn suggests, however: 'Probably at Brutus's urging, he read at a multitude of anti-apartheid rallies in London.' Bunn, '"Some Alien Native Land": Arthur Nortje, Literary History, and the Body in Exile', *World Literature Today* 70, no. 1 (Winter, 1996): 41. Dirk Klopper's timeline of Nortje's life indicates that he was invited by Brutus to address 'a Human Rights Day Poetry Meeting on 12 December [1970] at London University', but died in the days prior. See Klopper, ed., 'Chronology of Arthur Nortje's Life and Work', in *Anatomy of Dark: Collected Poems of Arthur Nortje* (Pretoria: UNISA, 2000), xxii.

[57] Arthur Nortje, *Oxford Journal*, 140. The full transcription is available online at the University of South Africa's Institutional Repository (UNISA): http://uir.unisa.ac.za/handle/10500/18648 [Accessed 25 October 2023].

[58] Ibid., 64.

The opening line is typical: the inverted word order delays and unsettles the identity of the subject, and allows the emphasis to fall on 'pass'. For the South African reader, this would immediately evoke the pass laws of the 1940s and 1950s, one of the key technologies of apartheid.[59] It also raises the question of racial 'passing', and Nortje's navigation of a different regime of race and colour. The poem as a whole unfolds under the shadow of 'White' in 'Whitehall', and takes in 'blue heavens', 'Gold Leaf', 'August green', a 'black bag', 'brown leaves' and 'big red buses'. Perhaps we shouldn't make too much of this, but the palette of the poem is built from, on the one hand, the red, white and blue of the Union Jack, and on the other the green, gold and black of the ANC flag. In the racial taxonomy of South Africa, Nortje's relationship to the ANC was complex. Officially, membership of the ANC was only open to Black Africans, and, as I've suggested above, the opening up of membership to Coloured, Indian and White comrades (who were free to join the SACP and MK) was a major source of tension within the London office.[60] Where then, does Nortje belong, and who does he belong with?

Even the beatnik, who – at least on the page – Nortje would later come to resemble, presents us with *difference* concealed by 'indifferent muscles'. The vigilance of the new arrival rings out in every line, with the 'paws' of the lion translating into the *pause* of the beatnik stretching, a little laziness emerging from the 'blaze of sun'. As he tells us later in the poem, 'The isle is full of Foreign Noises / that jangle in trafalgar square'. But instead of Caliban's twangling and humming, Nortje emphasises the jangling of loose change. Alluding to the sterling crisis of 1966, he writes: 'England expects every tourist / to do his duty now the Pound is sickly'. We see here that Nortje seems to think of himself, at least in this moment, as tourist rather than exile. He has coins in his pocket, and he seems, tentatively, to be more defined by his brand of cigarettes than his racial categorisation. He chooses not to mention the South African Embassy, on the Whitehall side of the square, the building he's presumably just walked out of.

But the shadow of this building follows him to Hyde Park. In the second section of the poem he has a confusing flirtatious encounter

---

[59] Nortje had inscribed his identity card details into an earlier poem, 'Hangover' (1963): 'In case of foul play, imprisonment, death / by drinking (identity is / 268430: KLEURLING / Pretoria register, male 1960)'. *Dead Roots*, 10. 'Kleurling' is Afrikaans for 'Coloured'.

[60] For a concise overview, see Nhlanhla Ndebele, 'The African National Congress and The Policy of Nonracialism: A Study of the Membership Issue', *Politikon: South African Journal of Political Studies* 29, no. 2 (2002): 133–46.

with a girl, who seems to signal to him with a mirror. By the time he's lit another cigarette 'the ugliest bloke that you have ever seen' has picked her up. They 'disappear / through the distance of August green', the poem dropping into doggerel couplets, like the cigarette stub being flicked away. When 'a huge Alsatian sniffs my loose boots', and we meet the 'gentleman with the leash', the reader tenses at a reminder of the police. But Nortje bursts out into a moment of great pathos:

> Sun, you are all I have:
> the grass already welcomes the brown leaves.
> I do not want to cross the road again,
> having learnt the value of other faces,
> acquired the pace and tone of other voices.

Nortje is a great poet of apostrophe. The whole scene, so carefully elaborated, drops out as the poet lies on his back, sinks into the ground. The temporal logic of the poem changes, and the sun seems to turn the leaves brown in the time it takes to read across the line break. The reluctance to 'cross the road again' is not the happy laziness of a summer's day, but rather a prospective image of further travel and exile. This thought repeoples the poem. The 'other faces' Nortje has learned to value are his friends, lovers and acquaintances in England; the 'pace and tone' of other voices are his new habits of speech and writing.[61] Yet despite negotiating his otherness and learning the codes of the English class system, Nortje remains painfully alone. He returns to the lost state of childhood, his recollection of wonder at London buses, here figured as a colonial pastiche of big game ('gentle monsters'). Unlike the statues of lions, these gentle monsters move. But the poem ends with another lost state, and the undertow of captivity: 'when I was young and shackled for my sharpness / in the Union of South Africa' (*Dead Roots* 57).

Though Brutus's estimation of Nortje's development is a general one, we might point to 'London Impressions' as the moment in which resignation to exile and aesthetic freedom reach their paradoxical settlement. Nortje made preparations to leave England in 1967, taking

---

[61] Anthony O'Brien has written about the 'Kaaps' Afrikaans dialect that Nortje uses in his letters and journal as 'a more risky exploration of foregone paths of hybridity and marginality that a later postcolonial writing would take up as a major theme'. O'Brien, *Against Normalisation: Writing Radical Democracy in South Africa* (Durham, NC: Duke UP, 2001), 239.

up a teaching post in Hope, British Columbia and subsequently also teaching in Toronto.[62] His extended poem 'Immigrant' finds him waiting at the departure gates, characteristically exasperated at the price of beer:

> Bitter costs exorbitantly at London
> airport in the neon heat
> waiting for the gates to open

But he also itemises the 'Bitter costs' of leaving, including the policing of his body by immigration officials:

> A maple leaf is in my pocket.
> X-rayed, doctored at immigration
> weighed in at the Embassy
> measured as to passport, smallpox, visa
>   (*Dead Roots* 92)

The poem is an uneasy attempt to empty out what he calls his 'mind's customs office'. Declaring himself 'Big boy breaking out of the masturbatory / era', he works himself up to a longer line, showing the influence of Allen Ginsberg's ambulatory poems of the mid-1960s.[63] I would also suggest that 'A maple leaf is in my pocket' is a nod to Frank O'Hara's 'My heart is in my pocket / it is poems by Pierre Reverdy'.[64] In fact, 'Immigrant' wouldn't be out of place in any of the mimeo magazines of the British Poetry Revival, where the influence of Ginsberg and O'Hara were beginning to be worked out. But set against the official documents, stamped with the insignia of the nation state, his visa and his vaccinations, Nortje writes:

> at last the efficient official informs me
> I am an acceptable soldier of fortune, don't

---

[62] See Craig W. McLuckie and Ross Tyner, '"The Raw and the Cooked": Arthur Kenneth Nortje, Canada, and a Comprehensive Bibliography', *English in Africa* 26, no. 2 (1999): 1–54. For the position of Canada in Nortje's imagination, see George Elliot Clarke, *Directions Home: Approaches to African-Canadian Literature* (Toronto: U of Toronto P, 2012), 143–53.

[63] In the *Oxford Journal*, Nortje makes approving reference to Peter Whitehead's film *Wholly Communion*, which documents the Royal Albert Hall reading in 1965: see the following chapter for a discussion of Ginsberg's visit to Britain and what it discloses.

[64] Frank O'Hara, 'A Step Away from Them', *Lunch Poems* (San Francisco: City Lights, 1964), 17. In his own rewrite of O'Hara's poem, the ANC activist Jeremy Cronin writes: 'my heart's in my packet: it's / one thousand / illegal pamphlets to be mailed'. Cronin, 'A Step Away From Them', *Inside* (Johannesburg: Ravan, 1983), 91–2.

> tell the Commissioner
> I have Oxford poetry in the satchel
> propped between my army surplus boots

These lines are teasing and ambiguous. Oxford poetry (the journal *Oxford Poetry*?) puts him under suspicion, casts doubt on his intentions and he navigates the border. Does this confirm Brutus's estimation? That Nortje is now the kind of poet whose writing might get him in trouble with the authorities? Or does Nortje here confess that his poetry is still insufficiently militant, revealing his army surplus boots as just so much costume? His address to the reader draws us in, conspiratorial, ironic.

Nortje returned from Canada in August 1970. Although struggling with alcohol dependency and mental health problems, he was set to pursue postgraduate study at Oxford and his poems were due to appear in his friend Cosmo Pieterse's anthology *Seven South African Poets*.[65] His last poems, like the long 'Nasser is Dead' and 'Questions and Answers' show a sustained political seriousness, and suggest how he might have developed had he lived. In the estimation of Romanus Egudu, writing in 1978, Nortje was simply 'concerned with self-pity' and 'therefore sentimental and tends to sap the energy for action'.[66] Perhaps this is so. But his papers suggest that while he was in Canada he was excited by the development of Black Power in the United States, writing with admiration about Stokely Carmichael, H. Rap Brown and Eldridge Cleaver.[67] With the greater prominence of Black writing in Britain following the Caribbean Artists Movement, it's possible he would have found a readership and a broader community. Most intriguingly, recent criticism has persuasively argued for the queerness of Nortje's writing, and his work could fit with and complicate the poets I look at in the following chapter.[68]

According to Brutus, at the time of his death by overdose on 11 December 1970, Nortje was facing problems with his immigration status:

---

[65] Cosmo Pieterse, ed., *Seven South African Poets* (London: Heinemann, 1971). Pieterse was a major figure in the South African exile community, and his poems, scattered in magazines and anthologies, await collection and re-publication.

[66] Romanus Egudu, *Modern Poetry and the African Predicament* (Basingstoke: Macmillan, 1978), 47.

[67] *Oxford Journal*, 333.

[68] See, for instance, Andrea Thorpe, 'The "Pleasure Streets" of Exile: Queer Subjectivities and the Body in Arthur Nortje's London Poems', *Journal of Literary Studies* 34, no. 1 (2018): 1–20; Diana Adesola Mafe, *Mixed Race Stereotypes in South African and American Literature* (New York: Palgrave, 2013), 85–112.

At that time, as he'd written to me in letters, his South African passport had expired, the British had agreed to issue him new documents on condition that he waited six years to get them and that he applied for them from South Africa.[69]

Dirk Klopper's extensive biographical research suggests that Nortje's South African passport was valid until October 1971 and his British visa was valid until July 1971. He was ineligible for automatic citizenship-by-residence because of his years abroad in Canada. It was likely that in order to apply for British citizenship he would have to return to South Africa, but it was unclear if his South African passport would be renewed.[70] Whatever the case, Nortje was clearly in a desperate situation. While Klopper has written of Nortje's 'elegies of alienation', it also makes sense to call them elegies of *alienage*.[71] Nortje, despite his scholarships, despite his 'Oxford poetry', despite his bursting heart, could neither move freely nor settle.

In one of his last poems, 'St Giles', Nortje rejects in advance the attempt to find pathos in his end. 'They, the dead, awaken / no sorrow / open / no fresh wound' he writes, of the churchyard in Oxford. And he rejects, too, any attempt to recuperate him for an English elegiac tradition, writing with perfect attitude:

>   Uncover in me no trauma:
> I piss behind telephone booths
>   watching stars, oh yes
> it is me, my
>   steam
>   risin'
>
>   (*Dead Roots* 144)

By the 1970s many of the South African exiles in London had gone to the United States. There were new political crises: the displacement of Ugandan Asians, who came to Britain in 1972; the war in newly independent Bangladesh. Other political fugitives would emerge, including members of European urban guerrilla groups, draft evaders from the United States and defectors from the British Army in Ireland. Nortje's name and the faint traces he left receded.

---

[69] Dennis Brutus, 'Poetry of Suffering: The Black Experience', *Ba Shiru* 4, no. 1 (1973): 2.
[70] Dirk Klopper, 'Arthur Nortje: A Life Story', in *Arthur Nortje: Poet and South African*, ed. Craig McLuckie and Ross Tyner (Pretoria: UNISA, 2004), 23–4.
[71] Dirk Klopper, 'Arthur Nortje and the Unhomely', *Alternation* 5, no. 2 (1988): 167.

The Avant-Garde of Their Own People: Poetry and Exile, 1959–1975   97

The Chilean poet and artist Cecilia Vicuña came to England in September 1972 to study at the Slade School of Fine Art. She was twenty-four years old. In an interview from 2017 she describes her first impressions:

> when the plane opened the door I felt immediately the horrendous grayness and sadness of the British soul, as if this was a world of pain and repression, where people didn't have an iota of the physical enjoyment that we had in Chile. So I never undid my suitcase, because I knew I had to return to the Americas that very first second I landed in England. I was there with a British Council scholarship to study art, but the minute my grant was over, I was going back. That was my plan. But three months before my grant came to an end, the military coup happened. So I had lost not only the joy of Chile, but the possibility of returning. I felt like it was the end of the world for me.[72]

The Chile Vicuña left behind was in the throes of revolutionary process. Salvador Allende's election as head of the Popular Unity (PU) coalition in 1970, the fruition of decades of class struggle, appeared to present a democratic and non-violent road to socialism. Vicuña was closely involved in the movement, and understood herself as a cultural worker in the service of a complete transformation of society. Though some leftists were sceptical of Allende's reluctance to dismantle the bourgeois state – as Régis Debray put it, 'What made the electoral victory possible also acts as a brake on its transformation into a complete victory' – Vicuña left during a highpoint of the thousand days of socialist government.[73] April 1972 saw the legal recognition of direct action on food distribution (the Local Councils for Provisions and Prices, known as JAPs); June saw the emergence of new forms of workers' control (the *cordones industriales*); September brought the passing of the *ley indígena* in tandem with land reform and expropriation, a major victory for the indigenous Mapuche peoples.[74] While all exile is traumatic, and while it was clear from the start that counter-revolution in Chile was

---

[72] Julia Bryan-Wilson, 'Awareness of Awareness: An Interview with Cecilia Vicuña', in Cecilia Vicuña, *About to Happen* (New York: Siglio, 2017), 116.
[73] Régis Debray, *Conversations with Allende: Socialism in Chile* (London: New Left Review, 1971), 46.
[74] See the chapter 'Popular Power', in Gabriel Smirnow, *The Revolution Disarmed: Chile 1970–73* (New York: Monthly Review, 1979), 81–99. For the context of indigenous rights and the Popular Unity movement, see Joanna Crow, 'Debates about Ethnicity, Class, and Nation in Allende's Chile (1970–73)', *Bulletin of Latin American Research* 26, no. 3 (2007): 319–38.

inevitable, a coup is a specific kind of catastrophe. This is to suggest that Vicuña's *becoming-exile* carried with it a visceral shock ('the end of the world') and required an immediate political response.

This came in the form of her book *Saborami*, constructed in the direct aftermath of the coup in September 1973. The book, which collects facets of her work as a poet, sculptor and painter, defies easy classification. It includes the reproduction of her iconographic paintings of Lenin and Marx, Allende and Castro; captions, or 'explanations' of the paintings appear in the form of prose-poems; reproductions of her *precarios* sculptures, made out of scraps of trash and organic material; extracts from a 1971 journal; pages from the parallel project, *Twelve Books for the Chilean Resistance*; thirty-eight pages of lineated verse in Spanish and fourteen pages of English translations. Referred to variously as SABORAMI, *Sabor a mí*, and *Saborami*, no one knows what it should be called, even now.[75] Certainly, its status as a multilingual artist's book produced by a Chilean exile has excluded it from the scant historical recall of socialist writing in Britain. But if it isn't a book of poems, exactly, it is undoubtedly a book of poetry. Vicuña celebrates the victories of the Popular Unity movement, mourns their destruction and reaffirms collective revolutionary desire among the wreckage.

The book was published by the Beau Geste Press, run by Felipe Ehrenberg, Martha Hellion and David Mayor from a commune in the Devon countryside. Ehrenberg and Hellion were themselves exiles, from Mexico, leaving after the massacre of students at Tlatelolco, Mexico City, in October 1968.[76] Beau Geste – named after the '*beau*tiful *Geste*tner' printing press – became a meeting point for radical writers and artists. Allen Fisher, who would become one of the major figures of the British Poetry Revival, stayed at the commune and helped to produce books and other ephemera. They produced journals including *Fluxshoe* and *Schmuck*, which printed the work of Czech dissidents, Japanese printmakers and many others. If there *was* an avant-garde of exiles in Britain, perhaps this was it. Along with Carolee Schneeman's *Parts of a Bodyhouse Book*

---

[75] The title is an allusion to a popular song, 'Sabor a Mí' ('A Taste of Me'). Vicuña has stated: 'I called it *Sabor a mí* in honour of my mother and her melodious voice singing the unforgettable bolero: *Pasarán más de mil años, muchos más* ...'; see Vicuña, 'Sabor a mí' in *Beau Geste Press*, ed. Alice Motard (Bordeaux: CAPC, 2017), 196–209 (196).

[76] They were affiliated to the magazine *El Corno Emplumado*, edited by Sergio Mondragón and the American radical Margaret Randall, which had published early writing by Vicuña and an international array of poets.

(1972), *Saborami* represents a highpoint in the output of the press. Vicuña was involved in all aspects of production, from the dying and treating of paper to the insertion of loose, found objects which made each copy unique.[77]

There are two aspects of the book that I want to emphasise. The first is Vicuña's insistence on an ecological and feminist socialism. In one of the most memorable passages she writes:

> the workers are the avant-garde in defending the
> ecological balance, natural resources, & fighting
> pollution.
>
> nationalized mines and industries won't follow the
> capitalist pattern of industrialization![78]

And elsewhere, years ahead of her time, 'Socialism and wild lands are the only thing that can save us'.[79] Though possibly a slip in translation ('las trabajadoras son la vanguardia'), the nomination of the workers as the avant-garde isn't merely sentiment. In an article for the British feminist magazine *Spare Rib*, Vicuña describes the formation of Centres of Popular Culture, where artists and artisans collaborated with trades unions to organise in the newly nationalised industries and agrarian districts. Though the artist would begin the process, 'instructors would emerge from the group of workers' and take the lead.[80] In the same article, she meditates on how her class position as a member of the intelligentsia made it harder for her to understand colonisation, and the need not only to be a leftist but to be a revolutionary. What Vicuña wants, and what seemed possible in the movement, is the reimagining of all social relationships. As she writes in one of *Saborami*'s internal commentaries: 'The second notebook includes what I don't know how to think.'[81] This statement reads two ways. The revolutionary process has made it possible to represent or to achieve what I don't know how to *think* but what I might know *how to do* or what I *know I desire* in transformative struggle for change. But read in the light of the coup, these scraps and destroyed projects might no longer seem possible; without

---

[77] Cecilia Vicuña, 'Fragments of Memory: An Afterward', in *Saborami* (Oakland: ChainLinks, 2011).
[78] Vicuña, *Saborami*, 36.
[79] Ibid., 43.
[80] Cecilia Vicuña, 'The coup came to kill what I love', *Spare Rib* 28 (1974): 37. Reprinted in Cecilia Vicuña, *Saborami: An Expanded Facsimile Editions*, ed. Luke Roberts and Amy Tobin (London: Book Works, 2024).
[81] Vicuña, *Saborami*, 55.

Allende, without Chile, without the movement, the artist *no longer knows how to think*.

But though *Saborami* is a painful, grief-stricken work, it isn't pessimistic. The other aspect I want to emphasise is joy: the book is joyful, refusing to submit to grayness and sadness, pain and repression. It takes joy seriously, imagining socialism as 'a combination / of joys', telling the reader that 'joy is a necessity' (66), stating 'joy could make people aware of the need to fight for joy', since 'the urgency of the present is the urgency of revolution' (67). Perhaps *Saborami* helps the reader to understand this, to think it through with other readers and with ourselves. Reflecting many years later on her position as an exile in Britain, Vicuña states:

> The migration is a double migration in the sense that you go to a place and it's the opposite of your place, because your place is not available to you any more, but you also migrate back to the source of who you are.[82]

One of the most joyful aspects of the book is that it ends with poems written when she was eighteen or nineteen, funny and erotic poems which were due to be published as a collection – *El Zen Surado* – in Chile.[83] Like Emma Goldman's demand for bread *and* roses, Vicuña wants both Lenin and 'the softest tools of love' (144). Surrounded by death, the book makes a commitment to life, and refuses to give up the projects of liberation. 'Repression has a dialectic, like everything else,' she wrote in *Spare Rib*, and 'the more the junta tries to supress us the stronger will be our response.'[84]

After *Saborami*, Vicuña threw herself into organisational work. She cofounded Artists for Democracy and in 1974 held the Artists Festival for Democracy in Chile. The British Council sanctioned her 'because according to them I was not doing "art" but "politics" and I was staying "outside of London". They said I was misspending the English taxpayer's money and withdrew the grant'.[85] A protest by young employees apparently worked to reverse the decision. Vicuña left England in 1975, heading to Bogotá and immediately making banner works such as 'Chile Salutes Vietnam', which celebrates the victory of the Viet Cong. Vicuña has returned to Britain many times since then, becoming an increasingly recognised artist and an

---

[82] Bryan-Wilson, 'Interview with Cecilia Vicuña', 117.
[83] See Juliet Lynd's 'Introduction' to Cecilia Vicuña, *El Zen Surado* (Editorial Catalonia, 2013).
[84] Vicuña, 'The coup came to kill what I love', 38.
[85] Vicuña, 'Sabor a mí', 200.

influence on subsequent generations of poets. Yet *Saborami* – so determinedly anti-monumental, but such an urgent memorial – still feels under-recognised, and insufficiently celebrated as a groundbreaking work of socialist, feminist, ecological and anti-colonial struggle. This is because what the work demands is not, finally, recognition of this kind. Like Claudia Jones, like Mazisi Kunene, like the bitter costs of Arthur Nortje, what *Saborami* asks for is the end of things as they are, the beginning of things as they could be.

Part II

Chapter 4

Driven Out of the Town: Homosexuality and The British Poetry Revival

How queer was *The New American Poetry*? Perhaps the only sensible answer to such a question is *not queer enough*. Yet Donald Allen's legendary 1960 anthology includes work by at least a dozen gay men, and several of the more prominent – including Allen Ginsberg, Robert Duncan, Jack Spicer and John Wieners – were, at different times, actively involved in the struggle for gay liberation. While this context hasn't always been legible in criticism, the reader doesn't have to search very hard to find something like a queer tradition, mercurial in outline but vivid enough.[1] In Britain these poets were read with enthusiasm and ardour. Their work circulated via little magazines and independent presses, commingling with European modernism and a rediscovered English romanticism to offer an alternative to the post-war literary establishment. The poet and critic Eric Mottram would come to christen this movement the British Poetry Revival.[2] But despite inspiring new formal experimentation and daring expansions of the poetic field, the American influence appears to have been chastened, straightened out from the start. If we ask how queer was the British Poetry Revival, the only sensible answer seems to be *not queer at all*.

I want to prise open this assessment. It's my contention that an indifference to the question of sex and sexuality has lingered over the reception of the new British poetries of the 1960s and 1970s. This is despite the fact that this flourishing of work coincided with

---

[1] For the paradoxical relationship between queerness and tradition, see Christopher Nealon, 'Queer Tradition', *GLQ* 14, no. 4 (2008): 617–22.
[2] Eric Mottram, 'The British Poetry Revival', in *New British Poetries: The Scope of the Possible*, ed. Robert Hampson and Peter Barry (Manchester: Manchester UP, 1993). The originator of the phrase was the poet and activist Dave Cunliffe.

major legislation about homosexuality in England and Wales, and that plenty of poets had queer relationships and wrote about those relationships. Unpicking the contours of homophobia and sexual repression within the cultural institutions and social formations that these poets moved in goes beyond the scope of the present chapter. So too does any direct explanation of the uneven articulation of desire between the American poets and their British counterparts. But in this chapter I elaborate two transatlantic meetings, arguing that the frictions, intimacies and silences they disclose might form a starting point for a queer, or at least queer-er reading of the British Poetry Revival.

Writing in the 1990s, Derek Jarman – a student of Mottram's in the 1960s – looked back at this formative moment:

> I remember the name of every boy I ever slept with in the sixties, even if it was for one night. These encounters took place in bedsits in an atmosphere of frustration. Long bus rides, and when you were there, shellshocked inability to love. Tortuous, stilted conversation until you got to the point. It was the Americans, at the end of the decade, who said 'Hi, let's fuck!'[3]

Here we're presented with a historical allegory. Jarman describes the emergence from a stigmatised and claustrophobic homosexual identity into the post-Stonewall activism of Gay Liberation. But the poets central to my discussion seem to have fallen out of this transformative embrace, and to have missed their moment of becoming. They have remained stifled in an atmosphere of frustration, the possibilities repeatedly foreclosed.

I want to begin by focusing on one of the formative public moments for the genealogy of the British Poetry Revival. In June 1965, Allen Ginsberg gave his star reading at the International Poetry Incarnation at the Royal Albert Hall. For many critics, this works as a convenient year-zero of the poetic counterculture in Britain. But the particular circumstances of Ginsberg's arrival – including his status as a gay man – tend to be overlooked. In May he'd been expelled from Prague after an incident with a presumed agent provocateur, who assaulted him in the street, yelling homophobic slurs.[4] The police intervention

---

[3] Derek Jarman, *At Your Own Risk* (Minneapolis: U of Minnesota P, 2010), 42.
[4] Allen Ginsberg, *Iron Curtain Journals*, ed. Michael Schumacher (Minneapolis: U of Minnesota P, 2018), 319.

resulted in the seizure of his notebooks, including a sexually explicit diary, which was used as the immediate pretext for his removal. This followed a pattern of harassment begun in Cuba earlier in the year. Within the typical Cold War narrative, Ginsberg's expulsions mark him as a Western dissident. But he was specifically a *sexual* dissident. His recently published journals from his stay in London record, among other things, cruising the Charing Cross underground toilets, where he enthusiastically noted down pages and pages of explicit graffiti. He paid at least as much attention to anonymous public sex as he did to the celebrity literati.[5]

As Juha Virtanen has argued, the reading at the Royal Albert Hall was far from free of ambivalences. He charts the 'myriad tensions' both between the performers and between the performers and their audience, both along political and aesthetic lines.[6] Daniel Kane, likewise, has analysed how the event laid bare 'the tensions between an English poetic tradition in the face of the growing hegemony of American literary culture'.[7] But neither critic remarks on the ambivalences of sexuality that the event might disclose. In the influential anthology *Children of Albion* (1969), these tensions are dispelled in rapturous self-congratulation: the reading takes on cosmic significance and Ginsberg is roundly adulated. In one of the poems written in the aftermath, the Welsh poet John James would write:

TO ALLEN GINSBERG

O fecund imagination, oh tender reader
    when you say "vagina" it
is a part of the human organism
    not a surgical name nor
a drawing on a lavatory wall
    & "cock" – whoever
could be revolted by
    your love for men
    loves no man, woman—[8]

---

[5] Ibid., 332–3. Piero Heliczer's great poem 'England' ends in 'a lavatory in regents park', where 'among the white tiles and urinals / we both though this would be the best place to meet gregory / and allen'. Michael Horovitz, ed., *Children of Albion: Poetry of the 'Underground' in Britain* (Harmondsworth: Penguin, 1969), 114.

[6] Juha Virtanen, *Poetry and Performance During the British Poetry Revival* (London: Palgrave Macmillan, 2017), 35.

[7] Daniel Kane, '"Wholly Communion": Literary Nationalism, and the Sorrows of the Counterculture', *Framework* 52, no. 1 (2011): 114.

[8] John James, *Mmm... Ah Yes* (London: Ferry, 1967), 23.

He is responding to the following lines of Ginsberg's 'Who Be Kind To', composed especially for the occasion:

> I want the orgy of our flesh, orgy
>   of all eyes happy, orgy of the soul
>   kissing and blessing its mortal-grown
>   body,
> orgy of tenderness beneath the neck, orgy of
>   kindness to thigh and vagina
> Desire given with meat hand
>   and cock, desire taken with
>   mouth and ass, desire returned
>   to the last sigh![9]

James's poem is a limited expression of tolerance and compassion. I have already observed Ginsberg's enthusiasm for the 'drawing on a lavatory wall', and we can note that while James pays attention to the 'vagina' and 'cock', he suppresses the anal eroticism of the lines immediately following. While James writes that disgust at Ginsberg's sexuality disqualifies the bearer of that disgust from love, he also locates homosexuality squarely within the totemic figure of the Beat poet. It is 'your love for men': there is little suggestion that the English audience might share or participate in Ginsberg's love of men. In the 1970s, inspired by the androgyny of stars such as David Bowie and Lou Reed, James would go on to write sophisticated and brilliant explorations of gender and sexuality. But despite his ostentatious address to Ginsberg, he was capable at the same time of casual homophobia, in a contemporary poem dismissively evoking 'a / middle-aged queer who'll never admit to his own / propensities'.[10] The queer potential of the American poet may be celebrated, but it is also warded off.[11]

Ginsberg shared the stage at the Royal Albert Hall with at least one other poet who loved men. Harry Fainlight, directly addressed in the opening of 'Who Be Kind To', is remembered now almost exclusively for his disastrous attempt to read his long LSD poem 'The

---

[9] Allen Ginsberg, 'Who Be Kind To', *Collected Poems: 1947–1980* (London: Viking, 1985), 361–2.

[10] John James, 'Poem of Inevitable September, or, I'm a City Boy at Heart', *The Small Henderson Room* (London: Ferry, 1969), 12.

[11] Ginsberg's identity is itself complicated. For example, Eileen Myles: 'Allen was more of a star than a homosexual. His great triumph was that you forgot he was gay.' Myles, 'A Speech About Allen (1998)', *The Importance of Being Iceland* (South Pasadena: Semiotexte, 2009), 181.

Spider'.¹² His reading, famously documented in Peter Whitehead's film *Wholly Communion*, was interrupted by the Dutch sound poet (and Ginsberg's translator) Simon Vinkenoog, high on mescaline, who shouted 'Love! Love! Love!' from the audience, derailing the performance. The young queer poet was literally heckled offstage by another poet yelling about love. If this sounds like a parable, let it sound like a parable. This fiasco has entirely eclipsed Fainlight's important early work, which deserves to be restored to view.

Fainlight writes during a transitional period of legal reform in England and Wales: the decade between the publication of the Wolfenden Report into Homosexuality and Prostitution in 1957 and the passing of the Sexual Offences Act of 1967. This legislative milestone was a limited victory. The 1967 Act decriminalised sex between men but only in private, and as long as they weren't members of the Armed Forces or Merchant Navy. It also set the age of consent at twenty-one, five years higher than the heterosexual equivalent. It sought to identify and specify the homosexual as a subject to be properly policed, and homosexuality as a threat to be contained.¹³ Fainlight's work both explores the boundaries of the public/private distinction and evinces a hesitant articulation of his identity as a homosexual. His pamphlet *Sussicran*, published in an edition of 150 copies in 1965, contains a dozen spare and intense lyrics. In Fainlight's early poetry it is always either morning or night. His lovers, when he can find them, are either coming or going. His themes are masturbation and cruising, and his tone veers between guarded happiness and anxiety over his future prospects, played out in the mirrored-Narcissus of his title.

The title itself is audacious. Fainlight takes on the pathologising construction of the homosexual-as-narcissist, and he both revels in it and flips it over. In the title poem he sets up the 'magical apparatus' of several mirrors, which assist in his erotic fantasy, 'unfocusing me, slowly sliding me into selves'. As he masturbates, the mirrors become a site of 'transfusion', 'flooding' and 'thawing'. After orgasm the poet wakes from his reverie with his mouth on the glass, 'as if washed up on a beach'.¹⁴ There are numerous precedents – think of

---

[12] Ginsberg writes, 'Be kind to yourself Harry, because unkindness / comes when the body explodes' (*Collected Poems*, 361). Fainlight's 'The Spider' was first published in *Fuck You: A Magazine of the Arts* 5, no. 7 (1964), unpaginated.

[13] See Jeffrey Weeks, *Coming Out: Homosexual Politics in Britain from the Nineteenth Century to the Present* (London: Quartet, 1977), 168–92.

[14] Harry Fainlight, *Sussicran* (London: Turret, 1965), 4. Further references will be given parenthetically in the text.

Hart Crane's 'O Janus-faced / As double as the hand that twists this glass'.[15] But the poem's formal arrangement – in two short prose stanzas – recalls Oscar Wilde's retelling of the Narcissus myth in his poem-in-prose 'The Disciple'. Wilde's poem ends by giving voice to the pool in which Narcissus gazed: 'And the pool answered, "But I loved Narcissus because, as he lay on my banks and looked at me, in the mirror of his eyes I saw my own beauty mirrored".'[16] This is the same paradoxical reversion that Fainlight presents in the *mise-en-abîme* of his title. The reflective surface has a life of its own, complicating, enriching and transforming the self rather than simply registering a regressive sameness. Fainlight dares to celebrate his love for himself, and he dares to fantasise that his image could be multiplied: there is no singular reflection. I can't help but wonder what would have happened had Fainlight read *this* poem at the Royal Albert Hall, and whether Simon Vinkenoog would still have yelled 'Love!', and if he had what that would have meant.

Across the sequence other figures come more solidly into view, as Fainlight cruises various sites which give him his titles: 'City Parks', 'Aristo Hotel', 'The Bayswater Road'. The untitled penultimate poem of the collection reads:

> Tonight, another one—
> first coming on so butch
> then turning right over in bed.
>
> Well, maybe I should be glad
> that these, who after all are experts,
> can see the man in me that I can't even yet.
>
> And who even if they're wrong
> at least give me a glimpse
> of the tricks one day I too may have to use.
>   (12)

Again, Fainlight is concerned with how he appears to others, how desire is to be read and how performances of masculinity are to

---

[15] Hart Crane, 'Recitative', *Complete Poems*, ed. Brom Weber (Newcastle Upon Tyne: Bloodaxe, 1984), 47. See Thomas E. Yingling's discussion in *Hart Crane and the Homosexual Text* (Chicago: U of Chicago P, 1990), 47–55.

[16] *The Complete Works of Oscar Wilde, vol. 1: Poems and Poems in Prose*, ed. Bobby Fong and Karl Beckson (Oxford: Oxford UP, 2000), 173. For a discussion of Wilde's poem in relation to Isaac Julien's film *Looking for Langston*, see Henry Louis Gates, Jr., 'The Black Man's Burden', in *Fear of a Queer Planet*, ed. Michael Warner (Minneapolis: U of Minnesota P, 1993), 230–8.

be interpreted. The 'man in me' is both figurative and literal: a pun about his unfulfilled desire for penetration. Three years later, Quentin Crisp would report the same situation in *The Naked Civil Servant*:

> Quite recently a male prostitute of my acquaintance, on one of his amateur nights, picked up a young soldier only to find at the crucial moment that he had lumbered himself with a passive sodomite. 'And, all of a sudden, he turned over. After all I'd done – flitting about the room in my wrap, making him coffee. You know, camping myself silly. My dear, I was disgusted. I made him get up and put on his clothes again.'[17]

Fainlight's poem is gentler and more forgiving than the hardened comedy of Crisp's hustler acquaintance. He is, as he says, non-expert. But it's important to stress how Fainlight looks ahead: in these poems he imagines not just the kind of man he may become, but the kind of homosexual he will one day become, laying claim to and contesting an emergent identity.

By the end of *Sussicran*, and across stray poems Fainlight published in the New York-based *Fuck You* magazine, Fainlight tentatively departs from the semi-private erotic confusions of the mirror. The multiplied 'selves' are replaced by the presence of 'our sweat-clammy bodies' in the still furtive environment of the public toilet. The final poem, 'Meeting', begins: 'Pacing beneath the glare of sodium I chanced on / some familiar urinal haunter's face borne towards me' (10). The bathroom, which contains mirrors, allows Fainlight to integrate the site of his private fantasy with the public encounter with another. The distinctions remain blurred; Fainlight seems to address himself when he writes:

> The face older now;
> worn thin by continual
> flickering of tunnel cables through
> its reflection opposite.
> (10)

These poems are not optimistic. Even as the Sexual Offences Bill made its slow passage through the House of Commons, passed eventually in July 1967, the threat of blackmail, police harassment and stigma continued. One poem imagines men lined up at a urinal as 'Prisoners waiting to be shot' (9). But Fainlight is neither tragic nor

---

[17] Quentin Crisp, *The Naked Civil Servant* (Harmondsworth: Penguin, 1997), 55–6.

paralysed by shame. He is interested and curious about who he is, and about who his lovers might be. The poem continues:

> Is this, then, forcing its way back against that fierce
> feature-distorting pressure, my own
> real and future face thrusting itself
> stiff and sodium-embalmed before me?
> Pitying it will not fight it off so easily.
> Soldered hard in lust no gesture now
> untwists this image into which we fused
>   (12)

The fused image of Fainlight's present and future self is also the real fusion of bodies, 'soldered' like an electrical current, which won't 'untwist'. The whole passage is charged with anguished eroticism. This cautious and still forming idea of an embodied collective identity is deflated by the final line: 'We pass without greeting' (12). But the flicker of utopia beneath the sodium lights remains.

Fainlight's poems remain mysterious, just out of reach. The problems and possibilities of identity and desire they explore remain unresolved. This is because there are no other book publications by Fainlight until his *Selected Poems*, thirty years later. Throughout his life, Fainlight had breakdowns, was incarcerated in mental hospitals and struggled with heavy drug use. He dropped out of the world of publishing and moved to rural Wales, dying in 1982. The *Selected* volume was overseen by his sister, the poet Ruth Fainlight, who chose – apparently in accordance with Harry's wishes – to concentrate on his later pastoral verse.[18] While she includes three poems from *Sussicran*, including the title poem, she excludes those dealing more frankly with homosexuality. The opening poem 'Pastorale', for example, which is surely a precursor to his later themes of nature and landscape, was presumably suppressed for its final lines:

> Ah faun
> the bitterness of sperm
> swallowed or spat out.
>   (3)

Fainlight's work was read enthusiastically in New York, where he intermittently lived in the early 1960s, and his work was championed

---

[18] Harry Fainlight, *Selected Poems* (London: Turret, 1986). For Harry Fainlight's 1981 letter to Ruth Fainlight, see *Wolf* magazine, online: https://web.archive.org/web/20111001215056/www.wolfmagazine.co.uk/17_hf.php [Accessed 20 April 2020].

in Britain by a range of poets including Ted Hughes and Stephen Spender, establishment figures who perhaps tainted his reputation within the British Poetry Revival and its legacies. The promise of *Sussicran* has remained obscure: dazzled on the one hand by the spectacle of the Royal Albert Hall, and shadowed on the other by editorial loss of nerve.

Lee Harwood noticed Harry Fainlight at a reading in January 1966. The event was a fundraiser for Dave Cunliffe, Arthur Moyse and Tina Morris, prosecuted on obscenity charges for publishing an anthology of erotic writing, *The Golden Convolvulus*.[19] We know Harwood noticed Harry Fainlight, because he kept a scrap of paper on which he wrote:

> Harry Fainlight (read extracts from journals/poems & 2 poems. one of which he wrote before he went to USA two years ago — & he dedicated it to me. I'm honestly flattered. we talked briefly before the reading & deep eyed each other. he is very beautiful & a wonderful poet.[20]

Harwood's archive is full of moments like this, if this is what you're looking for: the distributed evidence of desire across a life, sometimes more open, sometimes more hidden. When Harwood read with Fainlight he was in the middle of the most decisive relationship of his writing life: a love affair with John Ashbery. In the British Library there are thirty-seven letters from Ashbery to Harwood, one side of a correspondence lasting half a century. The rhythm of exchange is familiar: the first thrilling declarations of longing, urgent notes typed at work, frantic evocations of voice and touch to bridge the distance between one meeting and the next. Then the cooling off, the explanations, the redrawing and withdrawal of feelings. The letters become annual; plans to get together in one city or another fall to one side as life moves on; the gaps between the letters grow and grow, the traces of former passion hardly grazing the paper. As mortality approaches the men reconnect fondly, their now separate lives drawing to a close. Archival research can be dizzying; it can

---

[19] See Bruce Wilkinson, *Hidden Culture, Forgotten History* (Middlesbrough: Penniless Press, 2017), 74–9.
[20] 'Notes of Readings 1966–67', British Library Western Manuscripts, Lee Harwood Papers, MS Add 88998/2/8.

make you swoon. It's not only the hours of reading, delaying breaks for food or water in case the next letter or folder contains the scrap you've been searching for. The distortion of time is particular: you're absorbed in years and decades that don't belong to you, you lose track, glaze over, rushing back into the present as the library closes. Leaving aside the question of content, we might say it's the temporality of intimacy that such research transgresses.[21]

Harwood died in 2015 and Ashbery died two years later. Their relationship was never exactly a secret: as I'll show, *The Man With Blue Eyes* is a public acknowledgement of their affair. But both poets were reticent about their sexualities. Ashbery came out to escape the draft during the Korean War in the 1950s, and he belonged to male homosexual circles within the art worlds and poetry scenes of Paris and New York, but this context only became admissible in literary criticism after the advent of Queer theory. John Shoptaw's provocative book *On the Outside Looking Out* (1994) was the first study to focus on Ashbery's sexuality. He argues that the absence of direct homosexual content in Ashbery's poetry nevertheless leaves traces. Ashbery's distinct stylistic 'distortions, evasions, omissions, obscurities, and discontinuities' are evidence of a 'homotextual' poetics that the critic can work to excavate.[22] This line of enquiry – rejected by Ashbery himself – has been modified and extended, and there is now a body of queer interpretation of his work. But no American study has mentioned Harwood. This is despite the fact that their relationship bridged events of profound significance for Ashbery's life: his move back to the United States after ten years abroad, and the death of his great friend Frank O'Hara. It's only now, fifty years later, with Oli Hazzard's *John Ashbery and Anglo-American Exchange: The Minor Eras* (2018), that Harwood's name has entered the index.

From the other side, Harwood's critics have, if anything, focused almost to excess on Ashbery's stylistic and personal influence on the younger English poet. This is entirely licensed by Harwood himself, who consistently championed Ashbery's work and continually stressed his aesthetic debts to the New York School. Though the essays in *The Salt Companion to Lee Harwood* (2007) approach his work through several lenses, including a survey of his debts to French and English surrealism, his representation of women and an

---

[21] Susan Howe has called this 'mystic documentary telepathy' in *Spontaneous Particulars: The Telepathy of Archives* (New York: New Directions, 2014), 18.

[22] John Shoptaw, *On the Outside Looking Out: John Ashbery's Poetry* (Cambridge, MA: Harvard UP, 1994), 4.

ecocritical reading, Ashbery haunts the proceedings. When it comes to thinking about sexuality, this presents us with some difficulties. Hazzard, drawing on Shoptaw, argues that Harwood learned from Ashbery 'a way of articulating elements of his homosexual relationships through forms of representation that foreground vividly the necessity of their "encryption".'[23] But something here gets lost in translation. Ashbery's strategy of encryption – the term is Shoptaw's – was learned in 1940s and 1950s America. His discretion about his sexuality is historically and geographically contingent. Harwood's situation – married with a child in 1965, navigating a different city, different laws, a different class – was different. Harwood's agency as a sexual subject simply can't be understood if Ashbery remains such a privileged referent. For a long time, based on the criticism, I thought that Harwood's relationship was primarily opportunistic: what the critic Libbie Rifkin would call a 'career move', calculated to introduce the less well-known poet into the ascending glamorous coterie of New York.[24] With no available sense of the British context, Ashbery takes on something like the role of a queer centre of gravity, around which Harwood merely briefly orbits.

But I'm exaggerating. Two essays in *The Salt Companion* write extensively about Harwood's relationships without prioritising Ashbery. The first, by Alice Entwistle, focuses on gender rather than sexuality, but nevertheless traces Harwood's significant relationships with women, among others, Bobbie Louise Hawkins and Sandy Berrigan.[25] Mari Hughes-Edwards, meanwhile, grapples with passion, desire, lust, infidelity, the fragmentation of the body, loss, longing and finally love. Hughes-Edwards settles on, but never quite commits to, the idea of Harwood as a bisexual poet.[26] After considering the homoeroticism of Harwood's poetry, she writes: 'More accurate still might be the concept of bisexuality, for Harwood's love poetry is as frequently characterised by heterosexual desire as it is by the homoerotic.'[27] This much is true. But, she goes on:

---

[23] Oli Hazzard, *John Ashbery and Anglo-American Exchange: The Minor Eras* (Oxford: Oxford UP, 2018), 120.
[24] Libbie Rifkin, *Career Moves* (Madison: Wisconsin UP, 2000).
[25] Alice Entwistle, '"and . . . / not or": Gender and Relationship' in *The Salt Companion to Lee Harwood*, ed. Robert Sheppard (Cambridge: Salt, 2007).
[26] Robert Sheppard also writes strongly in his introductory essay of 'audaciously collapsing binaries' as a 'strategy of bisexual politics' in Harwood's poetry, but doesn't follow this up. See Sheppard, 'It's A Long Road' in *The Salt Companion to Lee Harwood*, 22.
[27] Mari Hughes-Edwards, '"Love . . . and other obsessions": the Poetry of Desire', in *The Salt Companion to Lee Harwood*, 136.

Yet even to regard Harwood's work as bisexual is to imply that the gender of his speakers and subjects is always identifiable, which is not the case. This is the crux of the matter. If the speaker's and the subject's gender are unidentifiable, it is impossible to identify the sexuality of a given poem (and consequently the sexual discourse of much of Harwood's poetry in general).[28]

It doesn't seem to occur to Hughes-Edwards that we can *choose* to read Harwood's poetry as bisexual, or gay, or that better yet by choosing to read Harwood as queer (a term she studiously avoids), we might loosen some of these problems of identification. The stumbling block here seems to be the assumption that poems have sexual identities. Hughes-Edwards attempts to resolve the contradictions of her approach by finally conflating textual ambiguity with homosexuality itself, arguing that prior to the limited decriminalisation of the 1967 Act, 'the textual sexual ambiguity of Harwood's poetry could be read as self-preservation'.[29]

Neither encryption nor ambiguity are satisfactory approaches because in his early work, Harwood's desires are hardly ambiguous or encrypted at all. There is no evidence of a concern for self-preservation or an obscuring of the objects of his sexual attraction. Harwood constantly tells the reader who he's sleeping with, he names his lovers, he describes sex acts. His earliest poetry, which he chose to exclude from the *Collected Poems* he prepared in 2004, are predominantly love poems addressed to men. In his first widely available collection *The White Room* (1968), three of the opening dozen poems are dedicated to a 'Harry'. We know this can't be Harry Fainlight, because these poems predate their meeting in 1966. We might speculate that they're addressed to Harwood's lifelong friend Harry Guest, whose own poetry in the 1960s contains numerous semi-coded references to gay relationships.[30] But we don't need to identify the recipient. The poems speak for themselves. Harwood almost seems to relish abandonment:

> the pain of your leaving
> and my love for you
>   as hopeless as ever[31]

---

[28] Ibid.
[29] Ibid., 137.
[30] See for instance 'Allegories' and the punningly titled 'Half Way Query' in Harry Guest, *The Cutting-Room* (London: Anvil, 1970).
[31] 'This Morning', *The White Room* (London: Fulcrum, 1968), 12. Collected in Lee Harwood, *New Collected Poems*, ed. Kelvin Corcoran and Robert Sheppard

In his vulnerability he fantasises about consuming his lover:

> a delicate hair has fallen
> into my coffee cup
> and
> thinking of you
>   I drink it.
>   (*NCP* 33)

And he wonders if the intensity of his feelings are reciprocated:

> can you smell me can you touch me
> can you taste me NOW in your
> dreams
>   (*NCP* 39)

When Harwood was writing these poems he was involved in publishing one-shot magazines with titles like *Soho*, *Night Train* and *Horde*. He was actively exploring the urban environment in London, a practice that would achieve its fullest expression in the long poem 'Cable Street'. This important early work draws on the anti-fascist and radical history of the East End of London, but it also includes at least one clear reference to gay sex: 'the strength of your loins / pressed to mine / our seed mingled' (*NCP* 53). In another poem, Harwood appears to drift to the West End, cruising:

> in this café
> where angels drift
> from table to table
> whispering their lovepoems
>
> waiting for my angel
> who's late as usual
> who never comes
>   ('angel rustling in the dry ditch', *NCP* 35)

While the gender identity of the 'angel' is unclear, as Maria Damon has argued 'angel' is a contemporary slang term for gay men.[32] But this speculation is unnecessary because the social situation Harwood depicts is so obviously evocative of the come-ons of drifting hustlers in the coffee houses of Piccadilly and Soho in the 1960s.

   (Swindon: Shearsman, 2023), 33. Hereafter *NCP*. Further references will be given in the text.
[32] Maria Damon, *At the Dark End of the Street: Margins in Contemporary American Poetry* (Minneapolis: U of Minnesota P, 1993), 167ff.

While this last poem comes close to the world that Fainlight explores in *Sussicran*, the two poets are very different. As I've argued, Fainlight is interested in both the perception and expression of a socially inscribed homosexual identity. For Fainlight, the kind of sex he has, who he has it with and where it takes place all form a basis of self-knowledge. Whether alone or with a partner, Fainlight deviates from the heterosexual norm, and he knows this. Harwood's work doesn't show the same interest in constructing or exploring a set of behaviours, affects and attitudes that could coalesce into a sexual identity. Nothing in his work suggests a permanent or fixed sexual orientation. He waits around in the café; he is, most typically, overthrown by love and hasty to declare it. His meeting with Ashbery is so important precisely because Ashbery loves him back. But if we follow the line of thinking which sees deviation from heterosexuality as marked by encryption and ambiguity, we would expect Harwood's poetry to become less open about his desires for men. These desires would be more remote, subject to distortion and evasion. But nothing could be further from the case.

While Ginsberg, Fainlight and everyone else were busy making countercultural history at the Royal Albert Hall, Harwood was in Paris with his new lover. They met in London in May 1965, and from Ashbery's letters it's clear they immediately fell in love. The twenty-five poems collected as *The Man With Blue Eyes*, published by the New York-based Angel Hair in September 1966, plot the consummation and dissolution of their affair. The opening poem, 'As Your Eyes Are Blue', is vivid and direct:

> As your eyes are blue
> you move me—and the thought of you—
> I imitate you[33]

The economy is insistent: of the first sixteen opening words, four are either 'you' or 'your'. The absent lover is called up in memory, the act of writing a substitute for physical contact. Critics have seized on the line 'I imitate you' as an admission of Harwood's stylistic

---

[33] Lee Harwood, *The Man With Blue Eyes* (New York: Angel Hair, 1966). Collected in Harwood, *Collected Poems* (Exeter: Shearsman, 2004), 65–97. The title is possibly an allusion to a line by Tristan Tzara: 'Captain! / beware of blue eyes'. Tzara, *Selected Poems*, trans. Lee Harwood (London: Trigram, 1975), 25.

debt to Ashbery: the lightly collaged digressive poem which moves in and out of the moment of composition through subtle changes of perspective. But we can also read these lines as a description of sexual play. The declared movement of the second line is the stirring of an erection; the imitation is mutual masturbation. The poem continues:

> & cities apart. yet a roof grey with slates
> or lead. the difference is little
> & even you could say as much
> through a foxtail of pain   even you

Is it significant that Harwood is thinking of imitation and difference? While he may be describing the different textures of lead and slate, Harwood is also thinking about and navigating his sexual object choices. What is the 'foxtail of pain'? A foxtail is a component of some species of grass, which works to disperse seeds, which we might interpret as a Whitmanesque metaphor for ejaculation. Fox's tails are also taken as a trophy in hunting, recalling the erotic chase and pursuit familiar to English poetry, stretching back at least as far as Wyatt's 'Whoso list to hunt'.[34] The anatomical position of the tail also hints at anal erogeneity.[35]

This might sound at first like the critical dynamic of encryption and decoding. If homosexuality remains something that we have to prove in the face of doubt or disinterest then, faced with pronominal ambiguity, we might go in search of fleshier territory. Hughes-Edwards tries this approach, but doesn't get very far, concluding: 'For the most part, however, the sexual organs are rarely revealed and dwelt upon textually.'[36] In a poem from *The Man With Blue Eyes*, excluded from the 2004 *Collected*, and addressed to the British poet Chris Torrance, Harwood writes:

---

[34] Though of course when Wyatt writes 'Whoso list to hunt, I know where is an hynde' the metaphor is of the deer hunt. *Collected Poems of Sir Thomas Wyatt*, ed. Kenneth Muir (London: Routledge, 1967), 7. In a blazon of disgust in Book 1 of Spenser's *The Faerie Queene*, Duessa is portrayed as having a fox's tail growing at her 'romp', covered in 'dong'; Jonathan Goldberg reads this as an emblem of 'unproductive, sodomitical sex' in *The Seeds of Things: Theorizing Sexuality and Materiality in Renaissance Representations* (New York: Fordham, 2009), 81.

[35] Compare Harwood's gloss on an F. T. Prince poem: 'He wrote a poem called "Words from Edmund Burke" – wonderfully pompous, long poem. In fact the whole poem is about being buggered, and he has this great line in it – "I am it would seem an acceptable tube." Well, it is just so genteel! I admired it very much.' Eric Mottram, 'Interview with Lee Harwood', *Poetry Information* 14 (Autumn/Winter 1975–1976): 12.

[36] Hughes-Edwards, '"Love . . . and other obsessions"', 140.

>   a new thing
>   coming
>   or dying
> (I must conceal) my unaimed erection (behind
> some bookshelf here at work)
>   (NCP 85)

But while Harwood has to conceal his erection while at work, he proudly displays it in the poem. Critics have tended to play along with this concealment. Much of the confusion about *The Man With Blue Eyes* comes from the long poem 'Summer', which is addressed to a woman and includes a description of cunnilingus: 'a tongue passing the length / of her clitoris' (*NCP* 74). Robert Sheppard argues:

> [T]he explicitness is arguably an over-compensation for the restraint of the gay poems with their lack of gender markers, and their focus on detached parts of the body: 'if only I could touch your naked shoulder' could easily be read as non-gender specific, or as heterosexual by default.[37]

One wonders about these apparently detachable body parts. At this point let me be clear about my position: it is a wilful misreading of *The Man With Blue Eyes* to consider it as anything other than a book of gay love poems. Presented in the 2004 *Collected*, with several poems dropped, the order changed, missing the bold dedication 'FOR JOHN' and the cover by Joe Brainard, perhaps this is understandable. The over-literal focus on genital sexuality has provoked a basic misunderstanding about the poem in question: four lines later lines in 'Summer' we're told that this takes place 'so long ago'. The scene of cunnilingus (which in any case is passively constructed: it's 'a tongue' rather than 'my tongue') is in the past; it belongs with other loves.

Regardless, both Hughes-Edwards and Sheppard ignore one of the plainest examples of homosexual desire in the book, from 'Journal May 20 1965':

> let his cock droop warm and clean
>   in his denims
>
> I don't know . mental fingers
>   goosing him in wood-shed
>   ecstasies

---

[37] Robert Sheppard, 'It's A Long Road', 20.

> why should the bandits want him
> >   —when I'm here
> the first to come in all situations.
> >   (NCP 86)

It seems necessary here to state the obvious: Lee Harwood is fantasising about John Ashbery. If we insist that Harwood is concealing his desires for men, it's as if we as critics are doing our best to keep these poems in the 'wood-shed' closet. One of the reasons *The Man With Blue Eyes* deserves to be celebrated is precisely for its vulnerability and clarity, and how it anticipates more open representations of queer desire in the 1970s. This vulnerability extends to how Harwood deals with the necessity of secrecy in his personal circumstance. He locates his sexual activity outside the family home, whether the apparently 'concealed' erection at work, or the fantasy space of the 'wood-shed'. At the time, Harwood was working at Better Books, and Ashbery's letters are addressed to him there. One letter refers with anxiety to the fact that Harwood's wife might have inadvertently intercepted their communications.

Better Books was an important space for queer cultural distribution: the first gay bookshop in London, Gay's the Word, didn't open until 1979, with the lesbian feminist Silver Moon books following in 1984.[38] Films by Kenneth Anger, Jack Smith and Andy Warhol were all shown in the basement, and the bookshop carried titles by John Rechy, William Burroughs, Jean Genet, and other American and European imports. We can understand Better Books as an important site for Harwood's relationships with men. As I've already mentioned, it provided the scene for his meeting with Fainlight in 1966, and for his correspondence with Ashbery. Perhaps it was there that he met the out gay Benedictine monk and concrete poet Dom Sylvester Houédard, known as 'dsh'. Harwood dedicates a poem to him in *The Man With Blue Eyes*, titled simply 'For D.S.H.', which reads in part:

---

[38] Robert K. Martin recounts a visit to Gay's the Word in the early 1980s, and gives a portrait of John Duncan, one of the first managers of the store. John, he writes, 'came to life when he met the gay poet Jonathan Williams as a student at Wake Forest College and subsequently fled to civilization and a job in a London bookstore'. See Martin, 'London Diary', in *The View From Christopher Street*, ed. Michael Denneny, Charles Ortleb and Thomas Steele (London: Chatto, 1984), 233. It's worth mentioning here that Sisterwrite feminist bookshop in Islington, which played a major role in distributing lesbian literature and in community support, opened in 1978.

> I can kneel here
>   with no special ritual
> but my own
> a carpet design
>   or a twisted heap of metal
> my obsession god this minute
>
> cymbals dulled drums
>   my clothing so ornate that
>   I have to move with ceremony
> gold and silver
>   silks at my throat
> a minute explosion puffing
> from a top window
>
>   (NCP 80)

The poem is charged with sexualised imagery: the ritual of kneeling, the eroticised attention to clothing, the silks at the throat. All are suggestive of a scene of fellatio. While Houédard's most famous typewriter works (typestracts) are not typified by queer content, he also made ingenious calligraphic 'reversal poems'.[39] These could be read as suggestive or innocuous, explicit or inscrutable, like 'pansyish nymphs / enhanced ideas', or 'blonde danes long to / of proud gayes love'.[40] Houédard was involved in the Gay Liberation Front, and acted as a mentor to younger artists and writers throughout his life.[41] Harwood's poem retained its dedication to dsh in *Children of Albion*, but by the time of his 2004 *Collected* this trace is gone, the poem titled after its first line: 'No–all the temple bells...'. The queer social context is erased.

But if Harwood was 'the first to come in all situations', perhaps it makes sense to think of *The Man With Blue Eyes* as premature. Ashbery had already made the decision to return to New York by the time the book appeared, permanently curtailing the relationship. How did Ashbery – so private, so restrained – receive this extraordinary work of open sexual detail? In a letter accompanying the jacket-text he wrote for the 1968 publication *The White Room*, he said:

---

[39] A collection was published in an extremely limited edition as Dom Sylvester Houédard, *begin again: a book of reversals and reflections by dsh* (Brampton: LYC Museum, 1975).

[40] For these examples, see William Allen Word & Image, online: https://williamallen wordandimage.wordpress.com/dom-sylvester-houedard/ [Accessed 20 April 2020].

[41] Charles Lambert has written of his complex feelings about being seduced by dsh while a student at a reading in Cambridge in 1973. See Charles Lambert, 'postfuck tristezza', *Cambridge Literary Review*, 1 (2010): 87–94.

> My only objection to your work is that I keep stumbling over myself in it and that I emerge as a kind of cross between the Dark Lady of the Sonnets and a CIA agent. Now you know I am joking and that I am actually very happy to figure in your work, though it always makes me feel guilty somehow and as though I ought to have been another kind of person.[42]

In some ways this is the perfect queer reading: Ashbery identifies with the Dark Lady, rather than the youthful boy, and his role as a CIA agent is like a character stepping out of Auden. The Shakespeare comparison is echoed by the poet Jeremy Reed, who writes that these poems are 'as important to [their] time as Shakespeare's androgynously sexed sonnets were to his'.[43] There are examples of contemporary reviews – of a later work – that comment dismissively on Harwood's sexuality. These are, interestingly, reviews of an LP of the poet reading *Landscapes*, issued by Stream Records in 1969. For the reviewer in *The Observer*, they are 'translucent, slightly fey, mildly homosexual poems, read with controlled hesitation, which fits'.[44] The *Audio and Record Review* is more strident:

> I found that the poet's voice, its South-East English accent just prettily tinged with North American, and a delivery that we should call 'little-girlish' if Mr. Harwood were a girl, combined to (with the text) make a mixture that was just too much for me. This record did not please. It may well appeal to some tastes, but they are not mine.[45]

For these critics, both Harwood's vocal performance and his poems are evidence of non-normative sexuality and gender. In some ways, they stand as proof of Reed's assessment: they demonstrate, albeit negatively, that Harwood's work was legibly queer in its contemporary moment. When I suggest the book is premature, I'm thinking of the emergence of gay print cultures post-Stonewall, and the kind of sympathetic audience *The Man With Blue Eyes* might have found in different circumstances. I combed Harwood's papers looking for reviews of later work, perhaps in *Gay News*, but with no luck. Reed's advocacy of the work is important because it suggests how the text may have circulated, accruing new meanings and new significance for queer readers in the 1970s and beyond.

---

[42] Ashbery, letter to Lee Harwood, 31 January 1968, British Library Western Manuscripts, Lee Harwood Papers Add MS 88998/2/2.
[43] Quoted in *The Salt Companion to Lee Harwood*, 20.
[44] Unsigned review, *The Observer Review*, 16 February 1969. Add MS 8898/1/7.
[45] Unsigned review, *The Audio and Record Review*, June 1969. Add MS 8898/1/7.

Harwood's visits to New York after the book was published were bittersweet. At least one trip coincided with the presence of Ashbery's long-term boyfriend, the poet Pierre Martory.[46] But the English poet was a hit all the same. Joe Brainard would later send him sweet, nervous letters declaring that he had a crush on him. Poems collected later in *The White Room* suggest that romantic liaisons with both men and women were in no short supply. One of the more important occluded relationships was with the poet and novelist Thomas M. Disch, who would go on to become a groundbreaking queer sci-fi writer. Harwood wrote him half a dozen poems that remain unpublished, but he broke off the proceedings abruptly. Disch would have his revenge in a brutal sonnet titled 'You & I', writing of a later meeting with Harwood in Exeter during 'the heroic phase of my chagrin, / That you could give me up for heroin'.[47] He also mentions 'Lee Harwood, the noted Anglo-American poet' in his novel *Camp Concentration*, which imagines a genocide against homosexuals in the near-future USA.[48] Disch's sonnet points to the massive emotional upheavals Harwood was going through during this period. The pressures of a looming divorce and his drug use contributed to a hospitalisation in a psychiatric ward in July 1967. In an autobiographical essay, he writes:

> The end of the sixties was both a bleak and prolific time for me. Put crudely, my life fell apart and I wrote a lot of books. [...] Amongst all this rushing around, I'd had a breakdown and spent two months in a locked ward of a London psychiatric hospital.[49]

The blunt historicist would note that this hospitalisation coincided with the passing of the Sexual Offences Act 1967.[50] But there's no

---

[46] In the original publication of *The Man With Blue Eyes*, the sequence ends with the magnificently passive-aggressive poem 'That Evening Pierre Insisted I had Two Roast Pigeons At Dinner'. The *Collected* sequencing ends with 'Landscape With Three People', which negotiates the break-up of Harwood's marriage, with its especially plaintive line 'I loved him and I loved her'.

[47] Thomas M. Disch, 'You and I: A Sonnet', *ABCDEFGHIJKLMNOPQRSTUVWXYZ* (London: Anvil, 1981), 78.

[48] Thomas M. Disch, *Camp Concentration* (London: Hart-Davis, 1968).

[49] 'Lee Harwood', *Gale Contemporary Authors Autobiography Series 19* (Detroit: Gale Research, 1994), 145.

[50] The only evidence I've found for how the poets may have registered (celebrated?) the 1967 Act is the re-publication that year of Auden's erotic poem *The Platonic Blow* (London: Fuck Press, 1967). Fuck Press, named in honour of Ed Sanders's *Fuck You* magazine, which originally unearthed and published the Auden poem, was edited by Bill Butler. See Terry Adams, *Bill Butler and the Unicorn Bookshop* (Binley Woods: Beat Scene Press, 2020).

reason to believe in a direct link between one and another: the temporality of any individual erotic life is surely only tenuously related to such changes in the superstructure. As I've already shown, the attempts to link Harwood's aesthetics with the illegality of homosexuality result in distorted interpretations of the text. We would expect, if the relationship between formal legality and his writing were so substantial, that after 1967 his poems would abandon evasiveness, heralding the liberalisation of the law with a new directness. But the reality is more complex.

It's not possible, here, to fully detail the books that followed *The Man With Blue Eyes* and *The White Room*. But I want to make a single claim, even risk a sweeping generalisation. In *Landscapes* (1969) and especially *The Sinking Colony* (1970), homosexual content is systematically displaced by a range of colonial fantasies. Half of this equation has been noted before. Sheppard identifies 'colonialism and erotic obsession' in the poem 'Animal Days' from *The Sinking Colony*.[51] Geoff Ward writes of the 'balanced and ambivalent representations of militarism as both a joke, a raid on the dressing-up box, and a lingering of something that could flare up again with unknown consequences'.[52] Tony Lopez describes this phase of Harwood's poetry as 'a beautiful but fading kind of colonial camp'.[53] But no critic has pointed out that this strange and melancholic imagery – a kind of aristocratic empire nostalgia – coincides with the significant reorientation of Harwood's sexual desires away from men.

Where *The Man With Blue Eyes* repeatedly named men, some of them Harwood's lovers – John, Chris Torrance, dsh, Michel Couturier, Peter Ruppell and Pierre Martory – in *Landscapes* the only dedicatee, the only name, is that of Marian O'Dwyer. In 'When the Geography Was Fixed', he writes:

> When I say 'I love you'—that means
> something. And what's in the past
> I don't know anymore—it was all ice-skating.
> (NCP 158)

---

[51] *Salt Companion to Lee Harwood*, 23.
[52] Ibid., 44.
[53] Ibid., 83.

His relationship with Ashbery – the author of 'The Skaters' – is consigned to a past now beyond knowledge. The poem continues with the redrawing of boundaries, into the apparent consolidation of heterosexuality:

> There is only one woman in the gallery now
> who knows what's really happening on the canvas—
> but she knew that already, and she
> also instinctively avoided all explanations.
> (NCP 159)

The canvas – and the numerous other poems in *Landscapes* featuring paintings – allows Harwood to emphasise his preference for surface over depth. Knowledge of 'what's really happening' is now the property of the desired and desiring woman, and one of the things that she knows, instinctively, is that explanations should be avoided.

Yet beneath the declared heterosexual address of these love poems, Harwood remains interested in the mutability of his object choices. This is also the cause of anxiety. We read of 'fingers and objects of superstition'[54] and we're told that 'the objects / are real enough, they have powers',[55] and in the poem 'The "utopia"' Harwood dramatises the work of selection at length. The poem begins with all options open: 'The table was filled with many objects.' While he tells us these objects are books, Harwood is interested in relational possibility, in 'fresh arrangements', and how these objects 'could not help but rouse a curiosity'. But figures intrude on the scene:

> There are at times people in this room
> —some go to the table—things are moved—
> but the atmosphere here is always that of quiet and calm
> —no one could disturb this.
> (NCP 164)

The poem seems to work to mitigate the threat that *people* pose to Harwood's own sense of his erotic life. When people intrude things get moved around, explanations are required, the libidinal order is disturbed. But here, in the poem, or at least in this poem, Harwood is in control. He goes on:

---

[54] 'When the Geography Was Fixed', NCP 99.
[55] 'Sea Coves', CP 102.

> Once the surveyors had abandoned their project
> the objects once more took over.
> It would be false to deny the sigh of relief
> there was when this happened and calm returned.
> (NCP 165)

Given that Harwood had been sectioned in 1967, we can assume that the question of his sexuality had been subject to the intrusion of psychiatric evaluation. The 'surveyors' here stand in for the regime of knowledge presided over and enforced by psychological and medical diagnostic criteria. That's to say: Harwood's work is only inflected by oppressive state invigilation *post*-1967. The poem ends with a deliberate withholding: 'The many details may appear evasive / but the purpose of the total was obvious / and uncompromising' (NCP, 166).

It will be obvious to the reader that these poems – unlike *The Man With Blue Eyes* – are stylistically resonant with Shoptaw's understanding of the homotextual, with its 'distortions, evasiveness, omissions, and discontinuities'. But Harwood insists that the 'purpose of the total' is both 'obvious' and 'uncompromising'. Perhaps we can understand these poems as registering the conflict between sexual identity and sexual desire. If in *Landscapes* he is orientated towards women, and one woman in particular, perhaps his desires refuse to conform to this compromise. His struggle to accept the fluidity of his desire, then, results in the 'beautiful colonial camp', as Lopez calls it, that at this point comes to dominate the imagery of his poems.

The most blatant example is the title poem of *The Sinking Colony*, which begins with an epigraph from André Gide's complex and riddling novel of homoeroticism, *The Counterfeiters*. We are launched into a narrative:

> At the time being a young geologist with the British Raj in India I
>   was somewhat limited in the actions I could take, you see
> The expeditions into the foothills and mountains to the north with
>   our mules strung out behind us along the mountain track
> (NCP 221)

Colonial homoerotics have a long and substantial history.[56] Harwood draws in *The Sinking Colony* on the narratives of writers such as Gide and E. M. Forster, for whom the colonial project provided

---

[56] For an account that focuses on the Middle East, see Joseph Allen Boone, *The Homoerotics of Orientalism* (New York: Columbia UP, 2014). See also Robert Aldrich, *Colonialism and Homosexuality* (London: Routledge, 2002).

the opportunity for sexualised contact with a mystified other.[57] For Joseph A. Boone, 'the imagined or actual encounter with exotic otherness engenders profound anxieties about one's ability to narrate'.[58] Is that what's happening here? Harwood's narrative in 'The Sinking Colony' skips between the Raj and Canada, 'base camp' and a 'mansion', and presents a disordered and fragmented series of events that refuse to add up. We don't know and we don't find out what 'actions' the 'young geologist' would like to take, though a few lines later we find that he and his wife like to listen to music. The narrative, what there is of it, foregrounds incoherence. The material remains curiously inert: what's most distinctive about them is a decisive lack of eroticism. It's as if Harwood has to journey in imagination to the periphery in order to banish his homosexual desires, leaving him free – at the table or the art gallery – to refocus on the permitted love object of the woman. Yet what remains is slight, a poetry wounded by the muting of desire.

Harwood's colonial aesthetics are at best dubious. They coincide, gratuitously, with the flowering of Black poetry in Britain following the Caribbean Artists Movement. They raise a question of the specific racial formations of his sexuality that would require a broader contextual analysis than this chapter allows. Harwood's return to a more sexually explicit mode of writing is evident in *The Long Black Veil*. This sequence charts his relationship with the writer Bobbie Louise Hawkins, who at the time was married to Robert Creeley. The poem brings with it the orientalised atmosphere of *The Sinking Colony*, making reference to the Egyptian Book of the Dead, and including hieroglyphs and passages again from Gide, and R. A. Nicholson's *A Literary History of the Arabs*. But in a note to himself included with the manuscript in his archive, we can see Harwood beginning to recognise – to narrate at least to himself – a view of sexuality as unfixed and polymorphous:

> sex relations are not this simple – roles if any are reversed & always opaque & misty – the edges at least.[59]

This note is scored through, but it stands as evidence of how Harwood was beginning to understand his relationships. While

---

[57] Gide is especially important: the front cover of the Fulcrum edition of *The Sinking Colony* (London: Fulcrum, 1970) features a photograph of Gide in the Congo with his lover, Marc Allégret.

[58] Joseph A. Boone, 'Vacation Cruises, or, the Homoerotics of Orientalism', *PMLA* 110, no. 1 (1995): 89–107.

[59] British Library Western Manuscripts, Lee Harwood Papers, Add MS 88998/5/7.

his relationship with Hawkins – like his relationship with Sandy Berrigan – have been taken as evidence of the predominance of heterosexuality in Harwood's 1970s work, Harwood reminds us, again, that desire is always unruly. His work is marked by the simple homo/heterosexual binary, but also offers resistance.

Yet what's clear in Harwood's writing of the late 1960s and early 1970s is that he doesn't come to identify with the emergence of a public gay presence post-Stonewall. He shows no apparent interest in the burgeoning militancy of Gay Liberation, despite, for example, spending time in Boston with John Wieners, who was at the time involved in the radical *Fag Rag* collective. Closer to home, the posthumous books of Mark Hyatt, who killed himself in 1972, began bringing his extraordinary queer lyrics to light.[60] Americans Jonathan Williams and Tom Meyer, dividing their time between North Carolina and the Dales, continued to publish riotously inventive work. Poets such as Alaric Sumner, associated with Writers Forum, began to involve themselves in practical activism with the Gay Liberation Front. The twenty-five-year-old Jeremy Reed arrived on the scene with a fully formed queer aesthetic in *The Isthmus of Samuel Greenberg* (1976). These poets, all gay, couldn't be more different: but critical recovery takes precedent over critical distinction.[61] Meanwhile poets including Denise Riley and Wendy Mulford, socialist feminists, began to think critically about sexuality and gender. Mulford would go on to do groundbreaking scholarly work on lesbian poets and novelists Sylvia Townsend Warner and Valentine Ackland, members of the Communist Party in the 1930s. Magazines such as Paul Buck and Glenda George's *Curtains* started to publish transgressive French writing by Bataille, Pierre Guyotat and others. Harwood seems to have been content with his Gide and his Forster, and to have retreated from the queer possibility opening up around him.

But there are important later examples of queer poems within his body of work. After Harwood moved to Brighton in 1968, he worked at Bill Butler's Unicorn Bookshop. Butler, who was gay, had

---

[60] See Sam Ladkin and Luke Roberts, eds., *So Much For Life: Poems by Mark Hyatt* (New York: Nightboat, 2023), and Mark Hyatt, *Love, Leda*, ed. Luke Roberts (London: Peninsula, 2023).

[61] One avenue worth following up would be the publication histories in England of queer American poets of colour. This might begin with two books by Stephen Jonas: *Transmutations* (London: Ferry, 1966) and *Exercises for Ear* (London: Ferry, 1967). It could include Alfred Celestine's *Confessions of Nat Turner* (London: The Many Press, 1978), and extend to the anthology including work by Essex Hemphill, *Tongues Untied*, ed. Martin Humphries (London: The Gay Men's Press, 1987).

lived in the Britain since the early 1960s, working at Better Books before setting up in Brighton. It's not clear if Harwood was present when the bookshop was raided by police, looking for and finding obscene publications. Butler, successfully prosecuted, was crushed by the legal costs. He moved to Wales, dying prematurely in 1977. His work deserves to be recovered. Harwood's elegy for Butler, 'Afterwords to a Poem by Jack Spicer', speaks with raging grief:

> That mean spirits and the dishonest man now hold sway
>   poison us all with their intrigue and venom
> Where no hand of kindness reaches out to touch
>   our lips as we pass
> As though love were driven out of the town
>   and only left alight in the quiet of a home
>   (*NCP* 408)

These lines offer an oblique self-commentary on the horizons of sexual freedom that Harwood had turned away from, and which we as critics might try to keep open. Love, says Harwood, shouldn't be relegated to bourgeois domesticity, but should be open and public, where an anonymous 'hand of kindness' might touch you as you pass. Queer love is transformative; its banishment has repercussions for the whole fabric of the social world. Critics of experimental poetry have tended to shy away from biographical readings, seeing the virtue of 'linguistically innovative poetry' in its opposition to the egotism of confessionalism. But in doing so, much of the collective life of the 1960s and 1970s has been left unexamined, and an assumed heteronormativity has been left undisturbed. As Samuel Delany has argued:

> Of course, there *are* no 'heterosexual' male preserves. There are social groups where gay and bisexual men feel safe acknowledging themselves – first to one another, then to pretty much everyone. And there are other social groups where they don't. By heterosexual preserve, you simply indicate the latter. The gay and bisexual men are there. But the homophobia in the group is high enough to make them wary of acknowledging their presence – sometimes even to themselves.[62]

The further recovery of Harwood's contemporaries is necessary if we are to understand the era. Without acknowledging and celebrating the presence of gay and bisexual men within the poetry scenes of the

---

[62] Samuel R. Delany, '*The Black Leather in Color* Interview', *Shorter Views: Queer Thoughts and the Politics of the Paraliterary* (London: Wesleyan, 1999), 115.

Driven Out of the Town: Homosexuality and The British Poetry Revival   131

1960s, we have no way of understanding the operation of homophobia both within that scene and in its legacy and reception.

During the 1980s Harwood continued to write. For our purposes, the most interesting publications he was involved in are three anthologies of gay poetry: *Not Love Alone: A Modern Gay Anthology* (1985); *The Penguin Book of Homosexual Verse* (1987); and *Take Any Train: A Book of Gay Men's Poetry* (1990). The precedent for these anthologies comes partly from American books like *Angels of the Lyre: A Gay Poetry Anthology* (1975), but also from the explosion of lesbian feminist poetry in Britain, collected in volumes like *One Foot on the Mountain: An Anthology of British Feminist Poetry, 1969–1979* (1979). When I first discovered Harwood's presence in these anthologies, I interpreted it as evidence of his belated coming out. Here at last was irrefutable evidence that Harwood was gay. But as my research deepened I became more secure in uncertainty. Martin Humphries, the editor of *Not Love Alone*, wrote in a letter soliciting poems from Harwood's 1981 book *All the Wrong Notes*: 'I felt that any or all of these would be fine for the collection except that I have no idea if you define yourself as gay.'[63] Harwood's reply is worth quoting at length:

> The pieces you mentioned in my book *All the Wrong Notes* are really to do with friendship rather than being 'gay' – though there's a pretty thin line between the two, I admit. But no, these days I don't think of myself as 'gay'.
>
> [...]
>
> If you do want to see work of mine that is directly gay then do look at my two early books – *The Man With Blue Eyes* (Angel Hair Books, New York, 1966) and *The White Room* (Fulcrum Press, London, 1968).[64]

We can note the falling away of the quotation marks around 'gay' when Harwood talks about his earlier writing. We can also note that Harwood doesn't offer any identification in place of '"gay"'. He instead acknowledges the 'thin line' that separates friendship from romance, or affection from desire, one kind of relationship from another.

Harwood's publication in these anthologies – perhaps especially the groundbreaking *Not Love Alone*, published by the Gay Men's

---

[63] Martin Humphries, Letter to Lee Harwood, 9 February 1985. Martin Humphries Papers, Bishopsgate Institute, London.

[64] Lee Harwood, Letter to Martin Humphries, 20 February 1985. Martin Humphries Papers, Bishopsgate Institute, London.

Press – is important for several reasons. Amid the AIDS crisis, Harwood sees no stigma in his inclusion.[65] Other poets during the same period weren't able to be so open. Peter Ackroyd, another English supporter of Ashbery, went as far as to change the pronouns from masculine to feminine in his 1987 *The Diversions of Purley*, explaining to a reporter in a recent profile:

> 'It was mainly for the sake of my family, who were still all alive. I thought this was maybe too much for them, because they had no idea, so I took the coward's way out. I sort of regret it now, but there you go.'
>
> They were the last poems he published. 'The muse left me. That was that.'[66]

One of the poems Harwood included, 'Just Friends', is a supremely melancholic detailing of the activities of two men, including visiting galleries, walking around cities and visiting the coast with another friend, sometimes more ('Two men and a woman', 'Three men and two women').[67] But the refrain, 'Two men ...', emphasises their shared intimacy, which extends to walking 'on a summer evening through the leafy streets of west London' where they 'discuss renting a studio'. It is by any accounts a kind of love poem, ending with naked sincerity:

> Two men scramble over a recent cliff fall searching for flints and
>   fossils, and then fade in the sea-mist.
>
> One man... the lush parks and mute statues.
>
> At this moment I feel close to tears.
>
> (NCP 410)

At the launch of the anthology at Dillon's bookshop in January 1986, a collective reading of 'Just Friends' closed out the proceedings, the

---

[65] Harwood later contributed a poem, 'The Old Question', to *Jugular Defences: An AIDS Anthology*, ed. Peter Daniels and Steve Anthony (London: The Oscars Press, 1994).

[66] Andrew Dickson, 'Peter Ackroyd: A Secret History – 2000 years of gay life in London', *The Guardian* (20 May 2017). Ackroyd tells this story slightly differently in different interviews. In most versions he changed the pronouns in the 1973 *London Lickpenny*, because he feared homophobia at the right-wing *Spectator* magazine, where he was about to take a job.

[67] For a reading of this poem in relation to the Whitman tradition, see Gregory Woods '"Still on My Lips": Walt Whitman in Britain', in *The Continuing Presence of Walt Whitman: The Life After the Life*, ed. Robert K. Martin (Iowa: U of Iowa P, 1992), 129–40.

headline event. In the Martin Humphries archive there are photographs of the readers at the launch and the reception. Harwood isn't among them.

As Isabel Waidner has recently argued, there has never been a 'queer and intersectional avant-garde writing movement in Britain', or at least, not one preserved in criticism. Waidner's explanations for this absence are hard to argue with, running from the entrenched upper class in British publishing, to Oxbridge gate-keeping and specific instances of censorship and prosecution.[68] Waidner looks with something like longing or envy to the United States and Canada, and recently recovered and celebrated movements such as New Narrative. But it's possible to imagine, unbound by linear temporality, a dazzling constellation, a presence in Britain if not always a movement: from H. D. and Bryher in Cornwall to Suniti Namjoshi in Devon; Alfred Celestine in London, Edward Carpenter in Bolton, Edwin Morgan in Glasgow, Hamish Henderson in Edinburgh; Essex Hemphill visiting Brixton and Audre Lorde talking with Maud Sulter and Jackie Kay. The configurations are endless. There are now more young queer, trans and non-binary avant-garde poets than ever, forming new traditions and sharpening history to a point. The militant political critique and formal experimentation of poets such as Verity Spott, Timothy Thornton, Nat Raha, Francesca Lisette, Lisa Jeschke, Laurel Uziell and countless others have changed the cadences of whatever came before.[69] As Uziell puts it in *T*, a work at once in the tradition of the British Poetry Revival and set against it in total opposition: 'The cracks in the firmament belong to everyone.'[70]

Lee Harwood lived to see at least some of this, giving one of his last public readings with Spott and Sam Solomon at Brighton's Hi Zero reading series. I don't know what he made of it. But there's a late poem of his called 'Gorgeous – yet another Brighton poem' which soars in glorious declaration. It is nothing less than a queer affirmation of undifferentiated desire, to which I give the last word:

---

[68] Isabel Waidner, 'Class, Queers, and the Avant-Garde', the Institute for Contemporary Arts (2019), online: www.ica.art/media/01901.pdf [Accessed 28 August 2022].
[69] For an overview of some of these poets, see Danny Hayward, *Wound Building: Dispatches From The Latest Disasters in British Poetry* ([n.p.]: Punctum Books, 2021), online: https://punctumbooks.com/titles/wound-building-dispatches-from-the-latest-disasters-in-uk-poetry/ [Accessed 25 October 2023].
[70] Laurel Uziell, *T* (London: Materials, 2020), unpaginated.

The summer's here.
Down to the beach
to swim and lounge and swim again.
Gorgeous bodies young and old.
Me too. Just gorgeous. Just feeling good
and happy and so at ease in the world.
                              (NCP 582)

Chapter 5

Living in Feminism: Denise Riley and Wendy Mulford

Here, by way of a beginning, is a poem by Denise Riley:

> the eyes of the girls are awash with violets
> pansies are flowering under their tongues
> they are grouped by the edge of the waves and are anxious to swim;
> each one is on fire with passion to achieve herself.[1]

First published without title in 1978, by the time of her 1985 collection *Dry Air* this poem was named 'In 1970', and it has stayed so ever since. The title suggests either that it was written in 1970 – and so speaks to us *from* 1970 – or that the poet is recalling the events of that year at a later date. These shifting temporalities thrum like the waves. Though there had been stirrings – Sheila Rowbotham's 'Women's Liberation and the New Politics' was circulating in 1969, along with publications such as *Socialist Woman* and *Shrew*, and the first workshop meetings – 1970 was the year zero for women's liberation in Britain.[2] At the end of February, some 600 women from across the country gathered at Ruskin College in Oxford for a three-day conference. It was a watershed moment both for newly politicised women and seasoned activists alike.[3] Riley was among

---

[1] The publication history is as follows: Denise Riley and Wendy Mulford, *No Fee: A Line or Two For Free* (Cambridge: Street Editions, 1978); Riley, *Dry Air* (London: Virago, 1985); Riley, *Selected Poems* (London: Reality Street, 2000); Riley, *Selected Poems* (Basingstoke: Picador, 2019).

[2] Sheila Rowbotham, 'Women's Liberation and the New Politics' (1969), reprinted in *The Body Politic: Women's Liberation in Britain, 1969–1972*, ed. Michelene Wandor (London: Stage 1, 1972). For the background, see Sheila Rowbotham, *Promise of a Dream* (London: Penguin, 2000), 210–55.

[3] See the interviews conducted by Michelene Wandor in *Once A Feminist: Stories of a Generation* (London: Virago, 1990).

the attendees. The conference formulated a list of demands, which would remain consistent (albeit contested, expanded and rephrased) over the decade: (1) equal pay; (2) equal education and opportunity; (3) 24-hour nurseries; (4) free contraception and abortion on demand.

This poem, which I suggest is directly 'about' the Women's Liberation Movement (WLM), a kind of testimony to it, does not make these demands.[4] It is not a demanding poem. But it is a surprising poem, full of swerves and durable ambiguities. The first two lines are balanced and parallel: one body part per line (eyes/tongues), one type of flower (violets/pansies), one verb (awash/flowering). The phrasing almost sounds like a translation exercise, luxurious examples of the passive voice. But then the perspective shifts: 'they are grouped by the edges of the waves ...', the line extending beyond itself and kept in check only by the semicolon. Here is the problem and possibility of the group; here is the prospect of feminism's second wave; here is the question of swimming.

Thinking of Riley's later references to the popular music and culture of her adolescence in the 1950s and 1960s, including the Everly Brothers and Little Eva, I've often wondered what kind of swimming happens in 'In 1970'. The colour palette of the violets reminds me of the MGM extravaganzas of Esther Williams, amazing choreography and camerawork, perilous dives and fabulous elegance. Is this the model for women's liberation? Surely not. But to misremember Frank O'Hara, perhaps feminist political organising, which had to invent itself as it went along, could be just as intoxicating and astonishing as the movies.[5] Riley leaves plenty of room for interpretation. Maybe it's a stretch to say that 'pansies are flowering under their tongues' holds some queer promise, transforming the injurious speech of 'pansy' into a moment of fleeting identification. Certainly, the violets appear to have been plucked directly from H. D.'s *Sea Garden*, which Riley read from at her first public reading in 1977.[6] There's also the residual memory of flower power, an LSD tab dissolving under the tongue. A final speculation, thinking of

---

[4] At a reading at the Feminist Emergency Conference, Birkbeck College, University of London, June 2017, Riley explained that 'it was written from the middle of the then-Women's Liberation as an affectionate, ironic tribute'.

[5] 'And after all, only Whitman, and Crane and Williams, of the American poets, are better than the movies.' Frank O'Hara, 'Personism: A Manifesto' in *Collected Poems*, ed. Donald Allen (Berkeley: U of California P, 1995), 498.

[6] See Juha Virtanen, *Poetry and Performance During the British Poetry Revival, 1960–1980*, 55–82. For H. D.'s violets, see 'The Gift', 'Sea-Violet' and 'Sea Gods' in *Sea Garden* (London: Constable, 1916).

the poem's feminist lineage: is there a playful deflation of Adrienne Rich's 1973 'Diving into the Wreck'? This is no lonely and murky retrieval, but a strange combination of wryness and joy.[7]

Writing in *The Feminist Review* in 1979, Rebecca O'Rourke identified, in passing, a kind of stumbling block: 'It's as if I still have some notion of The Feminist Text, a rarefied, perfect work which would balance and represent all the conflicts and contradictions of contemporary feminism.'[8] This burden of expectation is only compounded by time. We greet feminist texts from the 1970s with an embarrassment of feeling: gratitude and jealousy, nostalgia and suspicion, enthusiasm and disappointment, excitement, perhaps even love.[9] There are multiple conventions, sometimes contradictory, that we might want these texts to conform to or subvert. This brings with it doubt and worry. I have already tried, almost as a reflex action, to place Riley's poem at a precise point in time, to hint at a modernist genealogy, to disentangle it from certain feminist texts or cultural objects while associating it with others. And who's this 'we' I'm conjuring up, the phantom collective subject? On what grounds, with how much shared language and how many obligations do we meet?

Clare Hemmings has argued that our understanding of recent feminist history tends to be determined by 'political grammars' which take certain narrative shapes. These are: (1) *Progress*, which follows the shift from 'woman' as a unified subject to a category critically understood via theories of difference and differentiation (most importantly race and sexuality); (2) *Loss*, which sees the apparent fragmentation of a unified feminist subject as symptomatic of a weakened political momentum, hastened by a retreat into the academy; (3) *Return*, which forms a pragmatic approach to both 'Progress' and 'Loss', balancing the theoretical insights of post-structuralism against the concrete persistence of inequality and oppression.[10]

But feminist poetry, at least in the British context, often seems to elude history's grasp. The critical neglect is longstanding. There are

---

[7] The question of Rich's poetic influence in Britain is intriguing. Jan Montefiore, writing in 1983, suggests that 'Rich is much better known here for *Of Woman Born* and *On Lies, Secrets, & Silence* (both published by Virago) than for her poetry, which is mostly only available in imported U.S. editions'. Montefiore, 'Feminist Identity and the Poetic Tradition', *Feminist Review* 13 (Spring 1983): 69.

[8] Rebecca O'Rourke, 'Summer Reading', *The Feminist Review* 2 (1979): 8.

[9] For some of the problems of generation as a 'mechanism of temporal management' see Robyn Wiegman, 'On Being in Time With Feminism', *MLQ*, 65, no. 1 (2004): 165.

[10] Clare Hemmings, *Why Stories Matter: The Political Grammar of Feminist Theory* (Durham, NC: Duke UP, 2011).

no monographs on poetry and the WLM in Britain. Survey essays in edited collections on post-war poetry and literature are sporadic and often dutiful. In a recent 400-page study of post-war women's print cultures, there is no chapter dedicated to the publishing and circulation of poetry.[11] Perhaps, with Samuel Solomon's *Lyric Pedagogy and Marxist-Feminism*, we've now passed from the era of overview towards more sustained political analysis and textual scholarship.[12] But recovery and contextualisation is a constant task. One need only open a recent companion to contemporary literature to find feminist poets of the 1970s still being leadenly caricatured and belittled.[13] Meanwhile, even Riley herself – despite being one of the most influential feminist theorists and poets of the past four decades – has only ever been served by selected and uneven editions of her poems, each one bigger than the last but none of them sufficient.[14]

Faced with this marginality, it's tempting to imagine that poetry must have a distinct political grammar, messier than Hemmings's structure allows. After all, Hemmings is thinking specifically about the temporal experience of story and narrative, and how these forms shape our understanding of the past. One of poetry's virtues might be the stubborn lyric refusal of these scripts. I might even fantasise about a poem that could bring everything together and let it fall apart in a desire to be named *redemption*. But before I get carried away and start searching out, grail-like, for the rarefied and perfect Feminist Poem which could do this, I hear a sceptical note sounded by Riley in a poem from the 1980s: 'disturb the text; you don't disturb the world'.[15] Dating from deconstruction's heyday and the emergence of a freshly formalist 'Linguistically Innovative Poetry' in Britain, Riley's line is a salutary reminder of the limits to textual freedom.[16] But the implied reverse must also be true: that if you

---

[11] Laurel Foster and Joanne Hollows, eds., *Women's Periodicals and Print Culture in Britain, 1940s–2000s: The Postwar and Contemporary Period* (Edinburgh: Edinburgh UP, 2020).

[12] Samuel Solomon, *Lyric Pedagogy and Marxist-Feminism: Social Reproduction and the Institutions of Poetry* (London: Bloomsbury, 2019).

[13] 'As a matter of fact, fewer and fewer women poets are angry nowadays. The man-hating days are over and they know better than to fight battles that have already been fought and won.' So proclaims Marc Porée, 'Women Poets in the British Isles', in *A Companion to Contemporary British and Irish Poetry, 1960–2015* (Chichester: Wiley, 2021), 343.

[14] One suspects that this is the author's preference, but it poses problems for scholarship, nevertheless.

[15] Denise Riley, 'Ah, so', *Dry Air*, 48.

[16] For roughly contemporaneous pronouncements made on behalf of Linguistically Innovative Poetry, see Adrian Clarke and Robert Sheppard, 'Afterword', in *Floating Capital: New Poets from London*, (Elmwood: Potes and Poets Press Inc, 1991).

disturb the world through political organising, you disturb the text, changing what and how it means, expanding what's possible to write and say and think.

'In 1970' remains poised at this threshold of dawning political commitment, full to the brim with feeling. Being anxious *to* swim isn't the same as being anxious *about* swimming. The poem is not fearful but eager. Elsewhere, in the same era, Riley writes with equal parts deprecation and affection of a subject 'who lives in "feminism" like a warm square', and this poem is animated by a similar immersive longing.[17] But rather than a town or city square that gently traps the sun over the course of a morning or afternoon, here the movement into feminism is figured as a splash. Soon you will be in the water; soon you will be swimming; already you are on fire with passion. It's not so much metaphor as metamorphosis: somewhere beyond the semicolon in line three, the 'girls' become the wave which breaks in turn to show how 'each one' is transformed in self-achievement.

But for the reader who wants to turn the poem into a political artefact – The Feminist Text – there are knotty ambivalences that won't go away. If I am on fire with passion, surely swimming will douse my desire, leaving me washed out and bedraggled. Perhaps the atmosphere is surreptitiously baptismal, and the lyric contraries and lingering doubts simply dissolve in a form of ecstatic devotion. What about the group? We're told, with a little flex of absent authority, 'they are grouped', but we don't know by whom or according to what categories. Perhaps they have been arranged, as girls, into rows, by a teacher.[18] Perhaps they have grouped themselves according to friendship, loose loyalties and trust. Maybe there are differences that go unremarked: white girls and black girls, trans girls and cis girls, rich girls and poor girls, straight girls, bisexuals and lesbians. Does the poem think about disabled girls, non-disabled, those who swim and those who can't?

I want to say that it does. The category 'girls' is left deliberately vague, anonymous, capacious. They could be infants, teenagers or young adults, could be intimate in number or abundant. But the poem's final line insists on the recognition of their individuation. In Lisa Robertson's interpretation, this is the moment where 'the

---

[17] In *Selected Poems* (2019) this poem – originally untitled in *Marxism for Infants* – is called 'An Infant' (10).

[18] Recalling Riley's training in art history, we might also identify this as a painterly gesture: the grouping of figures in the foreground or background. As such, it would be possible to read the poem as a subversion of pictorial conventions relating to women bathers.

lyric image looks back' and meets the reader's gaze.[19] Swimming, figuratively, seems to represent the escape from being grouped, and to hold out the possibility of other forms of organisation. It brackets the formative and transient designation of girlhood, with each figure now stepping out, now turning inwards, now setting off. Swimming is a disciplined abandon, a loosening and a stretching both at once. The poem lets the categories fall apart and recombine, the waves coming and going out. Tellingly, nowhere does the poem demand that you, the reader, jump in; it is free from imperative. All of this folds back into the poem's nervous excitement, its magnetism and charisma. To use Hemmings's grammars, we call this progress.

More by way of complement than contrast, this is a poem by two schoolgirls, from 1964:

A Ditty

Snowdrops	Daffodils	Tulips	Crocus
			Narcissi!
Bluebells	Roses	Sunflowers	Violets
			Gardenias!
Orchids	Lavender	Fresias	Buttercups
Daisies	Dandelions		

And my new elastic swimming costume.

It was written by Celia Davies and Melanie Tompkins, and published by the avant-garde press Writers Forum in a collection of writing by schoolchildren from Barnet edited by Bob Cobbing and Jeff Nuttall (both working as schoolteachers at the time).[20] While literary history records that Cobbing and Nuttall became legends of the counterculture, Davies and Tompkins have joined the ranks of the more or less anonymous. The anthology doesn't record their ages, but perhaps by 1970 they would have been old enough to know about and to attend the Ruskin conference; or, indeed, perhaps they were still young enough to be taken along to it by their mothers.

---

[19] Lisa Robertson, 'On Denise Riley', online: https://lemonhound.com/2013/06/04/lisa-robertson-on-denise-riley/ [Accessed 25 October 2023]. Originally published in *The Globe and Mail*, 8 September 2001.

[20] Bob Cobbing and Jeff Nuttall, eds., *Barnet Poets: An Anthology by Children of the New Borough of Barnet* (London: Writers Forum, 1965), unpaginated.

Although 'A Ditty' isn't obviously proto-feminist in sentiment, our interpretation might emphasise how the formal process of collaboration works to dislodge the idea of a singular creative genius. If daffodils belong to William Wordsworth and sunflowers to William Blake, here the girls dart in and out of the flowers undeterred by literary history. As Cora Kaplan suggested in 1975: 'As women's poetry reflects the growing strength and assurance of women artists in the first part of the twentieth century there is a strong emphasis on women not *as* flowers, but in some kind of critical relationship *to* them.'[21] If, as I've suggested, Riley's 'In 1970' makes room to think with and against categories, here there's a playful intervention in taxonomy. The flowers are organised by intuition and pleasure, and the exclamatory register means that when spoken aloud it's as if each name rhymes with the other, equal in meaning and weight.

The final line is, again, important. Any notion of untroubled 'organic' femininity – of the equivalence between women and flowers – is undermined by the appearance of the commodity: 'my new elastic swimming costume'. Partly, this serves to remind us that flowers can be commodities, too. In some ways it's a sombre intrusion, marking the moment where collaboration reaches its limits: it's 'my' swimming costume, rather than 'our' swimming costumes, as ownership intrudes on companionship. One of the early actions of women's liberation in Britain, predating the Ruskin conference, was a sticker campaign and protest against Nelbarden swimwear, and perhaps in 'A Ditty' we wearily register the social inscription of gender roles.[22] But this would involve denying the sheer delight of this line, the happiness of the poem, how the violets in this poem might also flower, have flowered, under the tongues of the girls who wrote it.

I'm interested in how the ending of 'A Ditty' might illuminate the passion of self-achievement at the end of 'In 1970'. It's a similarity in texture: the tender gaudiness of 'my new elastic swimming costume' seems to correspond with the awkward grace of self-achievement. But one involves reaching for costume and the other doesn't. In the poems collected in *Mop Mop Georgette* (1993), Riley refers to a range of fabrics with exactitude: rayon, shantung silk, poplin.[23]

---

[21] Cora Kaplan, ed., *Salt Bitter and Good: Three Centuries of English and American Women Poets* (London: Paddington, 1975), 23.

[22] See the recollection by Lois Graessle in Wandor, *Once a Feminist: Stories of a Generation*, 131. The campaign is also mentioned by Rowbotham in 'Women's Liberation and the New Politics'.

[23] Riley's interest in fabrics continues: her newest collection is titled *Lurex* (London: Picador, 2022).

These tend to signal fleeting hopes and missed opportunity, a melancholy just beyond reach. As she writes in 'Rayon', 'Perhaps the passions that we feel don't quite belong to anyone / but hang outside us in the light like hoverflies'. Even these hoverflies are 'aping wasps'.[24] Yet the end of 'In 1970' gestures, surprisingly, to something like authenticity, where fiery passion will burn away all that's peripheral to reveal the core of achieved selfhood.

It is surprising because Riley's historical and philosophical work on language, selfhood and gender – from at least 1988's *'Am I That Name?': Feminism and the Category of 'Women' in History* through to the essays collected as *Impersonal Passion* (2005) – are exemplary in their scepticism of whether anything like an 'authentic' or coherent self could be achieved. Achievement implies a closure and completion that Riley's later work patiently shows to be always coming undone. Perhaps this is the poem's irony: the subject on fire with passion to achieve herself finds out she is, in fact, a 'fluctuating identity'.[25] Or perhaps it illustrates the ineradicable 'will to be', as she elaborates in a gloss on Sartre:

> To be and not be itself is self-consciousness's founding predicament. This ambiguity must always be fought out, for the ordinary relation of any self to itself can't escape the post-Hegelian restlessness in which the pursuit of self-definition, a will to be, is also its own undermining.[26]

It's difficult, if not impossible, to read Riley's earliest literary works without reference to her later critical writing. It isn't simply that Riley has 'kept up' or 'stayed relevant' in the passage from Women's Liberation to feminist philosophy, or the development of gender studies and Queer theory. It's that Riley's contributions have profoundly shaped the critical field in both Britain and the United States. If we try to think about feminist poetry in the 1970s, it's not simply that Riley is one of the objects of inquiry; her work is part of the methodology. The poetry, then, sometimes has an aura of prescience. It can also feel a little like a blueprint or architectural plan, with the prose standing in as the finished thought.

Close to hand, Riley provides us with a helpful phrase: 'a solidarity of disaggregation'.[27] This is an echo of a WLM campaign slogan,

---

[24] *Selected Poems* (2019), 82.
[25] Denise Riley, *'Am I That Name?': Feminism and the Category of 'Women' in History* (London: Macmillan, 1988), 1.
[26] Denise Riley, *The Words of Selves* (Stanford: Stanford UP, 2000), 119.
[27] Ibid., 175.

'Disaggregation now!', which emerged at the close of the 1970s.[28] Within the WLM, the disaggregation campaign fought for reforms to the benefit system, targeting the strictures which prevented married women (and any woman cohabiting with a man) from applying for supplementary assistance. State benefits were only allocated to the man of the house; they were his to distribute. This had far-reaching implications: single women claimants were disciplined by the structure because evidence of cohabitation, real or invented, could be used by the Social Security department as pretext for disqualification and sanction.[29] As the campaign argued, the demand for disaggregation raised 'fundamental issues about women's dependence in the family and the part the state plays in the subordination of women'.[30] It was part of a broader project of the WLM to understand how, in the words of Elizabeth Wilson, 'anti-feminism became so entrenched in our social policies', and how aspects of the architecture of the welfare state perpetuated forms of gendered inequality.[31]

Riley's conceptualisation of disaggregation is part of a cluster of desires that surface in her work from the 2000s: for 'demassification', for 'disintegrative liberty', for an agile rearrangement of selfhood that could loosen the determining bonds of identity.[32] This avoids what Gayatri Spivak calls the 'triumphalist mode' of solidarity, where subjects are uncritically celebrated rather than rigorously deconstructed.[33] I'm going to return to the question of solidarity and its limits in the WLM: but I want to proffer disaggregation as an alternative to the *bifurcation* that literary criticism often imposes on feminist poetry of the 1970s. Riley's work, along with that of her

---

[28] As Solomon has argued, 'Riley's work from the 1990s on is replete with echoes and returns of lines of prose, song and slogans'. *Lyric Pedagogy*, 163.

[29] Diana Scott records such a visit in her poem 'Social security visiting inspector semi-blues', in *One Foot on the Mountain: An Anthology of British Feminist Poetry, 1969–1979*, ed. Lilian Mohin (London: Onlywomen Press, 1979), 80–2.

[30] London WLM Campaign for Legal and Financial Independence and Rights of Women, 'Disaggregation Now! Another Battle For Women's Independence', first published in *Feminist Review* 2 (1979). Reprinted in Feminist Anthology Collective, *No Turning Back: Writings from the Women's Liberation Movement* (London: The Women's Press, 1981), 22. There's no question that Riley was aware of the slogan and campaign: her essay 'War in the Nursery' appears in the same issue of *Feminist Review*, and her essay 'Force of Circumstance' is in *No Turning Back*.

[31] Elizabeth Wilson, *Women and the Welfare State* (London: Tavistock, 1977), 98. See also Fran Bennett, 'The State, Welfare, and Women's Dependence', in *What is to be Done About the Family?*, ed. Lynne Segal (Harmondsworth: Penguin, 1983), 190–214.

[32] Riley, *Words of Selves*, 175.

[33] Gayatri Spivak, *A Critique of Postcolonial Reason* (Cambridge, MA: Harvard UP, 1999), 113.

less well-known collaborator Wendy Mulford, has come to represent Marxist feminism. It is au fait with post-structuralism but not ruined by it. It is too agile to be caught in the nets of essentialist thinking or the lures of lesbian separatism. It is modernist, critical, ironic, and pleasingly and playfully difficult. On the other side there are the poets conveniently grouped in Lilian Mohin's 1979 anthology *One Foot on the Mountain*, whose work is rooted in Consciousness-Raising (CR) groups, is less reflexive in its use of first-person and collective pronouns, and is decidedly not modernist, ironic or especially difficult. It has either aged badly or it hasn't aged at all, trapped in the aspic of feminism's second wave.[34]

My sense is that this distinction, which I'm exaggerating and caricaturing, serves an important purpose for scholars trying to re-evaluate the legacy of second-wave feminism in Britain. It makes a coherent narrative out of often intense contradictions, and it provides a holding space where the grammars of loss, return and progress can play out. In Britain the stakes of these grammars are high. The vocal transphobia of some feminists who passed through the WLM – along with some selective reading by younger recruits to what's called 'gender critical feminism' – has given second-wave feminism a bad name.[35] As I'll return to in the remainder of this chapter, the whiteness of the movement has become glaring, making the formal minutiae of experimental poetry rather less absorbing. But because the feminist poetry of the 1970s and 1980s remains under-read, and the textual history remains a problem, it's worth briefly surveying the literary landscape.

Despite access to mimeograph machines, women poets in the 1970s often started publishing much later than men and usually, burdened with the unequal distribution of reproductive labour, had less time for writing. Mulford, for instance, whose work I'll examine later in this chapter, published her first mimeographed collection

---

[34] This distinction is made very even-handedly in Claire Buck's essay 'Poetry and the Women's Movement in Britain' in *Contemporary British Poetry: Essays in Theory and Criticism*, ed. James Acheson and Romana Huk (New York: SUNY P, 1996), 81–111. It has circulated more recently as something of a truism, appearing in passing in work cited elsewhere in this chapter by Juha Virtanen, Samuel Solomon and Linda Kinnahan. I would argue that many more writers on Riley make this argument *tacitly*. Christine and David Kennedy are exceptions to the rule: they give a substantial reading of Riley in relation to rather than contrast with *One Foot on the Mountain* in their *Women's Experimental Poetry in Britain, 1970–2010* (Liverpool: Liverpool UP, 2013), 31–47.

[35] For an overview and riposte, see Sara Ahmed, 'An Affinity of Hammers', *Transgender Studies Quarterly* 3, nos. 1–2 (2016): 22–34.

Bravo to Girls and Heroes in 1977.[36] Her second husband, John James – only two years older – had, by that point, published eight books. Barry MacSweeney, six years her junior, had published more than a dozen. Although Mulford had edited a one-shot magazine, *The Anona Wynn*, in 1969, this was a rarity. Unlike the United States, where underground and avant-garde magazines such as *The Floating Bear*, *0 to 9* and *Angel Hair*, each with women editors, were active from the early 1960s, publishing of all stripes in Britain lagged behind.[37]

Though the bibliographies are sometimes hard to judge, in the lists of the most prominent presses of the British Poetry Revival women are usually represented by a single volume per press. Ferry, established in 1965 by Andrew Crozier, managed to go fifteen years before publishing Mulford's *Reactions to Sunsets*.[38] Grosseteste, edited by Tim Longville and John Riley from 1966 onwards, published what appears to be the sole book by Elizabeth Rothwell, *Brown Smoke and Dark Amber*, in 1976.[39] Tom Raworth and Barry Hall's Goliard printed Elaine Feinstein's *In a Green Eye* in 1966, but the amalgamated Cape Goliard appears to have published no books by women.[40] Trigram, edited by Asa Benveniste with Pip Benveniste, issued *Sphere of Light* by Roberta Elzey Berke in conjunction with Fire Books in 1974.[41] Fulcrum, co-edited by Stuart and Deirdre Montgomery, fared better than most: they managed to publish not one but two books by Lorine Niedecker.[42]

The exception to the rule is Writers Forum (WF), edited by Bob Cobbing with Jennifer Pike Cobbing. Along with the anthology of schoolchildren I cited above, WF published many books by women, ranging from concrete poetry by the feminist activist Michelene Wandor (the only poet, to my knowledge, to publish with both WF

---

[36] Wendy Mulford, *Bravo to Girls and Heroes* (Cambridge: Street Editions, 1977).

[37] *The Floating Bear* was edited by Diane Di Prima with Amiri Baraka, 1961–1969; *0 to 9* by Bernadette Mayer with Vito Acconci, 1967–1969; *Angel Hair* by Anne Waldman and Lewis Warsh, 1966–1969. For these and other examples, see Steven Clay and Rodney Phillips, *A Secret Location on the East Side: Adventures in Writing, 1960–80* (New York: Granary Books, 1998). An exception to the rule would be Tina Morris' work on BB Books and *Poetmeat* with her then-husband Dave Cunliffe.

[38] Wendy Mulford, *Reactions to Sunsets* (London: Ferry, 1980).

[39] Elizabeth Rothwell, *Brown Smoke and Dark Amber* (Pensnett: Grosseteste, 1976).

[40] Elaine Feinstein, *In a Green Eye* (London: Goliard, 1966). It should be noted that Margaret Randall was the translator for the Guatemalan guerrilla poet Otto René Castillo's *Let's Go* (London: Cape Goliard, 1971).

[41] Roberta Elzey Berke, *Sphere of Light* (London: Trigram / Fire, 1974).

[42] Lorine Niedecker, *North Central* (London: Fulcrum, 1968); *My Life By Water: Collected Poems* (London: Fulcrum, 1970).

and *Spare Rib*) to the sole book by Viennese/Danish sound poet Lily Greenham, and innumerable works by the irrepressible Paula Claire.[43] Of course, this doesn't make WF a feminist press. But we might note that the structure of the WF workshop – a space for small group sharing, grounded in listening rather than critique – resembles, at least in outline, the CR group.[44] By sheer dint of productivity, WF almost certainly published more work by women than all the other experimental presses combined.

As a latent genre, feminist poetry first circulated in the journals and magazines of the WLM, and then through the publishing work of figures such as Mulford, Wandor and Alison Fell – all of whom were involved in socialist feminist organising. Mulford began publishing work by women with her Street Editions in 1975, including volumes by Veronica Forrest-Thomson, Alice Notley, Riley and Mulford herself. Wandor, who learned to typeset while working on the socialist feminist journal *Red Rag*, published the chapbook anthology *Cutlasses & Earrings* with Michèle Roberts through her own Playbooks in 1977.[45] Fell issued *Licking the Bed Clean*, a collection of poems from her writing group, via her own Teeth Imprints in 1978, with layout and design by the contributors.[46]

This is to suggest that the *One Foot on the Mountain* anthology arrives, as anthologies tend to do, only after significant work had already taken place. The critical bifurcation I've described – which reads Riley and Mulford as modernists and socialist feminists entirely distinct from the apparently radical feminist anti-modernist poets of *One Foot on the Mountain* – tends to downplay the blurred edges of political formation and the sense of aesthetic transgression and possibility in much feminist poetry of the 1970s. After all, while Onlywomen *was* a separatist press, and Mohin's editorial line explicitly opposed feminism's 'overlap with other existing political

---

[43] See Michelene Wandor, *Lilac Flinder* (London: Writers Forum, 1973); Lily Greenham, *Tune in to Reality!* (London: Writers Forum, 1974 / London: Distance No Object, 2022); and, among many others, Paula Claire, *Stone Tones* (London: Writers Forum, 1974).

[44] One of Cobbing's closest friends and collaborators, John Rowan, became instrumental in the men against sexism movement of the 1970s. See John Rowan, '*Achilles Heel* and the anti-sexist men's movement', *Psychotherapy and Politics International* 3, no. 1 (2006): 58–71. Rowan's publications with WF include *The Clare Poems* (London: Writers Forum, 1975), which detail often painful attempts to experiment with communal living and contain some jaw-dropping moments of sexism.

[45] Michelene Wandor and Michèle Roberts, eds., *Cutlasses & Earrings* (London: Playbooks, 1977).

[46] Alison Fell, Stef Pixner, Tina Reid, Michele Roberts and Ann Oosthuizen, *Licking the Bed Clean* (London: Teeth Imprints, 1978).

ideologies (i.e. socialism)', several of the contributors – including Wandor, Rowbotham and Gill Hague – explicitly identify as socialists in their biographical notes.[47] Others, including Fell, Michèle Roberts and Zoë Fairbairns, were prominent in socialist feminist campaigning and publishing. The solidarity of disaggregation would allow us to trace these lively correspondences and shared political projects, as well as their schisms, disagreements and divergences, with more precision.

But what gets occluded here is the almost total absence of women of colour in critical accounts of poetry by women in the 1970s. This is explicable, to a certain extent, for two reasons. The first is the whiteness of the WLM itself. Although Black activists such as Gerlin Bean were in attendance at Ruskin, and the women's caucus of the Black Unity and Freedom Party (BUFP) did contribute to early WLM publications such as *The Body Politic*, by and large women of colour organised autonomously and at arm's length from what they perceived as the bourgeois and imperialist mainstream feminist movement.[48] The second is the substantial absence of a textual and bibliographic record. Very few full-length collections of poetry by women of colour were published in Britain between Una Marson's *Towards the Stars* in 1945 and the appearance, from 1984 onwards, of work by Grace Nichols, Amryl Johnson and Jackie Kay in the Virago Press poetry series.[49] As a result, this tends to be how surveys of feminist poetry end: by gesturing towards and celebrating the emergence of Black feminist poetry in the 1980s, without always having analysed how race registers in the work of white feminists, both politically and aesthetically.

The first poem in Riley's 1977 *Marxism for Infants* – her first book – is 'A note on sex and the reclaiming of language'. It is also the first poem

---

[47] Lilian Mohin, 'Introduction', *One Foot on the Mountain*, 2.
[48] For the BUFP statement, see 'The Black Woman', in *The Body Politic*, 84–90. For context, see also the writing collected in Valerie Amos, Gail Lewis, Amina Mama and Pratibha Parmar, eds., 'Many Voices, One Chant: Black Feminist Perspectives', *Feminist Review* 17 (1984): 1–118.
[49] One important exception is the Heritage Series of Black Poetry, edited from London by the Dutch expat Paul Breman. He was responsible for publishing books by Audre Lorde, Dolores Kendrick and Elleasse Southerland. Kendrick is especially interesting, because she worked as a teacher in Belfast in the mid-1960s, an experience occasionally reflected in her poems. Breman drew on the knowledge of another Dutch editor living in London: the socialist feminist Rosey Pool. See Lauri Ramey, ed., *The Heritage Series of Black Poetry, 1962–1975* (Aldershot: Ashgate, 2008).

148   *Living in History: Poetry in Britain, 1945–1979*

in her 1985 collection *Dry Air*, her *Selected Poems* of 2000 and her *Selected Poems* of 2019. At the time of writing, its most recent appearance was in *The Penguin Book of Feminist Writing*, sitting between the Combahee River Collective's 'A Black Feminist Statement' and Maya Angelou's 'Still I Rise'.[50] It is one of Riley's most well-known and widely discussed poems. In its original printing, it reads:

> <u>a note on sex and the reclaiming of language</u>
>
> The Savage is flying back home from the New Country
> in native-style dress with a baggage of sensibility
> to gaze on the ancestral plains with the myths thought up
> and dreamed in her kitchens as guides
>
>   She will be discovered
> as meaning is flocking densely around the words seeking a way
> any way in between the gaps,   like a fertilisation
>
>   The work is
> e.g. to write 'she' and for that to be a statement
> of fact only and not a strong image
> of everything which is not-you, which sees you
>
> The new land is colonised,   though its prospects are empty
>
> The Savage weeps as landing at the airport
> she is asked to buy wood carvings,   which represent herself[51]

This is a didactic poem which invites misreading. If I was feeling extravagant, I might say that the poem can *only* be misread. Certainly, as Solomon argues, the early critical reception of the poem appeared to take the latter part of the title as an earnest call to arms, rather than disavowal.[52] Stephanie Burt, too, has suggested that though 'Riley's handful of exegetes have rightly seized on the poem's illustrations of feminist theory', this has sometimes involved short-circuiting the poem's ironies.[53]

How does the poem work? Fourteen lines long, it carries the semantic aura of a sonnet, complete with a conceit concerning 'The

---

[50] *The Penguin Book of Feminist Writing*, ed. Hannah Dawson (Harmondsworth: Penguin, 2021).
[51] Denise Riley, *Marxism for Infants* (Cambridge: Street Editions, 1977), unpaginated. Later printings (post-2019) include scare quotes around 'Savage'.
[52] Solomon, *Lyric Pedagogy*, 97.
[53] Stephanie Burt, *Close Calls With Nonsense: Reading New Poetry* (Minneapolis: Graywolf, 2009), 179.

Savage' that I'll come to in a moment.[54] Enclosed within the clear narrative framing of take-off and landing there are several temporal dilations. The present tense of the opening line is almost immediately undermined by the evocation of generational time ('ancestral plains'), the unbound temporality of myth and dream, and the regulated time of the kitchen. This is paralleled by a move from outward display ('native-style dress') to the interiority of thought.

But the next stanza sharply confronts us with the anticipated future: 'She will be discovered'. There is, I think, some menace to this line. For the reader in the 2020s it's hard not to hear something of the border guard or airport security. But the ambiguities multiply as we shift, almost like a slideshow, to a presentation of 'meaning' as sperm struggling towards an egg. And like a lightbulb switching on above the writer's head, the third stanza – frequently quoted as the poem's standalone credo – foregrounds the scene of writing in a moment of deliberate alienation. It appears to comment, self-reflexively, on the introduction of the word 'She' in line five. But the desire for a 'statement / of fact' is to be fulfilled only in the blankly forlorn 'The new land is colonised'. We return in the concluding lines to 'The Savage', now confronted by the scene of commodity representation, her weeping given as proof of her sensibility.[55]

Solomon writes that 'These lines have been read by critics as a relatively straightforward polemical allegory for the misrecognitions of categorical identifications and interpellations'.[56] This allegory operates through several figures. The first is the relation between 'The Savage' and the subject implied by 'she' in the third stanza. Habitually, interpretations of the poem rest on drawing an analogy between the position of the gendered subject and the racialised, colonised one. This is, then, a stratified allegory, where 'woman' is explained by 'The Savage' without reciprocation. It is, after all, a note on *sex*. But it's important that the two figures – the racially

---

[54] For a sustained reading of the poem's form, see Natalie Pollard, *Poetry, Publishing, and Visual Culture from Late Modernism to the Twentieth-Century: Fugitive Pieces* (Oxford: Oxford UP, 2020), 197–8. We might also think of sonnets by Riley's key American contemporaries Alice Notley (*165 Meeting House Lane* (Chicago: C Press, 1971)) and Bernadette Mayer (*Sonnets: 25th Anniversary Edition* (New York: Tender Buttons, 2016)).

[55] As Schopenhauer writes: 'Weeping is by no means a direct expression of pain, for it occurs where there is very little pain. In my opinion, indeed, we never weep directly on account of the pain we experience, but merely always on account of its repetition in reflection.' Arthur Schopenhauer, *The World as Will and Representation*, Vol. 1, trans. Judith Norman, Alistair Welchman and Christopher Janaway (Cambridge: Cambridge UP, 2010), 403.

[56] Solomon, *Lyric Pedagogy*, 96.

unmarked 'Woman' and the racially marked 'Savage' – never wholly coincide. The slippage of identification is crucial to the poem's argument. But to complicate matters further, there is perhaps a second 'She' in operation: that which seems to strain against or move beyond the sex-gender system in the utopian flare of a desire for, in Amy De'Ath's phrase, 'a world where such categories do not exist'.[57]

This is to suggest that the poem can't easily be paraphrased without doing damage to Riley's strategy of ambiguity and contradiction. When Linda Kinnahan, for example, writes of 'a story line in which a woman (called "The Savage") returns home from a trip', this doesn't adequately acknowledge the fractures in gendered categories of analysis that Riley is enacting, nor the specific racialised dimension of the poem's conceit.[58] I am interested in how the critical reception of this poem, by and large, has worked to problematise and historicise the category of 'women', following Riley's later theoretical lead, but has avoided paying the same attention to 'The Savage'. Numerous critical discussions of Riley's work quote from the middle two stanzas, dispensing with the colonial bracketing altogether.[59] Is this simply because 'the peculiar role of the savage as an agent of European self-constitution' is so self-evident as to go unremarked?[60] Does 'The Savage' simply gesture towards anthropology and Enlightenment philosophy as a rhetorical ornament rather than central concern?

I want to suggest that Riley's specific target for critique in this poem is Hélène Cixous's 'The Laugh of the Medusa', first published in English in 1976.[61] In a key passage towards the start of the essay, Cixous works to 'reclaim' those metaphors which align femininity with colonial territory: 'because you are Africa, you are black.

---

[57] Amy De'Ath, 'Abolition in Poetry Since 1973', talk at the Marxist Literary Group Panel, MLA 2018, unpublished.
[58] Linda A. Kinnahan, *Lyric Interventions: Feminism, Experimental Poetry, and Contemporary Discourse* (Iowa: U of Iowa P, 2004), 212.
[59] To take only three recent examples: Ange Mlinko, 'Echo is a Fangirl', *London Review of Books* 42, no. 23 (3 December 2022); Peter Robinson, *The Sound Sense of Poetry* (Cambridge: Cambridge UP, 2018), 178; Andrea Brady, 'The Loneliness of the Long Distance Poet' in *The Oxford Handbook of Contemporary British and Irish Poetry* (Oxford: Oxford UP, 2013), 707–26 (717).
[60] Tony C. Brown, *The Primitive, the Aesthetic, and the Savage: An Enlightenment Problematic* (Minneapolis: U of Minnesota P, 2012), 64.
[61] Hélène Cixous, 'The Laugh of the Medusa', trans. Keith Cohen and Paula Cohen, *Signs* 1, no. 4 (1976): 875–93. For Cixous's interactions with Riley and Mulford, see Solomon, 'Forms of Reproduction in Wendy Mulford's Early Work', in *Modernist Legacies: Trends and Faultlines*, ed. Abigail Lang and David Nowell-Smith (London: Palgrave, 2014), 218–23.

Your continent is dark'.⁶² Her lyrical prose makes glancing reference to apartheid, oil production ('our naphtha will spread, throughout the world, without dollars – black or gold') and 'the colonised peoples of yesterday'.⁶³ Cixous was herself a displaced Algerian Jew. But as Anne McClintock has argued of feminist appropriations of Lacan, the subversion of Freud's 'dark continent' axiom rests 'on a glamorisation of the Woman as primitive'.⁶⁴ This is what Riley's opening stanza satirises. In fact, the opening line shares a specific textual overlap with Cixous's claim that 'Flying is woman's gesture – flying in language and making it fly'.⁶⁵ The airport bathetically restores us to earth. Formally, too, Riley works to resist any instigation towards volcanic eruptions of *l'écriture feminine*. The poem is held together by extremely vigilant sonority, with each word carefully weighted for disturbance. 'Savage' is distributed through rhyme and echo in 'native', 'baggage', 'e.g.', and 'image'; a similar operation holds together 'sensibility', 'ancestral', 'densely' and 'represent'. This is a domain of regulation, inhibition and scepticism rather than freedom.

So behind the laughing Medusa, Riley presents her reader with the weeping Savage. Partly this must stand for the argument that the figure of the 'Savage' is constitutive of the European humanist tradition. As David Lloyd has argued, 'The Savage is required as a permanent instance of the "not-subject", the object of heteronomy both in the form of external natural forces and in that of the immediate gratification of his own desires'.⁶⁶ If, historically, 'woman occupies the same threshold as the Savage', then the poem's highest irony must be located in the final lines, where to weep at wood carvings – a moment of sentimental education and aesthetic reflection – is to take a step towards incorporation in the project of a liberal universalism.⁶⁷ This is what I mean when I insist that differentiation of 'The Savage' and 'Woman' must be retained at the level of allegory. This is a costly poem, fully aware of the compromised narrative of progress, the empty prospects. In this mode, Riley's poem retains an awareness of

---

⁶² Cixous, 'The Laugh of the Medusa', 877–8. For an extended critique of this passage, see Uzoma Esonwanne, 'Feminist Theory and the Discourse of Colonialism', in *ReImagining Women: Representations of Women in Culture*, ed. Shirley Neuman and Glennis Stephenson (Toronto: U of Toronto P, 1993), 233–55.
⁶³ Cixous, 'The Laugh of the Medusa', 880, 888.
⁶⁴ Anne McClintock, *Imperial Leather: Race, Gender and Sexuality in the Colonial Conquest* (London: Routledge, 1995), 194.
⁶⁵ Cixous, 'The Laugh of the Medusa', 887.
⁶⁶ David Lloyd, *Under Representation: The Racial Regime of Aesthetics* (New York: Fordham, 2019), 51.
⁶⁷ Ibid., 64.

feminism's genealogical entanglement with the discourses of colonialism, rather than enacting a displacement.

But Riley's deployment of this racial figure, even within a mode of critique, carries some risks. French feminist theorists were far from alone in their use of colonial metaphors, and Riley's poem might draw on a broader history of problematic identification and attempted solidarity within the British WLM. This is to say that Riley consciously and deliberately uses a trope that seems to have been widespread. For instance, in Rowbotham's foundational 1969 text, 'Women's Liberation and the New Politics', we read: 'Women have been lying low for so long most of us cannot imagine how to get up. We have apparently acquiesced always in the imperial game and are so perfectly colonised that we are unable to consult ourselves.'[68] It's worth emphasising that Stage 1, the publisher of *The Body Politic* – in which this text widely circulated – also published speeches by Fidel Castro, Amilcar Cabral's *Revolution in Guinea* and Eldridge Cleaver's *Revolution in the Congo*. Indeed, as the artist and activist Mary Kelly explained in 1970, the History Group of the WLM had addressed itself early on to the question, 'How are national liberation struggles related to women's liberation?' Kelly's summary of the group discussion is based in material analysis, as she assesses the grounds for solidarity between women in imperialist nations and the liberation struggles in, for example, Palestine and Vietnam. She writes: 'Ultimately we live in a kind of international caste system with the white western ruling class male at the top and the non-white female of the colonized world at the bottom.'[69]

But anti-imperialism doesn't necessarily translate into anti-racism, and the federated and decentralised structure of the WLM meant that the clarity of this analysis progressed unevenly.[70] It's perhaps enough to state that the 'Four Demands' formulated at Ruskin make no mention of race or of imperialism. In the painful work of finding a language to articulate women's oppression, concrete reckoning with colonialism could easily give way to looser metaphor. In an essay from 1979 that I'll return to, we find Mulford repeating Rowbotham's line from ten years earlier:

---

[68] Rowbotham, *The Body Politic*, 5.
[69] Mary Kelly, 'National Liberation Movements and Women's Liberation', *Shrew* (December 1970). Reprinted in *Social Process / Collaborative Action: Mary Kelly, 1970–75*, ed. Judith Mastai (Vancouver: Charles H. Scott, 1997), 69.
[70] For an analysis of the failures of the women's movement to develop a serious anti-racist line, see Jenny Bourne, 'Towards an Anti-Racist Feminism', *Race & Class* 25, no. 1 (1983): 1–22.

> I have, as it were, only a colonial relationship to such texts, inhabiting a language and a culture which I'm not quite at ease in, which doesn't quite fit. The problem is obviously keyed in to the previous one of language itself, but it has a slightly different area of impact for it's particularly in *reading* that I'm made aware of it.[71]

This is, in part, the legacy of Simone de Beauvoir's Hegelianism, where the structure of subjectivity is understood through the dialectical allegory of master and slave.[72] Riley alludes to this directly in a contemporaneous poem, where the position of working-class mothers is 'taken straight out of colonial history, master and slave'.[73] But we see in Mulford's text that the terrain has been shifted onto the question of language, and how a language is inhabited, which seems to be precisely what 'A note on sex ...' was warning against and warding off.

Riley's later theoretical work has been critiqued for its allegorical use of racial figures. The historical essay *'Am I That Name?'* takes its title from a line in *Othello* and begins with a reference to the abolitionist and ex-slave Sojourner Truth.[74] Riley imagines 'a new Sojourner Truth' who, rather than asking 'Ain't I a woman?' – as Truth famously did at the Ohio Women's Rights Conference in 1851 – would ask: 'Ain't I a fluctuating identity?' Writing in 1995, Deborah E. McDowell argued:

> Riley's move to appropriate Sojourner Truth introduces a subtle racial marker that distinguishes between Truth's original words and Riley's displacement. A familiar move in literary-critical discussion, Riley's 'modernization' functions allegorically to make a common if subtle insinuation about black feminist thinking in general: it needs a new language. That language should serve a theory, preferably a poststructuralist theory, signaled in this context by the term *fluctuating identity*.[75]

---

[71] Wendy Mulford, 'Notes on Writing: A Marxist/Feminist Viewpoint', *Red Letters* 9 (1979): 40.

[72] 'Certain passages where Hegel's dialectic describes the relationship of master to slave would apply far better to the relationship of man to woman.' Simone De Beauvoir, *The Second Sex*, trans. Constance Borde and Sheila Malovany-Chevallier (New York: Vintage, 2011).

[73] Riley, 'Affections must not', *Selected Poems* (2019), 20.

[74] The opening chapter also includes a cluster of references to 'a Greek Cypriot', Hanif Kureishi's film *My Beautiful Launderette* and 'an elderly Cantonese woman'. Riley, *'Am I That Name?'*, 16–17.

[75] Deborah E. McDowell, 'Transferences: Black Feminist Discourse: The "Practice" of "Theory"', in *Feminism Beside Itself*, ed. Diane Elam and Robyn Wiegman (New York: Routledge, 1995), 95.

Is 'A note on sex ...' open to similar interpretation? In Claire Buck's critical reading, Riley uses the metaphor 'of an immigrant returning to her native land' to argue against an essentialist construction of subjectivity.[76] The feminist reader – implicitly white – ought to avoid the lure of an ersatz cultural nationalism and recognise instead her discursive production in language. But if this is so, under the terms of the poem, the racialised subject's alienation can only be reconfirmed and doubled, displaced in the circuit of allegory's imprecision.

I'll turn, in a moment, to a poem by Mulford which explores some of this fraught ground further. But I want briefly to address the historical moment in which 'A note on sex ...' was written. As Buck argues, 'the growth of a black immigrant population in postwar Britain' is a feature of 'the structural metaphors of the poem'.[77] What I've been calling the racial figure of 'The Savage' is an example of what Sara Ahmed calls 'sticky' language.[78] It goes in excess of itself, draws other signs into its orbit, and incorporates other racialised categories and caricatures. Significantly, in all recent printings of the poem Riley has enclosed 'Savage' in scare quotes, as if to simultaneously draw attention to the word and defray its capacity for offence. If, as I've been implying, 'The Savage' is the figure of indigeneity who haunts enlightenment philosophy – Arawak or Carib, Māori or Amerindian – the narrative of the poem gestures nevertheless to the contemporary racist discourse around voluntary and involuntary repatriation of migrants. The poem's numerous ambiguities – like the respective identities of 'the New Country' and 'home' – are open to be 'corrected' by the trace of the immigrant, or the child of immigrants, flying from Britain to the legally defined 'country of origin'.

Two years after *Marxism for Infants* was published, Heathrow airport became the site of sustained protests and political organising against the practice of 'virginity testing' South Asian women.[79] In that light, maybe the images of 'flocking densely' and the spectre of 'fertilisation' in 'A note on sex ...' also reflect the discourse of racist anxiety about immigration in the later 1970s. The text accumulates history, and the whole poem seems to come crashing down

---

[76] Buck, 'Poetry and the Women's Movement in Britain', 95.
[77] Ibid., 96.
[78] Sara Ahmed, *The Cultural Politics of Emotion* (Edinburgh: Edinburgh UP, 2014).
[79] For the earliest reporting see Amrit Wilson, 'Atrocity at Heathrow', *Spare Rib* 55 (1977): 20–1. For the broader history, see Evan Smith and Marinella Marmo, *Race, Gender, and the Body in British Immigration Control: Subject to Examination* (Basingstoke: Palgrave, 2014).

in the final lines, as the aesthetic gives way to the commodity and the border. This is what makes it such an enduringly significant work. The poem is willing to be a bad object, to take on wounding language and unassailable contradictions, and offer them back to the movement as provocation and stumbling block. As the poet mordantly throws her voice, the poem hums with intensity, by turns jarring and whimsical. It is a painful dramatisation of what Vron Ware called 'the perpetual crisis within women's politics over the negotiation of race and class differences', which have 'everything to do with racism and imperialism'.[80]

No Fee: A Line or Two for Free, initially produced to coincide with a joint reading at the Institute of Contemporary Arts (ICA) in 1978, collects eighteen pages of poems by Riley and Mulford. The book opens with the short poem that came to be known as 'In 1970', with which this chapter began. By 1978 perhaps this backwards glance at the movement's early years seemed melancholic: the final National Women's Conference would be held that year, full of acrimony between the radical feminists and socialist feminists about strategy and theory.[81] But the object feels urgent: side-stapled, mimeographed, most of the poems lack titles and none are attributed to either author. The precursor for this joint presentation is Sylvia Townsend Warner and Valentine Ackland's *Whether A Dove or a Seagull* (1933).[82] This still neglected volume of poems was written during the early stages of Warner and Ackland's romantic relationship, and published on the cusp of their joining the CPGB. As Mulford would write in her pathbreaking scholarship:

> The poems themselves were not written in collaboration: rather the reverse. They represent voice speaking to voice in antiphonal dialogue, each voice separate, distinct, clear-toned. As such, they grew out a shared and mutually creative life together. The project of the book, however, the selection and arrangement of the poems was a

---

[80] Vron Ware, *Beyond the Pale: White Women, Racism, and History* (London: Verso, 2015), 242.

[81] For an attempt at reconciliation and consolidation in the context of the first onslaught of Thatcherism, see Feminist Anthology Collective, *No Turning Back: Writings from the Women's Liberation Movement, 1975–1980* (London: The Women's Press, 1981).

[82] Jan Montefiore notes this in her 'Sylvia Townsend Warner and the Biographer's "Moral Sense"', in *Arguments of Heart and Mind: Selected Essays, 1977–2000* (Manchester: Manchester UP, 2002), 159.

collaborative process. *Whether a Dove or a Seagull* offers an exciting precedent for women poets to recover [...][83]

Collaboration in 'the project of the book' was in the air: as mentioned above, other feminist collaborations appearing at the same time included the multi-authored *Cutlasses & Earrings* (1977), edited and published by Michelene Wandor and Michèle Roberts, and *Licking the Bed Clean* (1978), edited and printed by Alison Fell. But as I'll show, Mulford's poems in *No Fee* are particularly interested in what it means to be 'voice speaking to voice'. She is particularly interested in what happens when the tones and distinctions blur.

The title of the volume announces Mulford and Riley's commitment to the priority of economic analyses. Riley was a libertarian socialist; Mulford an active member of the CPGB. Perhaps the absence of a fee raises the vexed question of whether writing poetry can be thought of as labour, and what the position of the writer is in relation to the process of production. By 1978, both authors would have been familiar with the arguments about women's unwaged work proposed by Wages For Housework.[84] Solomon's important and crucial scholarship has shown how Riley's *Marxism for Infants* contributes to her theorisation of 'socialised biology' as the contested site of reproduction's relation to production.[85] But 'no fee' also sounds like the promise of an opportunist lawyer – no win, no fee! – and 'a line or two for free' sounds a little like a drug dealer's special offer. More pertinently, the question of whether and how you get paid, what kind of fee you might charge, also relates to sex work. Advertised in the back of *Marxism for Infants* was a never-to-appear anthology of writing by American and British women poets titled *Streetwalkers*. While playing on the name of Mulford's press, Street Editions, it also reads as a problematic instance of appropriative identification. But it's tantalising, in any case, to speculate and wonder what the literary history of feminist poetry would look like had this book appeared, one step ahead of *One Foot on the Mountain*.

In an essay more frequently cited than any of her poems, Mulford writes with candour and difficulty about being a Marxist-feminist

---

[83] Wendy Mulford, *This Narrow Place: Sylvia Townsend Warner and Valentine Ackland* (London: Pandora, 1988), 44.

[84] Mulford's first husband, Jeremy Mulford – a contributor to *The English Intelligencer* – was the co-founder and editor of Bristol-based Falling Wall Press, the main British publisher of Selma James and other Wages for Housework activists.

[85] Solomon, *Lyric Pedagogy*, 81–110.

writer. 'Notes on Writing: A Marxist/Feminist Viewpoint' was first published in *Red Letters*, the literary journal of the CPGB, in 1979.[86] Mulford's prose is, for the most part, exploratory rather than proscriptive, but the notes are full of argument and intention:

> Polemically, I insist with other women critics against the majority of left male criticism that gender and class *are* equally-weighted determinants of any literary production. Polemically I insist with other modernist writers against the practice of most women that for the writer revolutionary practice necessitates revolutionary practice in the field of the signifier.[87]

Though Mulford states that Riley is the only woman she knows engaged in similar practice, I'd suggest that this revolutionary practice in the field of the signifier took many forms. Much of Mulford's feeling of distance from her contemporaries seems to stem from her reading of Hélène Cixous and Julia Kristeva, and a rethinking of her own writing in terms of semiotics.[88] From the present vantage point, these differences can often seem over-determined, as the techniques of disjunction, collage, estrangement come to lose their disruptive power over time.

More interestingly, as Linda Kinnahan points out, Mulford 'nevertheless seeks a coalition among feminist poets that would recognise her "voice"'.[89] I suggest we can view her work's use of unmarked quotation and citation as a kind of aesthetic coalition-building, where multiple voices coexist and correspond. Before detailing this further, it's worth emphasising that the reception history of 'Notes on Writing' typically reads a later version which excises two paragraphs of Mulford's self-analysis of her own poem,

---

[86] Mulford, 'Notes on Writing: A Marxist/Feminist Viewpoint', 35–44. Mulford's essay was republished in a significantly revised form in *On Gender and Writing*, ed. Michelene Wandor (London: Pandora, 1983). It's the latter version of the essay that is most frequently cited, which presents some problems that I discuss below.

[87] Mulford, 'Notes on Writing: A Marxist/Feminist Viewpoint', 38.

[88] In this respect, Mulford draws on the work of her contemporary Veronica Forrest-Thomson, whose *Poetic Artifice* was posthumously published in 1978. Mulford and Forrest-Thomson differ: as the late Callie Gardner notes, Forrest-Thomson's criticism 'tends to see explicit engagements with politics as an annoyance'. Gardner, *Poetry and Barthes: Anglophone Responses* (Liverpool: Liverpool UP, 2018), 45. Though she published Forrest-Thomson's *On the Periphery* (Cambridge: Street Editions, 1975), Mulford only met Forrest-Thomson once. For Mulford's biographical recollection, see 'Veronica Forrest-Thomson, 1947–1975', in *Calemadonnas – Women & Scotland*, ed. Helen Kidd (Dundee: Gairfish, 1994), 15–21.

[89] Linda Kinnahan, 'Feminism's experimental "work at the language-face"', in *The Cambridge Companion to Twentieth-Century British and Irish Women's Poetry*, ed. Jane Dowson (Cambridge: Cambridge UP, 2011), 157.

'In Praise of Women Singers'. The first poem in Mulford's half of *No Fee*, it begins:

> going to bed with your book
> if it falls to bits in my hands
> inspired insanity
> put your arms round me
> dance down the parapet
> round and around
> bodying behind walls
> after landlessness
> one of a range of good products
> going to bed in my mind

In this case, as the final lines disclose ('going drinking tonight may / your shadows never be less / alice') and as Mulford explains in the essay, the book is *Alice Ordered Me To Be Made* by the American poet Alice Notley.[90] There's a definite erotic charge to these lines, the desire to 'go to bed with' the work of other women, to even risk 'insanity' in inspiration. Though 'in my mind' emphasises the safety of fantasy, the poem bristles with the physical, from the desire to be embraced, the dancing on parapets and the great verb 'bodying' taking place behind walls.

Along with this textual come-on to the American poet, the poem cites the Phoebe Snow song 'Inspired Insanity', one of many songs that Mulford sometimes directly transposes into her poems. In the excised paragraphs in 'Notes on Writing', she explains that she likes to begin by writing freehand, letting 'the language flow in as far as I can make it, uncensored, unchecked, uncorrected'.[91] What she calls 'Stage two', is 'the return', where she gives shape and texture to the language and edits the poem. Lastly, she makes a decision about whether the poem is worth showing to anyone else. This compositional practice of writing, revision and editing is, I think, common enough. But what's interesting is that Mulford emphasises the material practice of her composition, the use of found language, the process of collage and most particularly the temporal delay. The

---

[90] Notley lived in England between 1973 and 1974 while her husband Ted Berrigan worked at the University of Essex. She composed her important long poem *Songs for the Unborn Second Baby* (Northampton, MA: United Artists, 1979 / London: Distance No Object, 2022) while living in Wivenhoe, and continued to edit her little magazine *Chicago*. Mulford published her *For Frank O'Hara's Birthday* (Cambridge: Street Editions, 1975). Riley has recently written of Notley's important example in her poem 'From "Alice, a fragment"', *Lurex*, 45.

[91] 'Notes on Writing', *Red Letters*, 42.

spontaneity of writing is tempered by the discipline of judgement and shaping – the necessary stages the poem has to pass through – so that what we're presented with as readers is a similar process of coming-to-consciousness as we might expect across any given feminist poem: the crucial difference is that this process begins in the language itself rather than originating in the interior experiences of the poet. Yet as Michèle Roberts noted in a review of Mulford's work, we as readers become part of the negotiation of sense and sense-making; we are invited to participate.[92]

In *No Fee* the references and use of found language proliferates. The penultimate poem 'noise levels' is also, in a way, in praise of women singers. The opening line begins with an unmarked quotation from the reggae hit 'Uptown Top Ranking' by the teenage duo Althea & Donna:

see me in my halter back
hate of the vowels in the vowels
depleting the silence

Is this a moment of identification? Althea & Donna's track is built from the Alton Ellis single 'I'm Still In Love With You' and is a reply to Trinity's 'Three Piece Suit' from 1975.[93] The intertextuality and remixing of Jamaican dancehall culture clearly held some general appeal for the sensibility of experimental British poets, with poets frequently quoting from and alluding to reggae in the later 1970s.[94] But specifically, Althea & Donna, like Riley & Mulford, sing a defiant song and insert themselves into a tradition. The song is about dressing 'dread' during the day – 'khaki suit an ting' – and the glamour of halterbacks and high heels at night-time which threaten to give the men on the street a 'heart attack'. It's a great song of agency and self-definition, as the singers assert that they're 'strictly roots' despite accusations of being 'pop'.

Mulford's writing in the later 1970s and early 1980s includes many other poems about women singers, including a sequence featuring Poly Styrene and Lora Logic from X-Ray Spex and members

---

[92] '[S]he is a generous and humble poet, leaving her poems open, insisting that the reader participates in constructing their meaning.' Michèle Roberts, 'Review of Wendy Mulford, *Bravo to Girls and Heroes*, and Denise Riley, *Marxism for Infants*', *Spare Rib* 73 (1977): 39. This is a typical claim made on behalf of avant-garde poetry; here it's being made from a politically engaged feminist position.

[93] See Heather Augustyn, *Women in Jamaican Music* (Jefferson: McFarland, 2020), 121–2.

[94] See, for example, *Toasting* by John James (Cambridge: Avocado, 1979), and Barry MacSweeney, *Far Cliff Babylon* (London: Writers Forum, 1978).

of the post-punk band The Raincoats.[95] Several of these singers were women of colour. As Margaretta Jolly writes, surveying the importance of music and song to the movement in the UK, this often involved 'the long history of white expropriation of black music'.[96] But it could also provide moments of solidarity, the acknowledgement and navigation of difference. Natalie Thomlinson, in her vital study, records an example of one of the few Black volunteers at the *London Women's Liberation Newsletter* sharing the music of the African American vocal group Sweet Honey in the Rock, and that this 'lessened her alienation from her environment'.[97] In 'noise levels' Mulford is thinking about race. She's writing and revising her work during the era of Rock Against Racism and the complicated forms of collectivity between and among youth subcultures, anti-fascist activists and the organised – mostly Trotskyist – left.[98] Mulford writes:

> the
> innocence of syllables the
> verb giddy to truth
> sister of suffering & silence the
> privileged recipient all
> whiteness is violence the
> dream betrays the violence of silence.

The 'sister of suffering' might be a patronising designation to extend to Althea & Donna, whose music is, as I've suggested, mainly self-assertive.[99] Perhaps Mulford is warily self-conscious, and aware of her (white) privilege as a recipient of – as she calls in 'In Praise of Women Singers' – 'a range of good products', the latest hit single. But the declarative statement 'all / whiteness is violence' suggests an understanding of and insistence on the systemic production of violence in racial capitalism, rather than relative questions of ethical consumerism.

But to complicate matters, the phrase 'whiteness is violence' and other aspects of this passage (the sister, for instance) are unmarked

---

[95] See the 1979 sequence 'Reactions to Sunsets', collected in Wendy Mulford, *and suddenly, supposing: selected poems* (Buckfastleigh: Etruscan, 2002), 71–5.
[96] Margaretta Jolly, *Sisterhood and After* (Oxford: Oxford UP, 2019), 221.
[97] Natalie Thomlinson, *Race, Ethnicity, and the Women's Movement in England* (London: Palgrave, 2016), 101.
[98] See Dave Renton, *Never Again: Rock Against Racism and the Anti-Nazi League, 1976–1982* (Abingdon: Routledge, 2019). See also Thomlinson, *Race, Ethnicity, and the Women's Movement in England*, 132–5.
[99] Of course, it's also an echo of the Rastafari designation 'sufferer'.

quotations from the Egyptian-French Jewish poet Edmond Jabès.[100] It's possible that Mulford was introduced to the work by her friend, the poet and publisher Rosmarie Waldrop, who translated much of Jabès's work into English.[101] For Jabès, whiteness always in part signals the page and the scene of writing, raising metaphysical questions of presence and absence. Yet as a displaced person, other in both Egypt and in France, whiteness is also the structuring form he writes against and subverts, complicates or disrupts.[102] A citation doesn't make a coalition, it's true, but we see Mulford bringing together Black women's artistic production with the post-Holocaust writing of Jabès, assisted by the work of other women poets. This is fraught with difficulty. But as Bernice Johnson Reagon, one of the founders of Sweet Honey in the Rock, said: 'Today whenever women gather it is not necessarily nurturing. It is coalition building. And if you feel the strain, you may be doing some good work.'[103]

We can compare Mulford's practice with an example of a more full-throated solidarity: Peggy Seeger's collaboration with Jayaben Desai, 'Union Woman', released on Seeger's 1979 record *Different Therefore Equal*. Seeger, who as I noted in Chapter 3 performed at Claudia Jones's funeral, was a longstanding activist, and her work bridged the old left and the feminist movement. On 'Union Woman' she sets and sings Desai's words to a bluegrass tune:

Born rich in the womb
As you say, with a silver spoon in the mouth.
Born female, learned early to work but never had to labour.
The luxury life is a knife in the heart and mind,
Every day, all day, nothing to do but waste your time.[104]

As the song unfolds, Desai tells the story of her journey from prosperity in Gujarat and Tanzania to her position as a migrant worker in England and her experience of racism. The centrepiece

---

[100] Edmond Jabès, *The Book of Questions: Yaël, Elya, Aely*, trans. Rosmarie Waldrop (Middletown: Wesleyan, 1983), 284.
[101] See also her extraordinary commentary: Rosmarie Waldrop, *Lavish Absence: Recalling and Rereading Edmond Jabès* (Middletown: Wesleyan, 2003).
[102] See Jabès, 'The Page as a Place to Both Subvert Whiteness and the World', in *The Little Book of Unsuspected Subversion*, trans. Rosmarie Waldrop (Stanford: Stanford UP, 1996).
[103] Bernice Johnson Reagon, 'Coalition Politics: Turning the Century', in *Home Girls: A Black Feminist Anthology*, ed. Barbara Smith (New York: Kitchen Table, 1983), 362.
[104] Peggy Seeger, 'Union Woman', *Different Therefore Equal* (Folkways Records FS 8561, 1979). For an anthology of songs including contributions from the women's movement, see *My Song is My Own: 100 Women's Songs*, ed. Kathy Henderson, Frankie Armstrong and Sandra Kerr (London: Pluto, 1979).

is, of course, Desai's role as the leader of the strike by the largely Asian women workforce at the Grunwick film processing plant in 1976–1978. The method of composition involved directly recording Desai talking about her life, and then editing the text into shape as a song. According to Seeger's biography, when she played her the song for the first time, Desai said, 'I can hear myself speaking.'[105]

Of course, Desai had given many speeches and interviews over the course of the Grunwick dispute. As the title of Amrit Wilson's anthology of writing by Asian women put it, the strike was pivotal for 'Finding a Voice'.[106] But in setting Desai in the context of a folk tradition, and hearing her words ring out – 'what matter that the strike was lost / the enemy showed his face: / employers, management, Labour and union leaders' – the song stands as an extraordinary and powerful form of political articulation. Desai takes her place at the head of British working-class struggle. This kind of collaborative solidarity was rarer than it should have been. But from Denise Riley and Wendy Mulford to the schoolgirls Celia Davies and Melanie Tompkins, Althea & Donna to Peggy Seeger and Jayaben Desai, we can see the strength in heterogeneity, multiplicity, experiment and correspondence.

But this brings us to the question of Black and Asian women poets and their place in the struggle. There is no flourish I can make which would point to a body of work from the 1970s, though I'll refer to some work by women of colour from that decade in Chapter 7. As I've already indicated, Black women tended to organise autonomously and at arm's length from what was perceived as the inhospitable white, bourgeois and imperialist feminist movement. Recalling the 'critical relationship to flowers' that Cora Kaplan saw emerging in women's poetry in the early twentieth century, we might cite the Jamaican communist Elean Thomas, who wrote in 1988:

> Some
> can wander
> unthinking
> in ready-made gardens
> speak with each other
> of daffodils
> delicate lillies
> rare orchids.

---

[105] Peggy Seeger, *First Time Ever: A Memoir* (London: Faber, 2017).
[106] Amrit Wilson, ed., *Finding a Voice: Asian Women in Britain* (London: Virago, 1978).

But others have to 'grasp cutlasses / to chop away / the choking vines [...] Before they / can speak of flowers'.[107] This work of clearing and preparing for growth was undertaken by activists like those involved in the Brixton Black Women's Group, and later the Organisation of Women of African and Asian Descent (OWAAD), who would begin to claim, redefine and transform feminist politics in the 1980s. We had to wait forty years for Claudia Jones's poetry to be edited and published, and longer still for Una Marson's *Selected Poems*. There is nothing if not work to be done.

---

[107] Elean Thomas, *Before They Can Speak of Flowers* (London: Karia, 1988), 19–20. Thomas studied at Goldsmiths, and lived in England in the 1980s and 1990s.

Chapter 6

Yout Rebels: Refusal and Self-Defence, 1970–1979

> our children will live happy
> when wi tear down Babylon
> PRINCE BUSTER[1]

In May 1971, Chris Searle was sacked from his teaching job at the Sir John Cass School in Stepney, South London. He had edited and published an anthology of his pupil's poetry, *Stepney Words*, against the wishes of the school governors, who felt that lines like 'My classroom is dim and dull / My teacher sits there thinking / She's so dim and dull' were unfit for publication.[2] The students responded by going on strike. Between 500 and 800 students walked out, sent delegations to negotiate with the headteacher, went door to door collecting signatures for a petition and eventually marched to Trafalgar Square. This was an era of intense class struggle. Postal workers had been on strike earlier in the year, and Searle remembers one parent at Stepney, active in the Communication Workers Union, teaching the pupils how to picket the school gate.[3] Soon the National Union of Mineworkers (NUM) would begin a series of confrontations with Edward Heath's Conservative Government. In this atmosphere of industrial militancy, the children won a resounding victory in their dispute: Searle was reinstated and *Stepney Words*, widely celebrated, became synonymous with the possibilities of radical education. The story was covered in newspaper tabloids and broadsheets, and Searle

---

[1] Prince Buster, 'Police Trim Rasta' (1971), cited in Linton Kwesi Johnson, 'The Politics of the Lyrics of Reggae Music', *The Black Liberator* 2, no. 4 (1975): 371.
[2] Susan Johnson, 'The World is Dim and Dull', in *Stepney Words 1 & 2*, ed. Chris Searle (London: Centerprise, 1973), 19.
[3] Chris Searle, 'The Story of Stepney Words', *Race and Class* 58, no. 4 (2017): 71.

became well known as an activist teacher, going on to author and edit many more books.

Vivian Usherwood, not yet a teenager, wrote his own poem about the school strike:

School Strike

After dinner I went over to the park
I saw a most peculiar thing:
Boys standing
I didn't take no notice
Until after I had a game of football.
I saw teachers trying to clear the boys
That were sitting in the streets
And on the pavements.
I asked the Ladybird
He said it was a strike
So I started laughing for it sounded funny:
Schoolboys on strike
Hackney Downs boys too.[4]

This poem, along with some forty-eight others by Usherwood, was published in a small book by the community arts organisation Centerprise, which had opened in Hackney the same month as the strike. The brainchild of the Harlem-born Glenn Thompson and his fellow youth worker Margaret Gosley, Centerprise – which when it opened was the only bookshop in Hackney – formed a vital part of the community until its closure in 2012.[5] Usherwood's book was the first in a series of successful publications by working-class writers from the area, who were encouraged through literacy programmes and writing groups to write about their lives. His *Poems* was in all likelihood one of the bestselling volumes of poetry in the 1970s, selling over 8,000 copies.[6]

As both publisher, social centre and organisation, Centerprise is an example of what Mark Nowak recently theorised as 'social poetics'. That's to say, 'a radically public poetics, a poetics for and by the working-class people who read it, analyze it, and produce it within their struggles to transform twenty-first century capitalism

---

[4] Vivian Usherwood, *Poems*, 2nd ed. (London: Centerprise, 1975), 21. Further reference will be given in the text.
[5] See Rosa Schling, *The Lime Green Mystery: An Oral History of the Centerprise Co-Op* (London: On the Record, 2017).
[6] By May 1977 it had sold 6,500 copies. See Ken Worpole, *Local Publishing and Local Culture* (London: Centerprise, 1977), 21.

into a more equitable, equal, and socialist system of relations'.[7] But Usherwood's poetry doesn't entirely conform to this project. In 'School Strike' he is surely tentative, even sceptical, about being 'radically public'. He was one of the 'Hackney Downs boys', and his teachers there – Ann Pettit and Ken Worpole, the latter of whom played an important role in Centerprise – were responsible for the publication of his poems. But though he plays football and jokes around, Usherwood remains an observer rather than participant in the strike. He's a little shy, nervous, turning to 'the Ladybird' for answers. This is likely a reference to the Ladybird books series, a prominent part of post-war children's publishing; but the joke remains private, part of an interior world that the reader doesn't necessarily have access to.[8] Moments of absurdity and inscrutability are, of course, part of what makes children's poetry enjoyable to read. But I want to suggest that the relation Usherwood explores – the joke adjacent to the strike – should be understood as a moment of resistance.[9] On whose terms do we become 'radically public'? How much do we share? Who, the poem asks, is this strike *for*?

Born in Jamaica in 1960, at the time of writing Usherwood was living in a care home, Montague House. One of the repeated complaints he makes in his poems is of other children 'ganging onto him', and of unfair punishments and impossible rules. He ends one poem returning in despair to 'the stinking shitting house' (18), with the expletives flashing as an attempt at rebellion. He enjoyed some celebrity following the publication of *Poems*, appearing on television in 1972 with his friend and fellow Hackney Downs pupil Phil Ramacon playing piano, but there were no further books of poetry before his death in a house fire in Stoke Newington in 1980.[10] In one of the most moving poems in the collection, 'My Heart is Broken', he writes:

---

[7] Mark Nowak, *Social Poetics* (Minneapolis: Coffee House, 2020), 2.
[8] In *The Forsaken Lover: White Words and Black People* (Harmondsworth: Penguin, 1973), Chris Searle notes the racist representations of blackness in the Ladybird 'Peter and Jane' primers (123). Karen Sands O'Connor argues that long into the 1990s, 'Britishness and whiteness are equated' in the Ladybird history books. *Children's Publishing and Black Britain* (London: Palgrave, 2017), 127.
[9] Or perhaps, as in Kevin Quashie's theorisation, a kind 'dynamic and ravishing' quietness and interiority that precisely lies beyond resistance. See Quashie, *The Sovereignty of Quiet: Beyond Resistance in Black Culture* (New Brunswick: Rutgers, 2012), 6.
[10] Phil Ramacon went on to perform with Neneh Cherry and to contribute arrangements to Mutabaruka's dub poetry masterpiece, *Check It!* (1983). For biographical details see: *Hackney Gazette* (12 October 2016), online: www.hackneygazette.co.uk/news/tragic-tale-of-young-hackney-poet-12-who-inspired-a-3534072 [Accessed 23 September 2021].

What does the name Vivian Earl Usherwood (Dixon) mean?
I think it means punch, spit, kick.
I was born to take it –
You can even do do on me
I have no shame, no pride, no luck,
No heart and no pride –
I was born to take it all.

Well they are wrong.
It is the wrong person
And that is no lie.
(9)

The poem is a desperate struggle with and against alienation and persecution. When Usherwood says plaintively 'they are wrong' he asserts himself, even if the syntax of the following lines throws that self again into doubt. One of the reasons Usherwood's work is important is because it articulates a complicated, ambivalent subjectivity, brimming with personality and feeling. This sets it in direct contrast to how children of colour are often presented in *Stepney Words*, usually figuring as inert objects for contemplation and identification by white students.[11] A poem like 'My Heart is Broken' hasn't been constructed under the watchful eye of the teacher, or written from a prompt. It is a work of spontaneity and absolute necessity.

But Centerprise unquestionably helped to instil a sense of pride in Usherwood and in other working-class writers, allowing their voices to be heard. In the present era of vicious gentrification and the destruction of working-class communities across London, it feels slightly treacherous to consider the project as anything other than heroic. But the dynamic of the organisation wasn't free from problems. Though Thompson, the founder, was African American, it was initially a mostly white organisation. There were no royalties for authors, because this could 'begin to encourage the professionalism of writing', yet the staff – often middle-class graduates – drew a salary in part funded by these book sales.[12] Of course, almost all relationships between authors and publishers are unequal, fraught with the imbalances of power. But in the final poem in his collection, 'School', Usherwood writes with prescience about how 'Wherever

[11] For example: 'I am just a Pakistani boy / No one likes me [...] I wish that I wasn't born / I wish I was in Pakistan chopping corn'; 'The little girl stood alone / The white kids called her names / I wondered why? / Then I realised ... she was a coloured child'; 'it's not his fault / he's black. / Nor is it our fault / we're white'. *Stepney Words*, 12.
[12] Ken Worpole, quoted in Schling, *Lime Green Mystery*, 139–40.

you go there are schools: / The teachers bother the schoolboys and girls heads in' (31). It's tempting to read this back as a critique of the limits to progressive organisations, and the mystification they can sometimes enact. A strike to restore a beloved teacher is all well and good, and nurturing creativity and the work of imagination is crucial to any radical politics: but Usherwood's work, passionate and wounded, demands something more.

Certainly, Searle's work – which was closely related to Centerprise's community arts initiative – came in for comradely critique from Black activists.[13] Writing in the Marxist-Leninist journal *The Black Liberator*, Cecil Gutzmore and Rudi Guyan reviewed Searle's *The Forsaken Lover: White Words, Black People* (1972). They diagnosed Searle's 'petty bourgeois radical-romantic psychologism' and argued that Searle relied on a homogenous category of 'black identity' rather than engaging in a more thorough analysis of class and class struggle.[14] In his response in the following issue, Searle largely accepts this criticism, and offers his definition of the role of the teacher:

> Our struggle in the schools is to challenge and undermine that ruling ideology at every turn, building up our children like fortresses against its power, prising open the contradictions in the classroom into huge chasms to protect our class, the working class, and giving them the confidence and support to struggle against and overcome the enemy culture.[15]

He would write to *Race Today* in very similar terms in 1975, describing how the teacher 'uses the cracks and contradictions of the school to deliver continuous body-blows to its function within capitalism'.[16] This is the rhetoric of vanguardism, in which the teacher builds and moulds the students until, with a flourish, they can overcome 'the enemy culture'. A letter in response from one reader, Bob Dent, pointed out that if Searle is treating the school as an analogue of the factory, this would surely place teachers in the position of foremen

---

[13] Centerprise published the expanded *Stepney Words 1 & 2* (London: Centerprise, 1973) and Searle worked with Ken Worpole in establishing The Federation of Worker Writers and Community Publishers (FWWCP) in 1976.

[14] Cecil Gutzmore and Rudi Guyan, 'Missing the Point', *The Black Liberator* 1, no. 4 (1973): 252.

[15] Searle, 'Responses', *The Black Liberator* 2, no. 1 (1973): 117. Editor of *The Black Liberator*, Alrick X. Cambridge, had been assistant to Claudia Jones. See Carol Boyce Davies, *Left of Karl Marx: The Political Life of Black Communist Claudia Jones* (Durham, NC: Duke UP, 2007), 85.

[16] Chris Searle, 'School as a Weapon', *Race Today* 7, no. 12 (1975): 281.

and managers: 'Radical teacher? To my mind that's a contradiction in terms. What next? Radical policemen?'[17]

The Race Today Collective (some of whom were teachers), writing from a position informed by the autonomist Marxism of C. L. R. James and Selma James, took a slightly different line. The concluding passage of a collectively signed review of Searle's 1976 volume *Classrooms of Resistance* is worth quoting at length:

> [F]our-fifths of the writing in his book concentrates on what the ruling classes are doing to white workers, to Chileans, to black South Africans and so on. The other fifth bows to trade-unionism as salvation and transfers the inanities of 'fight', 'smash', 'grab', 'struggle', and 'unite' from the white left press onto ILEA [Inner London Education Authority] paper. Somewhere the curriculum should have considered the pupils, not as they will be, with union cards and cloth caps, but as they are – a wageless, dependent, underprivileged section of the population, who have nevertheless shown themselves to be the most potent force for revolutionising the institutions that contain them today. We would like to see teachers participating in the movement towards autonomy and financial independence of school pupils rather than creating the freedom within a small part of the school curriculum to write poems about struggle.[18]

We'll return to *Race Today*'s important theorisation of the young, black and wageless later in the chapter. What's important here is the demand to think from the standpoint of the pupil rather than the teacher, and to recognise the specificity of the contemporary situation. Treating the students as recruits to the trades union of the imagination fundamentally misunderstands their independent revolutionary capacity. In this respect, the poetry of the classroom risks becoming a safety valve and brake in their struggle for autonomy.[19]

My intention here isn't to diminish Searle's work, but to reckon with the intense argument and fissures around education in the early to mid-1970s. This was a period of crisis. As Hazel Carby writes, 'expectations of what schooling in Britain would mean for the black community were shattered by the end of the sixties'.[20] In 1969,

---

[17] Bob Dent, 'Radical Teachers', *Race Today* 8, no. 1 (1976): 19.
[18] Race Today Collective, 'Review Notes', *Race Today* 8, no. 1 (1976): 22.
[19] As Althusser writes: 'the bourgeoisie imposes, in the Ideological State Apparatuses, *forms* meant to *forestall* the revolutionary activity of the working class or to subject it to itself [*s'asujettir*]'. Louis Althusser, 'Note on the ISAs' in *On the Reproduction of Capitalism*, trans. G. M. Goshgarian (London: Verso, 2014), 230.
[20] Hazel V. Carby, 'Schooling in Babylon', *The Empire Strikes Back: Race and Racism in Seventies Britain* (London: Hutchinson, 1982), 195.

picking up the pieces, John La Rose, Sarah White and the New Beacon Books collective set up the George Padmore and Albertina Sylvester supplementary schools. These networks organised to try and resist banding based on IQ tests in North London schools, and would go on to play pivotal roles in the Black Parents Movement.[21] New Beacon published Bernard Coard's crucial exposé of Educationally Subnormal (ESN) Schools in 1971, which demonstrated that schools were one of the key sites of the production and maintenance of racial inequality.[22] Thousands of black children had been removed from mainstream education and placed in ESN schools, which had been designed for pupils with severe learning difficulties. In addition to the ESN scandal, several districts in London maintained a policy of 'dispersal', designed to prevent any school intake becoming more than 33 per cent students of colour. The borough of Ealing continued to bus South Asian children until 1981, despite a 1975 ruling by the Race Relations Board declaring it a discriminatory practice.[23] Further, Bhupinder Bassi of the Birmingham Asian Youth Movement (AYM) remembers that as the composition of schools changed in the early 1970s, many British-born Asian students were moved into remedial English literacy classes for migrant children.[24]

Any study of 'radical education' which didn't begin by acknowledging and addressing the material realities of segregation, inequality and oppression – and the links between schooling, hostile immigration policies, policing, housing – was going to be met with scepticism. One of the minimal reforms offered as a solution was the introduction of the multicultural curriculum, which would modify the content of the classroom without directly addressing the form. In Carby's view, this trend in progressive education – often conceived by white anti-racist teachers – was in effect 'a method of social control over black children'.[25] As Beverley Bryan, Stella Dadzie and Suzanne Scafe asked in the mid-1980s:

---

[21] See Kehinde Andrews, *Resisting Racism: Race, Inequality, and the Black Supplementary School Movement* (London: Trentham / Institute of Education, 2013).
[22] Bernard Coard, *How the West Indian Child is Made Educationally Sub-Normal in the British School System* (London: New Beacon, 1971). See also Paul Warmington, *Black British Intellectuals and Education* (London: Taylor & Francis, 2014).
[23] See Brett Bebber, '"We were just unwanted": Bussing, Migrant Dispersal, and South Asians in London', *Journal of Social History* 48, no. 3 (2015): 635–61.
[24] Anandi Ramamurthy, *Black Star: Britain's Asian Youth Movements* (London: Pluto, 2013), 18.
[25] Carby, 'Schooling in Babylon', 195. See also Carby, 'Multi-Culture' (1980), in *The Screen Education Reader*, ed. Manuel Alverado, Edward Buscome and Richard Collins (London: Macmillan, 1993).

How many dub poems, for example, were really introduced into the classroom as a serious exercise in widening critical faculties; how many more as an easy answer to boredom and disobedience? The concerns of a few teachers made it easy for the liberalism and defeatism of many others to masquerade as care and concern.[26]

Wary of cooption and compromise, presses such as New Beacon and Bogle L'Ouverture and members of the Race Today Collective all produced their own material for young readers and learners; but did so, crucially, from within the ongoing political struggle. These books ranged from Andrew Salkey's young adult novel about Walter Rodney, *Joey Tyson*, to Farrukh Dhondy's short story collection *East End at Your Feet* and Odette Thomas's Caribbean rhymes and songs, *Rain Falling, Sun Shining*, with beautiful illustrations by Errol Lloyd.[27]

There was one book everyone could agree on: Accabre Huntley's *Today at School*, published by Bogle L'Ouverture in 1977. Accabre was the daughter of Jessica and Eric Huntley, proprietors of the press and bookshop, and her work represented a collective achievement of the movement. Like Vivian Usherwood, she presents a sharp critique of school:

> At school today I said
> I am BLACK, PROUD, AND BEAUTIFUL
> they said, not true
> I am going to test you.
>
> At school today
> the teacher hit me hard
> She shook me til I was dead in my heart
> Black mother, save me from my troubles
> And take me into your arms.[28]

Huntley presents an education system that tries to systematically deny her self-knowledge, and attempts to refute the fought-for position of Black pride through tests both literal and spiritual. The relationship to the teacher is underpinned by violence and the threat of violence. The poem ends with what bell hooks would later theorise

---

[26] Beverley Bryan, Stella Dadzie and Suzanne Scafe, *Heart of the Race: Black Women's Lives in Britain* (London: Verso, 2018), 80.
[27] Andrew Salkey, *Joey Tyson* (London: Bogle L'Ouverture, 1974); Farrukh Dhondy, *East End At Your Feet* (London: Macmillan, 1976); Odette Thomas, *Rain Falling, Sun Shining* (London: Bogle L'Ouverture, 1975).
[28] Accabre Huntley, *At School Today* (London: Bogle L'Ouverture, 1977).

as the resistance offered by the 'homeplace'.[29] The whole situation can be grasped from these stanzas.

For Linton Kwesi Johnson, emerging as a leading young voice in the movement, 'Accabre's poetry speaks for a generation of British born blacks who are confident about who they are and what they are about'.[30] Perhaps in this way she differs from Usherwood; only a few years younger, her confidence signals the nurturing of rebellion latent in his work. But who knows how Usherwood's despondency might have developed and transformed in the struggles of the later decade, had he lived. By the third edition of Johnson's *Dread, Beat, and Blood*, Bogle L'Ouverture would list Johnson together with Huntley as part of a series of 'young revolutionary poets':

> The poetry they write comes out of their experience of struggle and resistance against the fascists' attacks on us in this society; the intensity of awareness in the poetry written by an eight-year-old sister and a young brother is just as important as the revolutionary work of our older poets. It is a poetry that does more than lie on the page. It speaks to us and is spoken by us in our communities.[31]

I want to turn now to examine Johnson's own position within this new generation, following his participation in the Race Today Collective and his early poems. Johnson's work, from the beginning, theorised and articulated a politics of self-defence, which became increasingly important as police violence and fascist attacks intensified over the decade. But for context we need to look briefly at another school strike, in South London, 1973.

Tulse Hill school, just south of Brixton, was a large comprehensive school for boys, and in the early 1970s it was often in the news. In 1971, as part of the broad shift towards comprehensive education, the ILEA proposed that Tulse Hill should incorporate the nearby Strand Grammar. This was met with alarm by the more affluent Strand parents, whose racially coded anxieties were duly reported in

---

[29] bell hooks, 'Homeplace', in *Yearning: Race, Gender, and Cultural Politics* (London: Routledge, 2015).

[30] Linton Kwesi Johnson, 'The New Caribbean Poets', *Race Today* 9, no. 7 (November 1977): 166.

[31] Linton Kwesi Johnson, *Dread, Beat, and Blood*, 3rd ed. (London: Bogle L'Ouverture, 1975), backmatter.

The Times and *The Guardian*.³² Following interventions by Margaret Thatcher, then Secretary of State for Education, the plan was deferred.

The next event was more serious. On 19 June 1973, following a firework display at Brockwell Park and reports of a stabbing, police clashed with a large crowd. Three young Black people were arrested and beaten in retaliation by the police, including Robin Sterling, aged fourteen and a pupil at the school. Between the arrests and the trial in March 1974 – at which the 'Brockwell Three' were each handed sentences of three years for affray – the students of Tulse Hill and the local area began to organise.³³ As Farrukh Dhondy describes:

> They formed a committee, the Black Students' Action Collective (Black Sac) and invited participation from four other schools in the area in which they knew they had support and friends. They called a one day strike of pupils from schools.³⁴

This was considerably more antagonistic than the Stepney strike. These students were in daily confrontation with the repressive apparatus of the state, and their demands neither began nor ended in the classroom. Dhondy goes on to make two points: first, that the strike shows that students were capable of 'very fast, quickly organised agitation of a mass nature'. Second, he suggests that in his experience as both teacher and activist, the motivating contradictions for student protest were 'Work and police and money and the relative strength of black gangs and white gangs, self-defence against whites who attack them, feeling against racist teachers and an opposition to the boredom and routine and discipline of schooling'. This was not about 'tinkering with subject matter', but something much more volatile.³⁵

For the authors of *Policing the Crisis*, published in 1978, the Brockwell Three case 'prefigured a massive and dramatic news break in the beginning of 1975, exclusively oriented around the "black crime in South London" problem'.³⁶ A glance at the headlines bears this out: the month after the Brockwell Park incident, *The Times*

---

[32] 'School name "blackened"', *The Guardian* (26 November 1971; 'Growing fears of a blackboard jungle', *The Times* (26 November 1971). The story remained in the news into December.

[33] For a full account, see 'Move as a Community: The Brockwell Park Three', *Race Today* 6, no. 4 (June 1974): 167–73. See also Rob Waters, *Thinking Black: Britain, 1964–85* (Oakland: U of California P, 2019), 165–7.

[34] Farrukh Dhondy, 'Teaching Young Blacks', *Race Today* 10, no. 4 (1978): 82.

[35] Ibid., 83.

[36] Stuart Hall, Chas Critcher, Tony Jefferson, John Clarke and Brian Roberts, *Policing the Crisis: Mugging, the State, and Law and Order* (London: Macmillan, 1978), 329.

begins again to focus on Tulse Hill with 'Coloured children arrested after school gangs clash' making the front page, adjacent to news of a prison riot at Long Kesh.[37] But by September 1973, the newspaper is reporting on the school's implementation of Black Studies, which follows the logic outlined by Carby above, with curriculum reform working to pacify student unrest.[38] The following year the school was again in the news, this time because a maths teacher, Richard Edmonds, was standing as a National Front (NF) parliamentary candidate at the 1974 General Election.[39] Edmonds eventually resigned from his teaching job in July 1975, going on to become one of the most influential figures in post-war British fascism and taking roles in the leadership of both the NF and the British National Party. Faced with fascists in the classroom, racist policing in the street and a vampiric right-wing press, this is the generation of 'Yout Rebels' – taking 'new shapes / shaping new patterns / creatin new links' – whom Linton Kwesi Johnson would come to address in his poetry.[40]

Johnson was, himself, a former student of Tulse Hill. In Franco Rosso's 1979 documentary about the poet, we watch him make his way towards the building while speaking in voiceover:

> I came to England in 1963 and went straight to Tulse Hill school. Now for any black child coming from the Caribbean and entering the British school system, whether it's primary or secondary level, you're at a disadvantage – not because of any *language problem*, because we all speak English in the Caribbean. You're at a disadvantage because at that time, in 1963, and now, still now, racism was rife within the British school system, and they naturally assumed that being black and coming from the West Indies, you didn't know as much as the white kids here.[41]

He recalls elsewhere that 'school was initially a traumatic experience' because it was his first 'confrontation with racism'.[42]

---

[37] Clive Borrell, 'Coloured children arrested after school gangs clash'; Robert Fisk, '33 hurt in fierce riot at Long Kesh', *The Times* (5 July 1973).

[38] But Barbara Beese and Leila Hassan of *Race Today* argued that at Tulse Hill the students refused to cede control of Black Studies, and so it remained a site of political possibility. See Rob Waters, *Thinking Black*, 156–8.

[39] 'Call for investigation into National Front Teacher', *The Times* (30 August 1974). Edmonds won 4.5 per cent of the vote in Deptford.

[40] Linton Kwesi Johnson, *Selected Poems* (London: Penguin, 2006), 22. Hereafter *Selected*, with citations in text.

[41] Franco Rosso, *Dread Beat and Blood* (1979).

[42] 'Linton Kwesi Johnson in Conversation with John La Rose', in *Changing Britannia: Life Experience with Britain*, ed. Roxy Harris and Sarah White (London: New Beacon / George Padmore Institute, 1990), 53.

Though this took the most immediate form of abuse from white students, Johnson goes on to describe how the racist streaming and banding system – the structure of segregating students based on presumed ability – presented structural obstacles to his academic aspirations. He left the school in 1970, taking O Levels at home and going on to do a degree in sociology at Goldsmiths.

But as Darcus Howe would later recall, Tulse Hill was 'a nursery for the Black Panther Movement'.[43] After a visit to the school by Altheia Jones-LeCointe, a central and inspirational figure in the Panthers, Johnson joined the youth wing.[44] Through the party's library he encountered W. E. B. Du Bois and Fanon, and soon started a study group that counted among its members the feminist activist Beverley Bryan and the prison activist Shujaa Moshesh, then known as Wesley Dick.[45] Johnson's work as what he'd later theorise as a 'political-culturalist' proceeded on all fronts.[46] He made contact with John La Rose, who invited him to the Caribbean Artists Movement events at the Keskidee Centre, and La Rose and Andrew Salkey published his poems in the special 'Writing Away From Home' issue of *Savacou* in 1974, along with poems by Bryan, James Berry and the Brixton-based collective, The Fasimbas. Johnson's poems read like he's raising the alarm, especially the great exclamatory 'Time Come', which begins:

>   it soon come
>   it soon come
> look out! look out! look out!

As he memorialises victims of police brutality, he also draws sharp lines of confrontation:

>   When yu fling me ina prison
>   I did warn yu

---

[43] Darcus Howe, 'Bobby to Babylon: Brixton Before the Uprising', February 1982, in *Here to Fight, Here To Stay: A Race Today Anthology*, ed. Paul Field, Robin Bunce, Leila Hassan and Margaret Peacock (London: Pluto, 2019), 65.
[44] Linton Kwesi Johnson, interviewed by Nicholas Wroe, *The Guardian* (8 March 2008), online: www.theguardian.com/books/2008/mar/08/featuresreviews.guardianreview11 [Accessed 25 October 2023].
[45] For extracts of Moshesh's poetry, see Jenny Bourne, 'Spaghetti House Siege: Making the Rhetoric Real', *Race & Class* 53, no. 2 (2011).
[46] Kwesi Johnson, 'The Politics of the Lyrics of Reggae Music'. In this important essay, Johnson opposes the work of the 'political culturalist' – whose work is grounded in 'the historical experience of the oppressed' – against both propagandists for social democracy and neo-nationalists.

> When yu beat Joshua Francis
>   I did warn yu
> When yu kill Oluwale
>   I did warn yu
> When yu jack me up against the wall
>   ha didn't bawl
>   but I did warn yu[47]
>   (*Selected* 22–3)

The poems are completely poised: the poet may be jacked up against the wall, but this gives him a surface to push back from. The social memory of violence and oppression – what he describes elsewhere as 'the unbearable weight of the present' – is sharpened into a simultaneous lament and rallying cry.[48] The voice is collective, strong. At the Keskidee, where he worked as a librarian, he had experimented with the rhythmic basis of his writing through a drumming and poetry group, Rasta Love. The space also provided room for him to work on the performance text *Voices of the Living and the Dead*, which was published as a chapbook – Johnson's first – by Race Today in 1974.

Dhondy reviewed the book for the journal, immediately grasping the influences of Eliot, Brathwaite and Césaire, of the Bible and reggae, and recognising the importance of the local references to Brixton, from the Railton Road Youth Club to the Soferno B sound system. These references, Dhondy implies, could form the basis for a potent 'collective myth'. The stakes are high: 'The way in which it will be successful depends on whether Linton's poetry cannot only live within, but earn the love of the common people.'[49] Johnson's own involvement with *Race Today* was fundamental to this process. To put it in less transactional terms, the journal and the collective gave Johnson's poetry context and momentum, and it provided his earliest readers with a critical forum for discussion, feedback and debate. David Austin's recent study has made clear the centrality of *Race Today* to Johnson's political development, pivotal for his intellectual relationships with the work of Walter Rodney and

---

[47] 'Dread beat and blood', 'Time Come' in *Savacou* 9/10 (1974): 26–8. Rachel Gilmour discusses these poems in 'Voice/Print Transitions in Black British Poetry', in *British Literature in Transition: 1960–1980*, ed. Kate McGloughlin (Cambridge: Cambridge UP, 2018), 91–3.

[48] Johnson, 'Jamaican Rebel Music', *Race and Class* 17, no. 4 (1976): 402. Collected in Linton Kwesi Johnson, *Time Come: Selected Prose* (London: Picador, 2023), 3–28.

[49] Farrukh Dhondy, 'Review: *Voices of the Living and the Dead*', *Race Today* 6, no. 3 (1974): 92.

C. L. R. James.[50] For Robin Bunce and Paul Field, he was simply *'Race Today*'s poet'.[51]

The story of *Race Today*'s development from the rather conservative and staid journal of the Institute of Race Relations to an independent fighting paper has been rehearsed many times before. Johnson's account is nevertheless worth quoting:

> Darcus Howe, who had been in the Black Panther movement with me, was offered the editorship. He took it, and promptly, with the connivance of John La Rose and other people, hijacked the magazine, typesetter and everything, and went to an old house in Brixton and squatted, and built an organisation around the journal, transforming the journal, from a rag of the Institute of Race Relations, into a political weapon, which could be used to inform and to mobilise people around the struggles of blacks and Asians in Britain and the world over.[52]

This wasn't simply a changing of the editors. Perhaps we can think of it as a particularly militant form of 'social poetics': the taking of what's due, transforming the paper into a kind of collective amplifier, a sound system in itself. The *Race Today* squat at 74 Shakespeare Road was opened by Olive Morris, a comrade of Johnson's from the Panthers youth section. She was a founder member of the Brixton Black Women's Group, whose own premises at 65 Railton Road was just down the street. There were many other radical squats in the area, including the South London Gay Community Centre and the artist Pearl Alcock's queer basement shebeen, all within a few hundred feet.[53] Morris' death from cancer in 1979, aged twenty-seven, was a huge loss for the movement. Johnson's elegy, 'Jamaican Lullaby' is one of his most tender poems, writing with 'heart's hurt' how 'the memories hearts are keeping / will soon slide down in dreams'.[54]

---

[50] David Austin, *Dread Poetry & Freedom: Linton Kwesi Johnson and the Unfinished Revolution* (London: Pluto, 2018).

[51] Robin Bunce and Paul Field, *Darcus Howe: A Political Biography* (London: Bloomsbury, 2014), 178.

[52] 'Interview with Linton Kwesi Johnson by Mervyn Morris', in *Hinterland*, ed. E. A. Markham (Newcastle Upon Tyne: Bloodaxe, 1989), 251. For other accounts, see A. Sivanandan, *Race and Resistance: The IRR Story* (London: Race Today, 1975); Bunce and Field, *Darcus Howe: A Biography*, 148–9.

[53] The radical queer presence in Brixton also involved a commune at Athlone Road, whose members included Julian Hows – a sixth-form student at Tulse Hill, who was expelled for his activism – and the poet Alaric Sumner. In retaliation for harassment from Tulse Hill pupils, the Athlone commune staged a protest at the school in 1972. See Stuart Feather, *Blowing the Lid: Gay Liberation, Sexual Revolution, and Radical Queens* (London: Zero, 2015), 429–39.

[54] Linton Kwesi Johnson, *Inglan is a Bitch* (London: Race Today, 1980), 34–5.

Johnson was not, initially, a formal member of the Race Today Collective, which centred around Howe, Dhondy, Leila Hassan, Mala Sen, Barbara Beese, Jean Ambrose and Patricia Dick.[55] He joined officially in 1976. But in the first issue of *Race Today* under Howe's editorial control, Johnson makes an appearance both as a contributor and as news item. He reviews the Penguin anthology *You Better Believe It – Black Verse in English*, taking issue with the editor Paul Breman's preposterous claim that Amiri Baraka 'has never in his life written black poetry'. Johnson quotes from Baraka's 'Black Dada Nihilismus' and 'Black Art', and goes on to discuss the work of Haki R. Madhubuti (then Don L. Lee) and Sonia Sanchez.[56] In 'Dock Brief', meanwhile – a regular feature of the journal, covering ongoing legal cases – Johnson is mentioned in relation to the case of a young woman convicted for assaulting a police officer.[57] The reader learns that she had been a co-defendant of Johnson's the previous year in a relatively high-profile case.

As Johnson recounts in a later interview, he had witnessed the violent arrest of a young Black man in Brixton market in November 1972. He explains that in the Black Panther Movement he had been trained to find out the name and address of anyone being arrested, especially young people, because they were often detained twenty miles outside London, 'in Ashford Remand Centre for weeks without informing their parents'.[58] When he started taking notes on the arrest, he was promptly thrown in a police van, beaten up and then charged with assaulting an officer. The case went to trial in June 1973, and thanks to two Black jurors, the defendants were acquitted. Lewis Nkosi, the exiled South African writer, covered the case in *The Guardian*. He named the detectives responsible – Bloom, Farr and Levers – and described a pattern of baseless charges and acquittals that came 'dangerously close to persecution'.[59] As a result, Farr

---

[55] Variously, this brought together members or ex-members of the Black Unity and Freedom Party, the British Black Panther Movement, the Institute of Race Relations and defendants from the Mangrove Nine case. See Bunce and Field, *Darcus Howe: A Biography*, 150.
[56] Linton Kwesi Johnson, 'Review: *You Better Believe It – Black Verse in English*', *Race Today* 6, no. 1 (January 1974): 24–5.
[57] 'Dock Brief', *Race Today* 6, no. 1 (January 1974), 8.
[58] 'Linton Kwesi Johnson in Conversation', *Changing Britannia*, 58.
[59] Lewis Nkosi, 'Why blacks are blowing their tops in Brixton', *The Observer* (17 June 1973). In his acceptance speech for an honorary degree from Rhodes University, Johnson talks about Nkosi and two other South African exiles – his lawyer Barney Desai and Lionel Morrison, who later became the first Black president of the National Union of Journalists. See Johnson, 'South Africa Connections', *Time Come: Selected Prose*, 193–9.

and Leavers were transferred. But of course, police persecution of the Black community continued: in the same month as Johnson's acquittal and Nkosi's coverage, the Brockwell Three were arrested.

This cycle of police harassment and criminalisation has long been understood as one of Johnson's principal themes. In perhaps his most famous poem, 'Sonny's Lettah (an anti-sus poem)', he writes from the perspective of a young man who retaliates after 'tree policeman, / di hole a dem carryin batan' attack his friend Jim (*Selected* 28). Fighting back, Sonny takes on three policemen and one of them falls down dead. From Brixton Prison, arraigned on murder charges, Sonny writes to his mother, presumably in Jamaica, explaining his predicament. It is a subtle and devastating poem. We can read it as a modification – almost a negative image – of an earlier poem, 'Night of the Head', Johnson's first elegy for David Oluwale, a Nigerian-born homeless man murdered by police in Leeds.[60] Written in a surrealist mode he would soon abandon, the poem begins with news of 'a black tramp's death', and the subsequent discovery by the speaker of his body parts: first 'the dead man's head' and ultimately 'the dead man's prick'. Oluwale, we're told, 'on the last onslaught / just broke into pieces and died'. But the poem resists this disintegration, ending with the prick fantastically transformed into a machine gun, and the protagonist shattering a police station with 'black sperm'. From emasculation and victimisation comes the possibility of violent resistance, in a dynamic familiar to any reader of Fanon or Eldridge Cleaver. But the final lines end by telling us 'not a soul survived / so he cried, / as the mist screamed red / and he drank of it'.[61]

Both poems are, as Fred D'Aguiar describes one of Johnson's favoured modes, dramatisations of injustice.[62] In 'Sonny's Lettah' the reader observes the social destruction brought about by the stop and search 'sus' laws; 'Night of the Head' is nightmare realism, portraying the psychological violence of police terror. What is to be done? In both poems, individualised responses to police brutality – whether lashing out or dreaming of revenge through red mist – brings with it certain costs. For Johnson and the Race Today Collective, this is a question of analysis rather than moralism. It became crucial over the course of the 1970s to understand and theorise the activity of young Black people as they navigated a landscape of state violence and

---

[60] See Kester Aspden, *The Hounding of David Oluwale* (London: Vintage, 2007).
[61] Johnson, *Dread Beat and Blood* (London: Bogle L'Ouverture, 1975), 33–5.
[62] Fred D'Aguiar, 'Preface: Why Inglan is a Bitch', in Johnson, *Inglan is a Bitch*, 9–10.

systemic oppression. 'We sought to offer ideological clarity,' Johnson has stated, 'based on the conviction that working people had the capacity to organise their own struggles for change and win.'[63]

At the beginning of 1975, *Race Today* published an editorial, 'Police and the Black Wageless', in which Darcus Howe analyses the refusal of work:

> Within the West Indian working class there has developed a distinct grouping of unemployed young men and women which increases at the end of every school year. It is not a reserve army of labour – that is to say, held in reserve to be called upon at the will of London Transport, Fords, night cleaning agencies, hospitals and all other employers of black immigrant labour. Call as they might, the youths have uncompromisingly refused to budge. It is an overwhelming refusal of shit work.[64]

Howe's argument – his ideological clarity – is important for several reasons. First, he stresses the *active refusal* of work. This is conscious and deliberate activity, rather than a 'problem' to be solved. Howe does not portray unemployed young people as passive victims of circumstance, but rather emphasises their agency. Second, he avoids treating this section of the West Indian working class as lumpenproletariat, despite their association with informal economies of petty crime and various forms of hustling. Instead, Howe works with terms developed by Marxist feminists such as Selma James, arguing that they are simply *wageless*, and the emerging moral panic around 'mugging' is merely a distraction from the demand 'for a social wage for the unemployed'.[65] Lastly, their *uncompromising* refusal of work strengthens the class as a whole. Older immigrant workers engaged in 'shit work' face less competition in the labour market, and so are strengthened in their industrial disputes and their demand for improved pay and working conditions.

Johnson's 'Yout Rebels', published in *Race Today* in 1977, is a direct condensation of this argument:

---

[63] Linton Kwesi Johnson, '*Race Today* and British Politics: Introduction', in *Race Today Anthology*, 8.
[64] 'Editorial: Police and the Black Wageless', *Race Today* 7, no. 2 (February 1975), 27. This text also circulated as a single-sheet leaflet.
[65] See Selma James, 'Sex, Race, and Class', *Race Today* 6, no. 1 (January 1974).

a bran new breed of blacks
have now emerged,
leadin on the rough scene,
breakin away
takin the day,
sayin to capital neva
movin forwud hevva.[66]
    (*Selected* 22)

As David Austin has observed, this is an 'anti-capitalist poem'.[67] It bears repeating: this is a poem which emerges from a specific Marxist analysis of the Black working class in Britain, and which furthers a specific political argument about the autonomous struggle of young people. For Howe, Johnson and the Race Today Collective, the Black wageless are 'leadin on the rough scene', 'movin forwud' and showing the way. They are not potential recruits; they are not an audience to be won over. The 'neva' that they say to capital is, precisely, what Howe calls the refusal of 'shit work'. This is exactly the kind of labour that Johnson would depict in 'Inglan is a Bitch', where 'mi dhu day wok an' mi dhu nite wok / mi dhu clean wok an mi' dhu dutty wok', only to be made redundant aged fifty-five (*Selected* 40).[68]

Needless to say, 'Police and the Black Wageless' was controversial, provoking debate and comment in the ensuing issues and broader left. Predictably, some in the trades union movement felt that a defence of unemployment was in line with the policies of the Conservative Party; others were simply offended by the characterisation of jobs in nursing, cleaning, London Transport and so on as 'shit'; still more were offended by aims barbed at social workers, the race relations industry and other 'missionary' jobs. More generative criticism came from *The Black Liberator*, who argued through a structuralist analysis informed by Althusser that this type of autonomous struggle remained 'ideological' rather than strictly

---

[66] Linton Kwesi Johnson, 'Yout Rebels', *Race Today* 9, no. 1 (February 1977). It appears alongside 'Five Nights of Bleeding', 'Doun de Road', 'Double Scank' and 'Yout Scene', plus an interview between Johnson and Dread Fred. The occasion was the award of Johnson's Greater London Arts Council fellowship, which made him Lambeth Poet in Residence.
[67] Austin, *Dread Poetry & Freedom*, 84.
[68] Johnson uses the phrase directly in a 1980 interview: 'young blacks are saying that we are not prepared to live under the demoralised immigrant status that our parents lived under; we're not going to do the same shit work they did – still do: and we're not going to go through the demoralisation of the social security system. So we will survive by any means necessary, even if it means crime'. Johnson, quoted in Eddie Chambers, *Root and Culture: Cultural Politics in the Making of Black Britain* (London: I. B. Tauris, 2017), 118.

'political'. Sceptical of calls for a social wage, Alrick X. Cambridge insisted that this demand does not and cannot *directly* subvert the production of surplus value: rebellious, perhaps, but not yet revolutionary.[69] In the long concluding chapter of *Policing the Crisis*, Stuart Hall and his co-authors would mediate between these two positions – the spontaneity and autonomy of *Race Today* and the militant structuralism of *The Black Liberator* – beginning his crucial foray into what he later called 'Marxism without guarantees'.[70]

But whether rebellious or revolutionary, the Race Today Collective had identified the leading section of the working class. If *refusal* is part of working-class power – one way of saying 'neva' to capital – it accompanies an urgent question about self-defence. How would the 'Yout Rebels' defend their communities from the linked threats of police and fascist violence?

At least initially, it seems like the best form of defence is a riot. Throughout 1976, the Notting Hill Carnival was threatened and undermined by protests and petitions from white residents, threats from local councillors and intimidation by the police.[71] While the Carnival Committee managed to keep the event on the streets – rather than being contained in a park or a stadium – the police presence was raised from 60 officers in 1975 to more than 1200 deployments over the 1976 August bank holiday weekend.[72] This was a planned confrontation, and it was met with ferocious opposition on the streets. The coverage in *Race Today* draws parallels with the Soweto Uprising of the previous month, and describes how the police were repeatedly outmanoeuvred, attacked with bottles, bricks and sticks, and outrun by the crowd. As Johnson would write in 'All wi doin is defendin', a poem I'll return to:

> wi have
> a grievous blow fi blow
>
> wi will fite yu in di street wid we han
> wi hav a plan
> soh lissen man
> get ready fi tek some blows
> (*Selected* 11)

[69] See A. X. Cambridge, 'Black Workers and the State: A Debate Inside the Black Workers' Movement', *The Black Liberator* 2, no. 2 (1973–1974): 183–6.
[70] Hall et al., *Policing the Crisis*, 372–97. Excerpted in Stuart Hall, *Selected Writings on Marxism*, ed. Gregor McLennan (Durham, NC: Duke UP, 2021), 199–227.
[71] See the 'Carnival Belongs to Us', Special Issue, *Race Today* 8, no. 9 (September 1976).
[72] Bunce and Field, *Darcus Howe: A Political Biography*, 221.

This is the poetry of collective action, with the choreography of the crowd making itself felt in every line. In his *Race Today* editorial, Howe writes admiringly of 'this youthful majority, that saved the community from total humiliation', and goes on to describe their 'common purpose':

> Their togetherness arises from their common experience of what can or can't be done through schooling; of life within, or the battle to stay out of, other detentive places; of the realities of being offered, and refusing, the shitwork of the society.[73]

Open battle with the police – which had its antecedents in Brockwell Park and other skirmishes – is galvanising, because it consolidates the sense of 'togetherness' and 'common experience', and deepens and further politicises the politics of refusal. When Johnson writes 'wi', the whole struggle for collective agency is implied.

But 1976 also saw an intensification of violent racist attacks directed at the Asian communities in Southall and in the East End of London. Gurdip Chaggar was murdered in Southall on 4 June, and *Race Today* carried reports of Bengali factory workers being stabbed and beaten in the days after.[74] Despite important work by Stephen Watts and John Welch, there remains little work translated into English from either the Punjabi-speaking or Bengali migrant communities during this era.[75] But a 1978 article by Jogindar Shamsher collected extracts from more than a dozen Punjabi-language poets living in England, many of whom were affiliated with the Indian Workers Association, and some of whom were communists. Santokh Singh Santokh, who came to England in 1962 and worked at the Woolf rubber factory in Hayes, wrote militant anti-colonial poems:[76]

> The north points to Ireland
> The south to Vietnam
> The east to Bengal

---

[73] Howe, 'Editorial: Carnival Belongs To Us', *Race Today* 8, no. 9 (September 1976): 170.
[74] See *Race Today Anthology*, 109–15.
[75] But for work by Bangladesh-based poets, see Farida Majid, ed. and trans., *Take Me Home Rickshaw: Poems from Contemporary Bangladesh* (London: Salamander Press, 1974), and Majid, ed. and trans., *From Inside the Prison Camp: Bangladesh 1971* (London: Salamander, 1973). Notwithstanding Alison Busby's and Jessica Huntley's work, Majid has some claim to be the first woman of colour to edit a dedicated poetry small press in Britain.
[76] This biographical information is gleaned from Claire Wills, *Lovers and Strangers: An Immigrant History of Post-War Britain* (London: Penguin, 2017). Wills implies that Shamsher put her in touch with many of these authors. The Woolf factory was the site of significant industrial disputes in 1964 and 1965.

184 *Living in History: Poetry in Britain, 1945–1979*

> And who is in the West?
> *I* am there.
> All points of the compass radiate from my heart.[77]

Surjit Hans, another factory worker, writes:

> Black brothers of the world
> One day you must die, so unite.
> Tonight you must mount such a raid
> That tomorrow a different sun will rise.
> Break the chains of slavery
> Forget the ways of non-violence
> The age of blackness is the people's age.
> Make it the age of black power.[78]

Shamsher quotes other poems in support of the Vietcong and Palestinian liberation fighters, and one or two brief extracts supporting the Maoist Naxalite insurgency in India. These poems exemplify what Sivanandan called the 'mosaic of unities and organisations' which resolved into 'a pattern of black unity and black struggle'.[79] There are also poems about life in the factory, and love and relationships including poems by Kailash Puri – 'An embrace, a sensation in the limbs' – who would go on to become an important writer on sex and relationships.[80]

This is merely to emphasise and gesture towards the thriving and politically engaged culture of poetry and song among the Asian workers in Southall.[81] In the East End, we can turn again to Centerprise, and Savitri Hensman's *Flood at the Door* (1979). Hensman, born in Sri Lanka, grew up in Hackney and won the borough's poetry competition in 1976. *Flood at the Door*, written

---

[77] Jogindar Shamsher, 'Panjabi poetry in Britain', *New Community* 6, no. 3 (1978): 301. This article is reprinted in Jogindar Shamsher, *The Overtime People* (Jalandhar: ABS, 1989).

[78] Quoted in Shamsher, 'Panjabi poetry in Britain', 302.

[79] A. Sivanandan, 'From Resistance to Rebellion: Asian and Afro-Caribbean Struggles in Britain' (1981), *Catching History on the Wing: Race, Culture and Globalisation* (London: Pluto, 2008), 96.

[80] See Kailash Puri, *The Autobiography of a Punjabi Agony Aunt* (Brighton: Sussex Academic Press, 2013).

[81] For further context related to the IWA, see Virinder S. Kalra, 'Poetic Politics: From the Ghadar to the Indian Workers Association', in *The Routledge Handbook of the Asian Diaspora*, ed. Radha Hegde and Ajaya Sahoo (London: Routledge, 2018). For a useful reading of song and music, see Kalra, John Hutnyk and Sanjay Sharma, 'Re-Sounding (Anti)Racism, or Concordant Politics? Revolutionary Antecedents', in *Dis-Orienting Rhythms: The Politics of the New Asian Dance Music*, ed. Sanjay Sharma, John Hutnyk and Ashwani Sharma (London: Zed, 1996), 127–55.

while she was a teenager, often explores traditional forms, including ballads and haikus, a stray sonnet. Judith Kazantzis, reviewing it for *Spare Rib*, observed that they're 'neither self-absorbed nor flowery', and states: 'She has a passionate subject: racism ...'[82] In 'Just Another Asian', Hensman writes of the spate of violent attacks and racist murders:

> They stabbed him in the face and chest
> They stabbed him in the back
> They kicked him as he lay there
> And told him to go back

The poem ends with the police delivering what is, in effect, the same message:

> The police stand by the body
> Nothing much to say
> Just another Asian
> Has been killed today[83]

Anandi Ramamurthy's research suggests that this poem circulated widely among the AYM in the 1980s, appearing in publications from the Sheffield branch in 1983. It joined work by the great Faiz Ahmed Faiz, along with British-based poets such as Mahmood Jamal and Mumtaz Awan.[84]

In spring 1977, *Race Today* effectively declared an emergency. The Bogle L'Ouverture bookshop had been vandalised by fascists, with Jessica and Eric Huntley receiving threatening letters and phone calls; the same thing started happening to New Beacon. Centerprise, located just down the street from the NF headquarters, was firebombed; nobody was injured, but many publications by local writers were destroyed. The Joint Action Committee on Bookshops recorded more than two-dozen attacks over the course of the year. But the *Race Today* position focused particularly on the attacks on

---

[82] Judith Kazantzis, 'Review', *Spare Rib* 105 (1981): 46.
[83] Savitri Hensman, *Flood at Your Door* (London: Centerprise, 1979). Hensman would go on to be one of the founders of the London Black Lesbian and Gay Centre, established in 1985. She contributes to Valerie Mason-John and Anna Khambatta, *Lesbians Talk: Making Black Waves* (London: Scarlet, 1993).
[84] Ramamurthy, *Black Star: Britain's Asian Youth Movements*, 83. Jamal published English translations of Faiz and other communist Urdu poets in the radical arts publication *Black Phoenix*, which he edited with Rasheed Araeen. See Mahmood Jamal, 'An Introduction to Radical Urdu poetry', *Black Phoenix* 2 (1978): 28–9. The same issue prints documentation of Araeen's important performance piece, 'Paki Bastard: Portrait of the Artist as a Black Person'.

Asian workers in the East End, where Dhondy and Mala Sen had been organising in the Bengali Housing Action Group. The editorial 'Forward to a Command Council' lays out the situation:

> What is to be done? There is no indication that the government and the security forces have placed the protection of Asian lives high on their list of priorities. If they have then it must surely be the best kept secret in the land.
> [...]
> We have to protect ourselves. There is no alternative. We have no choice. More to the point, there is a general movement in the Asian community towards self-defence.[85]

It goes on to argue for a committed self-defence organisation, broken up into Active Service Units, each headed by a Commander who would report to the Command Council. Reminiscent of the tactics of the post-war East End Jewish antifascists known as the 43 Group, this would be augmented by an Intelligence Unit who would find out 'where in the white community the attackers were based'.[86]

It's in this increasingly urgent context that Johnson makes his turn to become a recording artist, re-presenting two poems from *Dread Beat and Blood* (1975) on the 12" single *All Wi Doin is Defendin* (1977). The A-side opens with the title track, and the seething declaration 'war ... war ... / mi seh lissen'. If, as I suggested above, Johnson's 'Yout Rebels' condenses the *Race Today* line on the wageless struggle of the Black working class, here Johnson's lyric concentrates, even sharpens, the atmosphere of rebellion and resistance. It really *is* war, a matter of life and death and survival. In this context, the shift in format – from the book or magazine to the audio recording – is significant. It presupposes and enacts the collective, the form of riotous togetherness. As Johnson wrote in his sociological study of reggae lyrics, he sets out 'to transform the consciousness of the sufferer, to politicize him culturally through music, song, and poetry' and so 'the lyricist contributes to the continuing struggle of the oppressed'.[87] The other track on the A-side, 'Five Nights of Bleeding', addresses 'war among the rebels' and the fratricidal violence of Brixton in the earlier 1970s. Johnson reminds the listener of 'rebellion rushing down the wrong road / storm blowing down the wrong tree'. Juxtaposed, the two tracks play out the transformation

---

[85] 'Forward to a Command Council', *Race Today* 9, no. 3 (April/May 1977): 51.

[86] See Morris Beckman, *The 43 Group: The Untold Story of Their Fight Against Fascism* (London: Centerprise, 1993).

[87] Johnson, 'Jamaican Rebel Music', 411.

of consciousness, from infighting to fighting back. In his stark representations of violence, Johnson makes violence an object; something to recognise and think with, something that can be understood and used. As he puts it in 'Reggae Sounds', as a lyricist he has to 'dig doun to the root of the pain; / shape it into violence for the people' (*Selected* 17).

All Wi Doin is Defendin was Johnson's first collaboration with the musician and producer Dennis Bovell, and the B-side features two dubs of the title track: 'Command Council Dub' and 'Defence Dub'.[88] As Keith La Rose and Michael La Rose of the People's War Soundsystem wrote in a review for *Race Today*: 'For the best effect it should be heard at full or on a soundsystem [...] both are heavy dub.'[89] Again, I want to emphasise that 'Command Council' is *named after* the Race Today Collective's position on community self-defence. This is the unity of theory and practice. Johnson's vocal track is echoed and fragmented, his phrases sinking, floating and darting in and out of the spare arrangement, like a Command Council on the move. The 'Defence Dub', likewise, isolates the line 'all oppression / can do is bring / passion to di heights of eruption', and the music stays at this point of excitement and alertness. We can read the improvisatory dub versions as a kind of sonic analogy for the process of organisation and spontaneity that the Race Today Collective explored in their analyses over the course of the 1970s. Sounds become autonomous and cluster; rhythms consolidate and dissolve. It is a highpoint of the era's political art: as direct as it is experimental, equal parts propaganda and lament, as serious as the reality demanded.[90]

The decade seems to accelerate towards its conclusion. On 23 April 1979, New Zealand-born schoolteacher and anti-racist activist Blair Peach – a colleague of Chris Searle's from the East London Teacher's

---

[88] It's worth mentioning that Bovell had been involved in an important legal case, arrested and tried as one of the 'Cricklewood Twelve' when a club he was performing at was invaded by police. He served six months in prison before being released on appeal. See 'Dennis Bovell in Conversation with Linton Kwesi Johnson', in *Building Britannia: Life Experience with Britain*, ed. Roxy Harris and Sarah White (London: New Beacon, 2009).

[89] Keith La Rose and Michael La Rose, 'Review', *Race Today* 10, no. 1 (1978): 15.

[90] Jordan Musser has written recently about Johnson's 'Popular Avant-Gardism'. See Musser, 'The Avant-Garde is in the Audience', *Twentieth-Century Music* 16, no. 3 (2019).

Association – was killed by the Special Patrol Group in Southall. He was there as part of a huge demonstration against an NF election meeting. The police, more than 2500 of them, were there to make sure the meeting went ahead. The circumstances around the killing were covered up for more than thirty years, and no officer has ever been held responsible. Denied access to key police evidence, a jury inquest would rule that Peach's death was the result of 'misadventure'.[91] Peach became a martyr. His body lay in state in the Dominion Theatre in Southall, a building owned by the local branch of the Indian Workers Association. Photographs of his funeral show his coffin being carried through a crowd of the Southall AYM, fists aloft in salute. He was the subject of many poems.[92] Johnson's 'Reggae fi Peach' fashions the 'talk of the day' – the common and collective knowledge of police culpability – into a powerful and direct refrain: 'The SPG them are murderers (murderers) / we can't make them get no furtherer.'[93]

Written thirty years later, Bhanu Kapil's *Ban en Banlieue*, dedicated to Peach, is built from the remnants of a planned novel about a girl walking home from school 'just as a protest starts to escalate'.[94] We follow Ban as she hovers at the periphery, returning again and again to the moment when the sound of breaking glass signals that 'the coming violence has begun' (20). The narrative isn't so much deconstructed as destroyed: a poetics of fragments and waste, ash and soot and smudges and blur. Kapil was born in Hayes, the borough next door to Southall, in 1968. The NF had been founded the previous year. The book moves in a state of traumatised vigilance, where violence is both constantly anticipated and already enacted: 'the event unfolds both after and before' (70). Peach's death comes to stand as a moment of 'sacrifice and rupture', drawn into

---

[91] See David Renton, *Who Killed Blair Peach?* (London: Defend the Right to Protest, 2010). The police's internal investigation – the Cass Report – was released in 2010 in the wake of the police killing of Ian Tomlinson, a bystander at a demonstration against the G8 in 2009.

[92] See for instance the conclusion to Wendy Mulford's *ABC of Writing* (Southampton: Torque, 1985): 'somewhere in Southall / – you and I were sleeping – / a young man died'. Lotte Moos, a Jewish wartime refugee, writes with scorn about the coroner's inquest in her 'Balance', *Time to be Bold* (London: Centerprise, 1981), 59. Chris Searle edited a collection, *One for Blair* (London: Young World, 1989).

[93] Linton Kwesi Johnson, 'Reggae fi Peach', on the *Bass Culture* LP (Virgin, 1980). Johnson and Dennis Bovell briefly discuss the poem in Daniel Rachel, *Walls Come Tumbling Down: The Music and Politics of Rock Against Racism, 2 Tone, and Red Wedge* (London: Pan Macmillan, 2016), 197.

[94] Bhanu Kapil, *Ban en Banlieue* (New York: Nightboat, 2015), 31. Further references given in text.

folds and parallels with Jyoti Singh, sexually assaulted and killed in Delhi in 2012, and with artist and writer Theresa Hak Kyung Cha, sexually assaulted and murdered in New York in 1982. It's as if these events happen simultaneously, as if the book is written from within the moment of occurrence, a blow and recoil that never ends. In repeated figures and gestures, Kapil shows us that exceptional violence is part of the routine violence of the nation, the state and the family. Each sentence is like a stone dropped in a pool, the ripples travelling out.

The collectively authored community analysis of the day and aftermath, *Southall: 23 April 1979*, is arranged in sequentially numbered paragraphs.[95] Minute by minute, hour by hour, street by street, we follow the movements of the police as they begin to attack protestors. It is jarring to read such a precise, measured account of out-of-control violence: the police destroying the People's Unite squat, severely injuring Clarence Baker, the manager of reggae group Misty in Roots; the police at Rochester Row station forcibly removing bangles and turbans from Sikh arrestees; the police charging horses into crowds. The reader is left with the strongest sense that the authorities were lucky to get away with only one fatality. Reading the report side by side with *Ban en Banlieue* is uncanny. Kapil often gets close to testimony, but veers away: 'It snows that April for a few minutes, early in the day. Children walking on Southall Broadway open their mouths to receive the aluminium snowflakes.' (29). Likewise, in a detail that leaves me stunned, we learn from *Southall: April 23 1979* that the ambulance driver who attended to Blair Peach as he lay dying was called Ivor Poet.[96] I'm reminded of Cinna, the Poet, in Shakespeare's *Julius Caesar*, mistaken for Cinna, the Conspirator, and killed by a crowd. The structure of tragedy keeps intruding, erupting, as if one genre had been transposed uneasily into another, where the likenesses won't stick and the positions don't hold.[97] This is injustice's formal disturbance.

Part of the power of *Ban en Banlieue* – we might call it Kapil's capacity to upset – comes from its perspectival shifts. We move not

---

[95] *Southall: 23 April 1979 – The Report of the Unofficial Committee of Enquiry* (London: National Council for Civil Liberties (NCCL), 1980).
[96] See ibid., §3.14.
[97] Perhaps, as a reader, I'm assembling here an example of what Lauren Berlant has theorised as 'genre flailing'. They write: 'Genre flailing is a mode of crisis management that arises after an object, or object world, becomes disturbed in a way that intrudes on one's confidence about how to move in it.' Berlant, 'Genre Flailing', *Capacious: Journal for Emerging Affect Inquiry* 2, no. 1 (2018): 157. Berlant discusses *Ban en Banlieue* in *On the Inconvenience of Other People* (Durham, NC: Duke UP, 2022), 149–72.

only between Ban the child and Bhanu the adult, but between close and dispersed family, the claustrophobia of next-door neighbours and hemmed-in streets, 'the bad sex of the riot' (7), the suburb and the ditch. It is a work which honours minor characters. At one point Kapil references Bruegel's *Landscape with the Fall of Icarus*, and the reader is unsure whether Ban or Peach is the boy falling from the sky (37). Though Peach *is* the martyr in both books, his death is the point at which memory and memorialisation begins, rather than where it reaches its conclusion. Before Blair Peach there was Gurdip Chaggar or David Oluwale, Altab Ali or Kelso Cochrane. There are too many to name, and still further whose names are lost to memory. Though this is a list of younger men – the oldest, Oluwale, was thirty-eight or thirty-nine – there's Aseta Simms, who died aged fifty in Stoke Newington Police Station in 1972, the death of Cynthia Jarrett and the police shooting of Cherry Croce in Brixton and Tottenham in 1985, through to Sarah Reed's death in Holloway Prison in 2016. As Vivian Usherwood wrote in 1972, 'This is the world we live in: / What a mean and miserable world.'[98] Until the abolition of the police, the prisons and racial capitalism, there is as yet no end.

Johnson's poetry, along with his work as a cultural theorist and activist, urges us to recognise that the horizon of liberation resides in present struggle. He declines the role of teacher, leader or spokesman: 'mi naw preach / mi naw teach / mi jus a show yu / ow me seit' (*Selected* 108). As I've shown throughout this chapter, Black activists in the 1970s proposed forms of collective and autonomous self-education that radically challenged both the ideological and repressive apparatus of the British state. The practice of self-defence, from the school strikes to the Black Panther Movement to the Command Council, resists and refuses a narrative of victimhood and passive suffering. But it also acknowledges the reality of martyrdom and sacrifice, refusing to turn away from the necessity of organised community response to violent attacks. Looking back and trying to trace the range of activity in the 1970s can be both galvanising and demoralising, inspiring and intimidating. As Johnson says 'histri biggah dan mi ar yu yu know' (*Selected* 108). But he writes, too, in the refrain to 'Reggae Sounds': 'bass history is a moving / is a hurting black story' (*Selected* 17).[99] Marx described the inertia and defeat of

---

[98] Usherwood, 'Rich Men and Poor Men', *Poems*, 23.
[99] We can compare Nathaniel Mackey's analysis: 'in the "bass notes" bottoming the work of these various writers – writers who, poet or novelist, black or white, from

the failed revolutions of 1848 as a history 'painted grey on grey'.[100] Linton Kwesi Johnson's 'hurting black story' proposes a kind of history from below: felt in the body, bass history is the movement of the past into the future, the pulse and possibility of revolutionary change.

---

the United States or from the Caribbean, produce work of a refractory, oppositional sort – one hears the rumblings of some such "place" of insubordination'. Mackey, *Discrepant Engagement: Dissonance, Cross-Culturality, and Experimental Writing* (Cambridge: Cambridge UP, 1993), 1.

[100] Karl Marx, *The Eighteenth Brumaire of Louis Bonaparte* (1852) (Moscow: Progress, 1977), 35.

Chapter 7

Grave Police Music: Anti-Carceral Poetics

Hey poet! are you much of a teacher?
I teach myself – not you.
                        BILL GRIFFITHS[1]

In the fifteen years since his death, the work of Bill Griffiths has received steady – if not always sustained – critical attention. Readers have benefited from *The Salt Companion to Bill Griffiths* (2007); a special issue of the *Journal of British and Irish Innovative Poetry* (2014); and most importantly, a three-volume *Collected Poems* (2010, 2014, 2016). The latter, lovingly edited by his fellow poet Alan Halsey, brings a substantial amount of the poetry back into print, and allows perhaps for the first time a comprehensive chronological overview. Griffiths was one of the more fugitive of the 1970s avant-garde, publishing his work almost exclusively through his own Pirate Press imprint in editions that rarely reached triple figures. He remains unwieldy. His literary production from the early 1970s until his death in 2007 was relentless. The *Collected Poems*, which stops in 1996, still runs to more than 1,200 pages. In addition to poetry, Griffiths compiled dialect dictionaries of the fishing and coal industries in the North of England; wrote pamphlets of local history, political tracts, ghost stories and satires; and translated and prepared scholarly editions of Old English texts. He was also an archivist, cataloguing the papers of his friend and sometime mentor Eric Mottram at King's College London (KCL) and the Northern Sinfonia at Northumbria University. For the reader and the researcher, the result

---

[1] Bill Griffiths, 'Terzetto', *Collected Earlier Poems: 1966–1980* (Hastings: Reality Street, 2010), 37. Further references will be given in the text as *CP1* with page numbers following.

of this boundless productivity can sometimes feel overwhelming. It's hard to know where to begin, and harder to find an ending: even in the more definitive form of the *Collected* the sequences blur into one another, the result of a lifelong process of thought and rethinking.

I have come to think of this material as a kind of labyrinth, and the guides to navigation full of their own puzzles and secrets. Readers with different interests will each find their own thread, but these threads tangle and overlap, and start to pull in different directions. But for as long as he was writing poetry, Bill Griffiths wrote about prison, prisoners and the law. This is the thread I follow here. I start by providing some historical context for Griffiths's work on prisons, and by positioning his work in relation to some contemporaries, including Tom Pickard, Basil Bunting and John James. I go on to give a reading of three texts from the early 1990s which, I suggest, emerge from and revisit his practice in the 1970s. Throughout, I try to reflect on the difficulties that Griffiths's poetry poses to criticism. I will begin with a letter.

In November 1993, Tony Blair wrote to Bill Griffiths thanking him for a copy of his essay 'on the difficulties of prison life', promising to study it closely.[2] Blair's letterhead gives his address as Myrobella House at Trimdon Colliery, about 15 miles south of 21 Alfred Street, Seaham, on the North East coast, where Griffiths had moved on Mayday 1990. Though this move was dictated by economic necessity, it was also a gesture of political solidarity. After a ruinous decade of Thatcherism, Griffiths chose to settle in one of the places most severely impacted by de-industrialisation. As Clive Bush has written, Griffiths held an 'absolute loyalty to the poor and dispossessed'.[3] During the 1970s he was involved in squatting across London, with a couple of spells as a labourer in Germany, and lived for much of the 1980s on a houseboat until it was destroyed in a fire while undergoing repairs.[4] Many of his

---

[2] Bill Griffiths Collection, Brunel University Library Special Collections, London. BG 16/1/5. Technically speaking, the letter is typed and signed on Blair's behalf by his secretary.

[3] Clive Bush, *Out of Dissent: A Study of Five Contemporary British Poets* (London: Talus, 1997), 212. Bush's chapter on Griffiths remains the best introduction to his work.

[4] The voyages of the boat and his life on the waterways of South England are recorded in *The Book of the Boat* (London: Writers Forum, 1988); collected in *Collected Poems & Sequences: 1981–91* (Hastings: Reality Street, 2014), 73–102.

papers were lost, but he still managed to complete his PhD in Old English at KCL.

The essay Blair mentions, which I'll return to, is almost certainly *HMP: Revising Prison*, a pamphlet issued by Griffiths in 1993 through his own Amra imprint. *HMP: Revising Prison* isn't so much about 'the difficulties of prison life' as it is a careful argument about abolishing the whole judicial system. Blair was then Shadow Home Secretary, working to move the Labour Party to the right on questions of law and order.[5] The first time I read his letter to Griffiths, in the Bill Griffiths Collection at Brunel University, it felt like an archival prank. The thought of Tony Blair holding a comb-bound copy of an Amra publication, with a hand-drawn cover, promising to study it closely, is laughable and improbable. Even after I got over the shock, I could still only conceive of it as an act of futile defiance, the DIY activist text designed to offend the slick rising star of New Labour. But the papers at Brunel contain correspondence with several other Members of Parliament. After Blair became leader of the Labour Party in 1994, Griffiths started writing to his successor, Jack Straw. There are exchanges with the British Medical Association about their policies concerning care and medication in prison; petitions to the European Parliament; and numerous letters to the editors of newspapers. Griffiths was an active campaigner, intervening both on behalf of individual prisoners and in protest at the conditions of British jails as a whole.

The intensity of Griffiths's activity in the early 1990s had a personal element. His friend Delvan, whom he'd met in Seaham, spent time incarcerated at HMP Wandsworth, London and at HMP Highpoint in Suffolk. Griffiths collaborated with him on a least four books: *Review of Brian Greenaway & Notes from Delvan*; *Delvan's Book*; *Star Fish Jail*; and *Seventy-Six Day Wanno, Mississippi and Highpoint Journal*. Each of these works relies on Delvan's account of racist police harassment, judicial procedure and prison.[6] The content of *Seventy-Six Day Wanno* includes reproductions of letters that are, in their original form, held in the Brunel papers. But within the archive, the access to these letters is restricted due to data protection

For a recent commentary on this text, see Robert Sheppard, *The Meaning of Form in Contemporary Innovative Poetry* (New York: Palgrave Macmillan, 2016), 175–81.

[5] In an article for the *New Statesman* in January 1993, Blair would first try out his famous slogan: 'Tough on crime, tough on the causes of crime.' Tony Blair, 'Why Crime is a Socialist Issue', *New Statesman and Society* (29 January 1993).

[6] The ethical question of Griffiths's use of prisoner testimony can only be touched on here. For an extensive critique of Foucault's comparable work in *Group d'Information sur les Prisons*, see Cecile Brich, 'The Groupe d'information sur les prisons: The voice of the prisoners? Or Foucault's?', *Foucault Studies* 5 (2008): 26–47.

laws. In the poem these laws don't apply, and in this way I want to think of the poetry as alchemical, only the metaphor doesn't hold. If this is a labyrinth, then I think I can only find my way by the lighting of archives: the dry overheads, or the more intimate lamps of the library. Or I think of the light in the flat where I live, a mile away from Pentonville Prison, and where I am in relation to the document, observing its circulations. In an interview with Will Rowe, Griffiths calls his poems about prison 'evidence' poems.[7] What kind of evidence is poetry? What does the experience of prison do to a poem? To answer these questions, we need some history.

The first poem in the first volume of Griffiths' *Collected Poems* – unpublished in his lifetime but preserved on a floppy disc of collected works compiled by the poet in 1991 – is called 'Apology'. It is a character sketch of one Barnaby Falk:

> Barnaby Falk was born into a more liberal age, that
> Gave, capable of choosing, opportunity to follow this or change at
> A better course for money, position.
>
> (CP1 13)

The gradient of rhyme in this opening passage (age/gave/change) is loosely maintained over the rest of the forty lines. We learn that Barnaby rides 'a bike whose gears break, / stick in top and take / more effort than a hill is actually worth'. He works a little in a garage, and when the pubs are shut he wanders the roads, 'drinking down whisky, joyful'. In its cadence and in its portrayal of working life, the poem is reminiscent of the early work of Edward Dorn. In the interview with Rowe, Griffiths states that his early models were 'Hopkins, Keats, [Michael] McClure', for their 'sense and sound balance', and that his aim was to find a poetry 'that would cover modern fairly dangerous and fraught themes'.[8] In this first surviving poem there is almost no danger at all. It's only in the closing lines, as Barnaby sleeps off his whisky down the lane, that Griffiths speculates:

> I wonder which first the day-
> Light or police will send him off. Happy
> In any ending anyway, Barnaby.

---

[7] 'Interview with Will Rowe', *Salt Companion to Bill Griffiths* (Cambridge: Salt, 2007), 193.
[8] Ibid., 171.

The police don't seem to threaten Barnaby's happiness or trespass the poet's distant affection for his subject. But from this point onwards, the police will never leave the poet's peripheral vision.[9]

Two sequences that Griffiths wrote in the 1970s, *Cycles* and *War W/Windsor*, deal more directly with the violence of the state apparatus. They are justly celebrated as some of the great achievements of the so-called British Poetry Revival. Published in various configurations and batches, mainly by Griffiths's Pirate Press imprint, the language of both remains radically fresh. Drawn from slang, thieves' cant, Romany, ballads and news reports, Griffiths makes his way in a compressed sprung rhythm. Description turns suddenly to declaration; snatches of talk transform into argument; song breaks out and goes silent. His concision can be brilliant, as in the two-line summary of state power and sovereignty from one of the warm-up poems to *Cycles*: 'watched the queen tell a cop break my nose / and the queen told the cops I was an animal' (*CP1* 48).[10] Though the poems are sometimes obscure and secretive, this laconic edge, with its strange emotional quality, keeps them open. Sometimes, especially reading the three-volume *Collected*, Griffiths seems to drift into distracted eclecticism. But even then the attention is generous, and the possibility of distillation and generative association remains.

Other than a couple of broadsides, Griffiths first appeared in print in the autumn 1972 edition of *Poetry Review*. Though he doesn't quite sound like anything else in the magazine at that point, there are commonalities with the other contributors: the West Indian speech rhythms of James Berry; the transcription experiments of David Antin; the minimalist wordplay of Aram Saroyan. He shares political affinities with Robert Duncan, Jack Hirschman and Tom Pickard. Griffiths became embedded in the London experimental poetry scene of the 1970s, working in the printshop of the National Poetry Centre and contributing to many little magazines. He was an active member of the radical faction of avant-garde poets, led by Eric Mottram,

---

[9] It seems apt to mention here the irony that Brian Bransom Griffiths chose to name himself 'Bill'. In English, 'the old Bill' is a colloquial term for the police.

[10] In Griffiths's obituary, Nicholas Johnson notes: 'His exhibitions of local history in Seaham town hall attracted national attention, and, in 2002, the Queen visited one of his displays. But when the poet Ian Hamilton Finlay was appointed CBE the same year Griffiths declared that there were built-in repellents in his poetry to prevent similar nominations.' Johnson, 'Bill Griffiths – Obituary', *The Independent* (19 September 2007), online: www.independent.co.uk/news/obituaries/bill-griffiths-402904.html [Accessed 26 August 2021].

who took over the Poetry Society for much of the 1970s.[11] His commitment to experimentation involved concrete poems, collaborative sound performances and multi-voice texts.[12] In critical accounts and reminiscences, Griffiths often stands in for something like the spirit of the age. To describe his appearance – tattooed knuckles, motorbike gear, later a uniform of shellsuits – is by now a critical commonplace. Griffiths represents a way of life, and a way of living poetry against the academy, against institutions, against celebrity and complacency. Iain Sinclair, in *Hackney, That Rose Red Empire*, calls Griffiths, 'the real thing, that human catastrophe called poet'.[13] But in this way, the poet becomes an institution or a hero, or a formula. Or at least that's the risk. The antagonisms of the wider social context recede from view.

January 1972 saw the beginning of a wave of protests in British prisons, which culminated in a national strike on 4 August involving 30 institutions and more than 10,000 prisoners. Though there had been riots and disturbances before, this was part of a broader pattern of unrest. The NUM began a six-week strike in January, a dispute which would lead to the collapse of Heath's Government in 1974, and lay the ground for Thatcher's war with the miners in 1984–1985. Between May and December the Angry Brigade prosecutions took place, tried by Justice Melford Stevenson, whom Griffiths would later satirise.[14] In Derry, Northern Ireland, British soldiers killed thirteen people during a Civil Rights demonstration on 30 January. The policy of internment without trial continued, and many Irish Republicans were imprisoned in English jails.[15]

The protests in England were both spontaneous and coordinated, and the demands of the prisoners were delivered to the press and the Home Office by a new organisation: Preservation of the Rights of Prisoners (PROP).[16] PROP tried to establish a union for prisoners,

---

[11] See Peter Barry, *Poetry Wars: British Poetry of the 1970s and the Battle for Earls Court* (Cambridge: Salt, 2006).
[12] See Paula Claire, 'Bill Griffiths: A Severe Case of Hypergraphia', in *The Salt Companion to Bill Griffiths*, 37–50.
[13] Iain Sinclair, *Hackney, That Rose Red Empire* (London: Hamish Hamilton, 2009).
[14] In 'The Praise Song of Justice Melford Stevenson', *CP1* 181. The poem dates from 1977.
[15] See Ruán O'Donnell, *Special Category: The IRA In English Prisons*, 2 vols. (Sallins: Irish Academic Press, 2015).
[16] The most extensive account of the formation of PROP – which I rely on here – is in Mike Fitzgerald, *Prisoners in Revolt* (Harmondsworth: Penguin, 1977). Fitzgerald, a founder member of the group, who later became Vice-Chancellor of Thames Valley University, tends to emphasise the role played by PROP in the protests. For a measured critique of PROP, its methods and legacy, see the unsigned article, 'Long Hot Summer of "72"', in *Taking Liberties* (May 1998).

taking inspiration from Californian prison struggles, especially the strike at Folsom in 1970 and the Attica uprising of 1971.[17] In a five-point statement from 1973, the London chapter of PROP explains that while they support 'alternative policies more constructive than imprisonment', they demand in the short term a programme of maximum rights for prisoners. These rights are set out in a list of twenty-four demands, relating to legal representation, education, visits, voting, parole and other elements of prison life. Full membership of PROP was reserved for 'any person who is or has been an inmate of any detention centre, remand centre, approved school, Borstal prison, or other penal establishment'.[18] Only full members were entitled to vote and hold official positions, which meant that – in theory – PROP was led by those with first-hand knowledge of incarceration. Griffiths himself spent some nights on remand at Brixton prison in 1971, suggesting in an interview that the experience left him 'determined never to write the sort of poem that is simply entertaining, that helps people to carry on enjoying the world as it is'.[19]

The protests of 1972 ended one by one. The Prison Officers Association (POA) initiated a 'get tough' policy in retribution, restricting visits, classes and entertainment. After further disturbances at Arbury and Dartmoor in late August and early September, the POA met the Home Secretary Robert Carr, who had consistently refused to recognise PROP. Prison officers were given permission to hand out further punishment to 1,700 men, including long stretches in solitary confinement and the loss of as much as two years' remission. While I have found no evidence Griffiths was involved in these events or in PROP, this is the atmosphere in which his first poems were published. When extracts from 'Cycles on Dover Borstal', 'Terzetto: Brixton Prison' and 'To Johnny Prez' appeared in *Poetry Review* in Autumn 1972, the memory of the most extensive prison demonstrations in British history would have been fresh in the reader's mind.

Following the setbacks in the protests, and a split within PROP itself (between the Hull and London factions), some of the most interesting work the organisation undertook was in publishing

---

[17] See Griffiths's late poem 'The Attica Retribution', collected in *The Lion Man & Others* (London: Veer, 2008).

[18] From a single sheet document, 'Statement by London Group of PROP/Prisoners' Charter', undated, *c.*1973. Collection of the author.

[19] Interview with Bill Griffiths by Bridget Penney and Paul Holman (14 September 1993), online: www.invisiblebooks.co.uk/?page_id=341 [Accessed 25 October 2023].

accounts of prison by prisoners. The first major example was Brian Stratton's *Who Guards the Guards?* (1973), recording the systematic brutality which led to the riot at Parkhurst Prison on the Isle of Wight in October 1969.[20] The second, *Don't Mark His Face: Hull Prison Riot 1976* (1976) features testimony and analysis smuggled out of various prisons in the aftermath of a major disturbance at Hull.[21] Another dozen pamphlets covering topical issues and controversies were issued between 1973 and 1974. These books are still powerful. This isn't only because of the violence they recount; in general, these works avoid sensationalism and never luxuriate in brutality. It's rare to hear the voice of prisoners at any length, and it's rarer still to hear them unedited and in a context of their own making. I want to suggest that Griffiths shared at least one aim with PROP: he wanted to amplify the prisoner, to make the prisoner heard over what one poem calls the 'grave police music' of the penal system ('Cycle Two (Dover Borstal)', *CP1*, 69).

Of course, Griffiths' loyalty to aesthetic experimentation places him at some distance from the documentary accounts of prison riots and investigative reports published by PROP. The poems in *Cycles* are concerned with perception, and the agitated dynamic of control and release. The opening of 'Cycle Three: H.M. Prison Brixton' is typical:

> To the sickish kids
> nothing. all the epileptics,
> taken like no monster swans
> prison
> like houses
> going in a sort of late dog
> watching, hey master –
> all built,
> blocks, octagons
>   (*CP1* 70)

This poetry poses serious challenges to interpretation. We can understand the 'sickish kids' to be the inmates, both subject to the socio-psychological category of 'deviancy' and the physical

---

[20] Brian Stratton, *Who Guards the Guards?* (London: PROP, 1973). The version I have seen, a slim red paperback, is described as the third edition, printed at the War on Want building on Caledonian Road, London. It gives thanks to rock band The Stranglers and the students of Oxford Polytechnic for helping to fund the publication.
[21] PROP, *Don't Mark His Face: Hull Prison Riot 1976* (London: PROP, 1976). This volume contains a contribution from Jake Prescott, convicted in 1972 as a member of the Angry Brigade.

side effects of imprisonment. They receive 'nothing', no treatment or alleviation for their suffering. The 1973 PROP pamphlet, *The Scandal of British Prisons* focuses on the maltreatment of prisoners with epilepsy in Canterbury, Stafford and Strangeways, and it's possible Griffiths is thinking of this issue. But Griffiths makes a negative comparison with 'monster swans': I imagine the swan spreading its wings, hard to control and to capture. The comparison is ironic because swans come under royal protection while the prisoner detained at Her Majesty's pleasure is in these circumstances more like a dog, tail between legs.[22] This situation, Griffiths reminds us, is 'all built': the prison is not natural, but can and should be changed.

Griffiths's work can be placed alongside several other sequences in the British experimental tradition that deal with incarceration and with the law. A provisional list would include Barry MacSweeney's *Jury Vet*, written between 1979 and 1981, a delirious and violent engagement with Official Secrets Act trials and the beginnings of Thatcherism; John James's *War* (1978) and *A Former Boiling* (1979), Eric Mottram's *Legal Poems* (1986) and Maggie O'Sullivan's *her/story:eye* (1994–1999), each of which deals in different ways with internment and the hunger strikes at Long Kesh in Northern Ireland; Geraldine Monk's *Interregnum* (1994), a treatment of witch trials in early modern England punctuated by 'Gaol Songs'; Anna Mendelssohn's entire oeuvre, which I'll look at in the following chapter; Tom Pickard's reconstruction of the story of a border outlaw and folk hero, *The Ballad of Jamie Allan* (2007); and most recently, the incandescent late work of Sean Bonney, whom Griffiths mentored in London in the early 2000s.

Pickard is perhaps closest to Griffiths in both aesthetic sensibility and lived experience.[23] His work spans genres, from the pulp novel

---

[22] Alan Halsey notes: 'Animals clearly fascinate Griffiths and appear in many of his poems. They are "outlaws" without being formally outlawed; they live outside human jurisdiction, although human jurisdiction does affect their lives and they have no choice in the matter. They live in human consciousness and at the same time far beyond it; they seem to us deeply emblematic but we suppose they inhabit a world without emblems.' Halsey, 'Pirate Press: A Bibliographical Excursion', *The Salt Companion to Bill Griffiths*, 60–1.

[23] The two published a book together, *Tyne Txts* (Seaham: Amra, 2004). Griffiths's section, 'Newcastle from a Van Window', is dedicated to Ray Gilbert, a member of the

Guttersnipe (1971) to the radio documentary *Jarrow March* (1976), the social history *We Make Ships* (1989), and film and television documentaries about fellow poets. With his first wife, Connie, he founded the Morden Tower reading series in Newcastle in 1964, a pivotal feature of the city's working class and politically committed art. Pickard's autobiographical writing records the struggle to maintain the autonomy of the Tower in the face of North Eastern Association of the Arts (NEAA) bureaucracy and the opportunism of regional politicians. It also records his struggle for independence and livelihood as a writer, faced with harassment and surveillance from the dole office and the police.[24] One early work – 'City Council Poem' – portrays Pickard's confrontation with the local Lord Sherriff:

> You said, when I asked you
> what your powers were
> that you could lock me up
> if I caused some disturbance
> in the town
>
> but who, proud pig,
> if you chose to knock me down
> would lock you up?[25]

Though he keeps his diction and syntax much closer to ordinary speech, Pickard, like Griffiths, writes with absolute disdain for authority and from a position informed by the realities of police harassment and imprisonment. We greet the young poet here as a representative of the class struggle, embodying Walter Benjamin's description of 'the courage, humour, cunning, and fortitude' which emerges in the 'fight for crude and material things'.[26]

Pickard's great Northumbrian predecessor was Basil Bunting, contemporary of Ezra Pound, Ford Madox Ford and Louis Zukofsky. When the younger poet made contact with him in the early 1960s, Bunting was working as a newspaper sub-editor and had written almost no poetry in the previous decade. With his long poem *Briggflatts*

Toxteth Two who spent thirty-six years in prison on alleged murder charges. Griffiths contributed to the campaign to free Gilbert with his long poem *Mr Tapscott* (Durham: Amra, 1998).

[24] Tom Pickard, 'From *Rough Music (Ruff Muzhik)*', *Chicago Review* 46, no. 1 (2000): 9–36. See also his first publication, 'Teenage Unemployment – What It Really Feels Like', *Anarchy* 35 (1963): 384–5.

[25] Tom Pickard, *Hero Dust* (London: Allison and Busby, 1979), 14.

[26] Walter Benjamin, 'Theses on the Philosophy of History', *Illuminations*, ed. Hannah Arendt, trans. Harry Zorn (London: Pimlico, 1999), 255.

(1966), he secured a place as a revered elder statesman of the modernist resurgence, particularly in the North of England, but also across Britain as a whole and into North America. Bunting, too, belongs to the lineage of anti-carceral poetics. A Quaker, he had been one of just over a thousand absolutist conscientious objectors during the First World War, meaning that he refused to undertake any form of national service and was imprisoned as a result. In his biography of the poet, Richard Burton argues convincingly that Bunting was probably one of the prisoners whose testimony was used in *English Prisons Today: Being the Report of the Prison System Enquiry Committee* (1922), a major text of early prison reform in England.[27] Bunting had several further brushes with the law, including his arrest while drunk and disorderly at a hotel in Paris in 1923, which resulted in several days in prison.[28] These events clearly inform his first great work, 'Villon', which unfolds his signature chiselled music after opening: 'In the dark, in fetters, / on bended elbows I supported my weak back / hulloing to muffled walls blank again, / unresonant.'[29] The poem, then, becomes the resonant space, achieved against this memory of incarceration.[30]

But Bunting differs, in crucial ways, from Pickard and Griffiths. Kenneth Cox gives an implicit character sketch in the concluding paragraphs of his obituary:

> Many of the persons approved of in Bunting's poetry as well as several of the writers he translated conform to a type: an upright man of modest origin, not inexperienced in the ways of power but excluded from office, devotes himself in retreat or retirement to moderate pleasures and the exercise of a skill he does not expect to see rewarded.[31]

This coyness about the 'ways of power' is an important aspect of Bunting's mystique. His literary neglect was real: he struggled to find

---

[27] Richard Burton, *A Strong Song Tows Us: The Life of Basil Bunting* (Oxford: Infinite Ideas, 2013), 73–4. Stephen Hobhouse and A. Fenner Brockway, eds., *English Prisons Today: Being the Report of the Prison System Enquiry Committee* (London: Longman, 1922).

[28] In a letter to Eric Mottram, Bunting states that his arrest was 'chiefly for kicking a cop'. Quoted in Bill Griffiths, 'Basil Bunting and Eric Mottram', *Chicago Review* 44, nos. 3–4 (1998): 112.

[29] Bunting, *Collected Poems* (London; Fulcrum, 1968), 13. See Claire Pascolini-Campbell, 'Prison Writing and Parody', *François Villon in English Poetry: Translation and Influence* (London: Boydell & Brewer, 2018), 114–40.

[30] Kenneth Cox observes: '"The architecture of my poems is", as he once remarked, "my first and last consideration".' Cox, 'Basil Bunting', *The Art of Language: Selected Essays*, ed. Jenny Petherby (Chicago: Flood, 2016), 92.

[31] Ibid., 94.

publishers; he never won awards; for his final three decades he lived in poverty, trying to support his family on an insufficient civil list pension and the occasional teaching and speaking tour of the United States and Canada.[32] Yet at the same time, Bunting was championed by younger poets, and died with his work in print and widely available. His gruff dislike of literary London, of academics, of fools, burnishes his anti-establishment credentials. But, as Alex Niven writes, 'Bunting's lifelong antipathy to the British establishment was conspicuously absent throughout the forties, as he undertook work in Persia for the R.A.F. and M.I.6.'[33]

The extent of Bunting's espionage is unknown, but his intermittent presence in Persia between 1944 and 1952 – first as Vice-Consul of Isfahan and then as a *Times* journalist – suggests that he was involved in furthering British colonial interests in the region, particularly regarding the Anglo-Iranian Oil Company.[34] His anecdotes are filled with escapades that suggest both his affiliation with power and his exercise of power. He smokes opium with the head of the Persian Secret Police.[35] He tells a story about his friend Ezra Horesh, the punchline of which is about hitting 'an Arab' with the handle of a jack for insubordination, and then paying off a magistrate.[36] We can only speculate about whether Bunting was directly responsible for anyone's arrest or incarceration during the increasingly chaotic lead-up to the CIA- and British-backed coup of 1953. He himself was expelled from the country in April 1952. Perhaps living in wartime tends to stretch idealism thin: but we saw that Bunting was unwavering in his ethical stance during the First World War. His compromises in the post-war period make him a much more politically ambiguous figure than Griffiths or Pickard. The comparison, in turn, allows us to grasp just how confrontational and antagonistic

[32] Peter Quartermain writes that 'In the middle 1950s Basil Bunting and his family, valued servants of the state, were supported with food parcels sent by Ezra Pound, inmate of St Elizabeth's Hospital for the Criminally Insane. The British treatment of Basil Bunting is a national disgrace.' See 'Six Plaints and a Lament for Basil Bunting', *Conjunctions* 8 (1985): 175.
[33] Alex Niven, 'Towards a New Architecture: Basil Bunting's Postwar Reconstruction', *ELH* 81, no. 1 (2014): 359.
[34] A recently discovered 1985 interview with Norman Darbyshire, a British spy directly involved in the removal of Mohammed Mossadegh in 1953, names Bunting (mistranscribed as 'Basil Bumley') as one of his associates. See 'Transcript of Interview with Norman Darbyshire for *End of Empire*, c. 1985', via the National Security Archive at George Washington University, online: https://nsarchive.gwu.edu/document/20489-national-security-archive [Accessed 25 October 2023].
[35] Burton, *A Strong Song Tows Us*, 312.
[36] Ibid., 315.

the poets and poetry of the 1960s and 1970s could become, and to understand this as part of their achievement. Their work is, politically speaking, an advance.[37]

By the mid-1970s Pickard was living in London. He was awarded a C. Day Lewis fellowship in 1976 – Linton Kwesi Johnson received one the following year – which involved teaching for one day a week at Rutherford School, West London.[38] Soon after beginning the fellowship, he was arrested on drug smuggling charges and held on remand in Brixton Prison. His wily account of the circumstances and trial, *More Pricks than Prizes*, concludes with 'Wing Commander Bunting' taking the stand as a character witness (along with Eric Mottram and the film-maker Lindsay Anderson).[39] Pickard was acquitted, but he records the experience of prison in a searing poem, 'Rat Palace', which begins:

> the ears are closed
> snapped off and blocked
> death behind the eyes
>
> how can we help each other?
>
> some lives can't be lived
> it's time to assume a more
> rational perspective[40]

Like Bunting's 'Villon' we begin with claustrophobia and limitations to sound and vision. Pickard's plaintive question – 'how can we help each other?' – is both an address to his loved ones outside the prison, and a preparing of the grounds of solidarity with his fellow prisoners. The poem makes direct accusations:

> the guard dogs in Brixton are better fed
> than the inmates
>
> 30 per cent of prison staff in Wandsworth
> are badge-wearing members of the National Front
>
> tax the dole   build more cells

---

[37] To make a schematic pairing: we can view Griffiths's work – as pamphleteer, translator, prisoner, theorist – as a kind of camp anarchist antithesis to the work of Ezra Pound. Pickard is like a class struggle adaptation of his mentor.

[38] Pickard talks about the award and his experiences of schooling more generally in 'In the Original: Angela Neustatter Meets Tom Pickard', *The Guardian* (12 October 1976).

[39] Tom Pickard, *More Pricks Than Prizes* (Boston: Pressed Wafer, 2010). For an overview of Pickard's 1970s work, see Eric Mottram, 'Tom Pickard', *Poetry Information* 18 (1978): 68.

[40] Pickard, 'Rat Palace', *Hero Dust* (London: Allison & Busby, 1979), 64.

The prison is presented as an instrument for the management of surplus populations and as a site for the consolidation of racism and fascism within the state apparatus. Refusing the work of collecting 'shit parcels' – bags of shit thrown from cell windows during lock-up – Pickard declines the role of the volunteer, stating 'I'm not one // these laws are meant to break us'. This shift into the collective is powerful: the prisoner isn't *one* but many, and the collective subject is where defiance comes to rest.

For John James, born in Cardiff to Irish immigrants in 1939, the prison also came to occupy a central place in his writing as the decade wore on. He announced in *War* (1978) the beginning of the 1980s:

the 80s
start here →

2,000 detainees

a very monotonous sound
propping you/head against the wall[41]

The 2,000 detainees were the prisoners at Long Kesh in Northern Ireland. Since the policy of internment without trial began in 1971, members of the Provisional IRA and Irish Nationalist Liberation Army (INLA) had been classified as prisoners of war. They were allowed freedom of congregation, they were not required to work and they were permitted to wear their own clothes rather than prison uniforms. But this status was withdrawn in 1976, leading to protests in which the Republican prisoners went naked, or wore only blankets, refusing to 'slop out' their cells. In 1980, this escalated into the hunger strikes, which climaxed with the death of twenty-seven-year-old Bobby Sands in May 1981. Ten other prisoners died during the course of the strike. The poetry John James wrote at the turn of the decade furiously confronts British foreign policy in Ireland, particularly the conditions at Long Kesh, linking it to the suppression of internal left-wing dissent.

Directly following the extract quoted above is a quotation from a newspaper:

Greater Manchester police chief James
Anderton has been in the news of late.
He has now acquired a new assistant

[41] John James, *Collected Poems* (Cambridge: Salt, 2002), 154. Further references will be given in the body of the text.

chief constable who was formerly Chief
Superintendent for operational training
of the Royal Ulster Constabulary in
Belfast, a Dermot O'Brien.
(154)

This use of documentary content mirrors Pickard's deployment of oral history and first-hand reporting in the text of *Jarrow March*. We can trace it back to a number of modernist precursors, including William Carlos Williams, who included local newspaper reports in his epic *Paterson* (1946–1958). As Williams wrote elsewhere, 'It is difficult / to get the news from poems', but clearly for James it is possible to get poems from the news.[42] The Romanian-French avant-garde poet Tristan Tzara, whom Lee Harwood had sought out in the early 1960s, and whose work James translated in *Letters from Sarah* (1973), gave instructions in one of his Dada manifestos to take scissors to the newspaper and begin assembling poetry from the language found there.[43] But the significance of the passage above is not simply formal. While James had always written about working-class life, and was a member of the Communist Party, *War* marked a sudden and aggressive politicisation of his poetry. In an atmosphere of escalating Cold War paranoia with fears of nuclear war, left-wing radicals entertained anxieties about the Emergency Powers Act of 1920 and the deployment of troops 'at home'.[44] James's highlighting of the links between the police forces in Manchester and Belfast emphasises the continuum between repressive features of the state, and this became the dominant theme of his work as the new decade began.

James responded to the atmosphere of crisis by throwing himself into youth subcultures, bringing the influence of punk and dub reggae into his writing.[45] The books he published at this time, stapled in the

[42] William Carlos Williams, 'Asphodel, That Greeny Flower', *Collected Poems, vol. 2: 1939–1962*, ed. Christopher MacGowan (Manchester: Carcanet, 2000), 318.

[43] Tristan Tzara, quoted in *Chanson Dada: Selected Poems*, ed. and trans. Lee Harwood (Toronto: Coach House, 1987), 125; John James, *Letters from Sarah* (London: Ferry, 1973).

[44] See Tony Bunyan, *The History and Practice of the Political Police in Britain* (London: Quartet, 1977), 257–88. Brigadier Frank Kitson's *Low Intensity Operations: Subversion, Insurgency, Peace-Keeping* (London: Faber & Faber, 1971) had outlined the policy of counterinsurgency in Ireland, tactics developed during colonial rule in Kenya.

[45] We might also point to Amiri Baraka's Marxist-Leninist works of the 1970s as a hitherto unacknowledged inspiration. Compare Baraka's line 'Black studies pimps in interesting tweed jackets' ('Today', *Hard Facts* (Newark: Revolutionary Communist League, 1975), 15) with James's 'Feminist studies pimp in interesting denim' in *War* (1978), *Collected Poems*, 144.

left-hand corner and mimeographed, have more in common with zines and lyric sheets than his earlier texts, handsomely produced with cover illustrations by contemporary British artists.[46] In his three long poems written in 1979 – 'A Former Boiling', 'Toasting' and 'Inaugural Address' – he surveys the history of British colonialism, comparing the brutal suppression of the Mau Mau revolt against British rule in Kenya in the 1950s with the situation in contemporary Ireland. The most extraordinary of these poems is 'A Former Boiling', which carries a dedication to The Human League, at that point an avant-garde New Wave band (founded in 1977), whose minimal synthesiser masterpiece 'Being Boiled' gives the poem its title.[47] While James treats the lyrics to a situationist process of *détournement*, describing 'a synthesiser whiplash that I couldn't hear' and naming the members of the band, the poem repeatedly names itself as a radio station: 'this is Radio Shack / calling | or if that's Radio Ethiopia / this is Radio Splott / calling'. Through this device, what James *does* hear is 'Voices / in the H-BLOCKS calling/ | saying DESTROY' (161). With the H-blocks of Long Kesh echoing with the punk call to 'destroy', the poem turns into a dirge or incantation lasting 150 lines, at the heart of which is the following denunciation:

> on the I&I line
> on the Kevin Barry line
> on the Tom Barry line
> on the Michael Collins line
> on the Who shot Michael Collins line
> on the how many boys in your school were called Michael Collins
>   line
> on the Lord Boyd of Merton line
> on the Alan Lennox-Boyd line
>
> HO   LA
> HO   LA
>   (164)

These lines require some unpacking. Kevin Barry, Tom Barry and Michael Collins were all prominent figures in the Irish War of Independence in the 1920s and members of the IRA. Kevin Barry

---

[46] For a detailed and sensitive account of James's engagement with visual art, see Peter Cartwright, '"art is a balm to the brain / & gives a certain resolution": The Impact of, and Engagement With, the Visual Arts in John James's Writing', in *The Salt Companion to John James*, ed. Simon Perril (Cambridge: Salt, 2010), 40–58.
[47] Human League, *Being Boiled / Circus of Death*, 7" single (Edinburgh: Fast Product, 1978).

was tortured and executed in 1920, and Michael Collins, Chairman of the Provisional Government, was killed by British troops in an ambush in 1922. Lord Boyd of Merton, meanwhile, was Secretary of State for the Colonies in the 1950s and was sent by Thatcher in 1979 to observe the elections in Rhodesia.[48] Later in the poem he is joined by Lord Carrington, Foreign Secretary in Thatcher's first cabinet, described by James as 'an unelected parasite on the Nation' (165). The Hola camp was a British prison in Kenya, the site of routine abuse and torture, culminating in the Hola massacre of 1959.[49] James's poem asserts with intensity that this is not simply history to be moved on from. It requires something more: 'THIS AIN'T NOSTALGIA / THIS IS EXORCISM' (162).

As these examples suggest, Griffiths wasn't alone in writing formally challenging and politically committed poetry about prison and prisoners. This militant working-class experimentation runs parallel to, and sometimes crosses over with, the activist texts by Linton Kwesi Johnson and others I looked at in the previous chapter. Both Pickard and Griffiths spent time at Brixton police station and in Brixton prison; and James, as I've argued, puts forward an electrifying critique of British imperialism. But Griffiths brought his prison poems to a temporary halt in 1978, in a work of desolate prose called *An Account of the End*. Published by Richard Tabor's Lobby Press, *An Account of the End* begins by narrating a series of arrests and the disintegration of the relationships of the poet's closest friends. Part Five turns to the deaths of men in prison and police custody:

> It is specific: Stephen Smith hanged himself in a punishment cell in Wormwood Scrubs on the 8th August 1974 following a programme of mistreatment including beatings, having his glasses smashed and so on, alleged that is by two hundred prisoners whose petition was smuggled out and then ignored.[50]

---

[48] Lord Lennox-Boyd's son, Mark Lennox-Boyd, became Parliamentary Private Secretary to Thatcher in 1988.

[49] See Caroline Elkins, *Imperial Reckoning: The Untold Story of Britain's Gulag in Kenya* (London: Jonathan Cape, 2005).

[50] Bill Griffiths, *An Account of the End* (Cambridge: Lobby Press, 1978), unpaginated. Griffiths also mentions the attempted suicide of George Ince, who was tried by Judge Melford Stevenson and convicted based solely on the visual identification of four witnesses. He was later acquitted. See the report by JAIL: Martin Walker and Bernadette Brittain, *Identification Evidence: Practices and Malpractices* (London: Jail, 1978), 4–5.

In December 1977, Griffiths had written to Eric Mottram asking him for a character reference in the hope that he could access the inquest report about the death of Michael Dell, who drowned while attempting to escape a Borstal in Cambridgeshire.[51] It's not clear if this application was successful, but in a multi-voiced text titled 'Novella Three', snatches of testimony related to a drowning are cut up and presented in increasingly complex arrangements. The final of the twenty sections reads:

in the main air pass– ages	lung uniformly much	no mark of re– straint
no external mark	simple immersion	immersion alive and

       *   *   *

at the lips & nostrils	Frothed watery fluid in the throat	normal of any kind
	Librium…present confirming	

(CP1 327)

The text explores contingency and chance, but there's a wariness and weariness in play. Griffiths mutes the passionate music of his earlier sequences, and instead subjects the source text to a kind of dissection. But this is aesthetically fussy, with a directive at the start explaining that 'Where two phrases are separated by a horizontal line, they are not to be read consecutively: the reader is to travel to another part of the section and then return to read the 2nd of the alternatives' (*CP1* 322). Rather than countering the violence of the carceral regime – to perform an 'exorcism', as John James would have it – this poem can only do the work of 'confirming', a seam at its end, the poet going through the motions.

---

[51] Eric Mottram Collection, King's College London. Mottram: 5/100/1–36.

In *An Account of the End*, Griffiths strips his work of invention, soberly judging his poetry against the traces these bodies leave behind. In one bitterly sarcastic passage he reflects both on the kinds of material I examined in the first part of this chapter and on the position of the avant-garde poetry culture:

> I take a look back through all the leaflets of the early 70's. They are so fierce and so straight [...] Now it's just a matter of pointing the worst law-breakers out and all will go well. There's a better state network too covering the arts for the whole country. If I'm favoured they may even print this for me, as there is no way I can afford it.[52]

The collapse of his faction's involvement in the Poetry Society – where Griffiths helped to run the printshop – brought about a crisis in Griffiths's writing. Commenting self-reflexively on his listing of the dead, Griffiths writes, 'The plain compilation is a danger'. But the work of poetry is suspended until 'its good rhythms get to mean more than every aeon-rub and tear of instituted obliteration'. At this point the thread goes slack. Though the law continues as a theme throughout his writing in the 1980s, especially seen through the work of Boethius, the prison itself falls away. To pick it up again we have to jump ahead to the 1990s.

On Sunday, 1 April 1990, prisoners staged a protest in the chapel of Strangeways Prison, Manchester. After the sermon they refused to leave, and as the anger mounted the prison officers began to evacuate the premises. After seizing keys from a guard, prisoners began unlocking the cells and quickly took control of the jail. The resulting siege and rooftop protest lasted twenty-five days.[53] As in 1972, the disturbances spread to other prisons and came at a time of national unrest. On 31 March in central London the Poll Tax riots had forced the final defeat of Thatcher's Government, leading to her resignation in November. Soon after, the UK signed the Maastricht Treaty, integrating economic and fiscal policy with the EU, and preparing the ground for EU conventions on human rights and justice. This is the context in which Griffiths returned to writing directly about prison.

---

[52] Griffiths, *An Account of the End*, unpaginated.
[53] The most extensive account of the events can be found in Nicki Jameson and Eric Allison, *Strangeways 1990: A Serious Disturbance* (London: Larkin Publications, 1995).

The essay Griffiths sent Tony Blair in 1993, *HMP: Revising Prison*, begins with the critique of a television programme about HMP Wandsworth. Though Griffiths doesn't name the film, it was a three-part series entitled *Turning the Screws* directed by the influential documentary maker and criminologist, Roger Graef. Graef came to prominence in the 1980s with a series of films about police and policing. The focus of the Wandsworth documentary is on an industrial dispute between the POA and the Home Office. In 1989, a new shift system had been introduced, leading to a ten-day strike by the POA, during which the Metropolitan Police were brought in to control the prison. The dispute was never completely resolved, and following the Strangeways uprising, the POA were concerned about the conditions for prisoner association, the time spent by inmates outside their cells. In the preface to *Star Fish Jail*, written at the same time as *HMP: Revising Prison*, Griffiths complains that under the pretence of neutrality, the film reproduces: 'a pre-established mythology of a three-tier society: a decision-making elite, a hard-working and dedicated corps of middle-men, and a substratum composed of characterless, nameless beings who inexplicably keep falling down stairs'.[54] This is an accurate description. The narrative of *Turning the Screws* revolves largely around the chain-smoking union rep and the reforming prison governor, who occasionally quotes *Macbeth*. Each hour-long episode removes us further from the prison, until the final hearing at the Home Office where a repeat of the 1989 strike is averted. Though Griffiths notes in *HMP: Revising Prison* that there are two moments where the façade slips and we are presented with shots of a wounded prisoner and an officer disciplining an inmate, these are at best light pricks of conscience. The protagonists are the prison officers, the antagonists are the management; the prisoners make little impression.

Where Graef starts from the standpoint of authority, Griffiths sides only and always with the prisoners.[55] In *HMP: Revising Prison*

---

[54] Bill Griffiths, *Star Fish Jail* (Seaham: Amra, 1993). There are many variances to this edition, some of which are recorded by Alan Halsey in *CP3* 513–14.

[55] Graef is also the author of two books of documentary narrative. The first, *Talking Blues: The Police in their Own Words* (London: Collins Harvill, 1989) is an 'emotional mosaic' of British and Northern Irish police officers (11). The second, *Living Dangerously* (London: HarperCollins, 1992), features interviews with young offenders on an 'extreme probation' course in South London. While he expresses sympathy with his young subjects, and offers them material assistance, his position is always that of the liberal reformer. As Foucault argues: 'Prison "reform" is virtually contemporary with the prison itself: it constitutes, as it were, its programme.' Michel Foucault, *Discipline and Punish*, trans. Alan Sheridan (London: Vintage Books, 1977), 234.

his argument moves both outwards and inwards, from solitary confinement and institutional violence to Britain's imperial past. The regime of the prison comes to rest as the keystone of the system, the point at which the state's dynamic of internal suppression and external aggression is forged and sustained. As he says: 'The use of prison to try and re-establish past ideals of submission and control seems more a model of extinction than any way forward.'[56] Griffiths arrives at this conclusion by way of the immediate materials at hand: television, newspapers and his own experiences. While he was certainly familiar with Foucault and other sociological studies, he does not rely on theory for his claims. His prose is restrained, as it is in other contemporary essays such as *In Rebuttal of the Guardian: On the Role of Solitary Confinement in British Prisons – Call for an Inquiry* (1994) and *Some Notes on the Metropolitan Police, London: With Some Footnotes on the Magistrates' Courts* (1994).[57] He avoids the rhetoric of pathos, preferring instead to present his case with gentle irony. In what may be his first published essay, *A Note on Democracy* (1974), he leaves a generous margin for notes and supplies a return address for feedback and improvement.

But it's possible that the essay Tony Blair promised to study closely wasn't an essay at all. The two texts written in collaboration with Delvan are hybrid works: both *Star Fish Jail* and *Seventy-Six Day Wanno* smuggle poetry in the guise of prose, letters and diaries in the guise of poems and spoken testimony shaped by hand. A casual glance would hardly register the complexity.

Seventy-Six Day Wanno, Mississippi and Highpoint Journal – to give its full title – begins on 23 April 1993. The previous day, the teenager Stephen Lawrence had been murdered by a racist gang at a bus stop in South London. The next day the Provisional IRA would bomb Bishopsgate. Neither event is mentioned in the text, which details Griffiths's friendship with the young prisoner, Delvan.[58] The book is laid out as A4 landscape, split into two even columns. On the left-hand side runs Delvan's journal, progressing chronologically, and beginning with his arrival at Wandsworth. He is almost immediately assaulted by prison guards:

---

[56] Bill Griffiths, *HMP: Revising Prison* (Seaham: Amra, 1994).
[57] Both of these pamphlets were self-issued: *In Rebuttal of the Guardian: On the Role of Solitary Confinement in British Prisons – Call for an Inquiry* (Seaham: Amra, 1994); *Some Notes on the Metropolitan Police, London: With Some Footnotes on the Magistrates' Courts* (Seaham: Amra, 1994).
[58] Though Delvan notes at one point that he sits next to an IRA supporter while being transported from Wandsworth to Highpoint.

> I got sentenced to five months today. I am in Wandsworth prison, not the greatest place on earth, have got off to a seemingly bad start. Got a little bit of hassle off a screw for blanking him, when asked if I was ready to get banged up. He was not happy about this, he called four of his mates up to my cell, walked in slapped me across the face three or four times. I had to hold my hands behind my back to stop myself lashing out.[59]

The incident is retold in more dramatic fashion in *Star Fish Jail*:

> He sort of went a bit wild, him: 'You black bastard,' he yells at me,
> 'You black shit: you see this whistle?
> All I need is blow on this, see: and there'll be eight of us
> all over you, yes, and: off to the block head-down [...][60]

The right-hand side of the page is varied. It begins with a letter from Delvan to Bill, and is followed by Bill's reply. These are the letters inaccessible at the archive in Brunel under data protection laws. As the book progresses, short poems from the incidents Delvan reports start to appear. Over the course of his seventy-six-day stretch, Delvan is moved to Highpoint Prison, and we read about the bureaucratic obstacles this creates: his visitors, who aren't informed of the move, turn up at a prison where he is no longer held; his money and other personal belongings aren't transferred with him; he has trouble getting help with his housing benefit forms. Between *76-Day Wanno* and *Star Fish Jail* we are presented with a racist, violent, petty institution, and a portrait of survival within its confines.

Griffiths is sensitive to the special status of documents within the prison system. Unlike Graef, he makes the material conditions and terms of the book's composition absolutely clear. In one passage, after Delvan has been transferred to Highpoint, we learn about the letters:

> Letters are safe.
> They are sealed, taken to Cambridge and posted.
> It's better and quicker than Wanno.
> The letters come in,
> and if there's one for you,
> your names posted on a noticeboard so

---

[59] Bill Griffiths with Delvan McIntosh, *Seventy-Six Day Wanno, Mississippi and Highpoint Journal* (Seaham: Amra, 1993), unpaginated.
[60] Bill Griffiths, *Star Fish Jail* (Seaham: Amra, 1993), collected in *CP3* 191–209 (193).

you know to go
and collect it.[61]

There is a strange tenderness to the poems. Though the content is drawn from Delvan's correspondence and conversation, the quotations aren't exact. Griffiths instead imitates his friend's voice, finding in it a weakened poetry. The prison routine is still too demeaning for the 'good rhythms' he put aside in *Account of the End*, the full music of *Cycles* or *War W/Windsor*. Instead, the march back and forth from the cell is marked by tired end-rhymes, 'Wanno', 'so', 'go'. Where the earlier sequences placed the burden of interpretation on the reader, here Griffiths emphasises the formal and structural devices of his writing. He makes the process of composition visible.

There is, however, one major exception: *76-Day Wanno* was published in two different variations, and only one features the poems. The editions are otherwise identical. It seems likely to me that the poems – later made into a longer standalone sequence called 'How Highpoint is Better Than Wandsworth' – were written to obscure the letters Bill sent to Delvan. These letters talk about a separate legal case under review in the Magistrates' Court: they are, perhaps, the wrong kind of evidence. The poems, then, are practical, necessary, tactical. Griffiths is a resourceful poet, and midway through *76-Day Wanno* he explains to Delvan that he's working on another sequence, which will be issued in a signed limited edition to raise funds for the outstanding magistrates' fine. This is *Star Fish Jail*, issued in forty copies as 'a gesture of support from the printing world'. A few pages later we learn that the book has raised £290.18. With full disclosure, Griffiths tells Delvan and his reader that the 18 pence was 'someone paying for a stamp'. He describes the book as 'my only successful publication ever'.

The text of *Star Fish Jail* is in two parts, telling the story of Delvan's imprisonment, his childhood and adolescence. It is a work of sustained anger, analysis and poetic invention, and deserves to be more widely known. It presents a kind of prison writing that recalls the political engagement of the 1970s, and it fuses documentary engagement with poetic experimentation in a tradition that stretches back to Muriel Rukeyser's *The Book of the Dead* (1938). At the highest points of intensity, the division between Bill and Delvan disappears, leaving the poem to speak with painful clarity:

---

[61] As discussed below, the poems only appear in some variants of *Seventy-Six Day Wanno, Mississippi and Highpoint Journal*. They were later published as a sequence in their own right, 'How Highpoint is Better than Wandsworth', CP3 465–72 (467).

Grave Police Music: Anti-Carceral Poetics **215**

Is it act? drama?: It's me causing it all?
and only I move?: yet you have not felt the weight of this ziggurat,
seen the slant: heard the broad cattle-groans,
been picked out: or bred to
or congratulated: or admired
for this grade of de-manning: this culture of sovereign shit:
the golden blood,
the complete overturning: that sets your taboos safe, outside,
keeps that normality self-placed: this is ritual.
Meaningless here: to make sense there.

(CP3 199)

The barbarity of the prison system is intolerable. The poem makes it impossible for the reader to forget the existence of the people incarcerated at Wandsworth or at Highpoint or across the prison estate. The European Committee for the Prevention of Torture found, in 2019, evidence of indiscriminate use of violence by staff on prisoners at the three prisons it visited (Wormwood Scrubs, Liverpool and Doncaster).[62] Since I first drafted this chapter some years ago, over 1,500 people have died in prison custody in England and Wales. This includes 368 self-inflicted fatalities. According to data collected by the campaign group Inquest, a prisoner dies by self-inflicted injuries approximately once every four days.[63] In March 2016, the BBC broadcast another documentary about Wandsworth, and though it showed the chaos of the prison rife with violence and drugs, the prisoners remained – as in 1992 – a 'substratum composed of characterless, nameless beings'.

Griffiths's work gives character, gives names, gives voices to the cold statistics of punishment and death at the hands of the state. In the middle of *76-Day Wanno* there's a moment that catches my breath every time I read it:

Come on, let me tell you
the effect of the radios.
Suppose several were all tuned in the same,
one same song playing on them
and you stood in the doorway
for a listen.
Well, that was the whole music roll

---

[62] Jamie Grierson, 'UK prison officers punching compliant inmates, report says', *The Guardian* (30 April 2020), online: www.theguardian.com/society/2020/apr/30/uk-prison-officers-punching-inmates [Accessed 25 October 2023].

[63] See Inquest, 'Deaths in Prison: A National Scandal' (January 2020), online: www.inquest.org.uk/deaths-in-prison-a-national-scandal [Accessed 25 October 2023].

>   about the landing
>   a proud sound,
>   something tinny and from wherever the bass
>   and running round and round the ears
>   back. (*CP3* 469)

The prisoners' radio is a weak and precarious instrument: but this is an image of solidarity, cooperation and collective life. The passive receiver can be transformed through collaboration into a device for broadcast. Together, the tinny amplifiers make the bass appear, make the proud sound, the prisoners themselves heard along the landing and the doorway into the world. I started by describing the sheer quantity of work Griffiths produced as like a labyrinth; but maybe this is a better image. Each sequence like a radio, ready to be used.

Chapter 8

Fear of Retribution: Anna Mendelssohn

I didn't know her, but I used to see Anna Mendelssohn in the Cambridge University Library. Always at the same desk, at the top of the North Wing corridor, between the courtyard, the Map Room and the tearoom. Anna sat opposite a painting of a destroyer at sea, which when I picture now I think of as blue-green and grey, with wisps of white clouds above and surf below surrounding the ship. When I picture Anna she's writing, fierce and protective, and she's looking up and I catch her eye.

But this is a fantasy of recognition.

Sam Ladkin gave me her address, and I wrote to her to ask for poems for a magazine I had started, because in Cambridge at that time it seemed like starting a magazine was how you got to be a poet. As Anna says in *Bernache Nonnette*: 'Xerox it!'.[1] I sent her some of my own poems, my first real poems, and I'm embarrassed now to think of how I might have addressed her, how I must have blended the act of asking her for her work with my own desire for legitimation. I didn't know her, and I don't even think I knew then that she had a *history*. This was 2007, 2008, and I didn't know enough about the 1970s, about politics, about feminism or the law, to be able to place Mendelssohn as anything other than a poet, sitting at a desk at the same library I occasionally had reason to go to.

Anna died in November 2009, and I came back to Cambridge in October 2010. We were almost immediately thrown into student

---

[1] Grace Lake, *Bernache Nonnette* (Cambridge: Equipage, 1993). Mendelssohn published under the pseudonym 'Grace Lake' until her collection *Implacable Art* (Cambridge: Folio / Equipage, 2000), which was followed by one further pamphlet during her lifetime, *py* (Hunstanton: Oystercatcher, 2009).

revolt. It's hard to write an impassive timeline of these events, because my fidelity to the experience still determines my feelings. The newly elected Conservative/Liberal Democrat coalition tabled proposals for a massive increase in university tuition fees and the abolition of the Education Maintenance Allowance, a grant that enabled working-class school students to continue their studies. These policies were an aggressive and successful attempt to enshrine the logic of market competition in the education system. They were also the warning shots for the implementation of austerity measures, which have since 2010 enacted systematic and punitive cuts to the state provision of welfare and public services. At a demonstration called by the National Union of Students on 10 November – almost exactly a year after Mendelssohn's death – a crowd stormed the headquarters of the Conservative Party at Millbank. Subsequent protests in London were met with ferocious police violence. There were waves of student occupations around the country. For stretches of days and weeks, it felt like the government might be forced to capitulate, and that this capitulation might even lead to the government's collapse. Thinking back to this period I often forget that it happened before the Arab Spring and before the Occupy movement. While the education policies were passed in Parliament on 9 December, the atmosphere of revolt continued through to the riots in London in summer 2011 and beyond.[2] In Cambridge there were protests that autumn against a visit by David Willetts, Minister of State for Universities and Science. His speech was disrupted by the reading of a call-and-response text, widely described in the media at the time as a poem. For me the final event of this particular arc was a large demonstration in March 2012, when Dominique Strauss-Kahn, head of the IMF and indicted on a sexual assault charge, was invited by right-wing students to speak at the Union Debating Society. Soon afterwards I moved to Brighton with another poet, and here my timeline diverges.

Within these interlocking structures of confrontation there were about two dozen of us who were seriously interested in poetry, and Anna was one of the poets we were interested in. She was part of the texture of the time. We knew she had published a handful of chapbooks under the pseudonym Grace Lake in the 1990s, which we read in the library. We had copies of her full-length book *Implacable Art*. We knew she had been involved with the anarchist political

---

[2] For a compelling oral history of the events of November and December 2010 and some of the aftermath, see Matt Myers, *Student Revolt: Voices of the Austerity Generation* (London: Pluto, 2017).

group the Angry Brigade, and we knew she had spent time in prison, though the dates were vague. The slightly older poets who had personal relationships with Anna guarded her secrets and respected her privacy. For those of us who had only known her at a distance, or wanted to have known her, or felt that we could know her through the work, she was a figure shrouded in mystery, danger and glamour. At the library, the desk where she used to sit was called Anna's desk, and sometimes we'd sit there, hoping to benefit from the memory of her intensity. Books from her personal collection ended up at a stall on the market, and you might show up at the library with Anna's copy of Dryden, only to find that someone else held a rarer prize, like Anna's copy of Laura Riding.

The legal ramifications of the protests we were involved in dragged out for months and months, for years. The personal ramifications – what it did to our social life, to our poetry, to the way we are with each other – are still unfolding. Our conversations were punctuated by news of trials, our horizons shaped by court cases and witness statements. Everyone knew someone who was on trial for something. I internalised at least one line of Anna's poetry, taking it as both truth and demand: 'I don't talk to the police except never.'[3] As we learned more of her history, she felt more and more like a contemporary, a peer.

Becoming a poet during a time of intense political excitement brings with it certain complications. The demand to give up poetry for activism, or to devote your poetry to a radical cause is well worn. But to face this dilemma (or we might say to have it framed *as* a dilemma) before you've even started makes the unfamiliar territory more hazardous. I'm certain that Anna Mendelssohn wrote poems throughout her life, but she only became a poet after the huge drama of her life was over. I mean that after her trial and imprisonment, Mendelssohn wanted only to be a poet and an artist. But this statement makes me uncertain: the huge drama of her life never really ended, and I didn't know her, so how can I make such pronouncements. But we learned through conversation and stories that after her release she had been wary of politics and political activism of any kind. Reading her as a contemporary sometimes meant overlooking this. Sean Bonney, during the thrill of the first waves of marches in London, wrote that

---

[3] Anna Mendelssohn, 'basalt', *Implacable Art*, 71.

it's tempting but mistaken to view Mendelssohn's work 'as a continuation of left-wing politics by other means'.[4] He goes on to detail the quality of confrontation and refusal that animates her poetry, signing off with the gift she offers us: 'a poem of objects that live by magic'.[5] Reading her now, I'm interested in the moments where she seems to draw away from the world of politics and police, and tries to construct or protect the world of poetry. In trying to separate these two spheres she gives us a diagram of their relation. She shows us how one moves into the other, a hard lesson of inextricability and suffering.

Let me illustrate these complications, by which I mean most of all a kind of awkwardness. One of the first things you might do when you're trying to be a poet is to negotiate your own earnestness: you want, at least, to make an object of your sincerity, to treat it with some kind of intelligence and sophistication. But student activism troubles this. What could be more earnest than a student occupation? My most vivid memories of the occupation at Cambridge in winter 2010 are of standing outside, on guard at the door in case the university security or bailiffs came to eject us. I liked this job because it indulged my aloofness, but it also meant that I got to know people coming in and out. I remember one night in the snow, hiding behind a giant urn outside the Old Schools Building with a megaphone and Justin Katko. Justin read Edward Dorn's 'Thesis' to the deserted streets, and we heard lone applause from a distant open window. 'Only the illegitimate are beautiful', wrote Dorn and said Justin, and so it was.[6] One day inside the building we were sitting around and a child was walking through the forty or fifty students who made up the occupation. At one point he shouted: 'I want to stay here and do nothing! Destroy everyone's work!', lines which Justin would later work into a poem.[7] We loved this moment of refusal most of all. It was confusing because we didn't know if the child was speaking to us or for us. It was liberating because while we were storing up all this experience for poems, the child beat us at our own game.

After the protests died down and during the long repercussions, I sometimes felt like the child whenever I was in discussion with poets

---

[4] Sean Bonney, '"Minds do exist to agitate and provoke / this is the reason I do not conform": Anna Mendelssohn', *Poetry Project Newsletter* 226 (February/March 2011): 17–19.

[5] Anna Mendelssohn, 'A man who snatches a ring ...', *Implacable Art*, 9.

[6] Edward Dorn, 'Thesis', *Collected Poems*, ed. Jennifer Dunbar Dorn, Justin Katko, Reitha Pattison and Kyle Waugh (Manchester: Carcanet, 2012), 223.

[7] Justin Katko, *Rhyme Against the Internet* (Brighton: Crater, 2011).

about politics. Better to refuse and reject, better to do nothing than to carry on as if we'd mastered or even understood what we'd been through. Even if the distinction between the world of poetry and the world of politics is a false one, there's something painful about the return to order and routine. The lost moment of rebellion was the real order, and the time afterwards felt empty. However much we might will it in seminars or in private and public arguments, the political vector of poetry is determined by the social moment in which it's written, it if gets written at all. And in this way, I came to appreciate Mendelssohn's protectiveness, her secrecy, how her anonymous honesty calls for more poetry, more writing, more art, implacable.

This personal account risks a kind of sentimental embarrassment, both on my part and the people I imagine reading it. I've used a collective pronoun here recklessly, because it's the only adequate one: the memory of crowds, passionate conversation and violent scenes of protest is never singular. But the judgements and reflections are my own experience, the squeamishness my own, also. But I attempt this narrative because I've been thinking about something the art historian Lisa Tickner writes in a footnote to her book about the occupation of Hornsey College of Art in 1968. Tickner, who participated in the unrest, says she wants to write 'good enough history', she wants to be 'impelled by the investments of the present but not disabled by them'.[8] What is 'good enough history'? Tickner's elaboration is tantalisingly brief. It seems to be a way of acknowledging personal investment in the material under discussion while allowing that material a life of its own. Rather than studied neutrality, good-enough history can be a method of open and self-reflexive mediation. Perhaps, in literary studies, we can think of good-enough history as a cousin or a sister to Eve Kosofsky Sedgwick's concept of reparative reading, which I'll come back to over the course of this chapter. Tickner's wonderful study of her 1968 involves meticulous archival work and reconstruction. She offers interpretation rather than anecdote. But the events that she writes about are older than the events I write about: the dust has settled. Where May 1968 is understood as an epoch-making political and cultural event, November 2010 remains half-formed. My archive of the recent past is dozens and

---

[8] Lisa Tickner, *Hornsey 1968: The Art School Revolution* (London: Frances Lincoln, 2008), 104. For her first use of the phrase, see Tickner, 'The Impossible Object?' in David Freeberg et al., 'The Object of Art History', *The Art Bulletin* 76, no. 3 (1994): 407.

dozens of poetry pamphlets, held together by the scattered network of those who were there at the time. What was in public circulation retreats, ready or not yet ready for study.

In the world of the psychoanalyst D. W. Winnicott, 'the good-enough mother' is essential to the maturation of the infant, and to the psychic well-being of the baby. The good-enough mother, in Winnicott's account, *knows what to do*: she doesn't need specialist information or unnecessary advice from neighbours, though the reassurances of a qualified physician may be helpful.[9] Here's what Winnicott says:

> The good-enough 'mother' (not necessarily the infant's own mother) is one who makes active adaptations to the infant's needs, an active adaptation that gradually lessens, according to the infant's growing ability to account for failure of adaptation and to tolerate the results of frustration.[10]

So one thing the good-enough mother must do is to temporarily suppress her psychic life, or rather, make her psychic life coincide with that of the baby. This is what Winnicott defines later as the work of 'primary maternal preoccupation'.[11] Through this easy natural bond, sustained and eventually rescinded as an act of devotion, the baby will come to learn the differences between self and other, and establish for itself the shape and tenor of reality. This is another type of separation, different from that of poetry and politics. The practice of historical inquiry doesn't map onto this theory in any exact way: the historian who practises good-enough history is neither the baby nor the mother, though she was once *a* baby and may well be *a* mother. We'll return to the figure of the mother at the conclusion of this chapter to discuss its limitations.

Mendelssohn's life and poetry pose distinct difficulties to literary criticism. These include problems in appellation and attribution (her use of pseudonyms); in textuality (the sheer density of allusion and joyful détournement); in dating both manuscripts and published work; and of understanding Mendelssohn's relationships to her editors, including Rod Mengham, Alastair Horne and Peter Hughes.

---

[9] Such as those offered in his most popular book, *The Child, The Family, and the Outside World* (Harmondsworth: Pelican, 1964). This is a condensed version of the two volumes, *The Child and the Family* and *The Outside World* (London: Tavistock, 1957).

[10] D. W. Winnicott, 'Transitional Objects and Transitional Phenomena' (1951), in *Collected Papers: Through Paediatrics to Psychoanalysis* (London: Tavistock, 1958).

[11] Winnicott, 'Primary Maternal Preoccupation' (1956), in *Collected Papers*.

This is to say nothing of the ideological decisions that the work confronts us with. With the accession of her archive to Sussex University and pathbreaking scholarly and bibliographic work by Sara Crangle, there are now great advancements in our understanding.[12] Some of the mysteries are beginning to be solved. But as Samuel Solomon has recently written, explaining her omission from his book *Lyric Pedagogy and Marxist-Feminism*, 'her relationship to feminism is ambivalent, at best'.[13] So too is her relationship to psychoanalysis. In her final published work she describes 'every other day / socking it to Oedipus', and to read back across her work would furnish many other examples.[14] But the purpose of this chapter is to stay with those ambivalences.

I should be careful to emphasise here that Winnicott's focus on the infant's relationship to the mother, following and modifying Melanie Klein, has at times provided tactical room for manoeuvre for feminist writers.[15] Throughout Winnicott's writing, he stresses the importance of keeping his concepts and terminology open to interpretation and transformation.[16] If he's vague, his vagueness is a kind of generosity, so when I speak of 'good enough history' it's better to be imprecise rather than attempt to prematurely codify or systematise. Political commitment complicates all of this and leaves me uncertain. There's a risk that the transposition of the idea of adaptation to reality – the necessary disillusionment that the good-enough mother instigates in the infant – will emerge in writing as fully fledged disenchantment. The 'adaptation to reality', in a different context, is a familiar refrain of conservative quietism. But what Lisa Tickner is describing, I think, is how to meet the peculiar frustrations that arise when one's own experiences become historical experiences. You may be aware of this process happening at the time, in the sudden shock of agency in the street or the square.

---

[12] See also the special Anna Mendelssohn issue of *The Journal of British and Irish Innovative Poetry*, edited by Eleanor Careless and Vicky Sparrow, online: https://poetry.openlibhums.org/collections/301/ [Accessed 1 November 2023].

[13] Samuel Solomon, *Lyric Pedagogy and Marxist-Feminism: Social Reproduction and the Institutions of Poetry* (London: Bloomsbury, 2019), 181.

[14] Mendelssohn, *py*.

[15] See Jacqueline Rose's analysis of works by Alison Bechdel and Maggie Nelson, among others, in *Mothers: An Essay on Love and Cruelty* (London: Faber, 2018).

[16] For Winnicott's most acute statement on this matter, see his letter to Melanie Klein, 17 November 1952, in which he argues: 'I personally think that it is very important that your work should be restated by people discovering in their own way and presenting what they discover in their own language. It is only in this way that the language will be kept alive.' Winnicott, *The Spontaneous Gesture: Selected Letters*, ed. F. Robert Rodman (London: Karnac, 1999), 34.

You may be aware also of the distortions when they arrive at a later date. The pressurised local movements of political antagonism often involve substantial personal cost. By departing from the fiction of objectivity, we risk becoming blunt accountants of difficult feelings. So you adapt to the necessity of self-scrutiny, and try to prepare the conditions in which history can stand on its own two feet, if only to be turned on its head.

In one important elaboration of Winnicott's theories concerning the maternal aesthetic and language acquisition, Christopher Bollas writes that the good-enough mother can establish 'generative transformations of internal and external realities'.[17] And one of the things Anna Mendelssohn's poetry does – and sometimes undoes or undermines – is to instigate something like this relationship. Sometimes I feel like I have to brave it with Anna, called on by the language to make deep interior connections, to make historical associations take shape in forms that both promise freedom and repeatedly withdraw that promise. The moment of aesthetic absorption, something like recognition or intimacy, is violated. Reading Anna Mendelssohn's poetry often makes me feel clumsy, like I'm trespassing in someone else's carefully arranged environment. I feel like I'll knock over the language, that I'll hear something I shouldn't have heard. That I'll be thrown out of the world of art, where internal and external reality can be examined and enjoyed and pleasurably tested, where unspoken rules can emerge and dissolve. What I'm trying to describe is the feeling of guilt; or more or less precisely, what Mendelssohn calls elsewhere *the fear of retribution*.[18] But it's something more than that: within the circuit of retribution I will be identified as one of the 'civilian detectives' who invade the house in *Viola Tricolor*.[19] That's to say, I will be the unwitting agent of retribution rather than its focus.

What I've just described shares some terrain with Eve Kosofsky Sedgwick's famous essay 'Paranoid and Reparative Reading, or, You're So Paranoid You Probably Think This Essay Is About You'.[20]

---

[17] Christopher Bollas, *The Shadow of the Object* (London: Tavistock, 1987), 34.

[18] Anna Mendelssohn, 'Art made me thin ...', *Implacable Art*, 42.

[19] Grace Lake, 'on challenge, positive attitudes, and "les peintures cubistes"', *Viola Tricolor* (Cambridge: Equipage, 1993): '& cramming "too much" onto 10 × 10 / before opening the door to a team of civilian detectives.'

[20] Eve Kosofsky Sedgwick, 'Paranoid and Reparative Reading, or, You're So Paranoid You Probably Think This Essay Is About You', in *Touching Feeling* (Durham, NC: Duke UP, 2002), 123–51. See also Sedgwick, 'Melanie Klein and the Difference Affect Makes' *South Atlantic Quarterly* 106, no. 3 (2007): 625–42. For an excellent reflection on this area of Sedgwick's thought, see Heather Love, 'Truth and Consequences: On

Again, the mapping isn't exact. Reading and living with poetry is, I would like to think, a distinct mesh of temporal problems and units of feeling and experience. The context of Sedgwick's essay – a foundational text for Queer theory, an intervention into critical debate, a profound reflection on the AIDS crisis – has its own contours and its own rich and complex history. But Sedgwick's terms are helpful for the reader of Anna Mendelssohn, or at least this reader of Anna Mendelssohn. Sedgwick's essay draws directly (and indirectly) on the work of Winnicott's analyst, mentor and sometimes adversary, Melanie Klein. For Klein, we develop over the course of our infancies two 'positions', which we oscillate between throughout our lives. The first is the paranoid-schizoid position, which is the earliest strategy for coping with the negative experiences and destructive impulses she believes to be innate. It works as a kind of defence mechanism, where objects are split into good and bad, and are then held apart for fear that their contamination will lead to the destruction of both the object and the self. We can also, Klein believes, fragment an object into many parts in order to mitigate the threat that the object represents. Although this sounds desperate and pessimistic, it's also a means of keeping open the possibility of relation. The paranoid-schizoid position is a way of withstanding unbearable feelings of destructiveness and persecution. The counterpart to this, and what Klein says is the most important aspect of our development, is the depressive position. The depressive position is the domain of guilt, where we can recognise our culpability for what has been lost or destroyed in fantasy, and we can begin to integrate the twin impulses of hatred and love into a whole sense of self and other. For Klein, these fundamental processes are a type of structural equipment for surviving intolerable ambivalence. This is the ongoing and fragile work of reparation. The figure that has to withstand all of this, apart from the baby itself, is of course the baby's mother.

In Sedgwick's late work, written after her diagnosis with cancer, depressive or reparative reading emerges as a volatile practice of ethical engagement. Privileging surprise, uncertainty and mistakes over mastery and suspicion, it gives permission to surrender critical distance and to acknowledge how involved we might be in the work that we read. If, as Sedgwick argues, the 'reparative impulse' is

---

Paranoid Reading and Reparative Reading', *Criticism* 52, no. 2 (2010): 235–41. See also Robyn Wiegman's important account of the textual history of 'Paranoid and Reparative Reading', in 'The Times We're In: Queer Feminist Criticism and the Reparative 'Turn'", *Feminist Theory* 15, no. 1 (2014): 4–25.

surrounded by a culture that is 'inadequate or inimical to its nurture', this form of relation might be – at its outer limit or inner core – a matter of survival.[21] Sedgwick's work has long been hegemonic in queer studies, but since the financial crash of 2008, the status of reparative reading has become a central point of reference for debates in the US academy about the function of literary criticism.[22] There are too many iterations to enumerate here, but the prevailing opposition is between those like Rita Felski – who strongly reject the flipside of reparative reading, which is to say the 'hermeneutics of suspicion' associated with Marx, Freud and Foucault – and those who see in the 'reparative turn' the accommodating logic of neo-liberalism and empire.[23] It will be clear from the arguments I've made throughout this book that I'm committed to suspicion and interested in how we might untangle occlusion and illuminate the obscure and the secretive. But I also believe that aesthetic objects – poems – contain and provoke the intense, violent, unmanageable feelings that Klein's analysis focuses on, and that poems also perform, resist and frustrate interpretive functions.[24] Paranoid and depressive processes – or suspicious and reparative impulses – are not simply tools to pick up and put down, choices on a menu, but are inextricable aspects of thought.

As a kind of elaborated close reading, the search for the reparative is one approach to marginalised or damaged texts, works that have been produced under conditions of violence and surveillance, lives that have been interrupted and lost. Anna Mendelssohn was twenty-four when she went on trial as part of the Stoke Newington Eight. She was arrested in August 1971 on fraud charges, for using stolen chequebooks and credit cards. By November, as Sara Crangle explains, 'the charges were augmented to conspiring to cause

---

[21] Sedgwick, 'Paranoid and Reparative Reading', 149.
[22] As Andrea Long Chu writes: 'I have read, and this is not exaggerating, some 40 or 50 accounts of what Sedgwick meant by paranoid and reparative reading; it is, within queer theory, a forest fully logged.' Andrea Long Chu, 'You've Heard This One Before', *Vulture* (7 September 2021), online: www.vulture.com/article/maggie-nelson-on-freedom-review.html [Accessed 25 October 2023].
[23] See Rita Felski, *The Limits of Critique* (Chicago: U of Chicago P, 2015) and Patricia Stuelke, *The Ruse of Repair: US Neoliberal Empire and the Turn from Critique* (Durham, NC: Duke UP, 2021).
[24] As Gila Ashtor writes: 'It is an enduring irony to find in Eve Sedgwick's essays on "Reparative reading" the figure of Melanie Klein representing more benevolent, less shame-inducing interpretive practices since, as a clinical modality, the single most distinctive feature of Kleinian technique is its relentlessly confrontational approach to identifying, without equivocation, the essential, infantile, "true" meaning of a patient's behaviour.' Ashtor, 'The *Mis*diagnosis of Critique', *Criticism* 61, no. 2 (2019): 191.

explosions to endanger life or property'.[25] The Angry Brigade – a British version of the Red Army Faction or the Red Brigades – were responsible for small-scale attacks on, among other targets, the Spanish Embassy, the Biba department store, the home of Tory politician Robert Carr and Paddington Police Station. They caused no fatalities. In December 1972, Mendelssohn was sentenced to ten years in prison. She was granted early parole in 1976, and on her release she was hounded by the tabloid press. Later in life, her position as a mother was subject to legal and juridical intervention, and she was unable to keep custody of her children. The state did not judge her to be a 'good-enough mother'. So there is an undeniable bitterness in bringing to this work the metaphorical framework of psychoanalysis, especially the psychological mechanism of guilt, given Mendelssohn's experience of punishment at the hands of the state. We encounter these poems only after the terms of reparation have been pulverised by incarceration. The manageable scale of the poem and person unravels in the face of the machinations of the courtroom and cell. And yet my experience of these poems is one where the reparative, against all odds, is maintained. The reader is invited to withstand dread, suspicion, aggression, and to discover creativity, resistance, even joy. We are always allowed back.

Here's an example of one of Mendelssohn's more amenable poems, which appears early on in her only widely available collection, *Implacable Art*:

> from.   Implacable Art
>
> In unlike minds soft verdancy
> reconnoîtred for barrack room politics
> . . . .
> . . . .
> When the fat coca-cola man lands
> on you in the night, fling open
> the shutters and yell for Paint,
> Sheet metal, burin & copper wire.

This poem has been familiar to me for a long time, but I can never remember it quite correctly. From the title onwards, it seems like

---

[25] Sara Crangle, 'Introduction', *I'm Working Here: The Collected Poems of Anna Mendelssohn* (Swindon: Shearsman, 2021), 21–109 (28).

something has been redacted. The poem is called 'from. Implacable Art' and it's in a book called *Implacable Art*: is this an excerpt from what would be the title sequence? Or does all of Mendelssohn's work go under the heading and sign of implacability? The opening couplet presents a kind of military exercise. The minds are the opposite of 'likeminded', so we expect that these minds – however many of them there are – will diverge on matters of taste, perhaps to disagree more seriously. I read the 'soft verdancy' as shared but unstable ground. The 'verdancy' is already suspect, too poetic, almost arch. Because the verdancy is soft, it's pliable: but when has anything verdant truly been hard? This material, both the unlike minds and the soft verdancy, is 'reconnoîtred': it's being, or has already been, scoped out for military purposes. I imagine someone in fatigues watching the minds from a distance through binoculars, blending into the scenery. We move from the green shade into the barrack room, where politics takes place. It's unclear whether this has already happened, or is yet to happen, or simply might happen as one possibility among many. But *something* happens in the following two lines of ellipses.

Where do these dots come from? They remind me of the presentation of Rimbaud's early poems, where missing text and skips in the narrative are indicated in this way. Take for example 'La Forgeron', or 'The Blacksmith', one of his last experiments in Victor Hugo-inspired realism. The majority of this poem is a monologue, spoken by the title character, who confronts Louis XVI at the Palace of Tuileries, 'about August 10 92', as the poem tells us. He passionately justifies the destruction of the Bastille, and describes taking to the streets armed with his work tools to defend and further the revolution. The first sequence of dots occurs in the following lines:

> Waving our bugles and oakleaves,
> With pikes in our hands; we had no hate,
> – We felt so strong, we wanted to be gentle!
> . . . .
> . . . .
> And since that day, we have been like madmen![26]

The poem exonerates and celebrates the workers, and ends with the blacksmith defiantly throwing his *bonnet rouge* at the King's head. For Jacques Rancière it is 'the poem of the century, the poem of

---

[26] Arthur Rimbaud, 'The Blacksmith', in *Rimbaud: Complete Works, Selected Letters*, trans. Wallace Fowlie, rev. Seth Widden (Chicago: U of Chicago P, 2005), 59.

the people, of the worker, of poverty and of revolution'.[27] I don't think it's far-fetched to introduce Rimbaud's aporia into the aporia in 'from. Implacable Art'. I want to suggest that these dots, both in Rimbaud's poem and in Mendelssohn's, stand for revolution itself. More specifically, they stand for the question of revolutionary violence. The terms for each poet are different: Rimbaud's formal breakthroughs will allow him, during and after the Paris Commune, to write the fabled poetry of the future. He will, in the poems to come, fill in the gaps. But for Mendelssohn, writing in the long aftermath of the violence of which she was judged to be in proximity, the ellipsis indicates what still can't be said. Her use of language is conditioned by the experience of arrest, trial and imprisonment. There is nothing to say about revolutionary violence; there is everything to say about revolutionary violence.

Mendelssohn was a student at the University of Essex in 1968, when Essex erupted into student protest and activism. In February, a visit by the racist Conservative MP Enoch Powell was resisted by hundreds of students; disciplinary actions were halted by a sit-in. The university continued its controversial invitations to visiting speakers by hosting scientists from Porton Down in May. In his account of the events, David Triesman describes Porton Down as 'the germ warfare establishment on Salisbury Plain'.[28] There was already an anti-Vietnam War campaign at Essex, which Mendelssohn was involved in. But the visit by the military to the university came just a few days after the events in Paris at Nanterre and the Sorbonne that would escalate into a General Strike. At Essex, three students were suspended following the demonstration, leading to a mass student occupation and the declaration of the Free University. Among other things, these protests led to the departure of Donald Davie, who had set up the Literatures Department only three years previously, for Stanford in the United States. In his memoirs he skips over the condition of his exile, noting only sourly in the final sentence that he's left out 'variously frenzied people known in Essex in the 1960s'.[29] The story of Essex Poetry, including Davie, Dorn, Tom Clark, Tom Raworth, Douglas Oliver, and later Ted Berrigan, Alice Notley, Ralph Hawkins and many others, will have to wait for another time.

---

[27] Jacques Rancière, *The Flesh of Words: The Politics of Writing*, trans. Charlotte Mandell (Stanford: Stanford UP, 2004), 58.

[28] David Triesman, 'Essex', *New Left Review* (July–August 1968). Adrian Mitchell wrote a protest poem about the facility following these events, titled 'Open Day at Porton' and published in *Black Dwarf* (19 July 1968).

[29] Donald Davie, *These The Companions* (Cambridge: Cambridge UP, 1982), 176.

I want briefly to follow how these events impacted on Mendelssohn, before returning to the second part of 'from. Implacable Art'.

In the burgeoning underground press, the role of students within revolutionary struggle was a much-discussed topic. The front cover of the influential socialist newspaper *Black Dwarf* in July 1968 featured an enormous splash headline reading: 'STUDENTS: THE NEW REVOLUTIONARY VANGUARD'.[30] In her memoirs, the feminist historian and activist Sheila Rowbotham – an editor and contributor – describes how this issue moved her to despair: 'I sat on a pile of papers in the *Dwarf* office and wept. I couldn't abide vanguards. Tariq [Ali] maintained that the designer had forgotten to put in a question mark.'[31] Issues that followed detailed the student unrest at Hull and at the LSE, and discussed the possibility of founding 'Campus Soviets'. These claims for the potential of student vanguardism were not entirely without merit. Between 1945 and 1964, student numbers in Britain had doubled, and by 1972 had doubled again to around 600,000.[32] But if they were to become the revolutionary vanguard, these students would have to dissolve the university itself, to reject the terms of the education it presented and to abolish 'the student' as a social category.[33] The events in Paris – which Mendelssohn attended with a cohort from Essex, including Dorn – had shown that student protest could present the conditions for a revolutionary situation. Mendelssohn, like many others involved in political activism at the time, refused to take her finals and dropped out. For an idea of how common this was, the events diary in the summer issues of *Black Dwarf* featured an icon of a calendar with 'FINALS' crossed out and 'BOYCOTT' inserted, along with a reminder to attend student meetings.

In a late uncollected poem, Mendelssohn writes disparagingly about the culture around *Black Dwarf*. It appears to be a self-portrait of the artist, described at first as a 'Lazy socialiste / A Lazy Lady Socialiste', then 'Oh parasite poetess', 'problematic dreamy poetess' and as a 'mild-mannered swot'. The poem continues:

> She had been asked to leave
> a 'Black Dwarf' household

---

[30] *Black Dwarf* (5 July 1968).
[31] Sheila Rowbotham, *Promise of a Dream* (London: Penguin, 2000), 191.
[32] Chris Harman, *The Fire Last Time: 1968 and After* (London: Bookmarks, 1988), 40.
[33] See for example, the Situationist International communiqué, 'On the Poverty of Student Life', *Situationist International Anthology*, rev. ed., ed. Ken Mabb (Berkeley: Bureau of Public Secrets, 2006); and André Gorz, 'Destroy the University', *Les Temps Modernes* 285 (1970).

> for writing, and folding poems
> in her blue satin jeans
>
> escorted to a more suitable household
> that's where they got her – There.[34]

After leaving Essex, Mendelssohn lived in radical squats in London, ending up at the Amhurst Road address where she was arrested in 1971 and charged with conspiracy to cause explosions. I want to take seriously the accusation she makes in the poem. It suggests that she came to believe that the attitude revolutionary socialists took to her poetry led to her persecution by the state. I'm not interested here in passing any sort of judgement on the methods of the Angry Brigade; I'm interested in the judgement Mendelssohn makes about the trajectory her life took after university. Wanting to be gentle, she finds that *she* is the one who has been 'reconnoîtred for barrack room politics'. In 'from. Implacable Art' it's the barrack room and the reconnoitring that are cause for alarm, rather than politics as such. Viewed in any light, Mendelssohn's work is resolutely political: she writes ferociously against domination, against power, against historical injustice. But she also struggles against other people's ideas about politics, about having politics thrust on her, of being used or otherwise exploited. The closest comparison I can think of is something Alice Notley says in *Tell Me Again*: 'The only real politics I have is write my poems and destroy anyone who tries to keep me from it.'[35]

The final quatrain of 'from. Implacable Art' reads at first something like an uneasy punch-line. The 'fat coca-cola man' sounds comical: I think of the Coca-Cola Father Christmas dropping out of the sky. But the image changes: it happens in the night, and it happens in textual proximity to what we're told is a barrack room. Recalling the formative context of the Vietnam War, perhaps behind the sickly sweet appearance of the 'coca-cola man' lies the weight of US imperialism. The joke isn't funny. The man landing on you in the middle of the night reads like an attempted assault, like that which some scholars identify in Rimbaud's 'Le Coeur Volé', or 'The Stolen Heart'.[36] Mendelssohn presents this either as inevitability or likelihood: '*When* the fat coca-cola man lands / on you in the night'. Within the world of male-dominated revolutionary politics

---

[34] Anna Mendelssohn, 'The Gong', *I'm Working Here*, 506–7.
[35] Alice Notley, *Tell Me Again* (Santa Barbara: Am Here, 1982), unpaginated.
[36] Rimbaud, *Complete Works, Selected Letters*, 73.

of the 1960s, the threat of gendered violence is ever present. Her following advice is to 'fling open / the shutters and yell for Paint, / Sheet metal, burin & copper wire.' These are the artist's materials and tools. Mendelssohn's advice, at least in this poem, is to resist assaults on the self by means of art. What's moving about this poem is that she asks for assistance. Anybody could be on the other side of the window; who knows what the shutter might open onto. In the act of publishing her work in a widely available volume, she lets strangers into the guarded room. As the first poem following the title page, she presents the reader with her life's dilemma: what to do when the possibility for political commitment has been taken away, has already been sacrificed.

But the poem remains inscrutable, full of residues that don't entirely add up. I want to try reading this poem more literally, and I imagine that it's an *image* of the 'fat coca-cola man' that falls from the wall in the middle of the night, and could be hung back up with the copper wire, the plaster painted over. But I remain over-vigilant: after all, this is a poem about waking up in alarm in the middle of the night. What's the sheet metal for? Are these the bedsheets, transformed now into something harder? I can't help but hear the police in the '*copper* wire', and even start hearing 'pain' in 'Paint', a slip of the key. The turn to art keeps turning back to the experience of incarceration. The flinging open of the shutters is the corollary of the cell-door being shut behind us. The alarm subsides, we start our reading again.

The difference between 1968 and 2010 is that we were neither offered nor won the mass support of organized labour. We found it hard to extend our demands to the abolition of the university and the transcendence of the category of the student because we were stuck trying to salvage these things. The campaign in Cambridge went under the heading of Defend Education, and while it was possible to go on the offence, it was only possible to go so far and no further. Rather than boycotting finals, many of us were embarking on PhDs, already saddled with undergraduate debts from the fees introduced by New Labour. Maybe this makes me a bad reader of Mendelssohn's work, testing her scepticism of revolutionary politics against my untested enthusiasm for revolutionary politics. But of course, circumstances change, and the legacy of the recent student movement remains to be told and honoured. I encountered Anna Mendelssohn's work in a period of open and sustained state repression and violence. Or rather, my encounter with Mendelssohn's work coincided with the moment where, from my position of privilege, I was made aware of what state violence sometimes looks and feels like. And I encounter it and continue to encounter it from within the scholastic part of the state apparatus, the university we defended in the snow. It's in this juncture, or at this crux, that the need for 'good enough history' seems to get more difficult, and where I'd like to think further about Winnicott and Sedgwick.

There are a series of significant feminist readings of Winnicott's theory that I'd like to outline before bringing this chapter to a close. In the early 1970s, Juliet Mitchell argued that developments at the Tavistock Institute during the Second World War produced a 'heritage of mother-child obsession'. She goes on: 'It does not amount to an estimation of the intrinsic merits or otherwise of the work if one points out that the development of child psychoanalysis contributed very neatly to the political demands of the epoch.'[37] The disturbances to the family unit in wartime, the mass entrance of women into the workforce and the accompanying state provision of childcare was met with a theory in which the mother, if she was to be good enough, remained in the home. The heteronormative family unit was to be preserved as the foundation of capitalist social reproduction. Denise Riley's *War In The Nursery*, based on articles and research undertaken in the late 1970s and early 1980s, refines and extends Mitchell's critique. Riley's meticulous study traces the points where social policy, psychology and psychoanalysis overlapped, examining the emergence of pre-war, wartime and post-war theories of the child and mother. Rather than claiming, as Mitchell does in the passage above, a direct contribution to the interests of the state, she focuses on how these ideas were disseminated and popularised. She emphasises moments of friction and contestation, and offers a materialist history of the regulating discourses surrounding and producing the mother and the child. What were their origins? What were their limits? What kinds of division did they perpetuate or obscure? At the risk of oversimplification, Mitchell's Lacanian account at times seems to suggest that psychoanalytic theory is one thing, and what the state does with that theory is another. Riley's work shows that this isn't the case: the two are too finely inter-related to hold apart in any clean separation. This is salutary, because it can be tempting – especially when thinking about confrontation with the police and

[37] Juliet Mitchell, *Psychoanalysis and Feminism* (Harmondsworth: Pelican, 1975), 229.

the experience of incarcerated subjects – to think of the state as the fundamental origin of power, domination and authority. In the situations I started this chapter with, the state often looks like a monolithic expression of dominant class interests, a blunt instrument of repression, *and that alone*, rather than the whole set of jostling social relations that it constitutes. The moving parts of the whole are rendered static: the state, the family, the mother – all of these definite articles loom large while the needs of real mothers, waged or unwaged, single or otherwise, are effaced and forgotten.[38] As Riley concludes: 'Great intricacies are wrapped up in the bland package labelled "motherhood"; stubborn and delicate histories, wants and attributions are concealed in it.'[39]

Winnicott's conceptualisation of the good-enough mother indeed conceals much. Perhaps the idea of 'good enough history' itself does more harm than good, working as an additional layer of mystification. In the considerably less nuanced work of Janice Doane and Devon Hodges, published in the early 1990s, Winnicott is more strongly identified as reactionary. His modification of Klein works to subdue the mother, creating a hierarchy within the mother–infant dyad in which the mother is always the subordinate partner. Winnicott not only 'naturalizes women's submission' but works to 'hide his own efforts to enforce their submission'.[40] Like Riley, Doane and Hodges are interested in how the ideas of the Independent Group of British psychoanalysts became popularised. Through his talks on the BBC and his albeit sceptical relationship with the NHS, Winnicott was involved in the more innocuous elements of the British state. Yet to bring even a shadow of the good-enough mother in the guise of good-enough history to Anna Mendelssohn's work is a fraught proposition. For the mother subject to incarceration, Winnicott's idea of the 'holding environment' brings with it uneasy connotations, to say nothing of his ideas about stealing; and his studies of social delinquency align him with the social worker who is forever being expelled from Mendelssohn's creative sanctuary.[41] As I

---

[38] For a helpful account of Riley's thinking around social needs see Solomon, *Lyric Pedagogy*, especially 81–110.

[39] Denise Riley, *War in the Nursery* (London: Virago, 1983), 196. For Riley's direct comments on Winnicott, see 80–90. Riley published two poems by Grace Lake, 'Rose-Gazing' and 'Prelude to an Imaginary Moorish Castle', in the collection *Poets on Writing: Britain, 1970–1991* (Basingstoke: Macmillan, 1992).

[40] Janice Doane and Devon Hodges, *From Klein to Kristeva: Psychoanalytic Feminism and the Search for the 'Good Enough Mother'* (Ann Arbor: U of Michigan P, 1992), 23.

[41] See D. W. Winnicott, *Deprivation and Delinquency*, ed. Clare Winnicott, Ray Shepherd and Madeleine Davis (London: Tavistock, 1984). Brooke Hopkins has

have said, Mendelssohn's motherhood was subject to extreme intervention by the state and social services, which runs as a profound wound throughout her writing. It's finally this fact, rather than any ambivalence towards feminism, that presents the greatest difficulty in bringing Mendelssohn's work into dialogue with her contemporaries and the theoretical apparatuses complicit in carceral practices.[42] An account of the life of the imprisoned mother – to say nothing of the imprisoned child – along with the role of the prison in social reproduction, remains an urgent and necessary element of Marxist-feminist inquiry.

While Mendelssohn became a mother only after her direct incarceration was over, the prison remained for her a devastating element of the maternal imaginary. As she writes in one of the most painful poems in *Tondo Aquatique*, addressed to her daughter, Poppy:

> By tonight I shall have lost you
> because I cannot hold you
> & be anything other than abused.[43]

Yet it's precisely at moments like this, where the terms of reparation seem entirely displaced by loss and abuse, that good-enough history might make us good-enough readers. In the ten years following Mendelssohn's death, her work has gained a steady and growing readership. The singular facts of her life ask for nothing less than a reorganisation of our acquired habits of reading and critical response. Her work demands an approach that stays conscious of our relative positions within the state and its institutions, and the ways in which poetry has both imagined and resisted those institutions. In *Viola Tricolor*, Mendelssohn presents us with a challenge:

> What is Art, O what is She, a baby dandled on a strange man's knee
> For a mother to sing a new history. Too close to impossibility.[44]

---

argued that the 'spatial metaphors that saturate [Winnicott's] writing' are concomitant with the logic of the prison. See Hopkins, 'Winnicott and Imprisonment', *American Imago* 62, no. 3 (2005): 269–83.

[42] For an ethnological investigation, including a brief mention of Winnicott, see Judith Clark, 'The Impact of The Prison Environment on Mothers', *The Prison Journal* 75, no. 3 (1995): 306–29. There are some parallels between Clark and Mendelssohn. Clark was a member of the Weather Underground, and was convicted for her part in a robbery in 1981. She was finally granted parole in April 2019.

[43] Grace Lake, 'Abschied', *Tondo Aquatique* (Cambridge: Equipage, 1997); Mendelssohn, *I'm Working Here*, 405.

[44] Grace Lake, 'for Bruno Alcaraz Massaz', *Viola Tricolor*; Mendelssohn, *I'm Working Here*, 317.

Is it impossible that Mendelssohn's work might sing a new history? Or that a new history might sing her history, in turn? For this to happen we have to listen as carefully as we can. If 'Art' here is imagined as a baby, then what other option do we have than to try to be good enough?

The risk in my approach is that by meeting Mendelssohn's negativity and aggression with the reparative impulse, we rush prematurely to fill in the gaps and restore equilibrium. We adapt to reality and forget to transform it, or our transformations come undone in the uneven temporalities of our history. In a work written towards the end of her life, Eve Sedgwick continued to explore the dimensions of the depressive and paranoid modes of relation. Reflecting on her own experience of political activism, she states:

> But as I understand my own political history, it has often happened that the propulsive energy of justification, of being or feeling joined with others in a right cause, tends to be structured very much in a paranoid/schizoid fashion, driven by attributed motives, fearful contempt of opponents, collective fantasies of powerlessness and/or omnipotence, scapegoating, purism and schism –paranoid/schizoid, in short, even as the motives that underlie political commitment have much more to do with the complex, mature ethical dimension of the depressive position.[45]

Although I'm wary of drawing parallels, my experience is the opposite. The student revolt of 2010 was a period of openness, rapid education in the truest sense of the word, and a way of being together that remains for me as a resource for thought and action The rest of it, all of it, came only after we were defeated. But the poetry we read at that time, like Anna's, gave form and shape to our political thinking. It holds open possibility, allowing fragments of bad fantasy to surface without being rejected, knowing always that no defeat was ever defeat the whole way through.

While I was working on this chapter, I had to revisit the library in Cambridge to do some archival research on another project. As always, I walked past Anna's desk and thought of it as Anna's desk. While I was in the archives room I received a message from someone

---

[45] Eve Kosofsky Sedgwick, 'Teaching / Depression', *The Scholar & Feminist* 4, no. 2 (2006), online: http://sfonline.barnard.edu/heilbrun/sedgwick_02.htm [Accessed 30 April 2023].

I hadn't heard from in a long time, asking if I'd seen a letter addressed to me discovered in her papers in Sussex. The letter, replying to my request for a contribution to my magazine, had never been sent. I received the scan, and there it was: my name in her handwriting, breaching the whole terms of my approach, collapsing the lost past into the present. I reproduce it here, transcribed from the original, with Rimbaud's dots to indicate illegible text:

Dear Luke Roberts

Thank you for your letter and writing. I wish you well in your projected magazine. The 1960's are still fashionable surprisingly enough. I hope that they improve with age as good wine should, then we should be drunk and sleepy, heavy and buzzing. There were people who were intellectuals involved and committed to poetry and art in the 1960s; I miss meeting individuals who didn't have a poetry book in their hands. What is there to "talk about"? However it is twenty years that I have found myself on strike and a stroke made me collapse, not for the first time. Although fear is not a subject that is admitted, or admissible apparently, I do suffer from it, terribly. It's difficult to know whether a woman has the right to admit to this "weakness". What was destructive culturally about the late sixties was the coruscation of poetry, its encroaching disappearance for economic reasons as much else in this society economics has taken precedent. Individuals are approached and mugged, although this can be done in the most sophisticated ways. The references are filmic. Death becomes scattered thus, diasporic. A teacher of mine once reminded me that great male scholars would not have written and organised their work without their wives and their wives' maids. I needed a chaperone when I left home and this unprotected state has left me in a position [...] of the Irish [...] who has nothing but her own good nature and the fresh air to sustain her. Unless I can organise the 24 hour small screen line of ubiquity, I don't see any hope. The screen light is too strong for me.[46]

The archive will change the kind of stories we can tell about Mendelssohn's life and work. In the vast repositories of notebooks and manuscripts, a new account will emerge, bringing details into sharper focus. What I've tried to articulate in this chapter are the significant challenges and opportunities that Mendelssohn's work poses to historically inclined literary criticism. While I've focused on the affective dimension, the resistances to chronology within her

---

[46] Anna Mendelssohn, undated letter to Luke Roberts. University of Sussex Special Collections, SxMs109/3.

publishing history compound this. Her poetry frustrates my desire for progression, however disorderly or damaged, from sequence to sequence and from book to book. My mind reels at the thought of the thousands of pages of undated notebooks in the archive. While her play between languages, her magnificent ventriloquy, sarcasm and jokes – aspects that I've hardly touched on here – mean that sometimes I don't know what I'm reading, more fundamentally I don't always know *when* I'm reading the work, what history we're in. So I arrange these last items in the screen light, time ringing in my ears.

Coda: The Kind of Poetry I Want

Throughout the writing of this book I've had a line by Bhanu Kapil stuck in my head: 'One thing next to another doesn't mean they touch.'[1] No matter the loose sense of political affiliation I've traced across the work of the preceding chapters, there's still little evidence of substantial overlap or creative exchange between the traditions and standpoints I've assembled. On the one hand, I believe that poetry is collective work, moving often in excess of an author's designs, capable of making unpredictable and vital connections, full of radical convergence and possibility. On the other, I know that poetry also records intransigent divisions and differences, holding to vital specificity under duress. Given the social stratifications enforced by capital, it shouldn't come as a surprise that the conditions of poetic production in any given age retain disparate trajectories. Breaching the terms of our subjugation requires immense and various effort. As Diane di Prima wrote: 'NO ONE WAY WORKS, it will take all of us / shoving at the thing from all sides / to bring it down.'[2]

But by stressing the common political commitments of the writers in this study, I'm suggesting that there are multiple intersecting traditions of left-wing poetry in Britain. Put simply, it *matters* that the Communist Party included both Claudia Jones in Notting Hill and later John James and Wendy Mulford in Cambridge. It is culturally and historically significant that Bill Griffiths and Linton Kwesi Johnson organised at different times against the police and prison system. This isn't to suggest that differences in aesthetics, let alone in

---

[1] Bhanu Kapil, *Ban En Banlieue* (New York: Nightboat, 2015), 13.
[2] Diane di Prima, *Revolutionary Letters: 50th Anniversary Edition* (San Francisco: City Lights, 2021), 14.

the lived experience of race, gender, class or sexuality, are rendered superficial in political struggle; only that a contemporary poetics of solidarity might learn from this history, find resources for going on with, mistakes to avoid repeating.

There is at least *some* evidence of the tenuous physical proximity of the British Poetry Revival, the Caribbean Artists Movement, the African National Congress and other writers and subjects I've touched on here.[3] During the 1970s, the National Poetry Centre in London featured an events programme at Earl's Court far more diverse than any 'poetry wars' narrative would imply. In autumn 1971 – the beginning of the radical takeover of the Poetry Society – readers included Kamau Brathwaite, Barry MacSweeney and a double-bill of John La Rose (co-founder of New Beacon Books) and Jim Burns (poet and journalist with the Labour Party newspaper *Tribune*). There were also talks by Mazisi Kunene and Bob Cobbing, and a presentation by the East End Communist Party organiser (and veteran of the anti-fascist Battle of Cable Street) Jack Dash. The gender disparity was as dismal as ever: of twenty-nine speakers, Shirley Toulson was the only woman reading her own work. But nevertheless, this was not quite the racially homogenous avant-garde I had come to expect.[4]

The programme in spring 1977 – when the outmanoeuvred radicals quit *en masse* – tells a similar story, marked by developments in Women's Liberation and Gay Liberation activism. Mulford read with Liliane Lijn as part of an evening of feminist poetry; Pat Arrowsmith, anti-nuclear activist and gay rights campaigner, led a discussion of poetry and prison; there was a benefit reading for *Gay News* – at that point facing prosecution for blasphemy after publishing a poem by James Kirkup – featuring readings by Elaine Randell and Asa Benveniste. There were also readings in solidarity with Chile, and a launch event for *Bluefoot Traveller: Poetry by West Indians in Britain*, edited by James Berry, with readings by E. A. Markham, Linton Kwesi Johnson and Jimi Rand.

I don't want to present these precarious links and cross-currents of literary cosmopolitanism as somehow heroic or redemptive. A list of names on a flyer is thin grounds for conciliation, and to reiterate:

---

[3] Matt Martin's doctoral thesis, 'Tides of Voice: Nation Language as Political Resistance in the Work of Kamau Brathwaite and Bill Griffiths' (Birkbeck College, University of London, 2022), provides several further points of contact and comparison.

[4] My information here comes from flyers in issues of *Poetry Review* held in the collection of the National Poetry Library at the Royal Festival Hall and in the collection of the author.

One thing next to another doesn't mean they touch. In fact, given that Berry was – as far as I'm aware – the only West Indian poet to publish in *Poetry Review* during Mottram's editorship, this might simply re-emphasise the fundamentally exclusionary project of a nationally defined avant-garde aesthetic movement.[5] Every time I think I've managed to bend the British Poetry Revival into something more malleable, with more porous edges, it seems to spring back into shape.

This problem is perpetuated in criticism. For example, we find in the opening encomium of Andrew Duncan's recent *Nothing is Being Suppressed: British Poetry of the 1970s* (2022) an elaboration of the 'culturally marginalised' position of the poets of the British Poetry Revival via a description of Dogon cosmology drawn from the cultural anthropologist Victor Turner.[6] This is an example of what Timothy Yu has called, in the US context, 'the ethnicization of the avant-garde'.[7] Yu suggests that in response to the emergence of new identity categories for writing based on gender, race and sexuality, the predominantly white avant-garde literary community recast itself 'not simply as an aesthetic movement but as a social identity'.[8] It's clear that a similar dynamic is sometimes operative in Britain, though as I've argued throughout this book we have to pay attention to the specific exigencies of the British state and the history of empire. These are vast edifices, present everywhere in our critical heritage. There are many more obstacles still yet to dislodge.

My ideal for criticism, as far-fetched as it might sound, is something like the form of a political demonstration or protest march. I wrote much of this book during the protracted lockdowns of the Covid-19 pandemic, punctuated by the experience of coming out into the streets during the George Floyd uprisings in 2020, the marches in solidarity with Gaza in 2021 and the annual United Friends and Family Campaign walk from Trafalgar Square to Downing Street to commemorate those killed in state custody. In those events,

---

[5] See *Poetry Review* 63, no. 3 (Autumn 1972): 253–61. According to Stephen Willey, Berry attended some of the earliest meetings of Bob Cobbing's Writers Forum. See Willey, '"This Face of Glee … This Terrifying Sound": Sean Bonney Through the Soundhole, Where Bonney IS', *Journal of British and Irish Innovative Poetry* 14, no. 1 (2022).

[6] Andrew Duncan, *Nothing is Being Suppressed: British Poetry of the 1970s* (Swindon: Shearsman, 2021), 10.

[7] Timothy Yu, *Race and the Avant-Garde: Experimental and Asian American Poetry Since 1965* (Stanford: Stanford UP, 2009), 38–72.

[8] Ibid., 71. See also Natalia Cecire, *Experimental: American Literature and the Aesthetics of Knowledge* (Baltimore: Johns Hopkins UP, 2019), 35–7.

being close but not touching was a sign of both trepidation and care around the virus. Being next to each other was overwhelming, enlivening, after months of being indoors. Discrete individuals in our related blocs, we join together in the transformative hours of collective presence, lived through and later recalled.

A recent poem by Jackie Kay, 'A Life in Protest', presents the reader with scene after scene of such events. From Gay Pride marches to Greenham Common, marches against the war in Iraq to one of Hortensia Allende's visits to Glasgow, Kay moves her reader between the loose music of conversation, the chant of slogans, through to the full flight of song. She remembers the formation of OWAAD with the intensity of 'a first kiss', and runs through Chaka Khan, Sister Sledge, Junior Murvin.[9] At every staging post more voices seem to circulate, more songs spring to mind. In the concluding stanzas her mother – secretary of the Scottish section of the Campaign for Nuclear Disarmament – sings Paul Robeson, accompanied by the jazz singer Suzanne Bonnar. Kay interweaves lines from Joan Armatrading, until the speakers all blur, both one and many. Written to accompany an installation by the photographer Ingrid Pollard, Kay's poem reverberates with memory and the kind of 'bass history' I outlined in Chapter 6.

I'd like to start drawing this book to a close by dwelling on a moment from the start of the poem. Kay describes being taken 'straight from Elise Inglis more or less' to a demo against the arrival of Polaris missiles at Holy Loch, east of Glasgow, in 1961. Thinking back to the argument I made in the Introduction, perhaps we can read this as an understanding of the relationship between the already compromised welfare state – the Elsie Inglis maternity hospital – and the imperialist warfare state.[10] Kay, born to a Nigerian father and Scottish mother, was given up for adoption in 1961: her adoptive parents, both members of the Communist Party, were white.[11] Though it makes little sense to think of her work as 'avant-garde' – she was the Makar, or National Poet of Scotland, from 2016 to 2021 – the appearance of Kay's earliest poetry in the 1980s unquestionably

---

[9] Jackie Kay, 'A Life in Protest' (2022), online: https://artuk.org/discover/stories/a-life-in-protest-jackie-kays-response-to-ingrid-pollard-at-glasgow-womens-library [Accessed 25 October 2023].

[10] For a historical analysis of the post-war welfare state as a 'maternal surrogate', see Shaul Bar-Haim, *The Maternalists: Psychoanalysis, Motherhood, and the British Welfare State* (Philadelphia: U of Pennsylvania P, 2021), 3.

[11] For the poet's autobiography, see Jackie Kay, *Red Dust Road* (London: Picador, 2017).

broke new ground, and her involvement with OWAAD and the Black Lesbian Group was politically radical.[12] Likewise, her 1998 novel, *Trumpet*, has been recognised for its complex presentation of racialised trans life and death.[13] When Kay looks back in 'A Life in Protest', she sees herself looking forward, part of the movement for justice, the transformation of society.

In the second stanza, as if studying a freeze-frame recording of the Holy Loch demo, she writes:

> My brand-new mum carrying wee me.
> My brother in a pram pushed by
> Hugh MacDiarmid, black beret on, bead eyes.
> Lined face, – *but greet and in yer tears*
> *ye'll droon the hale clanjamfrie!*

This moment is shot through with the contradictions and questions I've been exploring in this book. MacDiarmid – grand old man of twentieth-century modernism – is positioned within the family matrix, his appearance after the line break simultaneously surprising and inevitable. The last two lines here are from MacDiarmid's famous 'The Bonnie Broukit Bairn'. One of MacDiarmid's early feats in experimenting with diction and extremes of scale, Nancy K. Gish suggests that it 'acknowledges the triumphant importance of the small, human, and earthly in the face of cosmic self-assertion'.[14] In the context of the nuclear threat, Kay seems to resignify this poem: the infant's cry becomes a wail of protest against the global arms race of the Cold War. But moreover, the 'bonnie broukit bairn' – the beautiful, neglected infant – is here situated as a description of the adopted Black child, whose voice will be heard, amplified within the intimate political agency of the crowd.[15]

I'm interested in how Kay presents herself in relation to MacDiarmid. Being held by her mother, to his side, this isn't staged as a filial relationship of inheritance, but instead a comradely one. They move in time together. John McLeod has described the 'aesthetics of adoption' in Kay's work as part of 'a quest for new ways

---

[12] See Barbara Burford, Gabriela Pearse, Grace Nichols and Jackie Kay, *A Dangerous Knowing: Four Black Women Poets* (London: Sheba, 1985).
[13] For an influential reading of *Trumpet*, see Jack Halberstam, *In a Queer Time and Place* (Durham, NC: Duke UP, 2005), 56–61.
[14] Nany K. Gish, *Hugh MacDiarmid: The Man and His Work* (London: Palgrave Macmillan, 1984), 40.
[15] According to the Chambers *Scots Dictionary*, 'brouk' means literally 'to soil with soot'.

of being that can be pitted against the normative'.[16] Where elsewhere in her work the Communist Party is figured as 'an extended family', perhaps in this poem the terms are reversed: the chosen family is like a Party (and joyously a *party*, too).[17] The relationships in the poem are asserted as lateral, rather than horizontal, diagramming an expansive queer kinship of political commitment. Even her mother, by the final stanza, is figured as a 'call and response *sister*', the relations again transformed in song.

Though it's a respectful cameo, honouring MacDiarmid's lifetime of activism, the framing reminds me of Margaret Tait's *Hugh MacDiarmid: A Portrait* (1964). In Tait's film the notorious elder statesman, renowned and reviled in equal measure for his polemical nationalism and communism, appears as a boyish figure, playing up to the camera. We see him in the kitchen drying cutlery, reading lines from his masterpiece *The Kind of Poetry I Want* about the dialectical breadknife 'which cuts three slices at once'; he walks a determined straight line down an Edinburgh street, balancing on kerbs and church walls, before throwing his notebook in a dustbin; he ends picking stones from a river and throwing them uphill in a mock-Sisyphean gesture.[18]

Without wishing to position MacDiarmid at the head of the table, it's worth emphasising the things he has in common with each of the writers I've discussed in this book. Like Kamau Brathwaite, Mazisi Kunene and Cecilia Vicuña, he was engaged with questions about language, colonialism and anti-imperialist struggle.[19] With J. H. Prynne, he is often much closer to Friedrich Engels's speculative dialectics of nature than he is to the political economy of Marx.[20] His anti-establishment credentials would surely compete with Bill Griffiths and Tom Pickard, both working-class autodidacts like him. Like Anna Mendelssohn he was harassed by the British state; like Lee Harwood and Harry Fainlight he experienced crises in his

---

[16] John McLeod, 'Adoption Aesthetics', in *The Cambridge Companion to British Black and Asian Literature, 1945–2016*, ed. Deirdre Osborne (Cambridge: Cambridge UP, 2016), 211–24 (223).

[17] Kay, *Red Dust Road*, 32.

[18] For a reading of Tait's film see Sara Neely and Alan Riach, 'Demons in the Machine: Experimental Film, Poetry and Modernism in Twentieth-Century Scotland', in *Scottish Cinema Now*, ed. Jonathan Murray, Fidelma Farley and Rod Stoneman (Newcastle: Cambridge Scolars, 2009), 6–8.

[19] Matthew Hart reads MacDiarmid with Brathwaite in *Nations of Nothing But Poetry: Modernism, Transnationalism, and Synthetic Vernacular Writing* (Oxford: Oxford UP, 2010).

[20] John Wilkinson accuses Prynne and MacDiarmid of being invested in a 'totalitarian version of Marxist dialectic' in *Lyric and Its Times* (London: Bloomsbury, 2020), 113.

mental health.[21] Like Denise Riley and Linton Kwesi Johnson, he was involved in political organising and activism.

The same year as the Holy Loch protest that Kay's poem records, MacDiarmid's *The Kind of Poetry I Want* was published in a handsome limited edition.[22] The origins of this long poem lie in the build-up to the Second World War, when MacDiarmid was editing his paper *The Voice of Scotland*. Inspired by the Glaswegian Marxist John MacLean, the editorial line announced itself as 'anti-Fascist, anti-Imperialist, opposed to the Imperialist War, and to the conception of the supremacy of brute instinct over intelligence, the perversion of science for the myth of racial superiority and the deification of state'.[23] This period of his writing causes immense problems for critics because of the staggering outpouring of work. According to his wife Valda, MacDiarmid wrote over one million words in the late 1930s, and the sheer exertion made him physically shrink.[24]

The byzantine publication histories that have resulted from his collaging and rearranging of this material are too complicated to go into here. But *The Kind of Poetry I Want* is a poem radically open and inviting to the reader, despite also being erudite, repetitive and tedious. It has always struck me that it works as a provocation to the reader, in which we might be expected to write our own version by way of reply. As MacDiarmid puts it in an aside about Fred Astaire, 'So great an artist that he makes you feel / You could do the dance yourself – is that not great art?'[25] The listing-form of the poem is his own invention or discovery, recalling somewhat improbably the work of the second-generation New York School. It's like a gigantic counterpart to Ted Berrigan's '10 Things I Do Every Day', or an inflated and antagonistic uncle to Joe Brainard's masterpiece *I Remember*.[26]

The specific form the poem takes – as Adrienne Rich has observed – is the manifesto, even as it subjects the manifesto to

---

[21] See Scott Lyall, '"The Man is a Menace": MacDiarmid and Military Intelligence', *Scottish Studies Review* 8, no. 1 (2007): 37–52.

[22] Hugh MacDiarmid, *The Kind of Poetry I Want* (Edinburgh: K.D. Duvall, 1961). Collected as 'The Kind of Poetry I Want', *The Complete Poems of Hugh MacDiarmid*, ed. Michael Grieve and W. R. Aiken, 2 vols. (Harmondsworth: Penguin, 1978), vol. 2, 1003–35, and 'Further Passages From *The Kind of Poetry I Want*', *Complete Poems*, vol. 1, 607–27.

[23] Hugh MacDiarmid, 'The Red Scotland Thesis: Forward to the John MacLean Line', *The Voice of Scotland*, 1, no. 1 (1938): 13.

[24] Alan Bold, *MacDiarmid* (London: John Murray, 1988), 379.

[25] MacDiarmid 'The Kind of Poetry I Want', 1006.

[26] Ted Berrigan, '10 Things I Do Every Day', *The Collected Poems of Ted Berrigan*, ed. Alice Notley, Anselm Berrigan and Edmund Berrigan (Berkeley: U of California P, 2005), 164; Joe Brainard, *I Remember* (New York: Granary, 2001).

travesty and parody.[27] It's hard to summarise without simply joining in with MacDiarmid's game, but the logic of composition is clear enough. MacDiarmid writes a long list of analogy, metaphor, simile and allegory, a list of demands of the kind of poetry he wants. It's both a self-address – he wants his own poetry to be like, for example, Astaire's dancing or Byzantine architecture – and a generalised demand for a high level of cultural attainment, a poetry capable of withstanding comparison to the full range of human and social activity, whether fishing or music, wrestling or childbirth, dialectics or religion or mysticism. In one sense the poem is a bravura demonstration that MacDiarmid is already capable of writing the kind of poetry he wants. But he also states:

> Poetry of such an integration as cannot be effected
> Until a new and conscious organisation of society
> Generates a new view
> Of the world as a whole[28]

As Marx wrote in *Critique of the Gotha Programme*, 'one only demands what one has not got'.[29] Yet this lack never feels like an absence: the poem wants what's to come, rather than longing after lost objects. MacDiarmid's desires in *The Kind of Poetry I Want* are latent in the existing social world, and they can be realised by the revolutionary reorganisation of society.

After the outbreak of war, and while MacDiarmid was writing the poem, industrial conscription was introduced for men aged over fifty-one. He was soon working on Clydeside, where he would be quite seriously injured in a workplace accident.[30] In this light, perhaps we can read the poem as the work of a vulnerable subject, looking to transform the conditions that have made him so. When we read it we encounter a vision of abundance, leisure and intellectual stimulation, where nothing is thwarted. It comes close to the passage in *The German Ideology*, where Marx and Engels argue that if society regulates production we might hunt in the morning, fish in the afternoon, rear cattle in the evening and criticise after dinner:[31]

---

[27] Adrienne Rich, *Poetry and Commitment* (London: Norton, 2007).
[28] MacDiarmid, 'The Kind of Poetry I Want', 1025.
[29] Karl Marx, *The Critique of the Gotha Programme* (Moscow: Progress, 1971), 28.
[30] In Bold's brief account, MacDiarmid's arms and legs were injured by a heavy copper plate. Bold, *MacDiarmid*, 384–5.
[31] Karl Marx and Frederick Engels, *The German Ideology*, ed. C. J. Arthur (London: Lawrence & Wishart, 1991), 54.

> A poetry finding its universal material in the people,
> And the people in turn giving life and continuity
> To this poetry by its collective interest.

Or:

> [...] a poetry that stands for production, use and life,
> as opposed to property, profits, and death.[32]

The 'want' that animates MacDiarmid's poem goes far beyond the categories identified for amelioration by the Beveridge Report or by the Labour Party manifesto of 1945.[33] Poetry's utopian function leaps ahead, sweeps us up in its burning urgency.

In *The Kind of Poetry I Want* – a poem MacDiarmid did not, or could not finish, a poem in which he writes 'I have found in Marxism all that I need', a poem in which his communism outflanks his nationalism – the poet holds to the obstinate centrality of inexhaustible and intractable demands.[34] His inability to complete the poem is because the demands of the poem can't be completed in the aesthetic sphere alone: they demand nothing less than the abolition of the present state of things, rather than their temporary readjustment.

---

[32] MacDiarmid, 'The Kind of Poetry I Want', 1023.
[33] 'Want' – in the sense of 'deprivation' – appears as one of the 'Five Giants' to be slain along with Ignorance, Squalor, Idleness and Disease. See 'Labour Party General Election Manifesto 1945', *Labour Party General Election Manifestos, 1900–1997*, ed. Iain Dale (London: Routledge, 2000).
[34] MacDiarmid, 'Further Passages From *The Kind of Poetry I Want*', *Complete Poems*, 615.

Select Bibliography

Adams, Terry. *Bill Butler and the Unicorn Bookshop*. Binley Woods: Beat Scene Press, 2020.
Ahmed, Sara. *The Cultural Politics of Emotion*. Edinburgh: Edinburgh UP, 2014.
Arendt, Hannah. 'Active Patience' (1941). In *The Jewish Writings*, edited by Jerome Kohn and Ron H. Feldman, 139–42. New York: Shockhen, 2007.
Austin, David. *Dread Poetry & Freedom: Linton Kwesi Johnson and the Unfinished Revolution*. London: Pluto, 2018.
Barrett, James R. and David R. Roediger. 'Inbetween Peoples: Race, Nationality, and the "New Immigrant" Working Class'. In Barrett, *History from the Bottom Up*, 145–74. Durham, NC: Duke UP, 2017.
Barry, Peter. *Poetry Wars: British Poetry of the 1970s and the Battle for Earls Court*. Cambridge: Salt, 2006.
Bernstein, Hilda. *The Drift: The Exile Experience of South Africans*. London: Jonathan Cape, 1994.
Bold, Alan. *MacDiarmid*. London: John Murray, 1988.
Bollas, Christopher. *The Shadow of the Object*. London: Tavistock, 1987.
Brathwaite, Kamau. 'The African Presence in Caribbean Literature'. *Daedalus* 103, no. 2 (1974): 73–109.
———. *Ancestors*. New York: New Directions, 2001.
———. *The Arrivants: A New World Trilogy*. Oxford: Oxford UP, 1973.
———. *Barabajan Poems*. Kingston and New York: Savacou North, 1994.
———. *Contradictory Omens: Cultural Diversity and Integration in the Caribbean*. Mona: Savacou, 1974.
———. *ConVERSations*. With Nathaniel Mackey. Minneapolis: XCP (Cross Cultural Poetics), 1999.
———. 'Dialect and Dialectic'. *African Studies Association of the West Indies Bulletin* 6 (1973): 89–99.
———. *DS(2): Dreamstories*. New York: New Directions, 2007.
———. *Golokwati 2000*. Kingston and New York: Savacou North, 2002.
———. *The History of the Voice*. London: New Beacon, 1984.
———. 'The Love Axe/L: Developing a Caribbean Aesthetic, Part Two'. *Bim* 16, no. 2 (1977): 100–6.

———. 'Newstead to Neustadt'. *World Literature Today* 68, no. 4 (1994): 653–60.
———. *Other Exiles*. Oxford: Oxford UP, 1975.
———. *Roots*. Ann Arbor: U of Michigan P, 1993.
———. 'The Second Time of Salt'. *Scritture Migranti* 5 (2011): 6–18.
———. *Third World Poems*. Harlow: Longman, 1983.
———. 'Timehri'. *Savacou* 2 (1970): 35–44.
———. *Trench Town Rock*. Providence: Lost Road, 1994.
Brown, Stewart, ed. *The Art of Kamau Brathwaite*. Bridgend: Seren, 1995.
Brutus, Dennis. 'Poetry of Suffering: The Black Experience'. *Ba Shiru* 4, no. 1 (1973): 1–10.
———. 'Protest Against Apartheid'. In *Protest and Conflict in African Literature*, edited by Cosmo Pieterse and Donald Munro, 93–100. London: Heinemann, 1969.
Bryan, Beverley, Stella Dadzie and Suzanne Scafe. *Heart of the Race: Black Women's Lives in Britain*. London: Verso, 2018.
Bryan-Wilson, Julia. 'Awareness of Awareness: An Interview with Cecilia Vicuña'. In Cecilia Vicuña, *About to Happen*, 110–29. New York: Siglio, 2017.
Buck, Claire. 'Poetry and the Women's Movement in Britain'. In *Contemporary British Poetry: Essays in Theory and Criticism*, edited by James Acheson and Romana Huk, 81–111. New York: State U of New York P, 1996.
Bunce, Robin and Paul Field. *Darcus Howe: A Political Biography*. London: Bloomsbury, 2014.
Burton, Richard. *A Strong Song Tows Us: The Life of Basil Bunting*. Oxford: Infinite Ideas, 2013.
Bush, Clive. *Out of Dissent: A Study of Five Contemporary British Poets*. London: Talus, 1997.
Carby, Hazel V. 'Schooling in Babylon'. In *The Empire Strikes Back: Race and Racism in Seventies Britain*, Birmingham Centre for Cultural Studies, 182–211. London: Hutchinson, 1982.
Chang, Victor L., ed. *Three Caribbean Poets on Their Work*. Kingston: UWIP, 1993.
Cobbing, Bob and Jeff Nuttall, eds. *Barnet Poets: An Anthology by Children of the New Borough of Barnet*. London: Writers Forum, 1965.
Crangle, Sara. 'Introduction'. In *I'm Working Here: The Collected Poems of Anna Mendelssohn*, 21–109. Swindon: Shearsman, 2021.
Crisp, Quentin. *The Naked Civil Servant*. Harmondsworth: Penguin, 1997.
Crozier, Andrew. *All Where Each Is*. Edinburgh and London: Agneau 2, 1985.
———. 'Introduction'. In *A Various Art*, edited by Crozier and Tim Longville, 11–14. Manchester: Carcanet, 1987.
Currey, James. *Africa Writes Back: The African Writers Series & The Launch of African Literature*. Oxford: James Currey, 2008.

Davie, Donald. *These The Companions*. Cambridge: Cambridge UP, 1982.
Davies, Carol Boyce. *Left of Karl Marx: The Political Life of Black Communist Claudia Jones*. Durham, NC: Duke UP, 2007.
———, ed. *Claudia Jones: Beyond Containment*. Banbury: Ayebia, 2011.
Debray, Régis. *Conversations with Allende: Socialism in Chile*. London: New Left Review, 1971.
Delany, Samuel R. *Shorter Views: Queer Thoughts and the Politics of the Paraliterary*. London: Wesleyan, 1999.
Dhondy, Farrukh. 'Review: *Voices of the Living and the Dead*'. *Race Today* 6, no. 3 (1974): 92.
———. 'Teaching Young Blacks'. *Race Today* 10, no. 4 (1978): 80–6.
Doane, Janice and Devon Hodges. *From Klein to Kristeva: Psychoanalytic Feminism and the Search for the 'Good Enough Mother'*. Ann Arbor: U of Michigan P, 1992.
Dorn, Edward. *Collected Poems*. Edited by Jennifer Dunbar Dorn with Justin Katko, Reitha Pattison and Kyle Waugh. Manchester: Carcanet, 2012.
Eagleton, Terry. *Literary Theory: An Introduction*. Oxford: Blackwell, 1983.
———. 'Recent Poetry'. *Stand* 10, no. 1 (1968): 66–74.
Ellis, Stephen. *External Mission: The ANC in Exile, 1960–1990*. Oxford: Oxford UP, 2013.
Etsy, Jed. *A Sinking Island: Modernism and National Culture in England*. Princeton: Princeton UP, 2004.
Fainlight, Harry. *Sussicran*. London: Turret, 1965.
Fanon, Frantz. *Black Skin, White Masks*. Translated by Charles Lamm Markmann. London: Pluto, 2008.
———. *Black Skin, White Masks*. Translated by Richard Philcox. New York: Grove Press, 2008.
———. *The Wretched of the Earth*. Translated by Constance Farrington. New York: Grove Press, 2004.
Fell, Alison, Stef Pixner, Tina Reid, Michèle Roberts and Ann Oosthuizen. *Licking the Bed Clean*. London: Teeth Imprints, 1978.
Field, Paul, Robin Bunce, Leila Hassan and Margaret Peacock, eds. *Here to Fight, Here To Stay: A Race Today Anthology*. London: Pluto, 2019.
Fitzgerald, Mike. *Prisoners in Revolt*. Harmondsworth: Penguin, 1977.
Freud, Sigmund. *Civilization and Its Discontents* [1930]. Revised edition, translated by Joan Riviere. London: Hogarth, 1963.
Gilroy, Paul. *The Black Atlantic*. London: Verso, 1993.
———. *Postcolonial Melancholia*. New York: Columbia UP, 2004.
Ginsberg, Allen. *Collected Poems: 1947–1980*. London: Viking, 1985.
———. *Iron Curtain Journals*. Edited by Michael Schumacher. Minneapolis: U of Minnesota P, 2018.
Gish, Nancy K. *Hugh MacDiarmid: The Man and His Work*. London: Palgrave Macmillan, 1984.

Glissant, Édouard. *Poetics of Relation*. Translated by Betsy Wing. Ann Arbor: U of Michigan P, 1997.

Gopal, Priyamvada. *Insurgent Empire: Anticolonial Resistance and British Dissent*. London: Verso, 2019.

Green, Peter Morris, ed. *Poetry from Cambridge, 1947–1950*. London: The Fortune Press, 1951.

Griffiths, Bill. *An Account of the End*. Cambridge: Lobby Press, 1978.

———. 'Basil Bunting and Eric Mottram'. *Chicago Review* 44, nos. 3–4 (1998): 104–13.

———. *Collected Earlier Poems: 1966–1980*. Edited by Alan Halsey. Hastings: Reality Street, 2010.

———. *Collected Poems & Sequences: 1981–91*. Edited by Alan Halsey. Hastings: Reality Street, 2014.

———. *Collected Poems, vol. 3*. Edited by Alan Halsey. Hastings: Reality Street, 2016.

———. *HMP: Revising Prison*. Seaham: Amra, 1993.

———. *In Rebuttal of the Guardian: On the Role of Solitary Confinement in British Prisons – Call for an Inquiry*. Seaham: Amra, 1994.

———. 'Interview with Will Rowe'. *The Salt Companion to Bill Griffiths*, 171–96. Cambridge: Salt, 2007.

———. *The Lion Man & Others*. London: Veer, 2008.

———. *Seventy-Six Day Wanno, Mississippi and Highpoint Journal*. With Delvan McIntosh. Seaham: Amra, 1993.

———. *Some Notes on the Metropolitan Police, London: With Some Footnotes on the Magistrates' Courts*. Seaham: Amra, 1994.

———. *Star Fish Jail*. Seaham: Amra, 1993.

———. *Tyne Txts*. With Tom Pickard. Seaham: Amra, 2004.

Gutzmore, Cecil and Rudi Guyan. 'Missing the Point'. *The Black Liberator* 1, no. 4 (1973): 249–53.

Hall, Stuart. *Cultural Studies 1983: A Theoretical History*. Durham, NC: Duke UP, 2016.

———. 'The New Conservatism and the Old' (1957). In *Selected Political Writings*, edited by Sally Davidson, David Featherstone, Michael Rustin and Bill Schwarz, 18–27. Durham, NC: Duke UP, 2017.

———. 'Politics, Contingency, Strategy: An Interview with David Scott'. In *Essential Essays: vol. 2*, edited by David Morley, 235–62. Durham, NC: Duke UP, 2019.

———. *Selected Writings on Marxism*. Edited by Gregor McLennan. Durham, NC: Duke UP, 2021.

———. 'The State – Socialism's Old Caretaker'. In *The Hard Road To Renewal: Thatcherism and Crisis of the Left*, 220–32. London: Verso, 1988.

———. with Chas Critcher, Tony Jefferson, John Clarke and Brian Roberts. *Policing the Crisis: Mugging, the State, and Law and Order*. London: Macmillan, 1978.

Harwood, Lee. *Collected Poems*. Exeter: Shearsman, 2004.
———. Interviewed by Eric Mottram. *Poetry Information* 14 (Autumn/Winter 1975–6): 4–18.
———. *Landscapes*. London: Fulcrum, 1969.
———. 'Lee Harwood'. In *Gale Contemporary Authors Autobiography Series 19*, 135–53. Detroit: Gale Research, 1994.
———. *The Man With Blue Eyes*. New York: Angel Hair, 1966.
———. *New Collected Poems*. Edited by Kelvin Corcoran and Robert Sheppard. Swindon: Shearsman, 2023.
———. *The Sinking Colony*. London: Fulcrum, 1970.
———. *The White Room*. London: Fulcrum, 1968.
Hazzard, Oli. *John Ashbery and Anglo-American Exchange: The Minor Eras*. Oxford: Oxford UP, 2018.
Hegel, G. W. F. *Lectures on the Philosophy of World History: Introduction*. Translated by H. B. Nisbet. Cambridge: Cambridge UP, 1982.
———. *The Philosophy of History*. Translated by J. Sibree. Mineola: Dover, 1956.
Heller, Agnes. *The Theory of Need in Marx*. London: Verso, 2018.
Hemmings, Clare. *Why Stories Matter: The Political Grammar of Feminist Theory*. Durham, NC: Duke UP, 2011.
Hensman, Savitri. *Flood at Your Door*. London: Centerprise, 1979.
Hickman, Ben. *Crisis and the U.S. Avant-Garde: Poetry and Real Politics*. Edinburgh: Edinburgh UP, 2015.
Horovitz, Michael, ed. *Children of Albion: Poetry of the 'Underground' in Britain*. Harmondsworth: Penguin, 1969.
Huntley, Accabre. *At School Today*. London: Bogle L'Ouverture, 1977.
Israel, Mark. *South African Political Exile in the United Kingdom*. London: Palgrave, 1999.
Jabès, Edmond. *The Book of Questions: Yaël, Elya, Aely*. Translated by Rosmarie Waldrop. Middletown: Wesleyan, 1983.
James, C. L. R. *Notes on Dialectics: Hegel, Marx, Lenin*. Westport, CT: Lawrence Hill, 1981.
James, Selma. 'Sex, Race, and Class'. *Race Today* 6, no. 1 (January 1974): 12–15.
———, ed. *Strangers and Sisters: Women, Race, & Immigration*. Bristol: Falling Wall, 1985.
James, John. *Collected Poems*. Cambridge: Salt, 2002.
———. *Mmm... Ah Yes*. London: Ferry, 1967.
———. *The Small Henderson Room*. London: Ferry, 1969.
———. *Striking the Pavilion of Zero*. London: Ian McKelvie, 1975.
Jameson, Fredric. *Allegory and Ideology*. London: Verso, 2019.
———. *The Political Unconscious*. Abingdon: Routledge, 2002.
Jarman, Derek. *At Your Own Risk*. Minneapolis: U of Minnesota P, 2010.
Johnson, Linton Kwesi. *Dread, Beat, and Blood*. 3rd ed. London: Bogle L'Ouverture, 1975.

———. *Inglan is a Bitch*. London: Race Today, 1980.

———. 'Interview with Linton Kwesi Johnson by Mervyn Morris'. In *Hinterland: Caribbean Poetry From the West Indies and Britain*, edited by E. A. Markham, 250–61. Newcastle Upon Tyne: Bloodaxe, 1989.

———. 'Jamaican Rebel Music'. *Race and Class* 17, no. 4 (1976): 387–412.

———. 'Linton Kwesi Johnson in Conversation with John La Rose'. In *Changing Britannia: Life Experience with Britain*, edited by Roxy Harris and Sarah White, 51–79. London: New Beacon / George Padmore Institute, 1990.

———. 'The New Caribbean Poets'. *Race Today* 9, no. 7 (November 1977): 164–6.

———. 'The Politics of the Lyrics of Reggae Music'. *The Black Liberator* 2, no. 4 (1975): 363–73.

———. '*Race Today* and British Politics: Introduction'. *Here to Fight, Here to Stay: A Race Today Anthology*, 8–10.

———. 'Review: *You Better Believe It – Black Verse in English*'. *Race Today* 6, no. 1 (January 1974): 24–5.

———. *Selected Poems*. London: Penguin, 2006.

———. *Time Come: Selected Prose*. London: Picador, 2023.

Johnson, Buzz. *'I Think of My Mother': Notes on the Life and Times of Claudia Jones*. London: Karia, 1985.

Jolly, Margaretta. *Sisterhood and After*. Oxford: Oxford UP, 2019.

Jones, Claudia. 'The Caribbean Community in Britain' (1964). In *Claudia Jones: Beyond Containment*, edited by Carole Boyce Davies, 167–81. Banbury: Ayebia, 2011.

Kalliney, Peter J. *Commonwealth of Letters*. Oxford: Oxford UP, 2013.

Kapil, Bhanu. *Ban en Banlieue*. New York: Nightboat, 2015.

Keith, Joseph. *Unbecoming Americans: Writing Race and Nation from the Shadows of Citizenship, 1945–60*. New Brunswick: Rutgers, 2013.

Kennedy, David and Christine Kennedy. *Women's Experimental Poetry in Britain, 1970–2010*. Liverpool: Liverpool UP, 2013.

Kinnahan, Linda. 'Feminism's experimental "work at the language-face"'. In *The Cambridge Companion to Twentieth-Century British and Irish Women's Poetry*, edited by Jane Dowson, 54–178. Cambridge: Cambridge UP, 2011.

Klopper, Dirk. 'Arthur Nortje: A Life Story'. In *Arthur Nortje: Poet and South African*, edited by Craig McLuckie and Ross Tyner, 1–28. Pretoria: UNISA, 2004.

———. 'Arthur Nortje and the Unhomely'. *Alternation* 5, no. 2 (1988): 166–76.

———. 'Chronology of Arthur Nortje's Life and Work'. In *Anatomy of Dark: Collected Poems of Arthur Nortje*, xix–xxiii. Pretoria: UNISA, 2000.

Koram, Kojo. *Uncommon Wealth: Britain and the Aftermath of Empire*. London: John Murray, 2022.

Kunene, Mazisi. *Anthem of the Decades*. London: Heinemann, 1981.

———. 'An Interview With Mazisi Kunene'. *Commonwealth (Dijon)* 14, no. 2 (1992): 34–42.

———. 'Introduction'. In Aimé Césaire, *Return to My Native Land*, translated by John Berger and Anna Bostock, 7–33. Harmondsworth: Penguin, 1969.

——— [unsigned]. 'Literature and Resistance in South Africa'. *Sechaba* 1, no. 6 (June 1967): 17–18.

——— [unsigned]. 'Literature and Resistance in South Africa, Part Two'. *Sechaba* 1, no. 7 (July 1967): 12, 16–18.

———. 'Non-Violence: A Tactic Not a Doctrine'. *The New African* 4, no. 1 (March 1965): 4–7.

———. 'Problems in African Literature'. *Research in African Literatures* 23, no. 1 (Spring 1992): 27–44.

——— [Raymond Kunene]. 'World Liberation Movement Loss'. In Buzz Johnson, *'I Think of My Mother': Notes on the Life and Times of Claudia Jones*, 165. London: Karia, 1985.

———. *Zulu Poems*. New York: Africana, 1970.

Lambert, Charles. 'postfuck tristezza'. *Cambridge Literary Review* 1 (2010): 87–94.

Latter, Alex. *Late Modernism and the English Intelligencer: On the Poetics of Community*. London: Bloomsbury, 2015.

Leavis, F. R. *For Continuity*. Cambridge: The Minority Press, 1933.

———. *New Bearings in English Poetry*. London: Chatto, 1950.

Lebovic, Sam. 'From War Junk to Educational Exchange: The World War II Origins of the Fulbright Program and the Foundations of American Cultural Globalism, 1945–1950'. *Diplomatic History* 37, no. 2 (April 2013): 280–312.

London WLM Campaign for Legal and Financial Independence and Rights of Women. 'Disaggregation Now! Another Battle For Women's Independence' (1979). In *No Turning Back: Writings from the Women's Liberation Movement*, Feminist Anthology Collective, 15–23. London: The Women's Press, 1981.

Luna, Joe, ed. *The Correspondence of Douglas Oliver and J.H. Prynne*. Amsterdam: The Last Books, 2022.

MacDiarmid, Hugh. *The Battle Continues*. Edinburgh: Castle Wynd, 1957.

———. *The Complete Poems of Hugh MacDiarmid*. 2 vols. Edited by Michael Grieve and W. R. Aitken. Harmondsworth: Penguin, 1978.

———. 'Foreword'. In *Poets to the People: South African Freedom Poems*, edited by Barry Feinberg, 13–15. London: Allen & Unwin, 1974.

———. *The Kind of Poetry I Want*. Edinburgh: K.D. Duvall, 1961.

———. *Lucky Poet*. London: Methuen, 1943.

———. 'The Red Scotland Thesis: Forward to the John MacLean Line'. *The Voice of Scotland* 1, no. 1 (1938): 7–14.

MacDonald, Peter D. *The Literature Police: Apartheid Censorship and Its Cultural Consequences*. Oxford: Oxford UP, 2009.
MacSweeney, Barry. 'The British Poetry Revival, 1965–79'. *South East Arts Review* (1979): 33–46.
Marriott, David. *Haunted Life: Visual Culture and Black Modernity*. New Brunswick: Rutgers, 2007.
———. 'No Lords A-Leaping: Fanon, C.L.R. James, and the Politics of Invention'. *Humanities* 3, no. 4 (2014): 517–45.
Marshall, Alan. 'Drift, Loss, and Return in the Poetry of J.H. Prynne'. *Études Britanniques Contemporaines* 27 (2005): 137–52.
Marx, Karl. *The Critique of the Gotha Programme*. Moscow: Progress, 1971.
———. *Economic and Philosophic Manuscripts of 1844*. Moscow: Progress, 1959.
———. *The Eighteenth Brumaire of Louis Bonaparte* (1852). Moscow: Progress, 1954.
Maud, Ralph. *Charles Olson's Reading*. Carbondale: Southern Illinois UP, 1996.
McDowell, Deborah, E. 'Transferences: Black Feminist Discourse: The "Practice" of "Theory"'. In *Feminism Beside Itself*, edited by Diane Elam and Robyn Wiegman, 93–118. New York: Routledge, 1995.
Mendelssohn, Anna [Grace Lake]. *Bernache Nonnette*. Cambridge: Equipage, 1993.
———. *I'm Working Here: The Collected Poems of Anna Mendelssohn*. Edited by Sara Crangle. Swindon: Shearsman, 2021.
———. *Implacable Art*. Cambridge: Folio / Equipage, 2000.
———. *py*. Hunstanton: Oystercatcher, 2009.
——— [Grace Lake]. *Tondo Aquatique*. Cambridge: Equipage, 1997.
——— [Grace Lake]. *Viola Tricolor*. Cambridge: Equipage, 1993.
Ménil, René. 'Introduction to the Marvellous' (1941). *Refusal of the Shadow: Surrealism and the Caribbean*, translated by Krysztof Fijałowski and Michael Richardson, 89–95. London: Verso, 1996.
Miliband, Ralph. *The State and Capitalist Society*. London: Wiedenfield & Nicholson, 1969.
Mitchell, Juliet. *Psychoanalysis and Feminism*. Harmondsworth: Pelican, 1975.
Mohin, Lilian, ed. *One Foot on the Mountain: An Anthology of British Feminist Poetry, 1969–1979*. London: Onlywomen Press, 1979.
Montefiore, Jan. *Arguments of Heart and Mind: Selected Essays, 1977–2000*. Manchester: Manchester UP, 2002.
———. 'Feminist Identity and the Poetic Tradition'. *Feminist Review* 13 (1983): 69–84.
Motard, Alice, ed. *Beau Geste Press*. Bordeaux: CAPC, 2017.
Mottram, Eric. 'The British Poetry Revival'. In *New British Poetries: The Scope of the Possible*, edited by Robert Hampson and Peter Barry, 15–50. Manchester: Manchester UP, 1993.

———. 'Interview with Lee Harwood'. *Poetry Information* 14 (Autumn/Winter 1975–6): 4–18.

———. 'Tom Pickard'. *Poetry Information* 18 (1978): 69–79.

Mulford, Wendy. *ABC of Writing*. Southampton: Torque, 1985.

———. *and suddenly, supposing: selected poems*. Buckfastleigh: Etruscan, 2002.

———. *Bravo to Girls and Heroes*. Cambridge: Street Editions, 1977.

———. *No Fee: A Line or Two For Free*. With Denise Riley. Cambridge: Street Editions, 1978.

———. 'Notes on Writing: A Marxist/Feminist Viewpoint'. *Red Letters* 9 (1979): 35–44. Reprinted in *On Gender and Writing*, edited by Michelene Wandor, 31–41. London: Pandora, 1983.

———. *Reactions to Sunsets*. London: Ferry, 1980.

———. *This Narrow Place: Sylvia Townsend Warner and Valentine Ackland*. London: Pandora, 1988.

———. 'Veronica Forrest-Thomson, 1947–1975'. In *Calemadonnas – Women & Scotland*, edited by Helen Kidd, 15–21. Dundee: Gairfish, 1994.

Myers, Matt. *Student Revolt: Voices of the Austerity Generation*. London: Pluto, 2017.

Ndlovu, Sifiso Mxolisi. 'The ANC and the World, 1960–1970'. In *The Road to Democracy in South Africa, vol. 1, 1960–1970*, edited by SADET, 541–71. Cape Town: Zebra Press, 2004.

Nealon, Christopher. 'Queer Tradition'. *GLQ* 14, no. 4 (2008): 617–22.

Newsinger, John. *The Blood Never Dried: A People's History of the British Empire*. London: BookMarks, 2013.

Nielsen, Aldon Lynn. *Reading Race: White American Poets and the Racial Discourse in the Twentieth Century*. Athens, GA: U of Georgia P, 1990.

Nortje, Arthur. *Anatomy of Dark: Collected Poems*. Edited by Dirk Klopper. Pretoria: UNISA, 2000.

———. *Dead Roots*. London: Heinemann, 1973.

———. *Oxford Journal*. University of South Africa Institutional repository. Web. URL: http://uir.unisa.ac.za/handle/10500/18648

Nowak, Mark. *Social Poetics*. Minneapolis: Coffee House, 2020.

O'Brien, Anthony. *Against Normalisation: Writing Radical Democracy in South Africa*. Durham, NC: Duke UP, 2001.

O'Brien, Sean. 'Bizzaro's Bounty'. *Poetry Review* 91, no. 2 (2001): 110–11.

O'Rourke, Rebecca. 'Summer Reading'. *The Feminist Review* no. 2 (1979): 1–17.

Okoro, Dike. *New Perspectives on Mazisi Kunene*. Milwaukee: Cirrus, 2015.

Olson, Charles. *The Collected Letters of Charles Olson and J.H. Prynne*. Edited by Ryan Dobran. Albuquerque: U of New Mexico P, 2017.

———. *Collected Prose*. Edited by Donald Allen and Benjamin Friedlander. Berkeley: U of California P, 1997.

———. *The Complete Correspondence of Charles Olson and Robert Creeley*, vol. 1. Edited by George Butterick. Santa Rosa: Black Sparrow, 1980.

———. *The Maximus Poems*. Edited by George F. Butterick. Berkeley: U of California P, 1985.

———. *Muthologos*. Edited by Ralph Maud. Vancouver: Talonbooks, 2010.

———. *Selected Letters of Charles Olson*. Edited by Ralph Maud. Berkeley: U of California P, 2001.

Padmore, George. *Africa: Britain's Third Empire*. London: Dennis Dobson, 1949.

Pattison, Neil, Reitha Pattison and Luke Roberts, eds. *Certain Prose of the English Intelligencer*. Cambridge: Mountain, 2014.

Parmar, Sandeep. 'Still Not a British Subject: Race and UK Poetry'. *Journal of British and Irish Innovative Poetry* 12(1), no. 33 (2020): 1–44.

Perraton, Hilary. *A History of Foreign Students in Britain*. London: Palgrave, 2014.

Pickard, Tom. 'From *Rough Music (Ruff Muzhik)*'. *Chicago Review* 46, no. 1 (2000): 9–36.

———. *Hero Dust*. London: Allison and Busby, 1979.

———. 'In the Original: Angela Neustatter Meets Tom Pickard'. *The Guardian* (12 October 1976).

———. *More Pricks Than Prizes*. Boston, MA: Pressed Wafer, 2010.

———. 'Teenage Unemployment – What It Really Feels Like'. *Anarchy* 35 (1963): 384–5.

Pieterse, Cosmo, ed. *Seven South African Poets*. London: Heinemann, 1971.

Pisano, Claudia Moreno, ed. *Amiri Baraka and Edward Dorn: The Collected Letters*. Albuquerque: U of New Mexico P, 2013.

Posmentier, Sonya. *Cultivation and Catastrophe: The Lyric Ecology of Modern Black Literature*. Baltimore: Johns Hopkins UP, 2017.

Prynne, J. H. 'A Communication' (1966). In *Certain Prose of the English Intelligencer*, 5. Cambridge: Mountain, 2014.

———. 'A Note to Josh Kotin and Jeff Dolven'. *No Prizes* 4 (2015): 21–4.

———. 'Afterword'. In Edward Dorn, *Collected Poems*, 938–41. Manchester: Carcanet, 2012.

———. 'The Art of Poetry No. 101'. *The Paris Review*, no. 218 (Fall 2016): 174–207.

———. *The Collected Letters of Charles Olson and J.H. Prynne*. Edited by Ryan Dobran. Albuquerque: U of New Mexico P, 2017.

———. 'No Universal Plan for a Good Life'. In *Sahitya Ra Jeevan Darshan [A Collection of the Expressions]*, edited by Rajan Prasad Pokharel, 172–5. Kathmandu: Madan and Geeta, 2010.

———. 'On Peter Larkin'. *No Prizes* 2 (2013): 43–5.

———. *Poems*. 3rd ed. South Fremantle: Fremantle Arts Centre Press; Newcastle Upon Tyne: Bloodaxe Books, 2015.

———. 'Review of Charles Olson, *Maximus IV, V, VI* (London: Cape Goliard, 1968)'. *The Park* 4/5 (1969): 64–6.
Race Today Collective. 'Editorial: Carnival Belongs to Us'. *Race Today* 8, no. 9 (September 1976): 2.
———. 'Forward to a Command Council'. *Race Today* 9, no. 3 (April/May 1977): 51.
———. 'Move as a Community: The Brockwell Park Three'. *Race Today* 6, no. 4 (June 1974): 167–73.
———. 'Editorial: Police and the Black Wageless'. *Race Today* 7, no. 2 (February 1975): 27.
Ramamurthy, Anandi. *Black Star: Britain's Asian Youth Movements*. London: Pluto, 2013.
Ramchand, Kenneth. 'Concern for Criticism'. *Caribbean Quarterly* 16, no. 2 (June 1970): 51–60.
———. 'The Pounding in His Dark: Edward Brathwaite's Other Poetry'. *Tapia* (2 January 1977): 5–7.
Ramdin, Ron. *The Making of the Black Working Class in Britain*. London: Verso, 2017.
Rancière, Jacques. *The Flesh of Words: The Politics of Writing*. Translated by Charlotte Mandell. Stanford: Stanford UP, 2004.
Raworth, Tom. *Earn Your Milk: Collected Prose*. Cambridge: Salt, 2009.
Reagon, Bernice Johnson. 'Coalition Politics: Turning the Century'. In *Home Girls: A Black Feminist Anthology*, edited by Barbara Smith, 356–8. New York: Kitchen Table, 1983.
Report of the Commission on Higher Education in the Colonies. London: HM Stationery Office, 1945.
Riley, Denise. *'Am I That Name?': Feminism and the Category of 'Women' in History*. London: Macmillan, 1988.
———. *Dry Air*. London: Virago, 1985.
———. *Lurex*. London: Picador, 2022.
———. *No Fee: A Line or Two For Free*. With Wendy Mulford. Cambridge: Street Editions, 1978.
———. *Selected Poems*. London: Reality Street, 2000.
———. *Selected Poems*. Basingstoke: Picador, 2019.
———. *War in the Nursery: Theories of the Child and Mother*. London: Virago, 1983.
———. *The Words of Selves*. Stanford: Stanford UP, 2000.
———, ed. *Poets on Writing: Britain, 1970–1991*. Basingstoke: Macmillan, 1992.
Rimbaud, Arthur. *Complete Works, Selected Letters*. Translated by Wallace Fowlie, revision by Seth Widden. Chicago: U of Chicago P, 2005.
Roberts, Michèle. 'Review of Wendy Mulford, *Bravo to Girls and Heroes*, and Denise Riley, *Marxism for Infants*'. *Spare Rib* 73 (1977): 39.
Rodney, Walter. *The Groundings with My Brothers*. London: Bogle L'Ouverture, 1969.

Rogers, Asha. *State Sponsored Literature: Britain and Cultural Diversity After 1945*. Oxford: Oxford UP, 2020.
Rohlehr, Gordon. 'Afterthoughts'. *Tapia* 23 (26 December 1971). Reprinted in *My Strangled City and Other Essays*, 133–41. San Juan, Trinidad: Longman, 1992.
———. *Calypso & Society in Pre-Independence Trinidad*. Port of Spain: Rohlehr, 1990.
———. *Pathfinder: Black Awakening in the Arrivants of Edward Kamau Brathwaite*. Tunapuna: Gordon Rohlehr, 1981.
———. 'Trophy and Catastrophe'. In *The Shape of That Hurt*, 293–304. Port of Spain: Longman Trinidad, 1992.
Rose, Gillian. *Mourning Becomes the Law*. Cambridge: Cambridge UP, 1996.
Rowbotham, Sheila. *Promise of a Dream*. London: Allen Lane, 2000.
———. 'Women's Liberation and the New Politics' (1969). Reprinted in *The Body Politic: Women's Liberation in Britain*, edited by Michelene Wandor, 3–30. London: Stage 1, 1972.
Schling, Rosa. *The Lime Green Mystery: An Oral History of the Centerprise Co-Op*. London: On the Record, 2017.
Schwarz, Bill. 'Forgetfulness: England's Discontinuous Histories'. In *Embers of Empire in Brexit Britain*, edited by Stuart Ward and Astrid Rasch, 49–58. London: Bloomsbury, 2019.
Sedgwick, Eve Kosofsky. 'Melanie Klein and the Difference Affect Makes'. *South Atlantic Quarterly* 106, no. 3 (2007): 625–42.
———. 'Paranoid and Reparative Reading, or, You're So Paranoid You Probably Think This Essay Is About You'. In *Touching Feeling*, 123–51. Durham, NC: Duke UP, 2002.
———. 'Teaching / Depression'. *The Scholar & Feminist* 4, no. 2 (2006). Web. URL: http://sfonline.barnard.edu/heilbrun/sedgwick_02.htm
Searle, Chris. *The Forsaken Lover: White Words and Black People*. Harmondsworth: Penguin, 1973.
———. 'School as a Weapon'. *Race Today* 7, no. 12 (1975): 281.
———. 'The Story of Stepney Words'. *Race and Class* 58, no. 4 (2017): 57–75.
———, ed. *One for Blair*. London: Young World, 1989.
———, ed. *Stepney Words 1 & 2*. London: Centerprise, 1973.
Seeger, Peggy. *First Time Ever: A Memoir*. London: Faber, 2017.
Shamsher, Jogindar. 'Panjabi Poetry in Britain'. *New Community* 6, no. 3 (1978): 291–305.
Sheppard, Robert. *The Meaning of Form in Contemporary Innovative Poetry*. New York: Palgrave Macmillan, 2016.
———, ed. *The Salt Companion to Lee Harwood*. Cambridge: Salt, 2007.
Sherwood, Marika. *Claudia Jones: A Life in Exile*. London: Lawrence & Wishart, 1999.
Shoptaw, John. *On the Outside Looking Out: John Ashbery's Poetry*. Cambridge, MA: Harvard UP, 1994.

Sivanandan, A. 'From Resistance to Rebellion: Asian and Afro-Caribbean Struggles in Britain' (1981). In *Catching History on the Wing: Race, Culture and Globalisation*, 90–139. London: Pluto, 2008.

Smirnow, Gabriel. *The Revolution Disarmed: Chile 1970–73*. New York: Monthly Review, 1979.

Solomon, Samuel. *Lyric Pedagogy and Marxist-Feminism*. London: Bloomsbury, 2019.

Southall: 23 April 1979 – The Report of the Unofficial Committee of Enquiry. London: National Council for Civil Liberties (NCCL), 1980.

Spivak, Gayatri. *A Critique of Postcolonial Reason*. Cambridge, MA: Harvard UP, 1999.

Steedman, Carolyn. *Poetry for Historians*. Liverpool: Liverpool UP, 2018.

Stockwell, A. J. 'Leaders, Dissidents and the Disappointed: Colonial Students in Britain as Empire Ended'. *The Journal of Imperial and Commonwealth History* 36, no. 3 (2008): 487–507.

Stonebridge, Lyndsey. *Placeless People: Writing, Rights, and Refugees*. Oxford: Oxford UP, 2018.

Sutherland, Keston. 'XL Prynne'. In *Complicities: British Poetry, 1945–2007*, edited by Sam Ladkin and Robin Purves, 43–74. Prague: Litteraria Pragensia, 2007.

Tait, Margaret. *Selected Films: 1952–1976*. Lux / Scottish Screen DVD, 2006.

———. *Subjects and Sequences: A Margaret Tait Reader*. Edited by Peter Todd and Benjamin Cook. London: Lux, 2004.

Temple, John. *Rothschild's Lapwing*. London: Ferry, 1968.

Thomas, Elean. *Before They Can Speak of Flowers*. London: Karia, 1988.

Thomlinson, Natalie. *Race, Ethnicity, and the Women's Movement in England*. London: Palgrave Macmillan, 2016.

Thorpe, Andrea. 'The "Pleasure Streets" of Exile: Queer Subjectivities and the Body in Arthur Nortje's London Poems'. *Journal of Literary Studies* 34, no. 1 (2018): 1–20.

Tickner, Lisa. *Hornsey 1968: The Art School Revolution*. London: Frances Lincoln, 2008.

———. 'The Impossible Object?' In David Freeberg et al., 'The Object of Art History', *The Art Bulletin* 76, no. 3 (1994): 394–410.

Traverso, Enzo. *Left-Wing Melancholia: Marxism, History, and Memory*. New York: Columbia, 2016.

Tuma, Keith. 'Ed Dorn and England'. *The Gig*, no. 6 (2000): 41–54.

———. *Fishing By Obstinate Isles: Modern and Postmodern British Poetry and American Readers*. Evanston: Northwestern UP, 1998.

Usherwood, Vivian. *Poems*. 2nd ed. London: Centerprise, 1975.

Uziell, Laurel. *T*. London: Materials, 2020.

Veit-Wild, Flora. *Dambudzo Marechera: A Source-Book on His Life and Work*. Harare: U of Zimbabwe P, 1992.

Vicuña, Cecilia. *About to Happen*. New York: Siglio, 2017.

———. 'The coup came to kill what I love'. *Spare Rib* 28 (1974): 36–8.
———. 'Fragments of Memory: An Afterward'. In *Saborami*, 157–63. Oakland: ChainLinks, 2011.
———. *El Zen Surado*. Santiago: Editorial Catalonia, 2013.
———. 'Sabor a mí'. In *Beau Geste Press*, edited by Alice Motard, 196–209. Bordeaux: CAPC, 2017.
———. *Saborami*. Oakland: ChainLinks, 2011.
———. *Saborami: An Expanded Facsimile Edition*. Edited by Luke Roberts and Amy Tobin. London: Book Works, 2023.
Virtanen, Juha. *Poetry and Performance During the British Poetry Revival*. London: Palgrave Macmillan, 2017.
Waidner, Isabel. 'Class, Queers, and the Avant-Garde'. London: Institute for Contemporary Arts, 2019. Web. URL: www.ica.art/media/01901.pdf
Walmsley, Anne. *The Caribbean Artists Movement, 1966–1972*. London: New Beacon, 1992.
Wandor, Michelene. *Lilac Flinder*. London: Writers Forum, 1973.
———, ed. *The Body Politic: Women's Liberation in Britain, 1969–1972*. London: Stage 1, 1972.
———, ed. *On Gender and Writing*. London: Pandora, 1983.
———, ed. *Once A Feminist: Stories of a Generation*. London: Virago, 1990.
——— with Michèle Roberts, eds. *Cutlasses & Earrings*. London: Playbooks, 1977.
Ware, Vron. *Beyond the Pale: White Women, Racism, and History*. London: Verso, 2015.
WReC [Warwick Research Collective]. *Combined and Uneven Development: Towards a New Theory of World-Literature*. Liverpool: Liverpool UP, 2015.
Waters, Rob. *Thinking Black: Britain, 1964–85*. Oakland: U of California P, 2019.
Weeks, Jeffrey. *Coming Out: Homosexual Politics in Britain from the Nineteenth Century to the Present*. London: Quartet, 1977.
Wiegman, Robyn. 'On Being in Time With Feminism'. *MLQ* 65, no. 1 (2004): 161–76.
Wilkinson, Bruce. *Hidden Culture, Forgotten History*. Middlesbrough: Penniless Press, 2017.
Wilson, Amrit, ed. *Finding a Voice: Asian Women in Britain*. London: Virago, 1978.
Wilson, Elizabeth. *Women and the Welfare State*. London: Tavistock, 1977.
Winnicott, D. W. *The Child, The Family, and the Outside World*. Harmondsworth: Pelican, 1964.
———. *Deprivation and Delinquency*. Edited by Clare Winnicott, Ray Shepherd and Madeleine Davis. London: Tavistock, 1984.
———. 'Primary Maternal Preoccupation' (1956). In *Collected Papers: Through Paediatrics to Psychoanalysis*, 300–5. London: Tavistock, 1958.

———. *The Spontaneous Gesture: Selected Letters*. Edited by F. Robert Rodman. London: Karnac, 1999.

———. 'Transitional Objects and Transitional Phenomena' (1951). In *Collected Papers: Through Paediatrics to Psychoanalysis*, 237–8. London: Tavistock, 1958.

Woods, Gregory. '"Still on My Lips": Walt Whitman in Britain'. In *The Continuing Presence of Walt Whitman: The Life After the Life*, edited by Robert K. Martin, 129–40. Iowa City: U o Iowa P, 1992.

Woods, Tim. *African Pasts: Memory and History in African Literatures*. Manchester: Manchester UP, 2007.

Worpole, Ken. *Local Publishing and Local Culture*. London: Centerprise, 1977.

Wynter, Sylvia. 'Creole Criticism: A Critique'. *New World Quarterly* 4, no. 4 (1970): 12–36.

———. 'We Must Learn to Sit Down Together and Talk About a Little Culture'. *Jamaica Journal* 2, no. 4 (December 1968): 23–32.

Index

0 to 9 (magazine), 145

Ackland, Valentine, 129
  Whether A Dove or a Seagull, 155–6
Ackroyd, Peter, *The Diversions of Purley*, 132
Afghanistan, 44
African National Congress (ANC), 77, 78, 79, 83, 86–7
  and 'Gang of Eight', 89
  and MacDiarmid, 84–5
  and Nortje, 92
  and *Sechaba* (journal), 87–8
Afro-Asian Writers' Conference, 88
Ahmed, Sara, 154
AIDS crisis, 65, 132, 225
Alcide, Mantoani, 67, 75–6
Ali, Altab, 190
Ali, Tariq, 230
alienage, 79–81, 96
Allen, Donald, 105
  New American Poetry, 52
Allende, Salvador, 97, 100
Althea & Donna, 'Uptown Top Ranking', 159, 160
Ambrose, Jean, 178
Amis, Kingsley, 23
ANC *see* African National Congress (ANC)
Angel Hair (magazine), 145
Angelou, Maya, 'Still I Rise', 148
Angels of the Lyre: A Gay Poetry Anthology (anthology), 131

Anger, Kenneth, 121
Angry Brigade, 11, 197, 218–19, 227, 231
Anona Wynn, The (magazine), 145
Anti-Apartheid Movement (AAM), 83
anti-capitalism, 44, 180–1
anti-carceral *see* prisons
anti-colonial movements, 3, 44, 183–4
anti-humanism, 44
anti-Marxism, 32–3
Antin, David, 196
antisemitism, 50
apartheid, 83–5, 86, 92, 151
Arendt, Hannah, 76–7
Arlott, John, 26
Arnold, Matthew, 8
  'Dover Beach', 7
Arrowsmith, Pat, 240
Artists for Democracy, 100
Ashbery, John, 10, 113–15, 118–19, 121, 122–3
  'The Skaters', 126
Asian communities, 183–6
Asian Youth Movement (AYM), 170, 185, 188
Association for Commonwealth Literature and Language Studies (ACLALS), 40–1
Atlantic Ocean, 50, 53, 58, 62
Attlee, Clement, 4
austerity, 5, 6–7, 15–16, 218
Austin, David, 176–7, 181

avant-garde, 1, 2–3, 76–7, 98, 241–2
  and homosexuality, 133
  and whiteness, 4
Awan, Mumtaz, 185

Balkans wars, 65
Bangladesh, 96
Banton, Michael, 20–1
Baraka, Amiri, 46, 47, 65, 178
  The Dutchman, 67
Barbados, 16–17, 33, 54
Barrett, James R., 51
Barry, Kevin, 207–8
Barry, Tom, 207
Bassi, Bhupinder, 170
Bataille, Georges, 129
BBC, 32
Bean, Gerlin, 147
Beau Geste Press, 78, 98–9
Beese, Barbara, 178
Benjamin, Walter, 201
Bennett, Louise, 25
Benveniste, Asa, 145, 240
Benveniste, Pip, 145
Berger, John, 85
Berke, Roberta Elzey, *Sphere of Light*, 145
Bernard, Jay, 81
Berrigan, Sandy, 115, 129
Berrigan, Ted, 229
  '10 Things I Do Every Day', 245
Berry, Ian, 84
Berry, James, 175, 196, 240, 241
Better Books (bookshop), 121
Bevin, Ernest, 6
Bible, the, 176
Bim (journal), 21
Bion, Wilfred, 44
bisexuality, 115–16
Black Britons, 11; *see also* Caribbean Britons
Black Dwarf (newspaper), 230–1
Black Lesbian Group, 243

Black Liberator, The (journal), 168, 181–2
Black Lives Matter movement, 9, 17, 80
Black Mountain Poets, 52
Black Panther Movement, 3, 175, 178
Black Parents Movement, 170
Black Unity and Freedom Party (BUFP), 147
Blackman, Peter, 78
Blair, Tony, 193, 194, 211, 212
Blake, William, 141
  America, 64
Bloch, Ernst, 36
Bluefoot Traveller: Poetry by West Indians in Britain (anthology), 240
Bogle L'Ouverture, 171, 172, 185
Bollas, Christopher, 224
Bonney, Sean, 200, 219–20
bookshops, 121, 129–30; *see also* Centerprise
Boone, Joseph A., 128
borders, 6, 79
Bostock, Anna, 85
Bourdieu, Pierre, 32
Bovell, Dennis, 187
Bowie, David, 108
Boyce Davies, Carol, 78, 81
Boyd of Merton, Lord, 208
Brainard, Joe, 120, 124
  I Remember, 245
Brathwaite, (Edward) Kamau, 5, 16–17, 75, 240
  and Africa, 36–7
  and Britain, 18–19, 20–1, 31–2
  and Cambridge, 23–4
  and creolisation, 27–8
  and Johnson, 176
  and Leavis, 33–6
  and MacDiarmid, 244
Brathwaite, (Edward) Kamau (works)
  'Anvil', 39–40

The Arrivants, 17, 18
Barabajan Poems, 21, 23–4
'Calypso', 31
'Caribbean Theme', 31
Contradictory Omens: Cultural Diversity and Integration in the Caribbean, 27
'The Day the First Snow Fell', 21–3, 24–5, 26–7, 29–31, 34
The Development of Creole Society in Jamaica, 1770–1820, 27
Golokwati 2000, 21–2
The History of the Voice, 21, 25–7
Masks, 18, 37
'Ogun', 24
Other Exiles, 24, 30
'The Professor', 34–5
Rights of Passage, 16, 38
Sun Poem, 19
Third World Poems, 15
'Timehri', 34
Trench Town Rock, 16
Brazil, 67
Breman, Paul, 178
Brenner, Robert, 55, 58
British Commonwealth, 19
British National Party (BNP), 173
Brixton Black Women's Group, 163, 177
Brixton Prison (London), 11, 199–200, 208
Brockwell Park (London), 173–4, 183
Brotherston, Gordon, 71
Brown, H. Rap, 95
Brutus, Dennis, 90–1, 93, 95–6
Bryan, Beverley, 170–1, 175
Bryher, 133
Buck, Claire, 154
Buck, Paul, 129
Bunce, Robin, 177
Bunting, Basil, 66, 193, 202–4
  Briggflatts, 201–2

Burns, Jim, 240
Burroughs, William, 121
Burt, Stephanie, 148
Burton, Richard, 202
Bush, Clive, 193
Butler, Bill, 129–30
Butterick, George, 61

Cabral, Amilcar, *Revolution in Guinea*, 152
Cambridge, Alrick X., 182
Cambridge University, 45, 217–18
  and Brathwaite, 20–1, 26–7
  and Leavis, 32–6
  and protests, 220–2, 232, 236
Cameron, Earl, 78
Campbell, Roy, 84
Cape Goliard, 145
Capildeo, Anthony (Vahni), 16
capitalism, 4, 8, 33–4, 70–1; *see also* anti-capitalism
Carby, Hazel, 169, 170, 173
Carew, Jan, 86
Caribbean Artists Movement (CAM), 5, 16, 18, 38–9, 95, 175
Caribbean Britons, 15, 16–17
Caribbean Labour Congress, 78
Caribbean Quarterly (journal), 21
Carmichael, Stokely, 38, 95
Carpenter, Edward, 133
Carr, Robert, 198, 227
Carrington, Lord, 208
Carter, Martin, 'Death of a Comrade', 78
Castro, Fidel, 98, 152
Cattouse, Nadia, 78
Cecil Rhodes House (London), 80
Celestine, Alfred, 133
Centerprise, 10, 165, 166, 167, 185
Césaire, Aimé, 24, 34, 88, 176
  Return to My Native Land, 85–6
Cha, Theresa Hak Kyung, 189
Chaggar, Gurdip, 183, 190

Children of Albion (anthology), 107, 122
Chile, 77–8, 97–8, 100, 240
citizenship, 79, 96
Civil Rights movement, 45–6, 51
Cixous, Hélène, 157
   'The Laugh of Medusa', 150–1
Claire, Paula, 146
Clark, Tom, 49, 229
class, 3; *see also* working class
class struggle, 162, 164, 168, 197, 201
Cleaver, Eldridge, 95
   Revolution in the Congo, 152
Coard, Bernard, 170
Cobbing, Bob, 140, 145, 240
Cobbing, Jennifer Pike, 145
Cochrane, Kelso, 190
Cold War, 106–7
Collins, Canon John, 83, 85
Collins, Michael, 207–8
Collymore, Frank, 21
Colombia, 71
colonialism, 2, 4, 30
   and Bunting, 203
   and Caribbean, 25–6, 27–8
   and Cixous, 150–1
   and eroticism, 125, 127–8
   and Mulford, 152–3
   and Riley, 151–2
   and USA, 55–6
   see also decolonisation; neocolonialism
Colston, Edward, 17
Combahee River Collective, 'A Black Feminist Statement', 148
Commonwealth Immigration Act (1962), 38, 79
Commonwealth Sugar Agreement (1951), 36
communism, 6, 73–4, 87
Communist Party (CPGB), 3, 74, 78, 239
   and feminism, 155, 156, 157
continental drift, 60, 61–4, 68

Corbyn, Jeremy, 5, 9
Corman, Cid, 48
Couturier, Michel, 125
Covid-19 pandemic, 9, 15, 241–2
Cox, Kenneth, 202
CPGB *see* Communist Party
Craddock, Matthew, 55, 57, 58
Crane, Hart, 'O Janus-faced / As double as the hand that twists this glass', 110
Crangle, Sara, 223, 226–7
Creeley, Robert, 52, 70, 128
creolisation, 27–8
Cripps, Stafford, 6
Crisp, Quentin, *The Naked Civil Servant*, 111
Croce, Cherry, 190
Crozier, Andrew, 73, 145
   Loved Litter of Time Spent, 53–4
Cuba, 107
Cunliffe, Dave, 113
Currey, James, 82, 90–1
Curtains (magazine), 129
Cutlasses & Earrings (anthology), 146, 156
Cutteridge, J. O. 'Captain', 28
Cypriot War of Independence, 48

Dadzie, Stella, 170–1
D'Aguiar, Fred, 179
Damas, Léon, 34
Damon, Maria, 117
Dante Alighieri, *Paradiso*, 68–9
Dash, Jash, 240
Davenport, Guy, 62
Davie, Donald, 49, 66, 229
Davies, Celia, 'A Ditty', 140–1
De Beauvoir, Simone, 153
De'Ath, Amy, 150
Debord, Guy, 44
Debray, Régis, 97
decolonisation, 19–20
Delany, Samuel, 130
Dell, Michael, 209
Delta (magazine), 21, 22–3

Dent, Bob, 168
depressive position, 225, 226
Desai, Jayaben, 161–2
Dhondy, Farrukh, 173, 176, 178, 186
 East End at Your Feet, 171
Di Prima, Diane, 239
Dick, Patricia, 178
Dikobe, Modikwe, 91
disaggregation, 142–4, 147
Disch, Thomas M., 124
Dizzy, Ras, 41
Doane, Janice, 234
Dobran, Ryan, 55, 58–9
Don't Mark His Face: Hull Prison Riot 1976 (pamphlet), 199
Dorn, Edward, 5, 52, 60, 65–9, 75, 195
 and continental drift, 62, 63
 and Essex, 229
 and Prynne, 45, 55, 69–70
Dorn, Edward (works)
 'A Theory of Truth: The North Atlantic Turbine', 66–7, 68
 Geography, 66
 Gunslinger, 68
 From Idaho Out, 66
 The North Atlantic Turbine, 62, 66–9
 'Oxford', 67
 The Shoshoneans, 65
 'Thesis', 220
Du Bois, W. E. B., 175
Duncan, Andrew, *Nothing is Being Suppressed: British Poetry of the 1970s*, 241
Duncan, Robert, 105, 196

Eagleton, Terry, 32–3, 43, 70
economics, 6–7
Edmonds, Richard, 173
education, 4, 9, 218
 and Brathwaite, 17
 and Caribbean, 27, 28–9
 and race, 169–75
 and Searle, 164–5, 167–70
 and violence, 187–8
 see also student protests
Education Maintenance Allowance, 218
Educationally Subnormal (ESN) Schools, 170
Egudu, Romanus, 95
Egypt, 49
Ehrenberg, Felipe, 98
Eliot, T. S., 76, 176
 Gerontion, 34
Ellis, Alton, 'I'm Still In Love With You', 159
émigrés, 76
encryption, 115, 116, 118, 119
Engels, Friedrich, 44, 244
 The German Ideology, 246
English Intelligencer, The (magazine), 45, 52, 53, 54, 69
 and Dorn, 66
 and race, 71–3
English Prisons Today: Being the Report of the Prison System Enquiry Committee, 202
Entwistle, Alice, 115
Erasmus, François, 84
espionage, 203
Essex University, 229–30
European migration, 50–2
European Union (EU), 210
Everly Brothers, 136
Evers, Medgar, 46, 86
exile, 76, 78, 80
 and Davie, 229
 and Kunene, 89
 and Nortje, 90, 91–4
 and Vicuña, 97–8, 100

Faber & Faber, 3, 32
factory workers, 183–4
Fainlight, Harry, 10, 108–13, 118, 121, 244–5
 Selected Poems, 112

Fainlight Harry, (*cont.*)
  Sussicran, 109–12, 113, 118
  'The Spider', 108–9
Fainlight, Ruth, 112
Fairbairns, Zoë, 147
Faiz, Faiz Ahmed, 185
Fanon, Frantz, 5, 22, 175
  Black Skin, White Masks, 30, 31
fascism, 11, 50, 173
Fasimbas, The, 175
Feinstein, Elaine, 54, 71–2
  In a Green Eye, 145
Fell, Alison, 147
  Licking the Bed Clean, 146, 156
Felski, Rita, 226
feminism, 99, 131, 137–8, 145–7;
  see also Mulford, Wendy;
  Riley, Denise
Ferry, 145
Field, Paul, 177
First, Ruth, 91
Fisher, Allen, 98
floating, 29–31
Floating Bear, The (magazine), 145
Floyd, George, 241
Fluxshoe (journal), 98
folk culture, 33
Forrest-Thomson, Veronica, 73, 146
Forster, E. M., 127–8, 129
Fortune Press, 23
Foucault, Michel, 212, 226
France, 49
Frank Knox Memorial Fellowship, 48, 52
Freud, Sigmund, 59, 65, 151, 226
  Civilization and Its Discontents, 63
Fuck You (magazine), 111
Fulbright Fellowships, 5, 48
Fulcrum, 145

Gay Liberation, 106, 122, 129, 240
Gay News (newspaper), 123, 240
Gay's the Word (bookshop), 121
Gaza protests, 241–2
gender, 3, 4, 8, 149–50
Genet, Jean, 121
George, Glenda, 129
Ghana, 36, 37
Gide, André, 127–8, 129
Gilroy, Paul, 7, 58
  Small Acts, 15
Ginsberg, Allen, 94, 105, 106–8
  'Who Be Kind To', 108
Gish, Nancy K., 243
Glissant, Édouard, 60
Golden Convolvulus, The (anthology), 113
Goldman, Emma, 100
Gondwanaland, 61, 63
'good enough' concept, 221, 222, 223–4, 233, 234
Gosley, Margaret, 165
Graef, Roger, 211, 213
Gramsci, Antonio, 84
Greenham, Lily, 146
Griffiths, Bill, 8, 11, 192–7, 198, 239, 244
  An Account of the End, 208–9, 210
  'Apology', 195–6
  Collected Poems, 192, 193
  'Cycle Three: H.M. Prison Brixton', 199–200
  Cycles, 196
  'Cycles on Dover Borstal', 198
  HMP: Revising Prison, 194, 211–12
  A Note on Democracy, 212
  'Novella Three', 209
  In Rebuttal of the Guardian: On the Role of Solitary Confinement in British Prisons – Call for an Inquiry, 212
  Seventy-Six Day Wanno, Mississippi and Highpoint Journal, 212–14, 215–16
  Some Notes on the Metropolitan Police, London: With Some

Footnotes on the Magistrates' Courts, 212
Star Fish Jail, 211, 212, 213, 214–15
'Terzetto: Brixton Prison', 198
'To Johnny Prez', 198
War W/Windsor, 196
Griffiths, Jim, 20
Grosseteste, 145
Guest, Harry, 116
Guillén, Nicolás, 34
guilt, 224, 225, 227
Gunn, Thom, 24
Gurley Flynn, Elizabeth, 81
Gutzmore, Cecil, 168
Guyan, Rudi, 168
Guyotat, Pierre, 129

H. D., 133
Sea Garden, 136
Hague, Gill, 147
Haile Selassie, 38
Hall, Barry, 145
Hall, John, 66, 72
Hall, Stuart, 8, 9, 32, 41–2, 49
May Day Manifesto, 70
Policing the Crisis, 182
Halsey, Alan, 192
Hans, Surjit, 184
Harris, Wilson, 35
Harvard University, 48
Harwood, Lee, 10, 66, 113–25, 129–30
and anthologies, 131–3
and homoeroticism, 127–8
and MacDiarmid, 244–5
and women, 125–7, 128–9
Harwood, Lee (works)
'Afterwords to a Poem by Jack Spicer', 130
All the Wrong Notes, 131
'Cable Street', 117
'Gorgeous – yet another Brighton poem', 133–4
Landscapes, 125–7

The Long Black Veil, 128
The Man With Blue Eyes, 114, 118–25
The Sinking Colony, 125, 127–8
The White Room, 116–17, 122–3, 124
Hassan, Leila, 178
Hawkes, Jacquetta, *A Land*, 61
Hawkins, Bobbie Louise, 115, 128–9
Hawkins, Ralph, 229
Hazzard, Oli, *John Ashbery and the Anglo-American Exchange: The Minor Eras*, 114, 115
Heidegger, Martin, 44
Hellenism, 7–8
Heller, Agnes, 70
Hellion, Martha, 98
Hemmings, Clare, 137, 138
Hemphill, Essex, 133
Henderson, Hamish, 83, 84, 133
Hensman, Savitri
Flood at the Door, 184–5
'Just Another Asian', 185
Herd, David, 45
Hickman, Ben, 49–50
Hilferding, Rudolf, *Finance Capital*, 71
Hill, Christopher, 74
Hinds, Donald, *Journey to an Illusion: The West Indian in Britain*, 15
Hirschman, Jack, 196
Hobsbaum, Philip, 23
Hobsbawm, Eric, 74
Hodge, Merle, 28
Hodges, Devon, 234
Hollo, Anselm, 66
homoeroticism, 127–8
homophobia, 65, 106, 108, 131
homosexuality, 10, 130–1
and anthologies, 131–3
and Fainlight, 108–13
and Ginsberg, 106–8
and Harwood, 113–25, 133–4

hooks, bell, 171–2
Horne, Alastair, 222
Houédard, Dom Sylvester ('dsh'), 121–2, 125
Howe, Darcus, 175, 177, 178, 180, 183
Howe, Fanny, 9–10
  O'Clock, 1–3
Hughes, Langston, 34
  'Let America Be America Again', 78
Hughes, Peter, 222
Hughes, Ted, 23, 73, 113
Hughes-Edwards, Mari, 115–16, 119
Human League, The, 207
Humphries, Martin, 131, 133
Hunter, Walt, 81
Huntley, Accabre, *Today at School*, 171–2
Huntley, Jessica and Eric, 171, 185
Hyatt, Mark, 129

immigration policies, 6, 9, 38, 94–6, 154–5; *see also* Commonwealth Immigration Act
imperialism, 4, 70–1, 72
Indian Workers Association, 188
Industrial Relations Act (1971), 11
infancy, 222, 223, 224, 225
International Poetry Incarnation, 106–9, 110
Iraq, 8, 44
Irish Nationalist Liberation Army (INLA), 205
Irish Republican Army (IRA), 2, 205, 212
Israel, 49
Israel, Mark, 90

Jabès, Edmond, 161
Jamaica, 16, 38–9, 41–2, 54, 159
Jamal, Mahmood, 185

James, C. L. R., 6, 169, 177
  Beyond a Boundary, 32
James, John, 11, 73, 74, 206–7
  'A Former Boiling Point', 207–8
  and CPGB, 239
  A Former Boiling, 200
  and Griffiths, 193
  and Mulford, 145
  'To Allen Ginsberg', 107–8
  War, 200, 205–6
James, Selma, 45, 71, 169
Jameson, Fredric, 36, 81
Jarman, Derek, 106
Jarrett, Cynthia, 190
Jerry, Bongo, 25, 41
Jeschke, Lisa, 133
Johnson, Amryl, 147
Johnson, Linton Kwesi, 10–11, 173–80, 190–1, 240, 245
  and police, 239
  and recordings, 186–7
Johnson, Linton Kwesi (works)
  'All wi doing is defendin', 182–3, 186, 187
  Dread, Beat, and Blood, 172, 186
  'Inglan is a Bitch', 181
  'Jamaican Lullaby', 177
  'Night of the Head', 179
  'Reggae fi Peach', 188
  'Reggae Sounds', 190
  'Sonny's Lettah (an anti-sus poem)', 179
  'Time Come', 175–6
  Voices of the Living and the Dead, 176
  'Yout Rebels', 180–1, 182, 186
Johnson Reagon, Bernice, 161
Joint Action Committee Against Racial Intolerance (JACARI), 91
Jolly, Margaretta, 160
Jones, Claudia, 5, 77, 78–82, 163, 239
  and Kunene, 86, 87, 88

Jones-LeCointe, Altheia, 175
Jonson, Bari, 78
Joseph, Anthony, 16
Journal of British and Irish Innovative Poetry (anthology), 192
joy, 100

Kaiser, Elizabeth, 59
Kalliney, Peter J., *Commonwealth of Letters: British Literary Culture and the Emergence of Postcolonial Aesthetics*, 31–2, 33, 34, 39–41
Kane, Daniel, 107
Kapil, Bhanu, 239
    Ban en Banlieue, 188–90
Kaplan, Cora, 141, 162
Kasper, John, 50
Katko, Justin, 220
Kay, Jackie, 11, 133, 147
    'A Life in Protest', 242–4
    Trumpet, 243
Kazantzis, Judith, 185
Keane, Shake, 23, 35
Keats, John, 67
Keith, Joseph, 79–80
Kelly, Mary, 152
Kenya, 33, 48, 207, 208
King, Audvil, 41
Kinnahan, Linda, 150, 157
Kirkup, James, 240
Klein, Melanie, 223, 225, 226, 234
Klopper, Dirk, 96
Koram, Kojo, 5
Krishnavarma, Shyamji, 20
Kristeva, Julia, 157
Kunene, Mazisi, 5, 77, 82–9, 240, 244
    Anthem of the Decades, 82
    and Jones, 78, 79
    Shaka the Great, 82
    'This Day', 84
    Zulu Poems, 86

La Rose, John, 38, 170, 175, 177, 240
Labour Party, 4, 5, 6, 9, 38; *see also* New Labour
Ladkin, Sam, 217
Lake, Grace *see* Mendelssohn, Anna
Lamming, George, 20, 35
language, 25–6, 224
Larkin, Philip, 23, 73
Latter, Alex, 54
    Late Modernism and the English Intelligencer: On the Poetics of Community, 45
Lawrence, Stephen, 212
Leavis, F. R., 32–6, 40–1, 49
Leavis, Q. D., 35
Lenin, Vladimir, 70, 98, 100
lesbianism, 129, 131
Lijn, Liliane, 240
line breaks, 46–7
Linebaugh, Peter, 58
Lisette, Francesca, 133
Little Eva, 136
Lloyd, David, 151
Loach, Ken, 5
Lobby Press, 208
London Magazine, The, 21
London Women's Liberation Newsletter, 160
Longville, Tim, 145
Lopez, Tony, 125, 127
Lora Logic, 159
Lorde, Audre, 133
Louw, Eric, 84

Maastricht Treaty, 210
McClintock, Anne, 151
MacDiarmid, Hugh, 11, 83, 88
    The Kind of Poetry I Want, 244–7
    'Let Africa Flourish', 84–5
    'The Bonnie Broukit Bairn', 243
McDowell, Deborah E., 153

McKay, Claude, 'The Snow Fairy', 23
Mackey, Nathaniel, 34
MacLean, John, 245
McLeod, John, 243–4
McLucas, Leroy, 65, 68
Macmillan, Harold, 49
MacNeice, Louis, 84
MacSweeney, Barry, 66, 74, 145, 240
  Jury Vet, 200
Madhubuti, Haki R., 178
Malaya, 48
Malcolm X, 38, 53, 65
Mandela, Nelson, 84, 86–7
  No Easy Walk to Freedom, 91
Maoism, 43, 44
Marechera, Dambudzo, 77
Markham, E. A., 240
Marriott, D. S., 29–30
Marshall, Alan, 70
Marshall Plan, 6
Marson, Una
  Selected Poems, 163
  Towards the Stars, 147
Martory, Pierre, 124, 125
martyrdom, 85, 188, 190
Marx, Karl, 2, 9, 98, 190–1, 226
  Critique of the Gotha Programme, 246
  Economic and Philosophic Manuscripts, 70
  The German Ideology, 246
Marxism, 5, 36–7, 43, 47, 60; *see also* anti-Marxism
Marxist feminism, 144, 156–7
Masilela, Ntongela, 86
Maud, Ralph, 56
Mayor, David, 98
Mbeki, Govan, 84
Melville, Herman, 50, 56
memory, 80–2
Mendelssohn, Anna, 11, 217, 218–20, 221, 227–33, 236–8
  and fear of retribution, 224
  and imprisonment, 226–7
  and literary criticism, 222–3
  and MacDiarmid, 244
  and motherhood, 234–5
  and prisons, 200
Mendelssohn, Anna (works)
  Bernache Nonnette, 217
  'from. Implacable Art', 227–8, 229, 231–2
  Implacable Art, 218
  Tondo Aquatique, 235
  Viola Tricolor, 224, 235–6
Mengham, Rod, 222
Ménil, René, 28
metre, 25–7
Meyer, Tom, 129
Miliband, Ralph, 6
Miller, Kei, 16
mimeographs, 144–5
mirrors, 109–10, 111
Miss Queenie, 26
Mitchell, Juliet, 233
MK *see* Umkhonto We Sizwe (MK)
modernism, 76
Mohin, Lilian, *One Foot on the Mountain*, 131, 144, 146–7, 156
Monk, Geraldine, *Interregnum*, 200
Montgomery, Stuart and Deirdre, 145
Moody, Ronald, 38
Moore, Marianne, 26
Morgan, Edwin, 133
Morris, Olive, 177
Morris, Tina, 113
Moshesh, Shujaa, 175
motherhood, 222, 223, 224, 233–4
  and Mendelssohn, 227, 234–5
motion, 24–5, 29–31
Mottram, Eric, 3, 105, 106, 192, 196–7, 209
  Legal Poems, 200
Movement, The, 3
Moyse, Arthur, 113

Muhammad, Elijah, 38
Mulford, Wendy, 10, 144–5, 155–61, 240
  and colonialism, 152–3
  and communism, 74, 239
  and sexuality, 129
Mulford, Wendy (works)
  Bravo to Girls and Heroes, 144–5
  'In Praise of Women Singers', 157–9, 160
  No Fee: A Line or Two for Free, 155–6, 159
  'noise levels', 159, 160–1
  'Notes on Writing: A Marxist/Feminist Viewpoint', 157–8
  Reactions to Sunsets, 145

Naipaul, V. S., 28
Namjoshi, Suniti, 133
narcissism, 109–10
nation language, 25–6, 41
National Front (NF), 173, 188
National Health Service (NHS), 9
National Poetry Centre (London), 196, 240–1
National Service, 48, 49
National Union of Mine Workers (NUM), 164, 197
National Union of Students (NUS), 218
nationalisation, 4, 5
nationalism, 9
Ndlovu, Sfiso Mxolisi, 86, 87
Nelson's West Indian Reader, 28–9
neocolonialism, 70
Nepal, 44, 71
New American Poetry, The (anthology), 105
New Beacon Books, 170, 171, 185
New Labour, 72, 194, 232
New Narrative, 133
Nichols, Grace, 147
Nicholson, R. A., *A Literary History of the Arabs*, 128

Niedecker, Lorine, 145
Nielsen, Aldon, 57
Niven, Alex, 203
Nkosi, Lewis, 178
Nkrumah, Kwame, 70
Northern Ireland, 1, 2, 11, 72
  and Civil Rights campaigns, 54, 197
  and prisons, 200, 205, 207–8
Nortje, Arthur, 6, 77, 89–96
  Dead Roots, 90–1
  'Immigrant', 94–5
  'London Impressions', 91–3
  'Nasser is Dead', 95
  'Oxford Journal', 91
  'Questions and Answers', 95
  'St Giles', 96
Not Love Alone: A Modern Gay Anthology (anthology), 131–2
Notley, Alice, 146, 229
  Alice Ordered Me To Be Made, 158
  Tell Me Again, 231
Notting Hill Carnival, 78, 182–3
Nowak, Mark, 165–6
Nuttall, Jeff, 140

oceanic feeling, 63–4, 68
O'Dwyer, Marian, 125–6
Official Secrets Act, 200
O'Hara, Frank, 94, 114, 136
oil, 151
Oliver, Douglas, 229
Olson, Charles, 5, 49–53
  and continental drift, 61, 62, 63, 64–5
  and Port Books, 55–60, 69
  and Prynne, 45–6, 48, 54–5
Olson, Charles (works)
  Call Me Ishmael, 50, 51–2, 59
  The Maximus, 51, 54, 56, 58, 61, 62
  Mayan Letters, 57
Oluwale, David, 179, 190

Organisation of Women of African and Asian Descent (OWAAD), 163, 243
O'Rourke, Rebecca, 137
O'Sullivan, Maggie, *her/story:eye*, 200
Owens, Richard, 45
Owuor-Anyumba, Henry, 72
Oxbridge *see* Cambridge University; Oxford University
Oxford University, 67, 135–6, 152

Padmore, George, 80
Palestine, 77, 152, 184
Pangaea, 61, 63
paranoid-schizoid position, 224–5, 226
Paris student protests, 229, 230
Parmar, Sandeep, 4
Patterson, Orlando, 38
Pattison, Neil, *Certain Prose of the English Intelligencer*, 45
Peach, Blair, 187–9
Penguin Book of Feminist Writing, The (anthology), 148
Penguin Book of Homosexual Verse, The (anthology), 131
pentameter, 25–7
Perse, St-John, *Neiges*, 23
Persia, 203
Pettit, Ann, 166
Pickard, Tom, 11, 66, 193, 196, 200–1, 244
   Jarrow March, 206
   More Pricks than Prizes, 204
   'Rat Palace', 204–5
Pieterse, Cosmo, 95
Pirate Press, 192, 196
Plath, Sylvia, 23
POA *see* Prison Officers Association (POA)
Poetry Review (journal), 3, 196, 198
Poetry Society, 3, 197, 210, 240
Poets to the People: South African Freedom Poems (anthology), 85
police, 9, 11, 173–4
   and Asian communities, 185
   and Johnson, 175–6, 178–80
   and Notting Hill Carnival, 182–3
   and prisons, 211
   and student protests, 218
   and violence, 188, 189, 190
politics, 2, 3, 220–1
   and Brathwaite, 39–40
   and demonstrations, 241–2
   and Jones, 78
   and Kunene, 82–3
   and Mendelssohn, 231–2
   and Olson, 49–50
   and Prynne, 43–4, 45–6
   see also African National Congress (ANC); Marxism
Poll Tax riots, 210
Pollard, Ingrid, 242
Poly Styrene, 159
popular music, 136, 159–60, 242
Port Books, 55, 56–60, 69
Porton Down, 229
Pound, Ezra, 50, 76
Powell, Enoch, 38, 229
Prague (Czechoslovakia), 106–7
Preservation of the Rights of Prisoners (PROP), 197–200
Prison Officers Association (POA), 198, 211
prisons, 11, 193, 194–5, 198–9
   and Bunting, 202
   and Griffiths, 199–200, 208–16
   and James, 205–6, 207–8
   and Mendelssohn, 227, 235
   and Pickard, 204–5
   and protests, 197–9
PROP *see* Preservation of the Rights of Prisoners (PROP)
Prospect (magazine), 54
protests, 17–18; *see also* student protests

Prynne, J. H., 5, 43–9, 65, 75, 244
  and continental drift, 61, 62–5
  and Olson, 52, 54, 54–5, 56–60
Prynne, J. H. (works)
  'Die a Millionaire', 70–1
  Kazoo Dreamboats, Or, On What There Is, 44–5
  Kitchen Poems, 43, 62, 67, 69–70, 73
  'Living in History', 7–8
  'No Universal Plan for a Good Life', 44
  'The Wound, Day and Night', 62
  The White Stones, 46–7, 62, 63–4, 71, 73, 74
  Wound Response, 44, 71
psychoanalysis, 223, 227, 233, 234
public urinals, 111–12
Puri, Kailash, 184

queerness, 105–6, 108–9, 133, 136
  and Harwood, 114–15, 116, 121–2, 123, 129–30
  and kinship, 244
  and Nortje, 95
  and Sedgwick, 225–6
  and squats, 177
  see also homosexuality
quietism, 223

race, 3–4, 5, 8–9
  and Asian communities, 183–6
  and children, 167
  and Crozier, 53–4
  and Desai, 161–2
  and Dorn, 65–6, 68
  and education, 169–75
  and *The English Intelligencer*, 72–3
  and feminism, 147
  and Harwood, 128
  and London, 20
  and Mulford, 160–1
  and music, 159–60
  and Olson, 51–2
  and Oxbridge, 20–1, 26–7
  and 'passing', 92
  and police, 178–80, 182–3, 185, 188, 189, 190
  and Pound, 50
  and Powell, 38
  and prisons, 194
  and Prynne, 45–6, 47
  and Riley, 149–50, 151–2, 153–5
  and Searle, 168
  and women, 162–3
  and working classes, 180–2
  see also apartheid; Black Britons; whiteness
Race & Poetry & Poetics in the UK (RAPAPUK), 4
Race Today (journal), 11, 168, 169, 180–1
  and Asian communities, 185–6
  and Johnson, 176–7, 178
Race Today Collective, 169, 171, 182
Raha, Nat, 133
Raincoats, The, 160
Ramacon, Phil, 166
Ramamurthy, Anandi, 185
Ramchand, Kenneth, 30–1, 40–1
Rancière, Jacques, 228–9
Rand, Jimi, 240
Randell, Elaine, 240
Rastafarians, 38–9, 41
Raworth, Tom, 45, 66, 145, 229
Rechy, John, 121
recorded readings, 123
Redgrove, Peter, 23, 24
Rediker, Marcus, 58
Reed, Jeremy, 123
  The Isthmus of Samuel Greenberg, 129
Reed, Lou, 108
Reed, Sarah, 190
refugees, 8, 76–7
reggae, 159, 176, 186
reparation, 224–6, 227, 235
retribution, 224

revolution, 228–9, 230
Rhodes Must Fall campaign, 17
Rhodesia, 54, 208
Rich, Adrienne, 245
  'Diving into the Wreck', 137
Rifkin, Libbie, 115
Riley, Denise, 10, 135–7, 138–40, 141–3, 147–55
  and MacDiarmid, 245
  and Mulford, 146, 155–6, 157
  and sexuality, 129
Riley, Denise (works)
  'A note on sex and the reclaiming of language', 147–50, 151–2, 154–5
  'Am I That Name?': Feminism and the Category of 'Women' in History, 142, 153
  Dry Air, 135, 148
  Impersonal Passion, 142
  'In 1970', 135, 136–7, 139–40, 141
  Marxism for Infants, 147, 154, 156
  Mop Mop Georgette, 141–2
  No Fee: A Line or Two for Free, 155–6, 159
  Selected Poems, 148
  War In The Nursery, 233–4
Riley, John, 145
Rimbaud, Arthur
  'La Forgeron' ('The Blacksmith'), 228–9
  'Le Coeur Volé' ('The Stolen Heart'), 231
Rivonia trial, 84, 86–7
Roach, Eric, 35
Roberts, Michèle, 146, 147, 156, 159
Robertson, Lisa, 139–40
Robinson, Roger, 16
Rodney, Walter, 5, 16, 39, 41, 176
  How Europe Underdeveloped Africa, 36–7
  and Salkey novel, 171

Roediger, David R., 51
Rohlehr, Gordon, 16, 18, 41
Rolland, Romain, 63
romanticism, 3
Roosevelt, Franklin D., 49
Rose, Gillian, 44, 73
Rose-Troup, Frances, 58
Rosselli, Amelia, 77
Rosso, Franco, 173
Rothwell, Elizabeth, *Brown Smoke and Dark Amber*, 145
Rowbotham, Sheila, 147, 230
  The Body Politic, 147, 152
  'Women's Liberation and the New Politics', 135, 152
Rowe, Will, 195
Royal Albert Hall (London), 106–9, 110
Rukeyser, Muriel, *The Book of the Dead*, 214
Ruppell, Peter, 125
Ruskin College (Oxford), 135–6

Sachs, Albie, 91
Said, Edward, 89
Salkey, Andrew, 38, 84, 175
  Joey Tyson, 171
Salt Companion to Bill Griffiths, The (anthology), 192
Salt Companion to Lee Harwood, The (anthology), 114–15
Sanchez, Sonia, 178
Sands, Bobby, 205
Santokh, Santokh Singh, 183–4
Saroyan, Aram, 196
Sartre, Jean-Paul, 142
Savacou (journal), 175
'Savage' conceit, 148–51, 154
Scafe, Suzanne, 170–1
Scandal of British Prisons, The (pamphlet), 200
Schmuck (journal), 98
Schneeman, Carolee, *Parts of a Bodyhouse Book*, 98
Schwarz, Bill, 17

Schwitters, Kurt, 77
Searle, Chris, 164–5, 168–9
Second World War, 6, 233
Sedgwick, Eve Kosofsky, 221, 233, 236
   'Paranoid and Reparative Reading, or, You're So Paranoid You Probably Think This Essay Is About You', 224–6
Seeger, Peggy, 78
   'Union Woman', 161–2
Seeger, Pete, 78
Selvon, Sam, 20
Sen, Mala, 178, 186
September, Reg, 89
Seven South African Poets (anthology), 95
Sexual Offences Act (1967), 10, 109, 111, 124–5
sexuality, 4, 8, 125–7; see also homosexuality; queerness
Shakespeare, William, 123
   Julius Caesar, 189
   Othello, 153
Shamsher, Jogindar, 183, 184
Sharpeville massacre, 83, 84
Sheppard, Robert, 120, 125
Shoptaw, John, 127
   On the Outside Looking Out, 114, 115
Shrew (newspaper), 135
Silver Moon (bookshop), 121
Simms, Aseta, 190
Sinclair, Iain, *Hackney, That Rose Red Empire*, 197
Singer, Kirsty, 51
Singh, Jyoti, 189
Sisulu, Walter, 84
Situationist International, 44
Sivanandan, A., 79, 184
slavery, 17–18, 36, 50–1, 55, 56–60
Smith, Jack, 121
Smith, Michael, 16

Snow, Phoebe, 'Inspired Insanity', 158
snowfall, 22–3, 27
social poetics, 165–6, 177
socialism, 36–7, 97–8, 99
Socialist Woman (newspaper), 135
soft power, 5
solidarity, 143, 152, 162
Solomon, Samuel, 133, 148, 149, 156
   Lyric Pedagogy and Marxist-Feminism, 138, 223
South Africa, 77, 78, 79, 182; see also Kunene, Mazisi; Nortje, Arthur
Southall: 23 April 1979 (book), 189
Spanish Civil War, 84
Spare Rib (magazine), 99, 100
Sparrow, Mighty, 25
   'Dan is the Man in the Van', 28, 29
Spender, Stephen, 113
Spicer, Jack, 105
Spirit of '45, The (Loach documentary), 5
Spivak, Gayatri, 143
Spott, Verity, 133
state, the, 79, 80, 233–5; see also welfare state
statelessness, 76, 77
Steedman, Carolyn, 11
Stein, Gertrude, 68
Stephens, John Lloyd, 57
Stepney Words (anthology), 164–5, 166, 167
Sterling, Robin, 173
Stevenson, Justice Melford, 197
Stoke Newington Eight, 226–7
Stokes, Adrian, 63
stowaways, 75–6
Stratton, Brian, *Who Guards the Guards?*, 199
Strauss-Kahn, Dominique, 218
Straw, Jack, 194

Street Editions, 146, 156
street fascist organisations, 11
strikes, 162
　and prisons, 197, 205
　and schools, 164, 165, 166, 173
student protests, 218, 219–22, 229–30, 232–3, 236
Suez Crisis, 48–9
sugar, 28, 36, 57
Sulter, Maud, 133
Sumner, Alaric, 129
Sutherland, Keston, 45, 46, 47, 54, 58
swans, 24
Swanzy, Henry, 33
Sweden, 86
Sweet Honey in the Rock, 160, 161
swimming, 136, 139–40, 141
Symposium on Continental Drift, A, 61–2

Tabor, Richard, 208
Tait, Margaret, *Hugh MacDiarmid: A Portrait*, 244
Take Any Train: A Book of Gay Men's Poetry (anthology), 131
Tambo, Oliver, 86, 88
Tanzania, 36, 87, 89
Temple, John, 52–3
Tennyson, Alfred Lord, 7, 8
Thatcher, Margaret, 173, 208, 210
Thatcherism, 4, 8, 72, 193, 200
Thiong'o, Ngũgĩ wa, 33, 72
Thomas, Dylan, 23
Thomas, Elean, 162–3
Thomas, Odette, *Rain Falling, Sun Shining*, 171
Thomlinson, Natalie, 160
Thompson, E. P., 70, 74
Thompson, Glenn, 165
Thomson, Maurice, 55, 57, 58
Thornton, Timothy, 133
Tickner, Lisa, 221, 223
Tompkins, Melanie, 'A Ditty', 140–1

Torrance, Chris, 119–20, 125
Toulson, Shirley, 240
trade unions, 11, 38, 99, 161–2, 164, 181
transphobia, 144
Traverso, Enzo, 81
Triesman, David, 229
Trigram, 145
Trinidad, 28, 40, 54; *see also* Jones, Claudia
Trinity, 'Three Piece Suit', 159
Troubles *see* Northern Ireland
Truth, Sojourner, 153
Tulse Hill school (London), 172–5
Tuma, Keith, 6
Ture, Kwame, 38
Turner, Victor, 241
Turning the Screws (TV series), 211
Tzara, Tristan, 206

Ugandan Asians, 96
Umkhonto We Sizwe (MK), 87, 88–9
unemployment, 180–1
Unicorn Bookshop (Brighton), 129–30
United Friends and Family Campaign, 241–2
United States of America (USA), 3, 6, 16, 63
　and Black Power, 95
　and colonisation, 55–6
　and Crozier, 53–4
　and feminism, 145
　and Kunene, 89
　and prisons, 198
　and Prynne, 48
　and Suez Canal, 49
　see also Dorn, Edward; Olson, Charles; Vietnam War
University of West Indies (UWI), 19, 38–9, 40
university tuition fees, 218, 232
US Civil Rights Act (1964), 45–6
Usherwood, Vivian, 10, 172, 190

'My Heart is Broken', 166–7
'School', 167–8
'School Strike', 165, 166
Uziell, Laurel, 133

vanguardism, 168, 230
Various Art, A (anthology), 73
Vasquez Castario, Fabio, 71
Verwoerd, Hendrik, 67, 84
Vicuña, Cecilia, 5, 77–8, 97–101, 244
  Saborami, 77–8, 98–100, 101
Vietnam War, 8, 44, 65, 69, 71
  and Essex University, 229
  and imperialism, 72
  and India, 184
  and protests, 54
  and Tet Offensive, 88
  and Vicuña, 100
  and women, 152
Vinkenoog, Simon, 109, 110
violence, 8, 11, 78, 228–9
Virtanen, Juha, 107
Voice of Scotland, The (newspaper), 245

Wages for Housework, 156
Waidner, Isabel, 133
Walcott, Derek, 21, 35
Waldrop, Rosmarie, 161
Walmsley, Anne, 38
  The Caribbean Artists Movement, 1966–1972, 15
Wandor, Michelene, 145–6, 147, 156
Wandsworth, HMP (London), 194, 204, 211, 215
Ward, Geoff, 125
Ware, Vron, 155
Warhol, Andy, 121
Warner, Sylvia Townsend, 129
  Whether A Dove or a Seagull, 155–6
Warwick Research Collective, 33–4
Watts, Stephen, 183

Webster, Sheila, 21
Wegener, Alfred, 61, 62, 63
weightlessness, 29–31
Welch, John, 183
welfare state, 4, 5, 6, 9, 143
West Africa, 36–7
West African Student Union (WASU), 20
West Indian Gazette, 78
West Indian Students Union (WISU), 20
West Indies, 19, 27, 28–9, 36
White, Sarah, 170
white supremacy, 50
Whitehead, Peter, *Wholly Communion*, 109
whiteness, 4, 5, 25, 66, 160–1
  and WLM, 144, 147
Wieners, John, 52, 105, 129
Wilde, Oscar, 'The Disciple', 110
Willetts, David, 218
Williams, Aubrey, 38
Williams, Eric, 40
Williams, Jonathan, 52, 129
Williams, Raymond, 32, 47
  Culture and Society, 33
  May Day Manifesto, 70
Williams, William Carlos, *Paterson*, 206
Wilson, Amrit, 162
Wilson, Elizabeth, 143
Wilson, J. Tuzo, 61
Winnicott, D. W., 222, 223, 224, 233, 234
WLM *see* Women's Liberation Movement (WLM)
Wolfenden Report, 109
women *see* feminism
Women's Liberation Movement (WLM), 3, 136, 138, 144, 240
  and 'Disaggregation now!' slogan, 142–3
  and national liberation struggles, 152
  and race, 147

Woods, Tim, 82–3
Wordsworth, William, 141
　'Lines Written in Early Spring', 80–1
working class, 5, 6, 201
　and education, 218
　and migrants, 51
　and race, 180, 181–2
　and social poetics, 164–6
Worpole, Ken, 166
Writers Against Apartheid (newspaper), 83–5
Writers Forum (WF), 140, 145–6
Wynter, Sylvia, 20, 40

X-Ray Spex, 159

Yemen, 88
You Better Believe It – Black Verse in English (anthology), 178
Yu, Timothy, 241

Zimbabwean African People's Union (ZAPU), 87, 88–9
Zionism, 77
Zulu Inkatha Party, 89
Zulus, 82, 83
Zwelonke, D. M., 91